The Kentucky Barbecue Book

The Kentucky Barbecue Book

Wes Berry

UNIVERSITY PRESS OF KENTUCKY

Copyright © 2013 by The University Press of Kentucky

Scholarly publisher for the Commonwealth,
serving Bellarmine University, Berea College, Centre
College of Kentucky, Eastern Kentucky University,
The Filson Historical Society, Georgetown College,
Kentucky Historical Society, Kentucky State University,
Morehead State University, Murray State University,
Northern Kentucky University, Transylvania University,
University of Kentucky, University of Louisville,
and Western Kentucky University.
All rights reserved.

Editorial and Sales Offices: The University Press of Kentucky
663 South Limestone Street, Lexington, Kentucky 40508-4008
www.kentuckypress.com

17 16 15 14 13   5 4 3 2 1

Map by Dick Gilbreath, University of Kentucky Cartography Lab

Library of Congress Cataloging-in-Publication Data

Berry, Wes, 1969-
  The kentucky barbecue book / Wes Berry.
     pages   cm
  Includes bibliographical references and index.
  ISBN 978-0-8131-4179-4 (hardcover : alk. paper) —
  ISBN 978-0-8131-4180-0 (epub) (print) —
  ISBN 978-0-8131-4181-7 (pdf) (print)
  1. Barbecuing. I. Title.
  TX840.B3B47 2013
  641.7'6--dc23
                                        2012045882

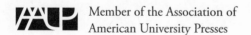

Member of the Association of
American University Presses

To

Elisa Berry, adopted Kentuckian and Jewish pig farmer—so proud to make country ham and bacon with you.

The memory of my uncle Roy Eason Williams, who colored my childhood with exaggerated belches, bawdy humor, and smoky treats from his cinder-block pit.

My barbecue companions, past and present. Love and peace to you all.

In memoriam: Ford Ranger, 1991–2012. I'll miss your company on my barbecue odysseys, mostly dependable rattletrap.

Contents

How to Chew the Fat

Bluegrass Barbecue Lingo

Baby back ribs: Small meaty ribs cut from the blade and center section of a hog's loin, called "baby" because they come from smaller (and usually younger) hogs. Larger loin back ribs are often called "baby backs" on restaurant menus.

Backwoods smoker: A manufactured cooking unit that makes use of water pans above the fire pit to add moisture to the cooking chamber.

Barbecue potato: A baked potato loaded with tasty fatty stuff like sour cream and butter and topped with barbecued meat and sauce.

Bark: The darkened exterior of smoked meats, favored by lovers of smoke and big flavors. Because of greater exposure to heat, bark is drier than the interior meat.

Beef brisket: A cut from the foreshank (breast or lower chest) of a beef cow, notoriously tough until tenderized by low and slow cooking. The "flat" cut is leaner than the "point" or "deckle." The tastiest cut is the full brisket, which has plenty of fat layered in.

Burgoo: An "everything but the kitchen sink" rich stew made with several meats and vegetables, cooked up in large quantities at Owensboro's International Bar-B-Q Festival and found at barbecue joints in Kentucky, especially those in the "Burgoo Belt" (my term) that includes the counties of Daviess, Hopkins, and Christian, among others.

Chip or chipped: A style of barbecue preparation popular in Union County and Henderson County, where heavily smoked exterior pieces of pork shoulders, hams, and mutton quarters are chopped and mixed with a thin, tangy dip sauce, a bold flavor creation that's salty and good as a sandwich.

City ham: Hams partially cured in sweet brine before being lightly smoked and cooked. Many western Kentucky barbecue joints smoke city hams and precooked turkey breasts to imbue them with a deeper smoked flavor.

Fast Eddy's by Cookshack: A meat-smoking apparatus that often utilizes wood pellets and a gas flame.

Hardwood: In tree talk, the wood from broad-leafed trees like oak, hickory, maple, and sassafras rather than conifers (like pine and cedar).

Hickory: One of the hardest of the hardwoods, hickory trees are nut-bearing friends of squirrels and Kentucky pit masters, who favor the smoke and heat imparted by hickory over all other woods. Several different species of hickory trees live in North America, including shagbark, shellbark, mockernut, bitternut, and pignut. Some pit masters claim they prefer one species of hickory—like shagbark—to others.

Masonry pits: Barbecue pits built out of cinderblocks (concrete blocks) and mortar, stacked a few blocks high and covered with flame-proof material like roofing metal. Meats cook on wire grates inside the pits. Once the blocks get hot, they hold heat well. Besides the oldest barbecuing methods, like digging a hole in the earth, masonry pits are the most traditional barbecue pits in Kentucky, favored by many pit masters in the western part of the state.

Monroe County dip: Sopping sauce favored in several south-central Kentucky counties, made with vinegar, butter, lard, salt, black and cayenne pepper, and sometimes other ingredients like tomato or mustard, used for basting meats as they cook slowly over hickory coals. Also served as a finishing sauce.

Monroe County style: Thin slices of pork shoulder grilled over hickory coals and sopped with the Monroe County dip. Shoulder is by far the best-selling meat, but joints cooking in the Monroe County style also serve grilled whole and half chickens, pork ribs, pork tenderloins, hamburgers, and hot dogs.

Mutton: Mature sheep, either female or castrated males. Mutton is Kentucky's claim to barbecue fame, although only 10 percent of the barbecue places in the state serve it.

Mutton dip: A Worcestershire sauce–based sop used to baste mutton during many hours of slow cooking, also used as a dipping sauce for cooked mutton.

Naked: Refers to pure meat served without the application of sauces or cooking tricks. For example, I'd call a whole pork shoulder seasoned with salt and smoked on a pit until tender, then served without sauce "naked." Or I'd call a beef brisket cooked without wrapping it in foil and served without sauce a "naked" brisket. If you start dressing it up too much, it's no longer naked, of course!

Ole Hickory Pit: A meat smoker made in Cape Girardeau, Missouri. A popular model utilizes a gas flame that burns sticks of wood to create heat and smoke in a firebox adjacent to the cooking chamber.

Pork shoulder: The cut of a pig or hog that includes the front leg and the area above it. Shoulders are often butchered as "Boston butt"—the meaty upper portion—and as "picnic" or "picnic shoulder," the upper part of the hog's foreleg. Whole pork shoulders are still favored by many western Kentucky barbecue places, although more places use Boston butts for their pulled pork.

Rick: A measurement of firewood stacked four feet tall by eight feet long. Kentuckians use the term loosely to name a goodly sized stack of wood; we aren't too particular about the precision of the measurements unless we're paying for it.

Sassafras: A North American hardwood tree with aromatic leaves, bark, and branches. Used as a smoking wood, sassafras imparts a bold smoke flavor and dark coloration to meats. Along with hickory, it's a favored wood—in small amounts—by Owensboro-area barbecue teams and restaurants.

Smoke ring: The pinkish hue imparted to smoked meats (a very good thing).

Southern Pride smoker: A meat smoker that works much like the Ole Hickory gas-fired pits, with a gas-flame-fueled firebox to the side of the cooking chamber. Smoke is generated by stoking the firebox with wood.

Spare ribs: The whole rib, including the bony end piece, cut from the belly side of the rib cage. They are flatter than baby back ribs and have more bone than meat. They also have more fat (and flavor).

St. Louis–style ribs: The whole rib with the bony end piece (the sternum bone, cartilage, and rib tips) removed. Removing the tips can aid in uniformity of cooking, since the tips can dry out and get tough quicker than the rest of the rib. St. Louis–style ribs happen to be the favorite pork rib cut of Wes Berry, author of *The Kentucky Barbecue Book*.

Texas crutch: A derogatory term to describe the wrapping of beef briskets in foil to steam and tenderize them.

West Kentucky style: Refers to whole pork shoulders or Boston butts cooked over a bed of hickory coals on masonry pits for many hours—usually from twelve to thirty—at temperatures ranging between 200 and 300°F. Lower and longer cooking usually yields a smokier meat with less shrinkage and more moisture and tenderness. Finished shoulders are served pulled, or pulled and chopped, often accompanied by a thin vinegar-pepper sauce, although sauce styles vary greatly by county.

Introduction

I am large, I contain multitudes of barbecue.

—**Walt Whitman**, speaking in a western Kentucky drawl, overheard in
a vision I had on May 27, 2012, while strolling near the confluence of
the Green and Barren rivers.

I've recently been diagnosed with Hyper Enthusiastic Barbecue Disorder
(HEBD). I'm supposed to drink eight ounces of KC Masterpiece daily to
make the cravings go away. The prescription isn't working very well. I still get
the nervous trembles when I think about deliciously smoked meats. But I
do know this: I'm not fond of KC Masterpiece and many other major-brand
sauces—thick concoctions sweetened with corn syrup and sometimes tainted
by unnatural-tasting liquid smoke.

My students sometimes tell me that their lives are so busy it's difficult
for them to turn in work on time. They ask for extended deadlines. I say, "You
think you've got it bad? I got HEBD. I can't even concentrate on what you're
saying to me right now. Sniff. Sniff. Is that the smell of pig flesh cooking over
wood smoke? You don't even know distraction until you got HEBD. Now
glue yourself to a chair and finish that essay."

Like a lot of barbecue lovers, I'll drive a good piece out of the way for
the chance of tasting some good smoked meats. In summer 2009 I drove
from Kentucky to Florida, on the way stopping at three barbecue joints to
check the fare. First stop: Fresh Air Barbecue and Brunswick Stew in Jackson, Georgia. I went there on the recommendation of Vince Staten and Greg

Johnson, authors of *Real Barbecue: The Classic Barbecue Guide,* what one blurber (*Glamour* magazine) calls "the ultimate barbecue book." Well, I'm fond of the writing of Vince Staten, having worn the cover off his *Jack Daniel's Old Time Barbecue Cookbook* since I bought it in the early 1990s, and I've eaten at the barbecue place bearing his name in Prospect, Kentucky, three times. (It recently closed after eighteen years in business.) I'm also thankful for his and Johnson's barbecue guidebook. How else can a road traveler feast on fine smoked meats without doing some serious Internet searching? Staten and Johnson make finding a good place pretty easy, as they describe in *Real Barbecue* their top one hundred restaurants, joints, and shacks they've found in twenty-eight states, coast to coast, over the past twenty years.

As I approached Fresh Air, my heart started thumping rapidly. Searching for the place, I'd accidentally driven off course for forty-five minutes, so by the time I reached the Promised Land my barbecue jitters had come on. It was past 1:00, and just a couple of pickup trucks were parked in the gravel lot. I admired the rustic architecture of Fresh Air, which has been in this same location since the 1920s. I smelled wood smoke and saw piled wood off to the south of the restaurant. A smoking chimney stuck up prominently from the center of the building.

Oh, Lord, I thought. *I'm going to savor some good barbecue today.*

Inside, I scanned the menu and was impressed by the limited offerings —simply chopped barbecue sandwiches and plates. I ordered a "deluxe plate," envisioning something outstanding (since *deluxe* suggests opulence), and here's what I received: a paper plate with a smallish portion of pork on it; a small cup of Brunswick stew; saltines; a small cup of slaw; a pickle. Two slices of white bread. Sweet tea. This was deluxe? The small portion of meat disappointed me. *False advertising,* I thought. Sure, I could have made a sandwich by shoveling the puny portion between the slices of bread, but I wanted to taste the meat. My assessment: good stuff, but not the best I've ever had. The sauce was a tangy, vinegary, tomato concoction, and the meat had a mild smokiness. According to Staten and Johnson, the pit tenders at Fresh Air smoke hams for over twenty hours.

Well, I've smoked whole hams and shoulders for over twenty hours at home, after having local Barren County farmer Joe Michael Moore (who makes and sells the best country sausage ever) kill a hog for me, and the result has been some deeply smoked barbecue with lots of good bark mixed in with the milder interior meat. At Fresh Air, the meat wasn't so smoky. The amount was smallish. The slaw was okay (mayo, green peppers, vinegar, cabbage). The Brunswick stew? I don't see what the big deal is. It's like veggie-pork soup cooked down to slurry, a less savory version of Kentucky burgoo. I liked the atmosphere of Fresh Air, and I liked the stripped-down menu. But after eating I felt less than satisfied.

What was missing? Smokiness. Quantity of meat. Interesting side dishes.

So even though I admire the good judgment of Staten and Johnson, I'm willing to admit that my tastes differ. And even though I haven't eaten at a thousand barbecue places, I've tripped around the country sampling many of them, and I've slow-smoked whole hams and shoulders and racks of ribs at my house. I've also judged at barbecue competitions in the Memphis Barbecue Network.

I lean toward a deeply smoked taste—not one of bitterness, which comes from cooking meat at too-high temperatures and using too much of certain types of wood like white and red oak, but the earthy, sweet-salty smokiness that comes from a whole pork shoulder smoked a long time at low temperatures using a goodly portion of hickory. I'm also fond of spices and I like dry rubs, but they aren't necessary if the pork shoulders or chicken halves or beef briskets have absorbed lots of smoke and there's some salt added to bring out the natural rich flavor of the meat. I love the bark of smoked meats. I usually prefer a vinegar sauce to a sugary one. I love black pepper, and I'm mighty fond of spicy heat.

In short, when I ate at Fresh Air, listed by Staten and Johnson as "As good as we've ever had," I thought, *I can tell you where to find some barbecue better than this!*

I'm here to tell you that Kentucky has some really fine barbecue, and that my home state's rich traditions of barbecue have been pretty much overlooked by food writers and the Travel Channel. Texas has been well covered, as has North Carolina. A recent television show had cowboys do blind tastings of various regional barbecue styles, and the styles represented were from North Carolina, Texas, Memphis, and Kansas City. In 2011 *Southern Living* did a story, "The South's 20 Best BBQ Joints," featuring what the authors considered to be "perfect plates of barbecue in four major regional styles."

These regional styles were, no surprise, the same ones mentioned above. The article was written by Matt and Ted Lee of Charleston, South Carolina, and while I admire their food expertise (I paid good money for a copy of their weighty *The Lee Bros. Southern Cookbook*), I've got a mutton bone to pick with them regarding this list of "the South's best" that doesn't include a single barbecue joint in Kentucky.

I read and watch these stories and think, *Now, hold on a durned minute here—where's my beloved Kentucky?* Off many barbecue aficionados' maps, apparently, and that's a shame since the Commonwealth/Bluegrass State has much to offer the barbecue thrill seeker. When hitting the roads of Kentucky in search of fabulous barbecue, I've discovered that many establishments, especially in the western part of the state, still cook old style, shoveling hot hardwood coals under meats elevated on grates inside cinderblock pits. Fat drips down onto the ashes and coals and sizzles back up into the meat, creating that special barbecue taste that smoke alone can't make. Of course, such a cooking style requires careful watching and long tending. Cooking with coals can also be dangerous. I talked with several people in my journeys whose barbecue places had suffered fire damage or burned down completely. Frances' Bar-B-Que down in Monroe County in south-central Kentucky burned in 2009. They've moved closer to the town of Tompkinsville and are back in business. Peak Bros. in Waverly also burned, but they continue smoking meats in a new restaurant. It's a risky business, this cooking with wood coals but, like I say, it produces a smoke flavor like no other.

The newfangled gas and wood hybrid cookers like the popular Southern Pride and Ole Hickory units that so many barbecue places have switched to can deliver a tasty product, especially if the meats are seasoned right. The big ovens hold a steady temperature and are fire safe, allowing restaurateurs to go home instead of needing to tend the pits all night, and most units are equipped with rotisseries to keep the meats moving for even cooking. The gas-cooked meats are usually moist and tender, and more often than not mild to moderately smoked. Outside the cooking chamber (an oven with rotisserie), a gas-fired flame creates smoke by torching sticks or chunks of wood. You can throw lots of wood into the firebox to create a more intense smoke flavor, but many folks using gas cookers don't because they want to conserve expensive wood and because regular firebox loading takes more work. Moreover, some places cater to mainstream tastes for less smoky meats. Ben Webb at Dave's Sticky Pig told me his wife wasn't fond of barbecue because she didn't want to "eat a campfire." No wonder some barbecue places cut back on wood.

Comparing old-fashioned pit barbecue with gas-cooked meats, I'd say the pros and cons are pretty clear. Old-fashioned methods are more labor intensive, more prone to pit fires, and more expensive (using wood for fuel costs much more than gas, at least in the long term). With both methods, you can get moist, tender meats if you cook at low temperatures for a long time using indirect heat. As for taste, the gas-wood hybrid cookers don't create the distinctive dripping-fat-and-sizzle, deeply smoked effect that comes from cooking over hardwood coals. When you try whole pork shoulders cooked a few feet above hickory coals for twenty-four hours at 200–220°F, you taste something that can't be reproduced in a gas oven. It's comparable to tasting a country ham that's aged in a barn through a year of Kentucky seasons instead of in a temperature-controlled warehouse.

On the Road to a Comprehensive Tour of Kentucky Barbecue

I've wanted to write a book on Kentucky's best barbecue since moving back to the green rolling hills of cave country in 2005, having sojourned for a while in the barbecue wastelands of the Midwest. My goal was simple enough: eat at every barbecue place in the Commonwealth and write a travel guide to direct readers to the best, describing and rating the food along the way.

After hitting the road in summer 2009, I soon realized the challenges of describing smoked meats, potato salad, baked beans, slaw, and sauces dozens and dozens of times without sounding like a broken record. How many words are there to describe the essential qualities of good barbecue: tenderness, moisture, and smokiness? I started boring myself pretty quickly when listening to my digital voice files from those early trips.

As I traveled more widely, I discovered that the stories of the people I met added depth, or *flavor,* that complemented my descriptions of the food

I ate. That's why I returned to Clinton in far-western Kentucky to revisit Nicky's and Grogan's nearly three years after my original trip. I wanted to get more stories about the places—not just the food. My original write-ups were scanty compared to the later ones. I wanted to give these places the attention they deserve.

I think of Kentuckians as a particularly rooted people, proud of their lands and customs, and touring the Commonwealth from the Mississippi River to Appalachia and most parts in between has reinforced this sense of pride in place. And no wonder! Kentucky is gorgeous, blessed with thousands of miles of freshwater streams, striking karst topography, green fields, diverse deciduous forests, and productive farmland. I feasted my eyes on fields of corn and soybeans, weathered tobacco barns, grass-covered roller coaster hills, pastures dotted with rolls of fresh hay and cattle. I stood on the banks of the Ohio River at Paducah, Uniontown, and Maysville, watching the water roll, and admired the sailboats on Kentucky Lake. I fell in love with the state all over again, and I've tried to capture a sense of the regional landscapes and local customs in these pages.

I began my tour of Kentucky barbecue in the western part of the state, the Mecca of smoked meats. Native Kentuckians identify with counties, as in, "I'm a native of Barren County." Ask someone from Chicago where they are from and they don't say Cook County. But ask a Kentuckian, especially one from a sparsely populated area, and you'll likely get an answer that includes a county name. Perhaps this is because we have so few big cities in Kentucky—only four with populations over fifty thousand—but our medium-sized state is divided into a whopping 120 counties. So I tried managing my barbecue research by making a county by county list, from west to east, and then checking the yellow pages for listings of restaurants (or shacks) that looked like they might serve barbecue. I also asked for recommendations from acquaintances across the state and called real estate offices, whose business is to make the customer happy, asking for their local recommendations. I quickly discovered that many places listed on the Internet are now closed. I called places and asked how long they'd been in business and also their opening hours. Then I set out in my rusty Ford Ranger to try the meats and, if finding them at least good, to interview the pit tenders and owners to learn about their cooking methods and history in barbecue.

Introduction

What strikes me most about Kentucky barbecue is the sheer variety of meats that individual joints smoke. In *Holy Smoke: The Big Book of North Carolina Barbecue* (a wonderful barbecue compendium), John Shelton Reed and Dale Volberg Reed define North Carolina barbecue as meat

1. that has been *barbecued*—that is, cooked for a long time at a low temperature with heat and smoke from a fire of hardwood and/or hardwood coals;
2. that meat being *pork*—whole hog, shoulder, or (occasionally) ham—
3. sometimes basted and always served with a thin *sauce* or "dip" that is at most only a slight variation on a traditional recipe including vinegar, red pepper, and maybe (or maybe not) tomato.

Note point number two: the meat must be pork to qualify as North Carolina barbecue. Well, pork is popular in western Kentucky, of course (we ain't fools), but the pit masters in this corner of the universe near the confluence of the Mississippi and Ohio rivers also smoke up mutton, beef brisket, chickens, city ham, precooked turkey breasts, and bologna. No kidding. Now I'm not liberal enough in my definition of barbecue to seriously give bologna— a meat that comes precooked before you throw it on the smoker—a spot on my list of "real barbecue." But mutton? Have you tried slow-smoked mature sheep? If not, you need to come visit us in western Kentucky, over to Owensboro and a few nearby counties to get your taste buds around the gamy taste of sheep slow smoked over hickory (and sometimes sassafras) for many hours. And while it's true that brisket is a Texas specialty, I've tasted some brisket in Kentucky that rivals in deliciousness the brisket I ate at McBee's Barbecue in Uvalde, Texas, or at Camphouse Barbecue in Ft. Stockton, Texas—both mystical brisket experiences in which the smoky, tender beef hit my taste buds and popped a huge grin on my face that didn't go away for many miles. I still smile lovingly when thinking of those beautiful meats, and fortunately I no longer have to drive to Texas to taste something comparable.

A conundrum anyone on a barbecue road trip has to deal with is the question of what to get. Apparently this isn't much of a problem in North Carolina. But in Kentucky, where meat smokers are throwing many varieties of animal flesh on the pit, a problem arises when you have only one stomach and many places to try before you sleep. My initial method when walking into a barbecue place was to ask the owners or meat smokers what they do best. What is their specialty? I would then evaluate the place based on what they recommended. I continue to use this method—trying to find out what places specialize in and the local favorite—but I've also been disappointed by the most popular items at certain barbecue establishments and preferred instead one of their less popular meats. This is especially true when trying pulled pork cooked on gas cookers—often recommended by proud employees at barbecue places, often a local favorite, and all too often disappointing to me. However, I sometimes found the ribs, brisket, and chicken wings smoked at these same places much more satisfying, even though they weren't recommended. When they were available, I often ordered sampler platters. At other times, like when I spied the beautiful pork ribs laid out underneath the glass at the ordering counter at Old Hickory Bar-B-Q in Owensboro, my anticipatory salivary glands and tummy-mind sent my brain a clear message: *Order these now!*

Another issue to confront while barbecue road tripping is side dishes. Should you fill valuable space in your stomach with mediocre pork and beans? When I first started my journey to discover Kentucky's best barbecue places, I stopped at Bad Bob's in Murray, having driven west from my home base in Bowling Green, and the head cook recommended his pork ribs. So I ordered a rib plate with mustard potato salad and "peach baked beans." The potato salad was good, but the beans weren't doctored up enough for me— didn't have the big flavor of baked beans loaded with lots of onions, peppers, spices, and at best, shreds of smoked meats. To this day I cannot understand why many barbecue places don't offer better side dishes. If a place wants to specialize in smoked meats only, fine. But if a place offers side dishes, then they should at least taste like something, right? My rule is to try side dishes if any place offers unusual ones, if my belly at that particular time can hold it. This becomes an issue when making the rounds of a county like McCracken (county seat: Paducah), which hosts at least six legitimate barbecue places. Even though I may see potato salad on the menu and want to sample it, I don't like wasting food, and if my belly is already swollen beyond repair for a particular day, then I'm going to leave off the side dishes, unless the menu includes something like homemade jalapeño peppers stuffed with country ham and goat cheese, rolled in batter and deep-fried. I'd probably make room for something like that.

At other times, like when I'm fortunate enough to eat at just one barbecue place during a day, I'll get side dishes, even though I'm rarely impressed by them. I'm a sucker for good potato salad, but unfortunately I've tasted only a few specimens that lodged in my food brain. I have to go out of state for my favorite potato salad, served at 17th Street Bar and Grill in southern Illinois. Mark's Feed Store in Louisville offers a comparable potato salad, with lots of sour cream and eggs. The loaded potato salads at Big R's and Shannon's in La Grange and at Pig in a Poke in Prestonsburg are also worthy of valuable stomach space.

If a place takes extra special pride in food preparation—making everything from scratch using the best ingredients possible—I'll let you know about it. Like I say (and if you've eaten at many barbecue places you know what I'm talking about), too many places dump pork and beans out of a can and heat them up. But there are wonderful exceptions, like Scotty's in Louisville, where the side dishes come from homemade recipes and not from industrial food service. Such places, if they can smoke good meats, get an extra feather in their cap for an overall good-eating sensory experience.

What I've Learned about Smoked Meats from the Barbecue Trail

When I began this indulgent quest, I'd already eaten plenty barbecue in my nearly forty years of living, and I thought I knew what I liked. I was a fan of thin-sliced pork shoulder grilled on an open pit over hickory coals and basted with a vinegar-pepper dip—the stuff we called "Monroe County style" that defined my earliest barbecue experiences. I knew I liked deeply smoked, tender, sliced beef brisket from my Texas travels. I loved dry-rubbed ribs, having eaten them in Memphis while living nearby in north Mississippi. I knew that thick, sweet sauces weren't my thing, and that my palate preferred meats without much sauce, especially if seasoned and smoked well. A vinegary, peppery sauce was my preference. I also thought that cooking over gas was inferior to cooking in traditional ways over wood coals or, second best, manufactured charcoal.

A little bit about my background: I grew up in Barren County, Kentucky, in the south-central part of the state, not far north of the Tennessee line. The barbecue style of my youth revolved mostly around what locals call "shoulder": oval slices of pork, bone in, cooked on an open pit over hickory coals and sopped with a dip of vinegar, butter, lard, black and cayenne pepper, and salt—closer to an eastern North Carolina sauce than what you'll find in western Kentucky. I ate plenty of that as a boy, as my Uncle Roy spent hours tending his homemade cinderblock pit, smoking sliced shoulder and chickens and kielbasa and hog ribs. In the spring Roy sent me off with a paper sack to cut pokeweed, and later he'd cook up a big mess of poke salad and we'd eat those rich greens with the meats he'd smoked up throughout a long day. So even though I cut my barbecue teeth on thin-sliced, vinegary pork shoulder grilled over hickory coals, my palate has always been open to trying new foods, and therefore I've been delighted by barbecue styles from far southwest Texas to Kansas City to middle Georgia. And I've eaten at least some decent stuff up near Chicago, although most of what I've had from that region depends too much upon thick sauce and not enough on long smoke.

As I've eaten around the Commonwealth, my tastes have changed a bit, but most of my original preferences—fashioned by what I ate in my youth, from my mother's excellent home cooking to Uncle Roy's vinegar-based meat smoking—have remained intact. My reverence for open-pit grilled sliced shoulder has declined somewhat after I've eaten the long-smoked, closed-pit pork shoulders of western Kentucky. And tasting the best of pork (tender, moist, and deeply smoked) from places like Prince Pit BBQ, Grogan's, Mr. BBQ & More, Leigh's, and Knockum Hill has set the bar high and made me more critical of other pulled and shredded pork styles. I've noticed a pattern in my reviews: in places lacking an excellent pulled-pork tradition, when I try several of the meats I often find myself disappointed with the so-called pulled pork (often finely chopped and sauced) and favoring instead such things as ribs, brisket, and half or quarter chickens (not "pulled chicken," which often comes from white breast meat and has never impressed me). Ribs, chicken, and brisket are more forgiving of gas cooking than larger pieces of meat (like whole pork shoulders or Boston butts) are. A rack of ribs, a chicken, and sliced shoulder can soak up a lot of smoke in a short time, and if you like smoke—a characteristic of real barbecue—then this is a good thing.

In my year(s) of meats, I discovered that precooked turkey breast, city ham, and bologna may taste good when smoked, but that I usually found myself saying, "Eh. It just tastes like deli ham or turkey with smoke added, nothing special. Not really barbecue." I believe that raw meats are best for soaking up smoke and creating the true barbecue flavor.

Approximately one-third of the places featured in this book smoke meat with some kind of gas or electric cooker. This makes Kentucky a better destination than North Carolina if you want meat cooked over wood or coals. My basis for this claim is Jim Early's comprehensive tour of North Carolina barbecue, laid out in his book *The Best Tar Heel Barbecue, Manteo to Murphy* (published in 2002). Early discovered that about 40 percent of North Carolina barbecue places use some kind of gas or electric hybrid ovens. As I traveled east in Kentucky—getting farther away from prime pulled-pork and mutton country—I found myself recommending brisket and ribs more often. Gas cooking is also more prominent east of I-65—more places using Southern Pride, Ole Hickory, Fast Eddy's by Cookshack, or some type of homemade gas cookers. I agree with the writers of *Holy Smoke* that the Southern Pride units are ironically named.

I still haven't grown to like "crock-pot pork" or "sloppy joe pork"— shredded and sauced pork that reminds me of the stuff served at my elementary school cafeteria. Why go to all the trouble of smoking a hunk of meat for twelve to twenty-four hours if you're going to mask the flavor with sauces? But see, that's a problem when cooking on the gas units, which—with a few exceptions—don't impart a distinctive smoky real barbecue flavor unless the pit tender keeps throwing logs into the gas burner. Since these units hold a steady temperature like an oven, I understand the temptation to go home and get a good night's sleep while the meats bake. Unfortunately, the results aren't as good, at least not for larger cuts like Boston butts and whole shoulders and quartered mutton. For those accustomed to sauced shredded pork, the long cooking doesn't matter as much. It's akin to putting lots of A-1 or Heinz 57 on a steak. Those sauces are just fine for a piece of chopped steak. But it's a shame to mask the flavor of a good rib eye with them.

A note on sauces: I like all kinds, but I do favor vinegar over sugar and tomato, and I always order hot if offered. (Full disclosure: in 2001 I won the jalapeño pepper–eating contest at Fiesta Hispana in Rockford, Illinois.) Sauces can too easily overwhelm smoked meats, which should have substantial flavor before the addition of sauces. This flavor can come largely from smoke and salt, or it can be enhanced by rubs and injections. Of course, if you like biting into a sandwich and tasting mostly bread and sauce (or slaw or pickles), then that's your business. Me? I want to taste smoky meat, tender and juicy, and I'm not opposed to the vinegary tang imparted by a drizzle of sauce. Maybe this is why I'm fond of mutton, as smoky, tender mutton marries well with the tangy black dip sauces you'll find at the four Owensboro barbecue places and at western Kentucky Catholic church picnics. There's nothing else like this flavor in the barbecue kingdom, and it's rare to find outside a few counties in western Kentucky.

By the way, my palate has broadened to appreciate a range of sweet sauces, like the complex melon sauce (which doesn't contain melon) at J. J. McBrewster's in Lexington, or the awesome, fruity "sweet Hawaiian" sauce at Big Kahuna in Leitchfield. I'm hardly a poster boy for moderation, but when it comes to sauces I can usually just say no. Such an attitude might brand you as an outsider in Prestonsburg where, according to Brian Cramer of Pig in a Poke, 99 percent of the barbecue-eating populace wants their meats heavily sauced.

An Abbreviated History of Kentucky Barbecue

"And God said, Let the earth bring forth the living creature after his kind, cattle, and creeping thing, and beast of the earth after his kind: and it was so." Then cattle, hogs, sheep, and other delicious things made of meat appeared on earth.

Fast-forward a few years to when Kentuckians, living when the United States was young, cooked God's creatures over fire and shared the smoky gifts at big celebratory socials. Virginians had squeezed through Cumberland Gap and brought with them into the Great Meadow (an early nickname for Kentucky) some barbecue know-how. One citizen of the young Republic, bird painter John James Audubon (who, ironically, killed the creatures he loved in order to paint them), wrote about a Fourth of July barbecue he observed in Kentucky in the early 1800s:

> The free, single-hearted Kentuckian, bold, erect, and proud of his Virginia descent, had, as usual, made arrangements for celebrating the day of his country's Independence. The whole neighborhood joined with one consent. No personal invitation was required where everyone was welcomed by his neighbor, and from the governor to the guider of the plough all met with light hearts and merry faces. . . .
>
> Now the waggons [*sic*] were seen slowly moving along under their load of provisions, which had been prepared for the common benefit. Each denizen had freely given his ox, his ham, his venison, his turkeys, and other fowls. Here were to be seen flagons of every beverage used in the country; "La belle Riviere" had opened her finny stores; the melons of all sorts, peaches, plums and pears, would have been sufficient to stock a market. In a word, Kentucky, the land of abundance, had supplied a feast for her children.
>
> A purling stream gave its water freely, while the grateful breezes cooled the air. Columns of smoke from the newly kindled fires rose above the trees; fifty cooks or more moved to and fro as they plied their trade; waiters of all qualities were disposing the dishes, the glasses, and the punch-bowls, amid vases filled with rich wines. "Old Monongahela" [whiskey] filled many a barrel for the crowd. And now, the roasted viands perfume the air, and all appearances conspire to predict the speedy commencement of a banquet such as may suit the vigorous appetite of American woodsmen.

Barbecue, according to Audubon's account (which is quoted in Robert Moss's book *Barbecue*), is cooked by the people, for the people—a communal food well befitting a commonwealth. I see here the early makings of the great community barbecues of present-day western Kentucky—the summertime picnics hosted by Catholic churches, for example, of which I'll say more later.

Moving ahead to the late 1800s, the *Louisville Courier-Journal,* on November 7, 1897, published an account of a big barbecue and burgoo shindig near Versailles in Woodford County, under the Twitter-disqualified title:

THE KENTUCKY BARBEQUE
Some of the Picturesque Phases
of the Great Political
Picnics.
NOTED ONES OF OTHER DAYS
How Whole Animals Were Cooked and
Vast Quantities of Burgoo Pre-pared and Eaten

Considering how the barbecue hotbed of contemporary Kentucky is the western part of the state, I'm struck by how the unnamed reporter, writing just over a century earlier, claims, "Although that noted Kentucky institution, the barbecue, is not by any means confined to the Bluegrass, yet it is only there that it reaches its happiest development." Woodford County, the writer continues, "is pre-eminently the favored spot for holding barbecues." These Bluegrass barbecues, held on the properties of wealthy men, "marked great epochs in Kentucky politics." For instance, in 1836 Kentuckian Henry Clay, a U.S. senator, returned from Washington for a big barbecue near Versailles, bringing with him Daniel Webster and Governor Poindexter of Mississippi. All three gave fiery speeches that day against President Andrew Jackson. Woodford County resident Colonel Thomas M. Field, present at the event, said, "It was about the first big barbecue ever held in Kentucky." In 1860, Colonel Field attended another huge political barbecue in the Bluegrass. He remembered it as

> probably the largest and most celebrated barbecue ever given in Kentucky or the South. [The event] was held in the pasture of Willis Jones, . . . one mile east of Versailles, and given by the old Whig Party and the Democratic Party, which stood in favor of Kentucky's neutrality, to John J. Crittenden, who was Kentucky's peace member in Congress. Crittenden that day was to make a great speech in which he was expected to outline a plan of reconciliation. It was more of a National than a State barbecue, and attracted men to Versailles from a dozen different States, especially from Virginia. . . . Mr. Crittenden spoke for two hours, and made a masterly speech. That barbecue and that speech were the turning point that caused Kentucky to delay action until the Union party had established camps and posts throughout the State. The crowd

present on that day was estimated at 25,000, and a magnificent feast was served to the multitude.

Nearly forty years later, the importance of political barbecues had decreased in the state because, the *Louisville Courier-Journal* reporter posits, Election Day had been changed from August to November (increasing the chances of bad weather and dampening barbecue spirits).

So Kentuckians have been barbecuing on a grand scale since their land became a state in 1792 (or soon thereafter, according to Audubon's account), and that tradition continues today with such massive events as the annual political picnic at Fancy Farm and at Owensboro's International Bar-B-Q Festival, where cooks prepare thousands of gallons of burgoo and roast thousands of pounds of meat, much as their ancestors did at that Bluegrass barbecue of fall 1897 I've been meandering toward. I'll close this abbreviated history with a description of that barbecue and burgoo feast:

The burgoo and the roasted (or barbecued) meats are even more essential features of the Kentucky barbecue than the speeches and are always associated with the occasion in the mind of the public. Preparation for this part of the entertainment usually begins the day before and continues throughout the night. For the meats, a pit or trench, from 100 to 150 feet in length, three feet deep, and three and one-half feet in width, is dug, in which hickory wood fires are kindled. The wood is burned down until nothing remains but the hot ashes, which generally takes five or six hours, and then the huge carcasses of beeves, mutton, and shoat, pinioned on either side by iron bars, are laid across the trench side by side and allowed to roast slowly. . . . The cooks stand by and baste the meats, constantly turning first one side and then the other to the fire. Occasionally the grease from the meats drips on the coals below, causing them to blaze and smoke. Buckets of water are kept conveniently near for the purpose of quenching the flames, for it would take only a few minutes for the meats to become smoked and utterly ruined. There is nothing so delicious as a juicy piece of barbecued mutton or shoat, done to a turn, unless it be a cup of Kentucky burgoo.

The making of good burgoo is even more difficult than the roasting of the meat, and requires more time. The burgoo at the Martin barbecue last week was made by M. Gustave Jaubert of Lexington, who also attended to the roasting of the meats, aided by ten assistant cooks. Jaubert has been at the business for thirty odd years, and is Kentucky's past grand master in the art of brewing burgoo. In fact, M. Jaubert claims to have made burgoo what it now is. It was originally a Welsh product, and for many years after its introduction into Kentucky was a watery soup made of beef, chicken, corn, tomatoes and other vegetables. M. Jaubert increased the number and quantity of its ingredients until he gave it its present consistency, and a distinctively Kentucky flavor. Burgoo is properly eaten from a tin cup with a spoon, and is a square meal in itself.

On that fine day in 1897, M. Jaubert and crew cooked up one thousand gallons of burgoo. Jaubert provided the *Courier-Journal* writer his recipe, which included "400 pounds of beef, six dozen chickens, four dozen rabbits, thirty cans of tomatoes, twenty dozens cans of corn, fifteen bushels of potatoes, and five bushels of onions. It takes burgoo ten or twelve hours to cook, and it requires constant stirring."

Jaubert said he was awake all night tending to the burgoo and barbecue: "First, I filled up the two big kettles—one containing 700, and the other 300, gallons—with water; then I put in the beef and the chickens, and let them boil until daybreak, when we skimmed off the froth of grease that had formed on the surface and took out all of the bones. The vegetables and the seasoning, including a quantity of red pepper, were than [*sic*] put in and allowed to cook for five hours, and the burgoo is ready to be served." At the time of the feast, each person present got a pint-sized tin cup and scooped his or her portion of burgoo out of large tubs, then walked to an "improvised table" and "there [was] served by waiters with bread and barbecued meats." At the big Bluegrass barbecue of 1897, the picnic table "was nearly half a mile in length," and the crowd, "which was estimated at from 5,000 to 7,000, made away with 5,000 loaves of bread, 56 sheep, 6 shoats, and 2 beeves, in addition to the 1,000 gallons of burgoo that failed to hold out."

Historical good times in the Land of Plenty, and the good news is that you can find similar scenes now, 115 years later, at Owensboro's International Bar-B-Q Festival every May, at the Fancy Farm picnic in August, or on a smaller scale at numerous picnics hosted by Catholic churches located mostly in the western counties of Kentucky during the barbecue season (spring through fall). Check out the church picnic schedule in this book for approximate dates (see "Bluegrass, Blues, and Barbecue Region"). The traditions have moved westward and evolved—through the Cumberland Gap, into the Bluegrass (where the burgoo got thicker), and on to the western Kentucky counties where, thankfully, they've rooted deeply.

Kentucky's Regional Barbecue Styles and Sauces

In the western counties, the preferred barbecue is pulled or chopped pork from whole pork shoulders or Boston butts. Traditionally, pork shoulders cooked on concrete block masonry pits for twelve to thirty hours, depending on the size of the shoulder, the type of wood used, the temperature inside the pits, the weather, and other factors like pit design. Pit masters burned down wood, mostly hickory, to coals and shoveled these underneath the meats every one to two hours, trying to keep a steady pit temperature. The most impressive pits have heavy thick insulated lids that are raised with the help of pulleys and cables. Many of the western counties are also fond of smoking cured hams (city hams) and precooked turkey breasts, slicing them thinly to serve on sandwiches. Sauce styles vary county by county. The Hickman County sauce is mostly vinegar and cayenne pepper. Some McCracken County sauces taste strongly of vinegar and chili powder. Union and Henderson counties favor a savory Worcestershire-based dip, while over in Christian County to the east the sauces turn again to vinegar and cayenne. It's safe to say that although Kentucky is most famous for mutton, pork is still king, dominating barbecue menus throughout the state.

Mutton, however, is our most distinctive claim to barbecue fame, although only 18 out of 160 places I visited serve it. The "Mutton Tree," as I'll call it, is concentrated in western Kentucky, with Christian County and Hopkins County forming the trunk of the tree, branching out into Union, Henderson, and Daviess counties for the upper foliage. Owensboro is mutton central, with all four barbecue restaurants serving it. Mutton is usually basted while smoking over hickory coals and served with a savory Worcestershire sauce–based dip, a thin, black potion that also contains vinegar and spices like black pepper and allspice.

Another noteworthy regional tradition—called Monroe County style— dominates barbecue menus in five south-central counties: Monroe, Barren, Cumberland, Allen, and Warren. This is the stuff I grew up eating. Locals refer to it as "shoulder." Boston butts—the thick end of a pork shoulder—are frozen and then cut into thin slices, bone in, with a meat saw. Pit masters traditionally burned down hickory wood to coals and shoveled the coals underneath iron grates that held dozens of slices of shoulder. As the meats cooked over hot coals, the pit tenders flipped and basted the pieces periodically with a "dip" of vinegar, lard, butter, cayenne and black pepper, and salt. Because of the small surface area, pieces of shoulder soak up a lot of smoke in a short amount of time. Preferred length of cooking is around forty-five minutes, but on a hot fire you can grill a piece of shoulder in fifteen minutes.

Beyond these three major regional barbecue styles, I've noted some general taste preferences and peculiar methods of barbecue preparation that I'll label "microregional flavors." I've learned, for instance, that a few Louisville barbecue places really slather on the sauce, and that this trend continues in the northern and eastern counties. The sauciest pork sandwich I encountered during my journeys was the "Big Smokehouse BBQ" at the Smokehouse in Tollesboro, way up in Lewis County, not far south of the Ohio River. The sandwich was shredded meat blended with a thick tomato sauce, like a porky sloppy joe. The most famous rib place in northern Kentucky is the Montgomery Inn, a Cincinnati-based franchise with a restaurant in Ft. Mitchell. Their ribs are basted in a thick, tomato-based sauce—and like I say, they're beloved by locals. Furthermore, barbecue is hard to find in Appalachia, but at Pig in a Poke in Prestonsburg, the local preference is for sauced barbecue. And in the same counties serving "Monroe County–style" grilled sliced shoulder, you'll find a menu item called "shredded." Lovers of naked smoked meats— beware! "Shredded" usually comes from Boston butts, often boiled and then drowned in a tomato-based sauce.

Something I do like is the barbecue on toast tradition of a few counties in the far west of the state, preferred in McCracken, Livingston, Lyon, and

KENTUCKY BARBECUE REGIONS

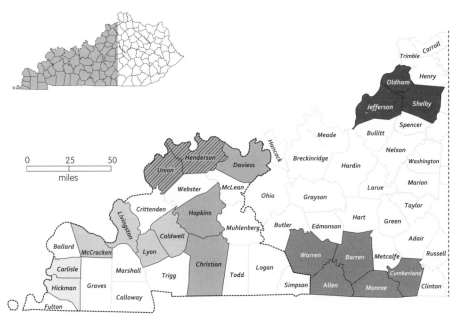

Hickory-smoked pork shoulder, city ham, and turkey breasts. Sauce varies by county, from vinegar to mustard to tomato.

Pork shoulder, pulled, with vinegar-cayenne table sauce

Pork on toast

Hickory-smoked mutton and mutton dip, burgoo

"Chipped" ham, pork, mutton

Monroe County style: pork shoulder and vinegar dip

Beef brisket, beef ribs—a blending of U.S. styles

Caldwell counties, although you can find it elsewhere, like in Graves County. Hickory-smoked pork or mutton is pulled or chopped and served on toasted bread with sliced raw onions and dill pickles.

I also like the "chipped" tradition of Union and Henderson counties, where the bark (the darkened and sometimes charred exterior pieces) of pork shoulders, hams, and mutton quarters are chopped and mixed with a thin, tangy sauce, which adds moisture back into the fire-dried meats. Because bark has so much smokiness, "chip" packs a wallop of flavor and is best eaten as a sandwich.

Burgoo, a stew made from many meats and vegetables, is found primarily in a funky triangle that runs from Owensboro (the burgoo capital) down to Madisonville, south to Hopkinsville, south to Guthrie, and back to Owensboro. You can find burgoo outside this region, but it's rare.

Finally, a note on Louisville and Lexington: I haven't detected any distinctive styles linking the barbecue places in these cities or their environs. Rather, they seem to be melting pots of barbecue styles, serving Texas brisket, Memphis-style dry-rubbed ribs, and western Kentucky–style pork and mutton. Indeed, two of the oldest restaurants, Ole Hickory Pit in Louisville and Billy's Bar-B-Q in Lexington, and newer places like J. J. McBrewster's and Sarah's Corner Cafe in Lexington, bill themselves as "west Kentucky–style" establishments. Two other urban upstarts, Hammerheads and Smoketown USA—both located in the appropriately named Smoketown area of old Louisville—blew my barbecued mind with their smoked lamb ribs, smoked duck, and smoked pork belly (masterminded by young chefs Adam Burress and Chase Mucerino of Hammerheads) and meaty Flintstone beef ribs (the creation of Smoketown's "Jewish redneck"—his words, not mine—pit master, Eric Gould). With so many new places opening up in both cities in the past few years, I'd say the future looks promising for barbecue in the Commonwealth. Surprisingly, many of them are cooking on tank units with external fireboxes, using a lot of wood to create what Vince Staten and Greg Johnson call *real barbecue*.

The Recipes

I hope you enjoy the recipes in this book, because getting them hasn't been easy. I've called places and asked sweetly. I've said sharing a recipe with the good people of Kentucky (and beyond) should be good advertising. When I make something good at home from a restaurant's recipe, it makes me want to go try the original. I own the great barbecue wonderworks Mike Mills and Amy Mills Tunnicliffe's *Peace, Love, and Barbecue* and Chris Lilly's *Big Bob Gibson's BBQ Book* and have used many of the recipes from both. When the dishes taste great, as they usually do, I don't say, "Now I can make this at home so I don't have to go to the restaurants." Instead, I'm saying, "Daggum! I wish we lived closer to the 17th Street Bar and Grill in Murphysboro, Illinois!" (owned by Mike Mills, coauthor of *Peace, Love, and Barbecue*) or "Don't we have some reason to drive to Decatur, Alabama?" (home of Big Bob Gibson Bar-B-Q).

Many people have a proprietary attachment to family recipes, and I understand that, especially in the realm of barbecue, which might coddle more secrets than all other cuisines combined. But do you really have to keep Aunt Suzie's recipe for mac and cheese tied up close to your chest, especially when multiple cookbooks and websites like epicurious.com and foodnetwork.com give easy access to recipes from great food minds like Alton Brown, Bobby Flay, Chris Lilly, Mike Mills, and the Neelys?

In short, I called many of my favorite barbecue places and requested recipes for this book. Some folks declined politely. Some needed reminding and ultimately delivered. And some, like Dave Webb of Dave's Sticky Pig in Madisonville, delivered in grand style.

I'm grateful to the generous folks who contributed recipes from across the Commonwealth. Dear Reader, I hope you'll get to travel to the different regions to sample the varied flavors and styles of the state, but even if you're bound to home, you can now taste what makes a Monroe County sauce different from a Land between the Lakes sauce and an Owensboro mutton dip.

The Ecology of Barbecue

Well, the short version is that it's hard to balance a love of barbecue with ecological sensibility. When I started my journey, I usually asked barbecue people where they got their meats, hoping to find some who bought from local butchers or small-scale hog farms, but after hearing "Sam's Club" numerous times, I stopped asking the question consistently. I know that Ross and Ross in Tompkinsville provides sliced shoulder to over forty barbecue places, and that Hampton Meats in Hopkinsville sells to several of the places I visited in western Kentucky. But where do these meat processors get their hogs? Does it even matter? Who cares where the meat comes from as long as it tastes good, right?

In *Holy Smoke,* the Reeds ask a similar question: "Is any other dish made with less attention to its basic ingredient than barbecue?" They encountered in North Carolina much of what I found in Kentucky: that "nearly all barbecue restaurants cook basically the same pork you can buy at Food Lion or Harris Teeter, most of which comes from Smithfield Foods or one of the other corporate giants that account for more than two-thirds of the pork produced in the United States." Thanks to economies of scale, these businesses—the Smithfields and Tysons—give us cheap meats while contributing to such environmental problems as water pollution from waste runoff and the depletion of aquifers (industrial hog farms, like those in the Texas Panhandle, require huge amounts of water). Animals are confined and get fed plenty of antibiotics. In *Pig Perfect,* Peter Kaminsky notes that "more than 80 percent of all the antibiotics consumed in the United States are used in the livestock industry; eleven million pounds per year by animals versus three million by people," and that concentrated animal feeding operations (CAFOs) rely heavily on them to keep packed-in animals from spreading sickness. You can read more about this sorry business in Ken Midkiff's *The Meat You Eat: How Corporate Farming Has Endangered America's Food Supply* and in Michael Pollan's *The Omnivore's Dilemma.*

So the question "Where do you get your meat?" became less interesting as I went along, but it still niggles me that something that tastes as good as barbecue often comes from animals that spend their brief lives in packed-in quarters.

My cousin Karen and her husband, Steve, down in Clinton County, Kentucky, used to raise some hogs on their small farm but stopped because they couldn't make a profit. The price of pork dropped so much because of the corporate supply that they could hardly break even on the costs of raising the hogs.

I know how expensive this can be, because my wife, Elisa, and I recently raised two Durocs. In April we bought the little brother-sister team from a farmer in Upton and transported them in a small dog kennel to our five-acre homestead here in Richardsville. Short Timer (the castrated male) and Red Bud (the female) slept and ate and rooted and played in a pen off the side of the shed, where they slept. They quickly ruined the goodly stand of grass, digging down deep for the cool earth in the dog days of summer. We fed them twice daily, often pizza from a local buffet and expired bagels from a shop in town; sometimes expired cakes and jams and hot dogs from a grocery store dumpster. Short Timer and Red Bud loved these surprise meals, just slurped the stuff up (we'd soak the pizza before feeding it to them). But we also had to buy several truckloads of pig feed at $20 for one hundred pounds, which, let me tell you, didn't last long.

When Joe Michael Moore (one of my high school football coaches—now a retired teacher and full-time farmer) guided us through the killing of our hogs in December, Red Bud tipped the digital scales at 444 pounds; Short Timer weighed 388. Elisa and I both teared up when Joe shot Red Bud with a .22 rifle. We skinned and butchered them, cured hams, made bacon and sausage, including salty jowl bacon. The work was exhausting, but we were fulfilled and felt we knew pigs so much better, inside and out. The four huge hams are hanging now in our garage. Hopefully they'll be wonderful this winter, after aging through a year of Kentucky seasons.

Point being, raising hogs is hard work, but I wish all the pork I ate from restaurants came from pigs that led lives as good as Short Timer and Red Bud. They seemed real content during their eight months with us—sort of like goofy dogs, with wagging tails and spastic circle turning in the pen when we turned the watering hose on them on hot afternoons. Short Timer liked rubbing his bulk on my leg like I was a fence post, just scratching off the dirt.

Back to the ecology of barbecue: most joints and shacks I've visited are also notorious wasters of polystyrene takeaway boxes, what everybody calls "Styrofoam." At many places, all "plates" are actually sectional polystyrene foam boxes, and one is served plastic forks and paper napkins. Cups are Styrofoam, too. This stuff is hardly ever recycled. Every time I go to Smokey Pig in Bowling Green I balk when disposing of the Styrofoam box in the trash receptacle by the door—often piled high with the voluminous boxes. Day after day, all this nonbiodegradable material goes to a landfill. No wonder it's so ubiquitous: you can buy the sectional containers in bulk for 18¢ each—probably cheaper than hiring someone to wash china or reusable plastic plates.

And then there's the wood issue. Good barbecue requires a lot of wood burning, which contributes to raising carbon emissions. All of this piles up to make barbecue restaurants pretty wasteful. Those of us who love it and also wish to live lightly on the planet just have to put blinders on. It does make me grateful for the few places that do little things to cut the waste. Coincidentally, two of my favorite places—Mr. BBQ in Grand Rivers and Mama Lou's in Uno—don't use much Styrofoam. Mr. BBQ eat-in meals come served on washable plastic plates; Mama Lou's uses paper plates that, at least, can be composted. Both use reusable stainless steel flatware instead of plastic forks. At Hammerheads in Louisville, the clamshell takeaway box was made from a compostable cardboard. I appreciate these touches of conservation.

How to Use This Book, and a Personal Note

Read it cover to cover, savoring every delectable, well-crafted sentence.

But seriously, I envision this book as an introduction to Kentucky's barbecue traditions and as a handy travel guide to steer you toward the best mom-and-pop smoked-meat destinations in the Commonwealth. Of course, I'd be delighted to meet someone who said, "Professor Porkbelly, I cracked the cover of your book on Kentucky barbecue before bed one night, and your book was so daggum interesting I stayed up until sunrise finishing it!"—but I expect this is a book most will dip into when traveling to certain regions of the state and hoping to score some great barbecue, or maybe—and I encourage this—to plan special barbecue road trips while the petroleum lasts.

At best, I hope this book kindles some long-overdue interest in the rich barbecue lore of Kentucky and drives some business toward these mom-and-pop places. We're fortunate to still have one-of-a-kind family businesses surviving in these days of corporate box stores and cooker-cutter chains. Every nonchain barbecue joint holds the potential for a singular experience. I still get excited when eating at new places and revisiting favorite haunts. I might try a new food or hear a new story.

And I hope you enjoy these stories about the characters from the barbecue trail: people like Red Seavers of Southern Red's in Pilot Oak, who traps (and sometimes barbecues) wild animals as a sideline job; and Cy and Jan Quarles, the sweetheart barbecue team of Mr. BBQ & More in Grand Rivers, still smokin' after all of these years; and "Jewish redneck" Eric Gould of Smoketown USA, tending his smoking pits in overalls and spouting philosophy; and the wonderful Wormie—maybe the most colorful character from my barbecue tripping—carrying his shovels full of hickory coals to his grilling pits, cigarette tucked behind his ear, telling me about the delights of pickled bologna and his support of the troops.

While writing about barbecue, sometimes personal stories leaked in—anecdotes about raising pigs, for instance.

Which goes to say: *this is an intensely personal book,* peppered with idiosyncratic biases, from sense of humor to speech patterns to slaw preferences. I suppose all food writing is subjective, and it seems to me my first stab at it is overwhelmingly so, as I haven't censored myself too much. Mostly I've written from the gut and the head, like I talk. That might charm you or irritate you. I hope more of the former.

As for food biases, I've already mentioned them above in the section "What I've Learned about Smoked Meats from the Barbecue Trail," but I'll try summarizing them here. Overwhelmingly, I favor savory over sweet, preferring potato salads with dill pickles rather than sweet ones, vinegar slaw over mayonnaise slaw, and real mayonnaise over Miracle Whip.

On Preferred Cuts and Tenderness

I confused a reviewer of this manuscript with my assessments of ribs. She asked me to clarify. "So, Wes, how do you *really* like your ribs?" Well, my favorite cut is the St. Louis–style spare rib, cut from the belly side of the rib cage, which has more fat (and flavor) than baby back ribs, trimmed of the tips. I like these because tips sometimes dry out quicker than the rest of the rib. Trimming the tips helps with even cooking. I also prefer dry-rubbed (spice-dusted) or naked (unsauced) ribs. When done, the meat should cling to the bone but pull off easily. If meat "falls off the bone," it's overcooked. Wrapping ribs in foil during cooking creates a steaming process that makes ribs very tender, but I dislike the "oven-baked" texture and flavor that often results from steamed ribs. Same with beef brisket, which can taste like roast beef instead of barbecue after lengthy wrapping and steaming. If pit masters succeed in tenderizing the meats by cooking low and slow without the use of wrapping, I congratulate them. It's my preferred method. Of course, I realize many people love ribs that require minimal chewing.

In a nutshell, I love richly smoked, tender meats, naked off the pit. Heavily sauced and overcooked (mushy) barbecue turns me off. But on most days I'd choose mushy barbecue over a fast-food burger.

BBQ, Bar-B-Q, Bar-B-Que, or Barbecue?

The multiple spellings of *barbecue* in this book are intentional. It's been a pain in the butt, but I've tried to remain true to the terms used by individual barbecue places on their menus and business cards. Sometimes a joint will use various spellings on the same menu, which makes consistency particularly difficult. In short, I'm just halfway confused, not entirely.

Dialect and the Kentucky Twang

I've used a bit of dialect in this book when trying to authentically re-create conversations I've had with barbecue people throughout the state. I'm not making fun of them. Hell, I love the way my people talk, our colorful flourishes and flexibility with the Queen's English. Maybe you can hear some of it in my voice. I hope so. Nevertheless, I've mostly avoided—or weeded out—much of the local dialect I wrote into an early draft while trying to capture the particular Kentucky-fried talk of barbecue people across the state. Written dialect can get annoying and appear condescending, after all. If you find some, it's just because I personally find that some particular "Kentuckyisms" like *'em* and *ye* help convey dialect without greatly complicating the flow of reading.

And the BEST BARBECUE IN KENTUCKY AWARD Goes To . . .

Don't you want to know? People ask me time and again, "Who's the best?" and I have to disappoint them. I could probably give you a Top 20 list, but then I'd agonize over #21, which nearly made the cut. Near the end of this book, I do include a subjective listing of superlatives, a kind of "greatest hits" of my barbecue travels, titled "Wes's Great Kentucky Barbecue Feast: Favorite Dishes from My Travels."

When I started this book, I considered a rating system similar to the one used by the authors of *Real Barbecue,* a scale of "good," "real good," and "as good as I've ever had." I like this clear, direct language, and you'll find it creeping into my reviews, especially the ones I wrote early on, but I intentionally left off a rating system because I want you to read about these places and decide for yourself where you'd like to visit. I think you'll know when a place is awesome from the words I use to describe it.

When people ask me to name the best, I usually say something like, "It depends on what kind of meat you want," because few places do everything at an excellent level. I might rate the half chicken at a particular restaurant as outstanding, for instance, but find the pulled pork too dry or lacking the smokiness I prefer. Or maybe a restaurant does stellar smoked meats but serves food-service potato salad and slaw. There are a few dear places that impressed me across the board, with quality smoky meats, fresh-tasting homemade sides, and good hospitality. You'll know these when you read about them. I don't try to temper my enthusiasm for these mom-and-pop barbecue wonderlands.

The Caveat That Must Be Written

And now I must make the disclaimer required of travel guides before sending you off into the blue yonder in search of good eats: *call before you drive out of your way to get to a place.* Or in these techie times, at least search the Internet to see if you can pull up recent food reviews. But calling is the safest bet. Established places close and new places keep popping up. I've done my best to give you up-to-date reviews and descriptions. I wish all these mom-and-pop shops would survive through several generations. Patronize them and they'll have a better chance. Give fast food the finger. Eat some love.

So Really, Let's Move on Already!

That's my introduction to Kentucky barbecue. I promise. I could yak on at length, but I'll get to the places, because I imagine that's why you cracked this book in the first place.

A note on how this book is set up: I've chosen a geographical orientation for the benefit of travelers. If you find yourself traveling in western Kentucky, for example, you can more easily locate a joint by such organization. For convenience, I've borrowed (stolen!) the terms used by the Kentucky Tourism Council to divide our 120-county state into sections.

And now for the good stuff.

Western Waterlands Region

Bardwell

Prince Pit BBQ

When driving on Highway 121 between Mayfield and Bardwell, or Highway 51 from Bardwell to Fulton in far western Kentucky, you get the feeling that industrialism has to a great extent passed the region by. Sure, you may come across some industry, like the "Hamtastic" Harper's Country Hams factory on Highway 51 between Bardwell and Clinton, but mostly the region features a gently rolling landscape of cornfields, barns, grain bins, and a few homes and businesses like Yoder's slaughterhouse. It's a lush, green agricultural region. If you decide to head to this part of the world, make sure you have plenty of gasoline in the tank. Stations are few and far between.

You'll find plenty of human industry, however, at Ricky's Prince's barbecue shack, and if you plan on getting any of his scrumptious smoked meats you better plan on getting there early. Ricky smokes Boston butts, mutton quarters, ribs, whole Smithfield hams, briskets, tenderloins, and chickens over hickory and red oak coals using old-fashioned methods—burning down wood in a big stove and shoveling the remaining hot coals underneath the meat every two hours. He'll also smoke whole pork shoulders if anyone wants them.

When I first visited Ricky's shack, it was 1:30 on a Friday afternoon and he'd already sold out of everything but pulled pork. I ordered a sandwich and sat down at one of two picnic tables nearby the ordering window. Whole fresh tomatoes covered one of the tables, telling me that they are hardly used. Indeed, Ricky's place is mostly a takeout shack, and he sells all his meats by the pound. He also sells plates and sandwiches.

Ricky was very busy tending his fire and pits, but he gave me a few minutes to explain his methods and show me the custom pits underneath a metal garage-like shelter out beside his selling shack. Huge slabs of twelve-foot-long hickory planks were stacked up behind the shack. He gets the wood from a sawmill up the road in Barlow as he's done for twenty years. Displayed nearby the ordering window was a photograph of Ricky with food-meister Alton Brown, who brought a caravan from the Food Network into Bardwell and filmed Ricky doing his work for the show *Feasting on Asphalt*. I hadn't realized before visiting that Ricky had already achieved fame as a barbecue man. And when I tasted his work I thought the accolades were well deserved.

From my seat at the picnic table I watched the heat shimmering off the stove used for burning down slabs of hickory. Ricky has to saw the slabs into smaller pieces to fit them into the stove. When I asked Ricky his specialty, he said, without blinking an eye, "All of it." The biggest local seller, though, is pulled pork and mutton. The Boston butts slowly soak up heat and pit smoke for eighteen hours. Briskets get fourteen hours. Mutton quarters—sixteen hours. Ribs and chickens—five hours.

Ricky got into barbecuing as a young man smoking meats with his father, Donald "Gene" Prince, on weekends when he wasn't working for the railroad. Gene's regular meats were chicken, ribs, pork, and mutton. Ricky was still in school when he came over and started helping. When Gene got tired of doing it, Ricky took over. I met Gene when I saw a small tank smoker off the side of the road in the small town of Barlow and stopped to check it out (Barlow was not on my list of places to visit). Ricky smokes everything down in Bardwell and then Gene picks meat up in coolers and brings it to Barlow, where he starts a wood fire in the smoker to keep the meat warm—a kind of family franchising. When I reached Gene's place at noon on a Saturday, he'd already sold out of everything but pulled pork. I asked Gene his personal history of barbecuing, and he told this story:

When I first got started there at Bardwell, I had a colored friend that had a barbecue pit over there. We'd been cooking out in the country, just a bunch of us boys and all, and I went down and asked him if I could rent his barbecue place and he said, "Nope, you can't rent it but you can use it." Me and him worked on the railroad together for a long time. I started that down there and he stayed with me about two weeks and he said, "Well, you don't need no help." I'd just cook on Friday. When I got off work at the railroad I'd come in and fire the pit up, load it up, cook on Friday and sell on Saturday. We sold out every day by dinner on Saturday most time.

The sandwich I ate that Friday at Ricky's shack was a hefty helping of pulled pork on a bun that was warmed and smashed flat with a spatula. The meat was lean, tender, and moist, with a smooth smokiness and distinctive sweetness from a sprinkling of sauce. The sandwich I ate on Saturday, up in Barlow, was magnificent—a very generous portion of tender pulled pork with some smoky bark mixed in, drizzled with a tangy-sweet vinegar sauce—sweeter than what you find down the road at Nicky's in Clinton—that mixes nicely with the meat. You can feel the weight of the sandwich in your hand. I loved the aftertaste—a lingering smokiness on my taste buds along with the tanginess and pleasant heat of the vinegar from the thin sauce. And all this magnificence for $2.50 per sandwich.

When I said to Ricky that his overhead should be pretty low—just a shack and all—he told me that Kentucky passed a law in May 2009 requiring roadside barbecue stands to have a bathroom. Ricky's place, lucky for us, was grandfathered in. So before true barbecue shacks become a thing of the past, get yourself down to Prince Pit BBQ and try some of Ricky's art. He says he plans to keep doing it all his life. In 2009 Ricky was just shy of forty. I hope longevity runs in his genes.

Open: Monday–Saturday, 9:00 a.m.–until he sells out
100 Elm Street (drive north of town on Highway 51; Ricky's shack is on the right, just after Highway 62 runs into 51); 270-445-0334

UPDATE: I returned to Prince Pit BBQ in May 2012, nearly three years after my initial visit, at 10:00 a.m. on a Wednesday. Gene had just pulled into the gravel parking lot of Ricky's shack ahead of me. I reintroduced myself, ordered a sandwich, and took some photos. Gene said to Ricky, "She ain't got much left over there, hon," referring to the woman selling Ricky's barbecue over in Barlow. "They hit her hard this morning early. They called and ordered three to four pounds and a whole butt and I don't know what all." Nearly sold out at 10:00! As I said, get there early.

Ricky cooks mutton only by special order now. The price of the meat has recently tripled, so he's not smoking it regularly.

Ricky believes the recent influx of Muslims into the region, concentrated in Mayfield and Murray, has boosted demand. Simple economics. "Used to you could buy mutton for 99¢ a pound on the hoof; now they're like $3.69 per pound."

Gene said, "I was talking to that old man, Blankenship, he got fifteen to twenty [sheep] out there in the field. I said, 'If you miss one, just don't say nothin' about it.' He said, 'Why?' I said, 'I might get one of 'em.' Blankenship said, 'I believe if you opened your trunk and throwed a little food in there they'd jump right up in there.'" Gene laughed.

Ricky now sells fried catfish on Thursdays and Fridays from 3:00–7:00 p.m., about a hundred pounds per week, cooked up in one little fryer inside the shack. People get fish and barbecue to go or sit on the weathered wood-slatted deck beside the ordering window or at the three picnic tables underneath a metal carport—a nice shady spot amid the oppressive summertime heat of the Mississippi River valley. I noted that Ricky had increased his picnic tables by one since my visit three years earlier. Seriously, you better get to Ricky's shack before he decides to go modern!

TRAVEL NOTE: Bardwell lies about six miles from the Big Muddy as the crow flies. When traveling in that far-flung corner of the state, you might as well venture down to Wickliffe to see where the river becomes "the Mighty Mississippi" after the Ohio River runs into it. Wickliffe stinks because of a Westvaco paper mill in town—a local fellow told me he thinks it smells like raw cabbage and that he'd "gotten used to it"—but despite the foul odor you can still enjoy the scenery. There's a big parking area by the river where you can watch the tugboats with their loud engines and accompanying barges. A brief drive west takes you over the big steel bridges over the Ohio and the Mississippi, and you can see where the rivers merge.

Cunningham

Hardware Cafe

Build it and they will come, I thought as I sat in this way-rural restaurant during a Wednesday lunch hour and watched tables fill with customers of all ages, male and female.

The cafe is located across the road from a car wash and near signs for a post office and for the Abracadabra Salon and Rudd Pecan Farm, the latter owned by Blair Rudd, owner and pit master at Hardware Cafe. Blair, along with cooking partner Shane Cornwell of Metropolis, Illinois, helms the Smokin' Hose Grillin' Team, a group of professional firefighters for the United States Enrichment Corporation (the uranium enrichment plant in Paducah) who first competed in Paducah's Barbecue on the River in 2006. They won the Reserve Grand Champion honor that first year in competition. They've developed their own distinctive rubs and sauces and sell their Smokin' Hose Grillin' sauce at the cafe. It's sweet, with a vinegar tang and pepper bite.

Blair opened the cafe on January 4, 2011. Business is booming. "When we done our business plan, we figured on a little bitty community like this at 70 people per day: 30 for breakfast, 40 for lunch. We've only had one day at 78, and the rest has been between 125 and 202 is the biggest day we've ever had in here, and you can't even get in here to sit down and eat." They serve a steady local crowd of farmers and are also getting people driving down from Paducah (about twenty-five miles away) and elsewhere. Blair said he strives to keep prices reasonable for this agricultural community, because he has farmers who will eat there for breakfast and lunch, and would come again for dinner if the place were open.

Out of high school, Blair worked as a cutter for family-owned Partin's Country Sausage in Cunningham, where he learned how to kill and cut up hogs. Such skills, plus his work as an EMT, have made him a master at cutting up competition whole hogs.

At the cafe, they cook Boston butts on an Ole Hickory gas-fired rotisserie using pecan wood from Blair's farm. He and his wife own two thousand pecan trees. Pecan smoke isn't as strong as hickory and oak and gives Blair's pulled pork, chickens, St. Louis–cut ribs, and beef briskets an earthy flavor. "I cook on green wood because it smokes better and you don't burn it up so fast," Blair said. "Pecan puts a beautiful ring on your meat, but it isn't overpowering. Oak throws a weird taste on meat and I never use it. I use exclusively pecan, and I will put some hickory on."

Pulled pork is available every day, and other meats are available depending on specials. For instance, Wednesday is fried chicken day (I relished the leg quarter I ate with mashed potatoes and rich gravy), and Thursday is the day for big barbecue baked potatoes, which I also ate (a day early, because Blair wanted me to try it).

They cook brisket flats unwrapped for fourteen to eighteen hours at 200°. Blair said when he first barbecued briskets he wrapped them, and that was a mistake because "it turns them into beef roasts. You can't slice them." They often serve brisket on Tuesdays. Fridays are often good days to get pork ribs.

The successes of the Smokin' Hose Grillin' Team are displayed inside the cafe, including a first-place trophy for chicken at the Jack Daniel's World Championship Invitational Barbecue.

Blair and company are on the ball to serve the highest-quality home cooking. "We cook fresh *every day*," Blair said. "We don't reserve *anything*. If we don't sell out, we'll let the girls [employees] take it home with them. Especially a rib or a chicken or brisket."

Considering the devoted local customer base, Blair said he wanted to remain flexible with his menu offerings. He doesn't want to burn people out. "I'd have thought by now that these barbecue potatoes would have fizzled a bit, but we're serving eighty every Thursday, so they haven't fizzled at all."

I can see why: a two-pound baking potato stuffed with all kinds of tasty stuff—butter, sour cream, abundant pulled pork, and cheddar, topped with Smokin' Hose sauce—all this goodness tipping the kitchen scale at just over three pounds! The potato took up most of the serving tray. I asked Blair if he'd ever done a nutritional analysis of this potato, and we both laughed.

"I'm afraid they'd shut me down," he said.

I loved that behemoth potato. To gloss the Big Lebowski, the reddish-orange peppery Smokin' Hose sauce crowning the potato and leaking down its beautiful skin really brought that tater together. The sauce has chardonnay in it. Not many people use wines in their sauces, and it works. Oh, yes, my friend, it works wonders.

If you're lucky, maybe you can get to the cafe on a day when they serve pecan cobbler—like a peach cobbler, but with pecans. Their pies, as with almost everything at the Hardware Cafe, are all homemade daily.

Open: Tuesday–Saturday, 6:00 a.m.–2:00 p.m.
7647 U.S. Highway 62; 270-642-2411

Clinton

Hickman County barbecue, as passed down by local legend Woody Smith, who got it from his father, one of the oldest remembered pit masters in these parts, is defined by whole pork shoulders cooked over hickory coals for a full day in covered cinderblock pits. The local sauce, served at all three barbecue places, is mostly white vinegar with a heavy cayenne pepper kick. Nicky's sauce reminds me of pepper vinegar, while Grogan's and Ruby Faye's sauces seem a bit sweeter. All three trace their roots back to Woody's original recipe.

In 2012 on the last weekend in April, Clinton hosted the Second Annual Clinton-Hickman County Spring Chicken Festival (A Feather Rufflin' Good Time) on the town square. This community-building event features a 5K run/walk, food vendors, arts and crafts, a chicken wing cook off, and an "egg-chunkin'" contest in which elementary school kids construct homemade catapults to throw eggs. Part of Hickman County's agricultural economy involves raising chickens. Gordon Samples at Ruby Faye's Bar-B-Que told me Hickman County has the highest per capita chicken barn count (over two hundred industrial chicken barns in a county of fewer than five thousand people) in the state.

While over in this sparsely populated region, take Highway 58 west of Clinton to Columbus-Belmont State Park, situated on a bluff overlooking the Mighty Mississippi, for excellent river views and Civil War history. In spring the songbirds were just a-gettin' it, and I sat on one of several park benches in the delicious shade of an ash tree on a weekday afternoon in May and watched the barges on the river. It's a relaxing place for a picnic, and I imagine—considering the high vista—that the western sunsets over the river are magnificent.

Nicky's B-B-Q

From the parking lot at Nicky's, you can't see much but corn, wheat, and sky. Fields stretch all around the cinderblock building. A man named Woody Smith opened the place in the 1930s. Current owner Nicky McClanahan has been here since 1974. Nicky, seventy-five years old in 2012, said he wakes at 4:30 and goes to sleep at 10:30 p.m., as he's done for the past thirty-eight years of owning this business.

Nicky cooks meats in an Ole Hickory gas-fired rotisserie unit, putting hickory wood only into the firebox, and he also uses old-fashioned masonry pits. He smokes whole pork shoulders, beef briskets, quarter chickens, pork tenderloin (cooked whole and sliced), precooked hams, and whole rolls of bologna. The shoulders and briskets cook for twenty-four hours, while the precooked hams smoke for six to eight hours. Nicky added brisket—not traditional in these parts—to the menu back in the early 1990s, and now it's a big seller.

Customers eat at the rectangular counter that runs the length of the building. Nicky's vinegar–cayenne pepper sauces sit in plastic squirt bottles beside napkin holders and bottles of Red Gold ketchup positioned evenly along the counter. A shelf in the middle of the employee area holds candy bars, Hostess cakes, and Wonder buns. A sign hanging from this shelf advertises the barbecue potato: a baked potato with butter, sour cream, cheese, bacon bits, and barbecue beef or pork for $5 (May 2012 pricing).

When I first stopped by Nicky's in summer 2009, my belly was so full by the time I arrived, having already eaten at three other barbecue places that day, I just got a pound of chopped pork to go. Later on that evening I sat with my friend John V. Glass III at his home in Mayfield and gave him a taste test. The pork was heavily seasoned and had some bark mixed in, and John appreciated the texture that comes from a less-fine chop. Some people unfortunately chop pork into "meat paste," he said.

I returned to Nicky's in May 2012 to get better photos and speak with the main man, who was away during my first stop. I'd learned some reporting skills during my three years of barbecue tripping, and I wanted to do a better write-up. I arrived at 10:00, before the lunch rush, and Nicky sat next to me at the counter and weaved his history in barbecue:

> I was in manufacturing for twenty years before this, and I didn't know anything about cooking. I hadn't even boiled water. But there was a man here, a black man named Woody Smith, that had been here several years, and he was retiring, and Harper's Hams owns the building. So Mr. Harper called me and said he wanted me to run it. I told him I didn't know anything about cooking, barbecuing, or anything. It took me about two months to make up my mind. Finally I called him and told him, I said, "I'll take it under one condition—that's if Woody will work with me a year." So he did and we cooked everything while he was here that year that he'd ever cooked. Then he retired and I'm still here. Barely.

Mr. Harper built the diner after Woody's original place up the road burned, and Woody relocated for his last decade of preretirement barbecuing.

"How long you plan to do this?" I asked.

Nicky said, "I guess till I die, I don't know. I'm healthy enough, but I'm seventy-five years old. It's going to break some day."

Nicky said the secrets to good barbecue are to "take your time, and have a good sauce and a good rub." Nicky's chickens, ribs, and briskets all get different seasonings.

"We'll build up the fire, build up the smoke, then take the main fire away from it and just let it smoke all night. We can't keep a live fire—don't want to burn the place down. We've had a couple of fires. We throw water on the coals before we leave and that steams and takes the oxygen out of the closed pits."

About his thirty-eight years in barbecue, Nicky said, "It's a lot of hard work, and it's hot in the summertime and cold in the wintertime. You gotta have a fan to pull the smoke out and when you pull the smoke out you pull the cold air in, and you can't air-condition because you are pulling the smoke out in the summertime. So it's hot in the summer, cold in the winter. Kinda like milking cows."

Nicky's delivers chopped pork seasoned with dry-rub spices that goes well with the thin vinegar sauce, with plenty of barky pieces that satisfy my desire for smoke. The cold slices of smoked city ham are good, and the bologna turns a dark brown color in the smoker. The sliced brisket, cut from the flat, was chewy and not very smoky. The tender, moist chopped pork, seasoned more heavily than at any other place I tried in the county, was my favorite of these. I recommend a chopped-pork sandwich on toast with some of the peppery vinegar sauce.

I asked Nicky if he'd had any problems from breathing in all that barbecue smoke over the years.

"Naw, naw," he said. "I eat the barbecue two to three times a day; that hasn't affected anything either."

Nicky said he wasn't even tired of barbecue yet. I told him I understood.

Open: Monday–Sunday, 6:00 a.m.–7:00 p.m.

3243 U.S. Highway 51 North; 270-653-6092

Red Grogan's Bar-B-Q

The pit behind Grogan's restaurant is the real deal. Hickory is burned down in a chimney and then hot coals are shoveled underneath the meat inside cinderblock pits. Thick smoke billows out the doors of the smokehouse. The meats smoke all night long, put directly on the pits without the addition of any salt or rubs. Red Grogan, owner, still makes his own secretive sauce learned from Woody Smith, son of the original Hickman County barbecue guru.

"Woody was the king," Red, now in his sixties, said. "When I was ten years old we didn't have a lot of food around the house, and I'd go sit up all night with Woody [while he tended the pits] and he'd feed me. I didn't think I was learning, but I did that until I was sixteen, and I guess I learned something."

Red said he reckoned he was the only one in the neighborhood still cooking with 100 percent hickory coals without the assistance of gas. "These young people come in here and they can't believe what I'm doing. I think the old-fashioned ways are dying. Hickory is hard to come by. A rick of hickory is awful expensive."

Red's outlook on the future of old-timey barbecue is not optimistic. "I expect if it ain't got a thermostat on it, it won't get cooked in the future."

When I first visited Grogan's in summer 2009, the barbecue was being served in a small market down the road from the big Hickman County courthouse in Clinton. I spoke with Red's granddaughter Taylor, who along with Lisa Powell was helping put fresh shoulders on the pits, and Taylor said they tried to keep Granddaddy Red away from the pits because he'd inhaled so much smoke over the years. Lisa said the smoke would kill you, and as my eyes burned because of the intense smoke inside the pit, I understood. Soon after my visit, the market burned and Red came out of retirement. He still uses the original pits, and he's back doing the barbecue. Red's a real carpe diem kind of fellow. In addition to his barbecue expertise, he's a three-time national truck-pulling champion and also a national fishing champion. One of Grogan's customers, Scott Smith, who says he eats there almost every day, testified that Red is "one of a kind, can do anything he wants to do. He's built houses for a living, owned a body shop, owned a restaurant more than once, done professional fishing, professional truck pulling . . ."

After the fire, Red rebuilt in style, fashioning a big open dining room with a dozen big tables and sturdy cushioned chairs, wood paneling on the walls (the knot holes and wood grain, along with the mounted wildlife hanging on the walls, recalls the decor of a hunting lodge). The wall menu, written on a white board and hung next to the head of a deer, listed extensive nonbarbecue offerings like fried chicken, kraut and Polish sausage, taco salad, grilled or fried bologna sandwiches, and burgers. Mr. Armbruster, curator of the museum at the Columbus-Belmont State Park overlooking the Mississippi River, bragged on the fried chicken at Grogan's, and it did look beautifully breaded and fried as I watched a neighboring customer eat a plate of it.

I got the pulled-pork plate with potato salad and fried okra. The okra was hot and crunchy. The potato salad was one of the best food corporation–produced salads I've tried—diced potatoes mixed with pieces of bacon, green onions, chives, and a sour cream dressing. The fabulous smoky pork comes without sauce, thank goodness, because this is as pure as smoked pork gets—tender pieces from the interior of the whole shoulder mixed with the flaky smoky exterior bark, moist enough to nearly melt in the mouth. I liked the vinegar sauce but found it unnecessary since the naked pork tasted so miraculous on its own. This sauce seemed less like pepper vinegar than Nicky's up the highway. More like straight vinegar with cayenne pepper in it. After getting a good taste of pure meat, I squirted some orange-red sauce onto the plate and dabbed the pork in it, and the combination was beautiful.

Even though I'd already eaten three times that day, I finished all the okra and pork, and most of the potato salad.

Open: Monday–Thursday, 10:00 a.m.–7:00 p.m.; Friday–Saturday, 10:00 a.m.–8:00 p.m.

211 South Washington Street; 270-653-4420

Ruby Faye's Bar-B-Que ("Home Style Comfort Food")

It took me nearly three years to finally eat a proper meal at Ruby Faye's. I first passed by this full-service restaurant in summer 2009, not long after it opened, and at that point in my early barbecue journeys I thought I might not include places that had been open for fewer than five years (one of the criteria set by Staten and Johnson in their book *Real Barbecue*). Plus, I was just too full to eat and figured I'd get there later on. Fast-forward to summer 2011, and I'm cruising up Highway 51 with buddies John Glass and Todd Chappel after eating at Southern Reds in Pilot Oak and at Deno's and Smoke House, both in Fulton. We stopped at Ruby Faye's briefly on the way to the Fancy Farm picnic, and I ordered a sandwich. It was a good sandwich that left me wanting more. As my book deadline approached in late May 2012, my failure to give Ruby Faye's a substantial evaluation nagged me, so I drove the two hundred miles west for a real sit-down meal.

Ruby Faye's is just off the highway south of Clinton. Huge grain silos next door and a tractor supply across the road speak to the agricultural base of this Mississippi River region. The exterior of the restaurant looks a bit like an old barn, with weathered wood and a covered porch. Big windows let in natural light, and pretty paneling and a cathedral ceiling (all wood) lend a classy feel to the large dining room that often accommodates parties after local sporting events. Regional high school athletic jerseys decorate the walls.

This time around, I sat in the front dining room, admiring the blue corduroy Hickman County FFA (Future Farmers of America) jacket hanging on the wall—taking me back to my younger years at Barren County High School, where many of my best friends, farm kids, wore FFA jackets to school—and sampled a quarter chicken, pork spareribs, brisket, pulled pork, slaw, baked beans, potato salad, burgoo, and homemade banana ice cream.

The in-house-made mayonnaise slaw isn't my preferred style, but the ingredients tasted fresh. I liked the creamy baked beans with meat mixed in, tasting of honey and brown sugar. I loved the sweet tea (not too sweet, so you can drink a bunch of it) and found the brisket to be a winner—a whole brisket with good rendered fat, full of flavor, tender and smoky. The ribs and chickens were both incredibly tender, and both had that distinct smoke flavor you get from long-smoked meats. The pulled and chopped pork came without sauce. The typical Hickman County vinegar-cayenne sauce on the table complemented the pork well. Gordon smokes Boston butts with no seasonings—just meat, heat from hickory coals, and wood smoke—for fourteen to sixteen hours. Ribs and chickens cook for four to five hours at around 225°F. Briskets smoke nine to ten hours.

Of the meats, the brisket was my favorite. The brisket gets a dry rub and baste, as do the chickens. I'd be real happy with a plate of that brisket, baked beans, and some fried okra. I also liked the savory, chunky burgoo—the only burgoo I found in far western Kentucky. Ruby Faye's menu is huge and includes an expansive list of vegetables, like black-eyed peas, turnip greens, and mashed potatoes. Save room for dessert, as their "Sweet Shoppe" menu lists a staggering array of homemade pies (pecan, chess, chocolate chess, coconut meringue), cobblers (blackberry or peach), cakes (strawberry or coconut), cookies (oatmeal raisin, Snicker Doodle), and—yes!—homemade ice creams (vanilla, chocolate, strawberry, banana). I finished my meal with a bowl of the super-creamy banana and just loved it.

Owner Gordon Samples sat down to talk with me. Gordon, like his local competition Nicky McClanahan and Red Grogan up the road, pays tribute to Woody Smith for early barbecue inspiration. On the Ruby Faye's menu, Gordon writes: "My first memory of barbecue was that cooked by 'Woody' Smith at the Springhill 'Y.' I loved the smell when we would go to pick up a barbecued pork shoulder from hogs that we had raised on our farm. The taste was equally satisfying. We are honored to continue the tradition and add to this legacy from our past." Gordon farmed for twenty years and then held a job in Clarksville, Tennessee, for eight years before moving back home to Hickman County and starting the restaurant. He said there wasn't much to do in Hickman County other than farming, unless you owned your own business. "I just came home and bought a job," he said of the restaurant venture.

His mother, Ruby Faye, was a schoolteacher who loved to cook and entertain. Most of what he learned about cooking came from watching her in the kitchen. The core concept at Ruby Faye's is "homemade." Before long they're going to start selling sourdough bread, because Ruby Faye always made sourdough bread and Gordon's eighty-nine-year-old father still makes it using his late wife's sourdough starter.

"My parents were married fifty-three years," Gordon said. "They never wore out a couch, but they sure didn't have any finish on the dining-room chairs. If you came to her house, she *would* feed you, and that's where you spent your time, around the table. If she were alive, she'd be here. She would be visiting tables and trying to get in the kitchen every once in a while—we couldn't keep her out—so my honoring my mother is keeping this place open and serving. This place is my memory to her. I think of that as far as our service and our food."

They've developed family recipes and created a menu with something for everyone. "We have way too many items on our menu," Gordon said. "But the whole population in this county is under five thousand. There are four restaurants in this town. Three of them are barbecue. There are three oth-

---

Ruby Faye's Sweet Shoppe Chocolate Torte

This sweet treat, courtesy of Gordon Samples, is from the kitchen of Ruby Faye Samples, inspiration for Ruby Faye's Bar-B-Que in Clinton.

1 large box (14 ounces) graham crackers
3 cups whole milk
2 packages (3.4 ounces each) vanilla instant pudding and pie filling
8 ounces Cool Whip
15-ounce can of milk chocolate frosting

Combine milk, pudding mix, and Cool Whip. Mix until smooth. Line bottom of 9 x 13–inch pan with graham crackers. Don't crush them. Add half of pudding mixture, and then cover with another layer of graham crackers. Add rest of pudding mixture. Cover this layer with graham crackers. Cover with milk chocolate frosting, thinning frosting with milk to make it spread easier. Refrigerate until pudding is set, 1–2 hours.

---

er restaurants in the county. There are way too many restaurants here for the number of people. But many of my loyal customers eat with me five to seven times a week, so I have to have variety because that's my market."

Gordon introduced burgoo to the community. "People around here didn't know what it was." He likes mutton, but said he doesn't sell it because he can't find a good supplier.

A note of interest: a Yamaha grand piano sits in the back dining room, owned by Don Nicholson, a transplant from Los Angeles who now lives in Hickman County and rebuilds and tunes pianos. As Gordon said, laughing, this might well be the only grand piano you'll find in a barbecue restaurant anywhere. They've been trying to have some regular piano music on weekends.

As Don left the restaurant, he stopped to say good-bye (I'd spoken with him earlier when ordering my food). I asked how he liked living in this out-of-the-way place after living in Los Angeles, Phoenix, and Memphis.

Don said, "It's God's country out here. I never thought I'd end up in a place like this, but now that I'm here I wouldn't change it for the world."

On behalf of proud Kentuckians everywhere, I say, thank you, and welcome, Don.

And thank you, Gordon, and the nice folks at Ruby Faye's for a filling and informative lunch and taste of Hickman County hospitality.

And before closing, please note that if you are a lover of ice cream, don't leave Ruby Faye's without trying some of their homemade concoctions, made in a White Mountain freezer.

Gordon said, "People ask me how we get our ice cream so creamy. I say *cream*. Lots of cream."

In May 2012, they added StrawBaNut ice cream, made with strawberries, bananas, and ground pecans, to the menu. Mama Ruby Faye mixed this up one day for a church function, and it's been a hit at local socials throughout the years. Now it's available to the public. Yet one more reason to return to Hickman County.

Open: Monday–Saturday, 11:00 a.m.–8:00 p.m.; Sunday, 11:00 a.m.–2:00 p.m.

155 U.S. Highway 51 South; 270-653-2271

Fulton

Deno's BBQ

Way on down in southwestern Kentucky, the town of Fulton straddles the Tennessee border. On the north side of the divide you'll find Deno's, barbecue so good that it—according to a local woman at the gasoline pumps at a nearby service station—will "make you want to smack your mama and then ask her forgiveness." Ricky Prince, from his barbecue place up in Bardwell, seemed to think I could get some good barbecue there as well. And Ricky knows his stuff.

I arrived at Deno's late on a Friday afternoon after a full day of barbecue sampling in western Kentucky, so I could make only a small dent in a large pork sandwich that was truly large, with nearly half a pound of meat heaped onto a white-bread bun. Local custom is slaw on the sandwich, so I got it. The overall effect was pleasurable, as the slaw added crunch and sweetness, but the combination of slaw and sauce did overwhelm the meat. The sauce is a tomato-vinegar base with a slight sweetness, moderately hot, delivering a slight bite at the end. The meat is pulled and chopped finely. They use hickory wood and charcoal and cook whole shoulders twenty hours, imparting a real nice smoke flavor to the meat. Valerie Minor and husband, Henry "Deno" Minor, have been serving barbecue since the early 1990s. They started out cooking in competitions, like at the Tennessee Soybean Festival down the road, across the border in Martin, and after many first-place wins they decided they wanted to collect money instead of trophies.

Several people stopped at Deno's concession stand for takeout orders of ribs and chopped pork while I ate my sandwich at one of several wooden picnic tables shaded by the protective roof of the pole barn. Hanging from the rafters were plastic bags filled with water to scare away the flies. A good warm breeze blew through the dining room. Valerie said when she and Deno were first talking about opening a barbecue place, Deno wanted to build or lease a building for a sit-down restaurant, but Valerie objected on the grounds of high overhead. The pole barn has been successful, keeping costs low while attracting a steady stream of mostly carry-away customers.

Valerie says that pork barbecue sandwiches are their specialty, and that they "cook with love" so you can taste it in your bites. They also sell a lot of ribs and half chickens. Another big seller is homemade deep-fried chicken on a stick—a kebab with potato, onion, pepper, chicken, and pickle.

While there I spoke with a man who drove up from Martin to get a slab of ribs, testifying to the Minors' smoking-with-love methods. I tried one of the ribs, and it was mighty tender and flavorful with impressive smoke penetration. The big sandwich was good, but the rib was even more flavorful. The ribs, after all, are what they've won awards for.

ADDENDUM: I returned to Deno's in August 2011 when over in that neck of the woods for the Fancy Farm picnic and ate another of those distinctive sandwiches. The open pole barn with picnic tables under it looked just as inviting as it had on that hot Friday afternoon two years before. Valerie remembered our conversation at the picnic table and how I'd enjoyed tasting the big rib and sandwich. I got another sandwich, this time sharing with friends Chappel and Glass, and it was as good as I remembered—juicy sweet meat piled high, creamy slaw, and a sauce that pulls it all together. That's right—I didn't leave the slaw off as I'd promised myself, and I didn't regret it. While waiting on the sandwich, I listened to Valerie's cleaver rapidly chopping the pork on a block, as a classic-hits station played "Freeze Frame" by the J. Geils Band over speakers loud enough to permeate the entire seating area. A steady breeze, cooler than two years before because of the morning rain, kept the flies away. Or maybe it was those plastic bags of water hanging from the rafters.

Henry introduced himself as Deno and quickly disappeared—not like a magician, but like a man with plenty to do. I heard a chainsaw roar up minutes later, and while sitting at a picnic table admiring the new fly-catching baskets they've hung from the rafters of the barn, we talked about the natural sweetness of the sandwich and watched Deno sawing long slabs of hickory into smaller pieces for his smoker. Noting the hanging bags, I told Valerie she was the one who showed me that home remedy for fly repellant two years ago. I said, "I learned this method from you but don't know how it works, but I got these bags hanging on my porch right now."

She answered, "It really works. You put a penny or a dime in there and they think it's a hornets' nest and [it] frightens them. And it keeps flies away."

I said, "Well maybe that's why mine hasn't worked, because I haven't put a coin in mine!"

Valerie laughed and said, "Ahhhhhhh, you have to put something in there! Put a penny or a dime—I was afraid to put a dime because, you know, it's hard times, and I don't want nobody stealing my stuff," and she laughed again.

Valerie said they were thinking about expanding the business to Mayfield—that people up there needed them—and they are looking for a location to set up their "Deno on Wheels" with a stainless steel refrigerator, double sinks, and a steam table. Valerie intends to stay in Fulton, and Deno will work the Mayfield spot three to four days per week. I thanked Valerie for the fine sandwich, and she said, "Y'all come back, next time when y'all can spend a little time—enjoy our chandelier," as she motioned up at the hanging water-filled plastic bags, "and have a wonderful time."

Open: Thursday–Saturday, 10:00 a.m.–8:30 p.m.
600 North Highland Drive; 270-472-2020

Future City

Leigh's Bar-B-Q

Not far off the new Highway 60 that runs between Paducah and Wickliffe, in the wonderfully named spot in the road called Future City, stands a green cinderblock building with a lunch counter and old-fashioned stools inside. Future City—I imagined the Jetsons flying around in a glass-bubble space buggy, but I'm guessing that whoever named this hamlet was just overly optimistic. The stripped-down menu at Leigh's includes pork, ham, chicken, and ribs (sandwiches and plates). Out back, several long rows of cut-up wood wait to fulfill the noble purpose of cooking some of the tastiest barbecue you'll ever put in your mouth.

Pay attention to the hours of operation. I've come to Leigh's a few times when they were closed and had to content myself with gazing longingly through the glass windows at the menu and empty bar stools. When I finally found them open one Friday afternoon around 2:00, they had just enough meat remaining to make me one sandwich. In other words, you should get there early.

Oh, but that sandwich ranks as the best I've ever had. Well-seasoned salty pulled pork, piping hot and deeply smoky with a lot of bark, topped by a thin and hot vinegar sauce between two pieces of bread they toast in an old-fashioned iron toaster. I love the hot crunchiness of the toast mixed with the real smokiness of the meat.

As I sat at the counter finishing off that magnificent sandwich, a woman came in and asked for a sandwich. Ray Leigh, who along with his father, Eddie, takes care of the meat smoking, told her they were out of pork. He said, "I got one and a half chickens if you want 'em."

"I'll take 'em," she answered promptly.

I said, "Is this pretty typical of you all, selling out on a Friday?"

"Pretty much, yeah," Ray said.

The woman getting the remaining chickens said to me, "That's what I had my heart set on, a barbecue sandwich."

"Don't make me feel guilty, now!" I said.

Then I learned that the chicken this woman scored was being held for someone who was supposed to have been there three hours before at 11:00 to pick it up. She said to Ray, "Just tell them I begged you out of it."

Ray said, "They was supposed to come up at 11:00 and I hadn't had a phone call or anything. Like I said, I got one sandwich left, and I wasn't going to sit for a chicken and a half until 4:00 waiting on them." Ray said he does ribs and chicken every day he's open, but "they go pretty quick," because they smoke only a certain amount of them since they refuse to sell day-old chicken and ribs.

Eddie said, "I run out of chicken and ribs intentionally. If you want some, just call ahead and I'll save some for you." They get a lot of local regulars, and Ray said they often have their orders fixed before they even get out of their cars.

The Leighs smoke whole shoulders over hickory on old-fashioned pits for twenty-four hours. The spareribs and chicken smoke for four hours. Ray said about the shoulders, "What you'll eat tomorrow I put on at 6:30 this morning." He salts the shoulders one time before putting them on the pits to "lock in the flavor" and flips them during the long smoking.

Eddie's father started the barbecue business in the 1950s to help feed the people who were building the atomic energy plant—"the bomb plant," Ray said. Then he passed it on down to Eddie, and now it has come to Ray—three generations of smoking expertise. They've been at their current location since 1964. Ray, who was thirty-nine years old when I talked with him, said he'd been helping make barbecue for thirty years, ever since he was old enough to do it.

I mentioned the large quantity of hickory stacked up out back. Ray said it came all the way from Van Buren, Missouri. I said, "No kidding?" and he said, "It's about like gold. It's getting harder to get because all the furniture companies have it bought up because all these doctors and lawyers now are wanting tongue-and-grooved ceilings and wood floors and it's hurting people who cook with it."

I loved everything about the sandwich I had at Leigh's. They set the bar real high for smoked pulled or chopped pork. I can't wait to get back there, *early* on one of their opening days, and try their ribs and chicken, too.

Open: Monday, Tuesday, Thursday, Friday, 8:00 a.m.–4:00 p.m.

9405 Old Highway 60 West (a hopskip south of the main drag of Highway 60); 270-488-3434

Paducah

Make a pilgrimage to McCracken County, where you can eat at a half dozen top-notch barbecue places and sit in the shade of willow oaks at Paducah's waterfront park and watch the Ohio River roll. Some tall birdhouses are set up to attract purple martins, and walls covered in painted murals depicting the history of the city stretch two hundred to three hundred yards along the river. Moving away from the river, you'll find local restaurants and arts and crafts shops, part of Paducah's successful downtown revitalization plans, including the only store I know devoted to the art of meat smoking, called bbQ & More. Paducah is also home to the National Quilt Museum, "a non-profit institution established to educate, promote, and honor today's quiltmaker."

Barbecue on the River: A Community Charitable Event

On the last weekend in September, Thursday through Saturday, Paducah hosts the Barbecue on the River festival, a "barbecue tournament and pig out" that raises big money for local charities. The streets of downtown are filled with wood smoke carrying the sweet aromas of sixty tons of slow-cooked chicken and pork. I went to the Seventeenth Ever Barbecue on the River festival in 2011, arriving late on a Friday afternoon on the twisty road from Marion where I'd eaten earlier at Hickory Heaven, belly full and happy to be a Kentuckian, soaking up the blue skies, fluffy white clouds, green farmland, and cool air after the recent rains. I crossed the Tennessee River just east of town on a narrow, butt-clenching old frame bridge, a single lane running each way and the steel beams stretching skyward. I'd seen the same river down in Chattanooga two weeks before, still running southward before making its odd northward turn in Alabama, grazing the northeast corner of Mississippi before heading straight north back through Tennessee and Kentucky, being impounded many times along the way and finally merging with the Ohio just east of the waterfront park in downtown Paducah—a good picnic spot if you wish to eat your barbecue in less-crowded surroundings than you'll find on the people-packed streets of the festival. The park is a short stroll away from the main action between North Second and Water streets.

Cruising into downtown, I saw the streets were lined with parked cars and roads were blocked off for pedestrians. Parking lots nearby the grounds charged $5 to hold your vehicle. Being frugal by nature and needing to walk off a bellyful of barbecue anyway, I parked farther away to the west side of the festival and saved a fiver. At 5:00 p.m., families walked along the levee of the Ohio River and funneled in to the festival, where children played carnival games and a young man climbed a tower with ropes around his body to catch him if he fell. Kids wearing harnesses attached to bungee cords leaped into the air, defying gravity, and vendors sold clothing and purses and many other things I ignored, because the delicious fragrance of barbecue smoke captured me, luring me along until I reached the distinctive shiny, red-painted barrel smoker of Deno's BBQ, one of my favorite sandwich places from way down the road on the southern border of the state in Fulton. Deno's was busy, with a line of people waiting to order. Out behind Deno's stand, I saw a striking image: two members of the Boudin Man BBQ Team from Louisiana and Arkansas prepping a whole hog for competition cooking. They told me they had until 9:00 in the morning to prep and cook the hog. They'd got a late start. Zydeco music filled the air, and the hairless pig looked almost comfortable resting on the table, its front hooves tucked back under its head, ears flopped out and alert like a young German shepherd, legs splayed out behind, and the hams looking oh so delicious. The naked pig drew a circle of admirers, mostly women snapping photos with cell phones. One of these ladies was Valerie Minor of Deno's BBQ. She gave me a hug and said I hadn't been down to see them in a while, although it was just over a month ago during the Fancy Farm picnic weekend. She tried talking me into buying their fried chicken on a stick, but I begged off on grounds of swollen belly as I'd already eaten at four places that day. Valerie tried twisting my arm, saying, "Make us five." I just smiled and told her I'd see her later.

I made my way along the facades of vendors, past Happy's Chili Parlor and Barbecue from Paducah, an establishment claiming it's been in business since 1929, and I wondered how I'd missed it during my research. A man out front offered me a Happy's rib tip and said the barbecue man had been away in California awhile but was now back in business, and the Barbecue on the River was his debut party. Their motto: "Takes No Teeth to Eat Happy's Barbecue Meat." They do "ribs, rib tips, beef brisket, pulled pork, and more." The rib tip was saucy and smoky, real good. They are known for their chili, the rib tip peddler said, but now do barbecue.

Down the street I stopped to chat with Rex Jewell, overseer of Rex's Kentucky B-B-Q-Express, a catering and concessions business out of Corydon in Henderson County. Rex was kicked back in a chair wearing a straw hat as younger men did the work of making curly fried potatoes by using an electric drill to force a whole potato through a mold to make it come out twisted. Rex, a native and lifelong Kentuckian, said, "I'm an old fart. I got tired and I sit here more than I get up there." He motioned to the potato-drilling activity. We talked Kentucky barbecue a while, and Rex said, "There's two things in America—barbecue and pizza. They're the only true American foods. They're still mom and pop. Nothing else is mom and pop. My barbecue sauce is a family recipe. Same with pizza. Every little town's got a guy who does pizza and he's got his own little recipe. To me, these are two true foods that if a man is going to get out and travel, anywhere you get a chance you should try them. Unbelievable how many unique flavors there are." On Texas barbecue, Rex said, "I'm not a big Texas barbecue fan. I think they smoke too long. Maybe that's just me. Maybe I'm wrong."

Rex said the Paducah festival is an atypical barbecue cook-off because teams don't use Southern Pride or Ole Hickory units but instead cook on open pits or on homemade smokers. "This is truly a unique cooking area," Rex said. "These guys are burning wood off and shoveling ash and cooking true open-pit barbecue. If I remember right, the dictionary says barbecue is food cooked over an open fire. So they truly are barbecue, where if you use a Southern Pride or Ole Hickory cooker, you're really getting into smoked meats. And Ole Hickory, I can't knock it—I think it does a hell of a job—but I mean it's a lazy man's piece of equipment, and I *am* a lazy man." I laughed at that.

Rex went on, "My living's made on an open grill, not barbecue." He was talking about the large number of pork chops they sell at festivals. Rex noted the regional preference for spareribs over baby backs, saying that in Henderson, Kentucky, he'd sell six cases of spareribs to one case of baby backs. I'm thinking the people of Henderson have good taste—spareribs have more marbled fat (and hence a richer flavor).

As I said good-bye to Rex, he told me that when in Owensboro I should get me a fried hot dog, a local specialty. I said I would if the cholesterol police would get off my back.

Susie Coiner, president of Barbecue on the River, Inc. and cofounder of the festival, summed up their mission succinctly: "We want to cook the best barbecue in the world, raise the most money for charity, and draw the biggest crowd." The 2011 festival hosted forty-five thousand people and raised over $400,000 for charities. For example, the Paducah Symphony averages about $25,000 every year with proceeds from its beer garden. Other barbecue teams have built new churches with proceeds. Susie added that she and the executive director of Barbecue on the River, David Boggs, strive to keep the quality of their main product, barbecue, high by carefully evaluating vendors before allowing them to compete and sell at the festival. All vendors have to sell to the public for three full days and cook in at least one category—whole pork shoulder, ribs, chicken, and whole hog—as a backyard (amateur) or circuit (professional) competitor. Grand champion and reserve awards go to two teams that submit barbecue entries in all four categories. Andrew Coiner, Susie's husband, confirmed what Rex Jewell had told me earlier: "We've been told by some of our competitors that our festival is probably the largest hardwood barbecue competition still left in the country. Whereas other competitions use gas and pellets, most of our teams still use hardwoods."

Barbecue on the River is particularly special because the public can taste real competition barbecue. I've been disappointed by other so-called barbecue festivals where the only people eating the great stuff were barbecue judges. Susie said each competition team and food vendor is inspected every day by the health department.

"They're treated like eighty little individual restaurants out there," said David Boggs. "Whereas most contests benefit one organizing body, we benefit seventy-five different charitable organizations."

I recommend going to the festival hungry, because you'll be tempted with more treats than you can reasonably taste in a weekend, vendor after vendor selling sandwiches and ribs and such heart-stopping carnival foods as deep-fried Oreos and Twinkies. Many of the barbecue vendors had won awards at previous competitions and decorated their booths with trophies and banners, and people stood in long lines to sample their wares. One of these was Smoke Shack BBQ from Columbus, Ohio, whose colorful motto is "Follow the Smoke and Get Your Bone On." I admired the red barn facade of Cookie's Grill, lit up beautifully in the pre-dusk sunlight, and I read the banners on top hanging from white-painted plumbing pipes: first place for "Backyard Chicken" at the 2008 Barbecue on the River festival, second place for "Backyard Ribs" in 2008, 2009, and 2010, and third place for "Backyard Whole Hog" in 2009. A large pink plywood pig outside wore a black scarf with a menu scribbled in white letters.

Nearby, the Pathway Baptist Church displayed a sense of humor by naming their barbecue team "Certified Holy Smoke." Their previous awards for "backyard" whole hog, chicken, and ribs were also displayed proudly on the top of their storefront. And on down the line, the Good Ole Boys BBQ Team displayed a sign announcing, "To get a better piece of Chicken than ours, you've gotta be a Rooster."

Throngs of people moved like a wave down the streets. The pretty old brick storefronts of Paducah lead down to the river, and kids and senior citizens alike stretched their necks to see into a portable aquarium displaying "Fishes of the Ohio" right there in the street. Just a couple hundred yards away rolled the real river, and the colorful big murals of Paducah's history stretching along the concrete flood walls show men arriving in wooden boats, men surveying the land, a pioneer cabin near the river, an early settle-ment map, a steam engine leaving a train depot belching smoke from an iron chimney, and pop-art scenes of modern Paducah with old-timey automobiles cruising a neon-lit commercial district. Lew Jetton and 61 South played their Southern Fried Chicago Blues on Water Street with the big river as a back-drop, across from a booth selling pigsicles (pork kabobs).

Paducah's BBQ on the River festival is a great street party, with enter-tainments for young and old alike, superb people-watching opportunities, and more barbecue than you can possibly sock into your gullet. What more, this is a charitable event, and vendors display their charities proudly. The Riv-er City Rib Ticklers, for example—"Smokin' for a cure"—donate 100 per-cent of profits to the Laurel Foundation, an organization that funds cancer research. Raising money for good causes, goodwill shared among people, a ra-cially diverse crowd, and everyone from kids to seniors meandering the streets and savoring the smoky offerings—Paducah's river fest ranks highly on my list of barbecue "must dos."

bbQ & More

"We can decorate your hog and your house," Susie Coiner told me when I walked into this commercial shrine to barbecue in downtown Paducah. "We can dress your hog—we can supply all the sauces, rubs, injections, and tools you'll need to barbecue."

Susie's husband, Andrew—a lawyer by vocation and barbecue judge by passion—showed me a wall of sauces and explained that many of them were developed by competition cooking teams southwest of Paducah in Carlisle County, where I'd eaten lunch shortly before at the Hardware Cafe in Cun-ningham. "They are the reason this store opened," Susie said. "This was our barbecue office for the festival, and we thought we should sell some of our competitors' sauces. We originally intended to just have a little retail nook in front, but then our city commissioner said, 'Why don't you really go for it and put in a kitchen and be like Williams-Sonoma.' Now we're a licensed res-taurant with the ability to do cooking demonstrations." They plan to do more of these now that they're selling Memphis brand pellet grills—computerized high-end meat smokers.

I'm usually allergic to shopping. The Christmastime commercial frenzy makes me grumpy. I avoid shopping mauls [*sic*] like the plague. Exceptions are food and beverage stores. I can get happily lost in those.

So it was with bbQ & More. I wandered about the store like a kid in Candyland, feasting my eyes on gourmet coffee beans, multicolored bottles of barbecue sauces, pepper sauces, and many Kentucky Proud products, like sea salts flavored with bourbon and smoked on a charcoal grill by a nurse in Louisville. Now that's unique. Susie and co-owner David Boggs have also developed a line of products under the Quilted Pig label, a tribute to Paducah's two major tourist draws: barbecue and the National Quilt Museum. David is actually an accomplished quilter. I took home a bottle of Quilted Pig BBQ sauce, an orange-colored mustard sauce that goes well with pulled pork. They also sell lampshades and pillows bearing the brand's memorable image: a standing pig marked with the pattern of a hand-pieced quilt.

Open: Monday–Saturday, 10:00 a.m.–5:00 p.m.

321 Broadway; 270-534-5951

Backwoods Bar-B-Que

Backwoods' award-winning barbecue (voted #1 in the *Paducah Sun* Readers' Choice poll in 2012) has two locations in Paducah. Ballard County native Sudie Holdman, a former tobacco farmer, and sons Tristan and Matthew run this family business, open since October 2000. I spoke with Matthew, who has a passion for the cultural history of food (he wrote his M.A. thesis on the Columbian Exchange—the movement of plants, animals, and diseases between Europe and the Americas after Columbus's arrival in the Caribbean—which includes a discussion of barbecue).

"What makes Backwoods special?" I asked.

Matthew said their hash brown casserole "launched us into regional superstardom," and that their homemade pies, like coconut and chocolate with tall meringues, are also a big hit. They also have pecan, chess, and Dutch apple. Pie expert Connie Peyton has made them daily for twelve years. "She's irreplaceable," Matthew said.

They smoke whole shoulders on custom cookers made in Clinton, Kentucky, by a do-it-yourself ironworker. An electric rotisserie keeps the meat moving, and a firebox on the side ignites wood on an electric burner. They

Backwoods Bar-B-Que's Coleslaw for a Crowd

The following recipe and description are offered courtesy of Matthew Holdman, a member of the family at Backwoods Bar-B-Que in Paducah: "This recipe was originally intended for large southern gatherings such as receptions and family reunions. Mrs. Connie Peyton has worked in kitchens for over thirty years and restaurants for nearly her entire adult life. She loves cooking and making eaters smile, and says that southern cooking and soul food are one in the same and include many of the same elements: grease and love.

"The original coleslaw recipe at Backwoods was missing something crucial, and Connie used her experience to change it into what it is today. I witnessed this change, and today the coleslaw at Backwoods is not only my favorite, but also reminds me of the many fresh slaws I ate in the Caribbean, notably Belize and Quitana Roo, Mexico (the connection I'm sure could be explained through African influences). This side dish is simply wonderful, and goes best with a splash of hot sauce."

10 pounds shredded cabbage
4 cups sugar
1 cup distilled vinegar
⅛ cup celery seed
⅛ cup black pepper
⅙ cup salt
½ cup minced onion
3½ cups mayonnaise

Combine sugar and vinegar and stir until fully dissolved. Toss spices over one quarter of the cabbage. Pour sugar and vinegar mixture over spice and cabbage mixture. Add mayo and onions and mix thoroughly. Gradually add remaining cabbage and mix until well incorporated.

buy hickory from an ax handle company in the Ozarks. Matthew said customers didn't mind when they switched the shoulders from open pits to this electric cooker.

Ribs and chickens, prepared daily, cook on an open pit over hot hickory coals for five hours. Additionally, they cook whole pork tenderloins and slice them an eighth of an inch thick after chilling them; smoke city hams in the regional fashion; and sell the Paducah favorite, an open-faced chili cheese dog.

"The ribs are our *pièce de résistance*," Matthew said. They dry rub St. Louis–cut spareribs and cook them on the pit, then apply sauce, wrap them in foil, and leave them in a 170° warmer for five hours until serving. They do fall apart after that long steaming. (Note: This method is similar to Ol Joe's World Champion Ribs recipe included in this book.) Country music stud Vince Gill stopped by in 2007 and "really tore into a slab of them."

These are the kind of spareribs that most people love: extremely tender and flavorful. Those who prefer competition-style ribs—where the meat is supposed to cling to the bone and pull off it easily, not fall off it—will think these ribs are overcooked. I'm not a huge fan of wrapping ribs, as steaming dilutes the smoke flavor, but I'll still eat them and like them. Maybe we could name these "old man ribs," since you don't need strong teeth to eat them.

The hash brown casserole was creamy, cheesy, and hot, with crumbled cornflakes baked on top. The pork on toast was a good portion of tender, moist pulled pork with hardly any bark drizzled with a sweet and tangy vinegar sauce with flecks of black pepper and spices on two pieces of lightly toasted white bread. The sauce is prepared in house. Because of the sweetness, I'd call this closer to a Memphis or St. Louis sauce than to the thinnest of the western Kentucky vinegar-pepper sauces. The bread wasn't buttered before toasting (as it is at Jewell's Open Pit in Princeton), so didn't add anything to my enjoyment. I picked the meat off the toast. The pork by itself with the sweet and tangy sauce was good, though.

Recommendation: get ribs, hash brown casserole, and a piece of pie. And by the way, a local guy told me Backwoods has the reputation for having the coldest bottled beer in town.

Open: Monday–Thursday, 11:00 a.m.–8:00 p.m.; Friday–Saturday, 11:00 a.m.–9:00 p.m.

5172 Hinkleville Road; 270-441-7427

O'Tyme Hickory Pit

Faye Tinsley, owner of O'Tyme Hickory Pit, comes from a barbecue dynasty. Her brother, Kenny Ramage, owns Ole Hickory Pit in Louisville. Their father, Murvin, worked at Kountry Kastle and owned the Plantation Barbecue drive-in restaurant in Paducah back in the day. Murvin built many of the masonry pits at barbecue joints in western Kentucky, including the old pit behind this restaurant. The pits look strikingly similar to those at Ole Hickory Pit in Louisville: long rectangular structures with thick firebricks for insulation and steel around the top for stability, with steel grates about halfway up from the ground to hold the meat, and a heavy steel lid operated by a pulley to keep the heat in. Of course, there's an access underneath to burn the wood and shovel coals.

In July 2009, Faye had been doing the smoking at the restaurant for over twelve years, while managing to drive a school bus full-time as well. She recently retired from the driving job and said she'd turn sixty-nine her next birthday, and yet she was still tending the pits.

I sidled up to the counter and spoke with Pawnee Dennis, Faye's daughter and assistant manager. The interior is homey, especially if you're a fan of University of Kentucky basketball. Posters of Kentucky basketball players going back many years line the walls, and you can tell the time by a Kentucky Wildcats clock. Ceramic pigs and figurines of various sizes line shelves, alongside two regal statues of American Indians carved from wood by Jerry Ramage, Faye and Kenny's brother, a hobbyist woodcarver.

The pork sandwich was a nice portion of meat on a bun—you can also get it on Texas toast—with a medium smokiness and a vinegary-pepper sauce to give heat. The meat is served "dry" instead of "wet," because Paducah folks—with their good tastes that agree with my own—don't like their meat overpowered by sauce. They smoke whole pork shoulders over hickory with a little oak. Unfortunately, they were sold out of ribs when I visited on a late afternoon, so I didn't get to try them, but I'm impressed by a place that cooks only enough ribs to sell on the day of smoking. Their beans are a mixture of brown sugar, Worcestershire sauce, onions, bell peppers, and ketchup, baked in the oven. The barbecue ham is a round of boneless ham smoked on the pit for six hours. They sell a lot of ham.

I asked Ms. Pawnee what the locals liked, and she said, "The barbecue is good and everybody loves our chili cheese dogs—we split a hot dog open and serve it on a round bun with chili on it." She said Kenny didn't sell many dogs in Louisville, but that in Paducah they "sell 'em like crazy." Well. I guess locals can get good barbecue anytime they want it, so I can't blame them for craving variety.

When I posed my often-asked question, "Why is barbecue such a tradition in western Kentucky?" Pawnee deferred to Debbie, who served up my sandwich, and she said, "We just like to eat out a lot. Paducah people are outdoorsy people, with the river and Kentucky Lake and Lake Barkley."

I loved the comfortable family atmosphere and sweet hospitality given by the genuine folks who keep this barbecue tradition going. Pawnee told me the restaurant was up for sale—that her mama Faye was tough but ready to retire from the hard work of smoking meats, and that she, having managed the place for nearly two decades, was getting a little tired, too. Fearing the worst—that the family would have sold the place, and that a franchise restaurant would move in—I called them months later, and Ms. Faye answered the phone early one morning. She said her son was probably going to take the place over and keep it going. I sure hope so.

Open: Monday–Wednesday, 10:00 a.m.–5:30 p.m.; Thursday, 10:00 a.m.–6:00 p.m.; Friday, 10:00 a.m.–8:00 p.m.

1535 Broad Street; 270-442-1680

Starnes

This is one of the most famous barbecue joints in Paducah. The pork sandwich, in the distinctive regional style, is smoked meat served on toasted white bread. The meat was chopped fine, tender, a little mushy, and served with a vinegary pepper sauce and a sprinkling of salt on top. The sandwich comes served on wax paper. I ate it right off the wood-toned laminate countertop while sitting at a barstool at the U-shaped counter in the center of the diner. The sandwich was good, but I prefer a more intense smoke flavor.

The simple menu includes sandwiches of pork, beef, ham, bologna, and turkey, with sides of potato salad and slaw. The diner's decor is simple as well, with tiled floors and cinderblock walls painted the color of pistachio pudding. Out back of the building, a huge fan blows smoke out from the pits, which I didn't see, and stack upon stack of wood stand near a brick chimney that vents the pits. The smoke smells wonderful. In short, Starnes has all the makings of an authentic barbecue joint. Indeed, Vince Staten and Greg Johnson rate it as "real good" in their guidebook *Real Barbecue*. I like their thin tomatoey-vinegary pepper sauce, which they sell in bottles. If you're in the Paducah area, Starnes is surely worth a visit for its old-fashioned flavor, tradition, and simple style.

Open: Tuesday–Saturday, 8:00 a.m.–6:00 p.m.

1008 Joe Clifton Drive; 270-441-9555

Kountry Kastle

This place ranks highly on my "BBQ Places with Character" list. American flags fly from two castle turrets at the top of the brown-painted wooden facade. Inside, especially on a hot summer Friday afternoon like when I first visited, you'll find a darkened pub atmosphere with air-conditioning and a jukebox and bar patrons, even though Kountry Kastle is a family joint. Living in Baptist-heavy Kentucky, in which 30 percent of its 120 counties are still dry, I don't expect to find beer served at barbecue joints, but locals tell me Paducah has been a destination for thirsty travelers going back many decades.

Lake Edwards founded the business in 1939, and he served beer from the beginning. When Lake died in 1964, his son Max took over. Now, the torch has passed to Lake Edwards's grandson A. J., who said he liked their electric cooker—which bakes meat and creates smoke by burning hickory blocks on a heating element—because you don't have to babysit the meat so much. He said a lot of times people can't tell the difference between traditional and electric, and that pretty soon nobody would be able to afford traditional smoking methods because wood prices were going up. A. J. took me back to the pits and showed me their meats and explained how they doctor their beans and smoke them, too. They cook whole pork shoulders skin up at 210° for fourteen hours and sheep quarters for eight hours. A. J.'s father makes up the spice mixture for the secret sauce. When I asked what they do best, A. J. said, "Barbecue on toast is the biggest seller. That and the chili cheese dogs." They'll pull or chop your meat "any way you want it." By the way, "barbecue" here means pork. If you want to sound like a local, ask for "barbecue on toast."

Kountry Kastle has an extensive menu of burgers, chili dogs, Polish kraut dogs, fried seafood, Philly beef and Swiss sandwiches, and cold beer on tap. The waitresses know people by name. I sat at the bar and ordered a mutton sandwich. The meat was rich and tender, a little chewy but gamy in the good mutton way, and heaped between two slices of toast. The thin sauce had a lot of chili powder in it and good heat. They also offer country-style ribs (sauced or without), chicken and pork dinners, beans, slaw, and potato salad.

I revisited the Kastle in May 2012 and found the place hadn't changed since my first visit three years earlier. The interior was still darkened and illuminated with neon beer signs, flat-screened televisions, and the jukebox. In late afternoon a few patrons, mostly middle-aged men, drank mugs of beer and talked. I asked for A. J. They hollered for him, and he came to the counter and greeted me like an old friend. He said that even though the price of mutton has gone way up, they'd hardly raised their prices.

I walked beyond the bar area and discovered that Kountry Kastle is huge. They have a room near the back where a young boy was shooting basketball. The ball went through the hoop high on the wall and then rolled back to him. Nets keep the ball from going wonky and disturbing patrons at nearby tables. They've also put in a smoking patio, now that Paducah has banned indoor smoking. The restaurant is like a maze once you get beyond the bar area. They've added on several times, and now the Kastle sits 275 people.

In a little nook off the bar area, I happened upon Eddie Guess, quietly sipping a mug of beer. Eddie has patronized the Kastle daily for years. He said, "This is my table. They take care of it for me. The Kastle is about family. Gooood people. It's *Cheers* in Paducah. *Coldest beer in town.* Put that in your book." Marvin Gaye played softly in the background. "When you walk in this place you can feel it," said Eddie, relaxing in the untroubled atmosphere of the pub after his workday at Progressive Rail, a company that builds locomotives. "Always stop at a railroad crossing—because I do the air and the brakes on 'em," Eddie said. He paused a second for that to sink in and then laughed.

His conclusion? "When I'm feeling real bad, I stop in here. When I leave here, I'm smiling. It's not like you're a customer. This is a family."

Open: Monday–Wednesday, 10:00 a.m.–10:00 p.m.; Thursday, 10:00 a.m.–11:00 p.m.; Friday–Saturday, 10:00 a.m.–12:00 a.m.

3415 Clarks River Road; 270-443-9978

Side Dish: Where Is the Mutton Line?

There's no mutton in Murray or Mayfield, which seems odd since the annual Fancy Farm picnic—where they cook up nearly ten thousand pounds of it—is nearby these western Kentucky towns. But there is mutton at Woodshed in Hopkinsville, and you can get it in Lexington at J. J. McBrewster's and in Louisville at Ole Hickory Pit (the owners at both these places have roots in western Kentucky). There seems little rhyme or reason about which counties favor mutton and which ones shun it. The most I can say is that with a few strange exceptions (like the random places in Louisville and Lexington), Hopkinsville forms the eastern border of the mutton line. It stretches up to Owensboro—mutton central, with Moonlite serving the most and Old Hickory serving some of the best—and goes all the way over to Bardwell, not many miles away from the Mississippi River, where Ricky Prince cooks up whole mutton quarters on special order. But it just gets haphazard between these poles, with some counties cooking up plenty of mutton and others treating it like some ugly stepchild to be shut away in the basement.

My math says that eighteen barbecue establishments in Kentucky serve mutton. This list shows that, like burgoo, mutton is a rare find, which means try it when you get the chance. For the record, the cost of mutton has skyrocketed. Several restaurant owners tell me they make little to no profit on it, but keep it around for the customers who want it. In short, expect to pay more for mutton, and be glad to do it.

As of February 2012, these places smoke and sell mutton. For convenience, my list begins in the far west and moves east.

Bardwell: Prince Pit BBQ (by special order)
Paducah: Kountry Kastle
Uniontown: Uniontown Food Mart
Waverly: Peak Bros.
Henderson: J & B Barbecue; Thomason's Barbecue
Slaughters: Good Ole Boys
Madisonville: Dave's Sticky Pig
Hopkinsville: Bar B Que Shack; Woodshed Pit BBQ

Owensboro: Dee's BBQ and Diner; Moonlite Bar-B-Q Inn; Old Hickory Bar-B-Q; Ole South Barbecue
Russellville: Roy's Bar B Q
Louisville: Ole Hickory Pit
Lexington: Billy's Bar-B-Q; J. J. McBrewster's

By the way, I've heard Kentuckians claim that we're the only ones barbecuing mutton—I've even said it myself—but in the book *America's Best BBQ: 100 Recipes from America's Best Smokehouses, Pits, Shacks, Rib Joints, Roadhouses, and Restaurants*, Ardie A. Davis and Chef Paul Kirk note that many central Texas barbecue joints serve it, and that it was once served at Boyd 'n' Son Bar-B-Q, a joint that's now closed, in Kansas City. So I reckon we aren't the only ones chowing down on mature sheep—but I'm wagering we eat more of it.

Harned's Drive In

On the road between Paducah and Reidland, just west of where Highways 60 and 62 split off from each other, sits a little square, white-painted cinderblock building that houses the only barbecue drive-in restaurant in Kentucky. A wall of wood runs behind the drive-in, and their sign promises, "OLD FASHION BAR*B*Q." I was surprised when I pulled into a space and a young woman walked over and asked if she could take my order. The menu hanging on the outside of the building displays the kinds of foods you'd expect from drive-ins, like burgers, hot dogs, chuck wagon sandwiches, and ice cream products, in addition to barbecue sandwiches and plates with fries, onion rings, beans, slaw, and potato salad. "Cash only" signs are posted at several spots inside the diner's windows. I visited at 6:00 p.m. on a Saturday and most of the parking spots were filled with cars, trucks, and motorcycles.

The large barbecue sandwich was pulled meat, slightly chopped, on a large bun. The meat was tender and had a moderate smokiness. Nice little pieces of fat were mixed in with the lean. When you pull the sandwich apart, chili pepper sauce clings to the bun and meat. The sauce is what makes this barbecue sandwich stand out. It's a thinner cousin to Arthur Bryant's Kansas

City sauce, with the taste and color of cumin and dried ground chili peppers. My friend John Glass said the sauce tastes like taco seasoning mix, which might sound pretty crappy if you don't like tacos, but pretty interesting if you want a sauced sandwich different from the regional norm.

On another trip to Paducah in 2012, I ate inside the drive-in and spoke with Rock Harned, one of four brothers who have managed the place over the years, and he gave me some history:

My granddaddy built it in 1955. He had a place down on Eleventh Street called Slim's Barbecue, and my uncle took it over when grand-daddy moved out here. My uncle continues to run that one, and when my dad came home from the Korean War, him and mama took this one over. Back then we were a long way out in the country, but the city just keeps bringing it to us.

The four of us brothers were all born on this piece of ground, and you started working in the restaurant when you turned five. A year before you started school you started weighing French fries and hauling in wood. We went to school, do what we do, come back home and went back to work. Matter of fact, some days you'd be sick and want to stay home from school, and about 10:00 Dad would come up there and go, "Get your work stuff on, boy, and come down and help us through lunch."

Rock laughed and said, "It got to be where you just might as well go on to school."

The brothers have a tight-knit relationship and see each other every day. There's Rick, the oldest, and then Rock, Rhet, and Rob, who passed away in 2011. "We're blessed," Rock said. "I know lot of guys don't see their brothers but twice a year."

When the brothers were younger and got mad at each other while working the drive-in, Daddy Harned would send them out back to work out their differences. "He'd say, 'Just get after it,' and I mean you'd just wear each other out, and you'd get done and he'd go, 'Okay, you done? Go in there and wash the blood off and get you another shirt and come back to work.' Well sooner or later you learned it just really wasn't worth going out there fightin' cause you was going to come back to work anyway, so you's just best to get over it. It wasn't a bad lesson," Rock said, laughing. "Just get it done."

They cook whole shoulders and sugar-cured hams on open pits and sell lots of "Paducah dogs" with the same chili recipe used by Rock's grandmother. In a rare shift from my barbecue monomania, I broke down and tried the Rock-recommended chili cheese dog: a chubby old-style frankfurter sliced in half and splayed on a toasted hamburger bun, topped with thin, spicy chili and goopy cheese. I raised the top bun to peek at the wicked goodness inside and said, "Man alive—heart attack on a plate." Two wide frankfurter slices laid side-by-side spanned the width of the hamburger bun, bathed in melted cheese and chili—so hot, gooey, and decadent I nearly broke into "The Star-Spangled Banner."

Additionally, knowing more about what to eat in Paducah than I did three years earlier, I asked for the pulled pork *on toast* this time around. My friend Cy Quarles, the septuagenarian barbecue master from Grand Rivers who smokes whole shoulders for twenty-four hours over hickory coals, had recommended Harned's pork during one of my visits to his restaurant, Mr. BBQ & More, and biting into the pork on toast this time around I understood Cy's admiration. The pork was pulled in good-sized strips and had some browned barky pieces mixed in and tasted deeply of hickory smoke. I requested no sauce so got the full flavor of that righteous pork. The white bread was toasted to a lovely golden, and the chili powder–laden vinegar sauce—their single sauce—made for a good palate cleanser when I dabbed bites of sandwich into it.

As I raved about the sandwiches, a heavyset man sitting on a barstool at the counter said, "I don't come here for the food—I come for the hospitality."

Rock said, "That's right, that's what I'm looking for. To be honest with you, that's the best thing I love about our restaurant is during lunch, when people come in, I bet 85 percent of them I call by name as they walk through the door. They've eaten with me since I was little bitty, and then they bring their grandbabies with them, and next thing you know, well, they're coming in too. They just can't wait to eat here again."

I said, "Is this *Cheers* without the beer?"

Rock laughed. "We're just cheerful people."

The future looks good for Harned's. The man who made my sandwiches was Rock's nephew Aaron, a recent graduate of Western Kentucky University who in sixth grade worked at the drive-in for fifteen hours weekly. When he was even younger he came in to weigh fries: measuring five-and-a-half-ounce portions of frozen fries from five-pound bags for cooking to order. "We don't cook a whole bunch of fries and leave 'em back here to get cold," Aaron said. He studied agriculture and minored in business administration at WKU, but he seems happy working at the drive-in. "It's what he's always wanted to do. It's his for the taking as we all go," Rock laughed.

When leaving I totally got my redneck on and purchased a camouflage ball cap with their logo—HARNED stitched in red letters inside the shape of a pig, above the words "The South's Best Bar-B-Q." That's a mighty big boast, but that pork on toast surely ranks up with the best sandwiches in the state of Kentucky, which means it's as good as you'll find anywhere. I wear it proudly.

Open: Monday–Saturday, 11:00 a.m.–9:00 p.m.
4421 Clarks River Road; 270-898-3164

Graves County

Graves County is home to several great barbecue places plus the annual Fancy Farm picnic—once named the largest in the world by the Guinness record keepers—where in 2011, the 131st of these events, they smoked ten thousand pounds of pork and nine thousand pounds of mutton at this church fund-raiser that's a mixture of carnival games, bingo, and political rally. I don't know why Graves County deserves so much fine barbecue. My friend John V. Glass III, a devout Catholic who lives in the county seat of Mayfield, would probably chalk it up to providence. I can't argue with him: the mutton and pork the Catholics smoked for twenty-four hours at Fancy Farm were truly divine. The people in this part of Kentucky appear fond of some items rarely seen on barbecue menus outside the region: stuff like precooked turkey breast and city ham smoked for additional flavor (on the menus at Hoskins' and Carr's) and also—wonder of wonders—"barbecue" bologna.

Micah Seavers of Southern Red's Bar-B-Que in Pilot Oak sums up the regional tastes this way: "Western Kentucky as a whole, everybody's pretty open to eatin' a little bit of anything, and so everybody's learned to be pretty open to cooking a little bit of anything." Let's go on a tour of a county that, while not boasting status as a "Barbecue Capital," deserves it.

Fancy Farm Picnic and Barbecue

The small town of Fancy Farm seems an unlikely location for the largest picnic in the world. American flags hung from light poles and political signs rose up from many front yards on the weekend of this famous picnic, the official kickoff to the Kentucky election season. Cars were parked all up and down the highway, on the baseball field owned by St. Jerome, the big Catholic church in the center of town, and everywhere else I looked. I drove there for the barbecue and left with a $5 raffle ticket for a 2011 Dodge Challenger and two pounds of the nineteen thousand pounds of meat the men of the Knights of Columbus from St. Jerome Catholic Church cooked up for this charity event. The yellow church building stood out beautifully against the blue sky on this perfect sunny picnic day.

As we parked at the Fancy Farm Elementary School, my friend Glass spoke some old Kentucky Catholic folklore: "This school has the unique distinction of being the only public school in Kentucky that was run and taught by nuns. The parish had a school, and when the state came and built the public school, the only teachers available in Fancy Farm were the nuns from the church school, so they just took all their students down the street to the new building and taught there. The only place it ever happened. In Kentucky."

We walked onto the picnic grounds, and first thing I noted was a huge covered building full of people. I thought this was the political rally until I heard a man barking bingo numbers. Beyond the bingo was the rowdier political rally. Rand Paul, Kentucky's newest U.S. senator, was pontificating as I walked the perimeter of the crowd, and Tea Party backers yelled support and held up outdated signs like "Rand Paul U.S. Senate 2010." Paul said, "The American dream is not about dividing a shrinking pie but *enlarging* that pie."

All this talk about pie made me hungry, so I quickly headed to the concession stand to see their offerings. The menu, sponsored by Pepsi Cola, said:

WELCOME TO FANCY FARM
ICE COLD PEPSI 20 OUNCES 1.00
CHIPS .50
BBQ SANDWICH 3.00
BURGER 2.50
HOT DOG 1.50
BOTTLED BBQ SAUCE 3.00

Real simple. The mutton, cooked on pits out back of the concession stand, smoked overnight for twenty-four hours. It was finely chopped, and the smoke flavor was distinct. It was dry enough to need some sauce.

I returned to the rally, and in the spirit of the big Bluegrass barbecues of the 1800s, fiery rhetoric burst from the mouths of politicians and boomed from big speakers. Current Kentucky governor Steve Beshear talked about his recent trip to Afghanistan and Iraq and praised the men and women in military service without saying anything specific about how to solve Kentucky's problems like unemployment or the destruction of Appalachian forests and streams by mountaintop-removal coal mining. Then Republican challenger David Williams stood up. "You know, if I was Steve Beshear I wouldn't want to talk about my record either. The old lawyers used to say, 'Now if you have the facts, beat on the facts, and if you have the law, beat on the law, and if you have neither beat on the table,' and it looks like Governor Beshear has chosen to beat on the table!" Williams's speech was interrupted by an audience member shouting, "Stop the war on workers!" His voice blended with others shouting the same, and Williams stepped back and talked to some policemen guarding the speakers' platform. The police left the stage and walked into the audience to remove the heckler. Williams stepped back up to the microphone and said, "That's okay. Leave the guy alone. I remember what it was like when I had my first beer. You'll be okay tomorrow, buddy." Audience members variously booed and cheered and waved small American flags, and some had Old Glory mounted from their baseball caps, and one woman used Old Glory as a hairpin.

Gatewood Galbraith, the independent candidate for governor, followed Williams with the most folksy speech of the afternoon. "People say, 'Gal-

R.I.P Gatewood

Gatewood Galbraith died January 4, 2012, five months after I heard him speechifying at Fancy Farm. I'll miss your populist platform and defense of civil liberties, Gatewood.

braith, you're a perennial candidate,' and I say, 'Well, Kentucky's got perennial problems.' If the people had picked me the first time to solve the problems I wouldn't have had to run again!" and "The leadership of both parties has their horns locked up like two white-tailed bucks fightin' over territory while our business lays dead in the dust!"

After listening to a few speeches, I fetched a Sun Drop cola from the concession stand and walked down the hill to talk with the men who smoked the meats for the picnic. The chief in charge, Mr. Eddie Carrico, said they barbecued 11,090 pounds of whole pork shoulders and 8,600 pounds of mutton halves. The pork came from Paducah, and the mutton came from Owensboro's famous Moonlite Bar-B-Q Inn, which, according to manager Pat Bosley, "semi-truck[s] it in—five thousand to six thousand pounds—two times per week" from three suppliers in the Midwest "where they raise sheep."

The Carrico family has been cooking at the picnic for thirty-two years. "Every family does the same thing for generation after generation, you know," he said.

They began on Friday morning with Mass at the church and then put the meat on after 8:00 a.m. and fired the pits by 9:00. "Then we stayed with it all day, all night. We had another crew come in at 5:00 this morning and kept it warm and basted. We basted it during the night five or six times with a vinegar base: two gallons of vinegar to one gallon of water, plus cayenne pepper, salt, and sugar." They have to strain the basting liquid in order to squeeze it through a sprayer, because nearly nineteen thousand pounds of meat is too much to sop with mops. With the sprayer, they can baste over three hundred feet of pits in less than thirty minutes.

The pits at Fancy Farm are truly impressive: cinderblock and masonry brick pits covered with heavy-duty corrugated steel roofing with steel panels on the side to remove for the shoveling of coals underneath the meat. Eddie said every time you remove the steel tops to baste the meat you lose heat, so they have a system where guys remove the tin, another sprays the meat, and they put the tin right back on to keep the heat in. They burned down seventy bundles of hickory shipped in from Missouri to fire the pits. Eddie said, "We liked to not got any [hickory] because after the river got out after all that flooding, they couldn't get in to get any trees. We was kindly gettin' worried."

I asked Eddie about the tradition of Catholics smoking meats at these community picnics, and he gave me an abbreviated history of Fancy Farm: "The picnic started with families eating fried chicken on the creek. But it got a little too big, so they moved it up to the school grounds. St. Jerome owns all these school buildings, so they moved it up here. The first picnic they had was a political speaking, barbecue, and a gander pull. You know what that is, don't you? It's a goose. Pulling down. Then it just growed into a big political thing, and here we are. We can't get any bigger. This little town can only hold so much."

Eddie said they have five hundred families at St. Jerome, and family tradition is strong. So the young people at least fifteen years old were helping all night with the barbecue. He said the young'uns thought it was great until about 5:00 in the morning. "We do this for the church and the kids," he said, pointing out that they'd built two baseball diamonds with money raised at the picnic.

As we talked, strong young men removed the tin from the pits and, wearing thick rubber gloves, hoisted out the pork shoulders and carted them off in wheelbarrows to be chopped by a team of men and women wielding cleavers in a covered area where you, the lucky eater, can buy as much as you want (if you get there early enough). The prices in 2011 were $10/pound for mutton and $8/pound for pork. Eddie said they'd be lucky if they broke even on the mutton because prices for wholesale mutton have risen so much. "But the people expect it," he said, "so we got to have it."

I didn't win the Dodge Challenger, but I left Fancy Farm with my belly full of hickory-smoked pork and mutton, my head full of political rhetoric, and a deepening respect for the Catholics of western Kentucky and their sense of family and community tradition. It was a really good time, and I'll be back.

Boaz (pronounced "Boze")

Hoskins' Bar-B-Que

Hoskins' is sort of stuck out in the middle of nowhere between Mayfield (about ten miles north) and Paducah, a cute little country house restaurant with a red metal roof in a rural neighborhood (there's another house next door). Open for over forty years, they serve mostly barbecue, fried catfish, standard barbecue side dishes, and some great-looking pies. I arrived around dinner time on a Friday and got a pork plate and struck up a conversation with a local fellow eating fried catfish, which looked real good, and he said it was. The finely chopped pork—pulled from Boston butts smoked twelve hours—had a real nice smoke smell and rich flavor with a lot of bark mixed in by my special request. The pork plate comes with a quarter pound of pork (the portion they measured for me was a generous quarter pound) and two side dishes chosen from baked beans, potato salad, slaw, macaroni salad, french fries, onion rings, and potato wedges. The fries were thick cut. On Friday and Saturday they have all-you-can-eat spareribs. They also offer smoked city ham, beef brisket, and smoked turkey breast. Table sauces included a sweet sauce with a lot of mustard flavor and a hot sauce with a vinegary–chili powder flavor with a consistency thicker than bottled hot sauce like Tabasco but thinner than commercial barbecue sauces. The macaroni salad was creamy and pickley, and the fried onion rings were crispy. While I sat there jawboning with the locals, I saw a lady eating a piece of coconut cream pie, and she said it was very fine.

While eating the pulled pork, I got to talking with a man at the next table about barbecue. This fellow, probably up in his sixties, had plenty of opinions about who had the best barbecue—and some real strong opinions about those places that are using electric or gas cookers. "That's not barbecue," he said. "They use electricity and put one stick of wood in there. That's not right." As he talked, the sounds of a knife chopping meat on a block provided background ambiance. He told me that back in the late 1940s and early '50s, Kountry Kastle in Paducah "sold their stuff out the back door," meaning they were bootleggers. "That was about the last place you could get beer," he said. "And whiskey—you had to get whiskey up in Paducah." He also informed me that people in Paducah loved hot dogs.

As I stood at the counter to pay, a man placed a very specific order. "I want one beef brisket sandwich with no sauce and a little fat on it. And I want one of them with mild sauce—no fat on that one. And the other two I want hot with a little fat on 'em."

I asked the man if the brisket was sliced or chopped.

He said, "They'll do it any way you want to, and it is *good*." He said Earl Hoskins, the original owner, was a sheriff down in Texas who moved back to Kentucky, and they just kept his name on the restaurant over the years. At this man's recommendation, I got some beef brisket to go, and when sitting in the parking lot in my truck couldn't help but taste it, even though I was full. It was a flavor explosion—pulled beef with plenty of fat, salt, and spices.

John Latch had done the smoking of the pulled pork I ate, as he'd been doing at Hoskins' for over thirty years. Mr. Latch wasn't there when I had dinner, but I was allowed to go outside and see the pits. There were four old-fashioned masonry pits under the roof of a garage-like building. Ash covered the floor, and the cinderblock walls were blackened by smoke. A single incandescent bulb burned from the ceiling. The pits were cool, but had obviously been well used for a long time.

UPDATE: I returned to Hoskins' around 5:30 on a Friday afternoon in early August 2011. I ordered a beef (brisket) sandwich and pork sandwich and asked if they pulled the meat or chopped it, and the lady at the counter said, "Any way you want it." I told her pulled and added that I like bark. The brisket wasn't ready, so I ordered a ham sandwich out of curiosity. I learned that the brisket would not be ready for two more hours, and at that point the restaurant would already be closed. Why wasn't the brisket ready? Because the woman doing the smoking (apparently John isn't doing it now) didn't get the meat on the pits until Friday morning. At least they aren't rushing the process. While waiting for my made-to-order sandwiches, I heard the chop-chop-chop sounds of a cleaver on a wood block coming from the kitchen. A sign on the wall beckoned to my inner sweet tooth by listing a string of scrumptious desserts (which you can see on display in the glass counter by the register; particularly eye-catching are the pies blooming with lofty meringues): coconut pie, chocolate pie, peanut butter pie, banana pudding, coconut cake, lemon icebox pie, and carrot cake. They also sell their sauces in bottles. The old wooden floors in the dining room and University of Kentucky sports decorations on the walls, along with the non-fancy tables and chairs and booths, make for a homey eating space, and indeed, several middle-aged couples were already eating dinner at this early hour, as they were when I had visited on a Friday two years earlier.

I took my sandwiches outside and ate at a picnic table. The ham sandwich was good, but it wasn't really barbecue in my humble opinion—just precooked ham (what I've always known as "city ham" to distinguish it from heavily salted and cured country ham) sliced and served warm on a hamburger bun with some thin hot sauce. The pork sandwich surely satisfied my desire for smoky bark. Some pieces were dry but balanced out with a tongue-numbing vinegary hot sauce with ample black and red pepper. The meat itself appears seasoned primarily by smoke. The hot sauce complemented the pork, adding pepper and saltiness that brings out the flavor of the meat. The generic bun it's served on is a waste of belly space.

After eating the sandwiches, I decided I had enough room for the Friday night special—two meaty spareribs with tips attached, slaw, beans, and two slices of white bread for $5.95. The ribs were tender and nicely smoked, sweet on the front end and spicy on the back. The vinegar slaw was medium-chopped cabbage with slivers of carrot and celery seed—a sweet and crunchy palate cleanser. The baked beans were nothing special. Hoskins' sweet sauce is thick and studded with pepper flakes. I preferred it to the hot sauce (something that rarely happens), and I liked how it enhanced the flavor of the smoky tender rib meat and then tingled in the throat.

The prices at Hoskins' are reasonable, and the ribs were great. The pulled pork was also really good. I missed the brisket, durn it, but will have to get that next time around. And if I ever have room, I'm going in for a slice of one of those beautiful pies.

Open: Monday–Thursday, 10:00 a.m.–3:00 p.m.; Friday–Saturday, 10:00 a.m.–7:00 p.m.

1015 State Road 849 East; 270-856-3400

Mayfield

Carr's Barn and Carr's Steakhouse

I ate at the original Carr's Barn in summer 2009 and enjoyed the half-century-old rustic diner. Soon after my visit, Carr's opened a new steakhouse across the street. The diner is still open, serving breakfast and lunch, and the barbecue you eat at the steakhouse is still cooked on the original pits behind Carr's Barn. I'm including here my original take on the Barn, followed by an update on the new place.

Smoke poured from the rustic shack behind Carr's Barn, and inside it the forty-year-old brick masonry pits were as well used as I've seen. Suzanne Flint, whose family has owned Carr's Barn since 1951, was feeding the fire with chunks of hickory when I visited during a hot summer lunch hour. Her grandfather, Wayne Carr, ran the place back in the day.

Located just off Mayfield's town square with its magnificent courthouse, the original Carr's is easy to find, a long, red-painted cinderblock structure with greenish asphalt shingles on top that looks like a barn. Inside, a single line of customers ate at the counter that stretches the length of the diner, seating only twelve people. Suzanne called customers by name. She said some of them have been coming there for fifty years.

I ordered a pork sandwich with potato salad, recommended by Suzanne. The potato salad was fluffy and had nice pickle and onion flavor. The sandwich was a generous helping of sweet and moist smoked pork—probably piled an inch thick—on a slightly toasted bun, with a sweet tomato-vinegar sauce on the side. They cook whole pork shoulders overnight on the already-hot masonry pits. When Suzanne comes in at 6:00 she takes off the shoulders and fires the pits again, adding coals underneath the meat every two hours, and by the time they close in the afternoon the firebricks have soaked up enough heat to keep the new batch of shoulders cooking overnight.

On Fridays they serve chicken and smoked hand-patted hamburgers. Pork barbecue and smoked sliced city ham are served daily.

Thank you, Suzanne and Carr's Barn, for keeping it simple and real.

Open: Monday–Friday, 6:00 a.m.–2:00 p.m.; Saturday, 6:00 a.m.–1:00 p.m.

216 West Broadway; 270-247-8959

UPDATE: Perhaps I should feel foolish for writing that final line two years before. First, you can find the phrase "keep it real" in the Urban Dictionary, and I'm hardly that hip. It's also a song by the Jonas Brothers—not my taste in music. Second, I'd no sooner congratulated Carr's Barn for keeping it simple when they decided to go upscale at the bigger, swankier place across the road. They continue to smoke meats on the rustic pits out back of the original building, but their new location holds 149 people (and they can serve alcoholic beverages), whereas the old place only seats a dozen. For a while they boasted the big chicken featured on the set of the film *In Country*, based on the famous novel by Graves County native Bobbie Ann Mason. The chicken has traveled around Mayfield a bit since the filming in the late 1980s. Ask a local to tell you about it.

I walked into the new place on a Friday evening and had to wait five minutes for a table to clear before a hostess—this isn't your typical barbecue shack—could seat my friend Todd Chappel and me. Carr's Steakhouse is located in a remodeled car shop. The high ceilings and the old original brick walls make for a classy ambiance. We sat at a booth in the main dining room and ordered the "west Kentucky combo," a choice of three meats (barbecue pork, ham, turkey, or rag bologna) and two sides. Rag bologna is an old southern staple found behind the counter of country stores where they'll slice off a thick piece and throw it between two slices of white bread, so named because it was traditionally sold in a cloth bag instead of a plastic casing. Rag bologna is typically saltier than mainstream brands like Oscar Meyer and often has a higher cereal content (so it's cheaper to make—you know, like dough burgers or slug burgers cut with such fillers as bread, crackers, eggs, or oatmeal). The Carr's menu says their rag bologna is "cooked slowly on our hickory pit."

We waited over thirty minutes for the order to arrive, which gave us plenty of time to snack on the four hot buttered rolls with whipped strawberry butter and regular whipped butter our waitress brought, gratis, to the table after we ordered drinks. The new restaurant has an upscale feel, but the clientele were dressed in regular-folks clothes like shorts, jeans, and T-shirts. One middle-aged guy wore a sleeveless shirt and a camouflage cap. I saw families eating steaks and potatoes and young adults eating burgers. The noise level in the main dining room was high because of the acoustics (one big open room separated by a half wall). Ceiling fans above us kept us cool. We sat in a high-backed, burgundy-colored pleather booth with decent wood rimming, and fake but attractive houseplants sat on a shelf above our booth. Todd, a.k.a. Asian Lad (he was adopted from Korea as a child and was raised in Dawson Springs, Kentucky), noted that people of significant girth should request a table, because even he, with his 150-pound frame, felt cramped in the booth.

A potential disadvantage of a barbecue shack moving upscale is that it's hard to find someone who can honestly tell you about the meats. Such was the case here at Carr's Steakhouse. I asked the friendly young woman who served us some questions about the ham—trying to figure out if it was a smoked fresh ham (the back quarter of a hog) or a sugar-cured ham—and she said, "It's really good."

To my question "Is it the kind of ham you eat at Christmas?" she replied, "Yeah, something like that."

I asked how the smoked bologna was prepared, and she said, "I hear it's really good." She then confessed that she really didn't like barbecue much. Fair enough. On the other hand, when I ate at the original Carr's Barn, the pit master, Suzanne Flint, was the same person who served me at the counter. She answered all my questions with authority. Again, it's the problem of economies of scale. Perhaps I should know better than to ask a teenage server specific barbecue questions, but sometimes I luck out and find one who knows the meats. For example, the young woman who took my order at Smoke Shack in Scottsville told me that everything on the meat menu was grilled except for the pork tenderloin, ribs, and Boston butts—meaning that the word "barbecue" in her mind designated slow, long smoking at low temperatures.

Side items at the new Carr's include steak fries, baked potatoes, mashed potatoes, sweet baked potatoes, homemade potato salad, green beans, white beans, sautéed broccoli, baked beans, coleslaw, and homemade mac and cheese. I asked the waitress why the potato salad and mac and cheese were the only items that said "homemade," but she didn't know. In addition to an eighteen-ounce rib eye, they also have salmon, tilapia, coconut shrimp, pasta dishes, grilled chicken, and so on. As I pondered the menu—which tilted away from "grub" toward "cuisine"—the tune from *The Jeffersons* danced in my head. "We're moving on up!"

Our meal finally came. The smoked turkey was sliced thinly and appeared to be cut from a precooked turkey breast (the kind you'd order at a deli counter). We also chose rag bologna because I'd already tried the ham at Hoskins' Bar-B-Que in Boaz and wasn't terribly impressed; it tasted like what it is, slices of city ham on a bun with a bit of smoke flavor—a good ham sandwich but not barbecue. So we got the bologna by default (I'd gladly order ribs or chicken if those were options on the combo plate). What came on the plate was a slice of bologna about three-fourths of an inch thick with a darkened exterior rim from the smoking. It tasted like—well, you guessed it—bologna! Todd sliced it into triangles and said, "This is like a bologna pie."

Like the smoked city ham that seems so popular in these western Kentucky counties, the bologna tasted as good as bologna can taste. Growing up, some of my first cooking experiments involved fried bologna sandwiches, and when I worked on a dairy farm in high school I used to order for lunch cold, thick-sliced bologna sandwiches from Zack's Food Mart in Lucas, Kentucky. In short, I'm no stranger to bologna, and as bologna goes the stuff at Carr's Steakhouse is great. But it pales in comparison to the pulled pork, which was even better than I remembered from my initial visit to Carr's Barn. The pork was pulled in big pieces, incredibly moist on the inside, with a great smoky flavor. Carr's sauce is vinegary-thin with strong tomato notes and red pepper for heat. A dab goes nicely with the pork. Mostly, I just liked the smoky flavor of the pulled pork, especially the flavorful exterior pieces.

The smoky sliced turkey breast was coated with diced caramelized onions, and I even found a sliver of steak mixed in, which makes me think they heated the turkey on the same flat top as they use for the steaks and hamburgers. The addition of the onions, if not intentional, should be (there's nothing about onions mentioned on the menu description of the barbecued turkey). The turkey and bologna were both very salty and would work better between pieces of good bread to balance the saltiness. The potato salad was whipped, almost like mashed potatoes, with the dominating flavor of pickles, maybe bread-and-butter pickles—a cross between sweet and dill.

I'd save a bit of money and just order the pulled-pork plate, heavy on the bark, and forget the bologna and turkey. Save those meats for sandwiches on a day when you're not craving real barbecue. Carr's pulled pork with bark and a drizzle of the thin sauce ranks right on up there with the best pulled pork I've ever eaten.

Worth noting is that off the dining room is a long bar area—the first bar in Mayfield's history and a source of local controversy. I listened to laughter coming from that farther room and thought, "Those folks are having a really good time." I watched a young waitress wearing high-heeled shoes carrying a full shot of liquor in her hand—sort of tiptoeing to keep the full shot from running over the glass. Carr's Steakhouse even offers Schlafly beer from St. Louis.

I missed the intimate diner atmosphere of the original Carr's Barn, but the new steakhouse offers big tables for group dining and an extensive menu with many nonbarbecue options, including burgers and salads. Still, if you want to keep it simple, head to the Barn for breakfast and lunch.

Open: Monday–Thursday, 10:30 a.m.–9:00 p.m.; Friday–Saturday, 10:30 a.m.–10:00 p.m.

213 West Broadway Street; 270-247-1111

Larry, Darrell & Darrell

My buddy John told me I had to try the barbecue here and talk with Mr. James "Juggie" Stovall, who was passionate about his work, and because I trust John's barbecue judgment, I went.

The pork sandwich I ate at Larry, Darrell & Darrell came with two very large pieces of pulled pork topped with a tangy tomato-vinegar hot sauce served on a bun warmed on a flat top. It's a hefty sandwich for the price. You know you're eating meat when you bite into it because the pork is pulled into such large pieces. The sandwich had a pleasant sweet-smokiness that lingered in the mouth five minutes after tasting. I loved the sweet and smoky spareribs, which may be glazed with honey. The moist meats, both the pulled pork and the ribs, conveyed excellent flavor even without a sauce. The brisket sandwich was a heap of meat, chopped and well seasoned, on a bun grilled on both sides—the most flavorful item I tried. Tasty fat pieces were mixed in with the leaner meat. LDD also smokes precooked city hams "until they fall apart." Side dishes include beans, potato salad, slaw, apple sticks, corn nuggets, fried okra, and white beans.

Mr. Stovall has been smoking meats for over thirty years. He started at home and then refined his craft while cooking to raise money to take some boys on a church trip. He smokes with hickory, red oak, cherry, and pecan. Whole pork shoulders cook at 225–250°F, three to four hours per side. The dry-rubbed St. Louis–style ribs smoke for three to four hours. Mr. Stovall credits his rub for the sweetness of the ribs. He sears beef briskets on the meat side first, then flips them and cooks the fat side up so that the fat saturates and tenderizes the leaner meat. "We season the fire out of it," he said.

Talking about what makes barbecue, Mr. Stovall said, "I don't want the taste of a sloppy joe. I want to taste the meat, so sauce should just enhance the meat, but you should be able to taste the meat first."

Amen.

Inside the restaurant, you can see numerous trophies and plaques that Larry, Darrell & Darrell—"The Smokin' Pigs" barbecue team—has won over the years, including five grand championships from Paducah's Barbecue on the River festival. They won the whole-hog category five years in a row. Mr. Stovall said there's a fair amount of comedy that goes into their competition cooking, and the triple-named team—Larry, Darrell & Darrell—seemed comical, so they adopted the name. We talked a bit about cooking with wood versus gas, and he said you just can't beat the flavor of hickory. He said folks serving barbecue who cook with gas could get sued for false advertising, because he thinks "barbecue" must be cooked with wood. But he admitted that when traveling he sometimes eats at places that use gas cookers. "It's decent, but just different," he said.

Finally, Mr. Stovall said he wants to give people hefty portions, because money's tight, and so when customers get up from his table they should feel well fed, especially from one of the plate lunches. "I want you to have a meal when you set down to one," he said, "and you'll think more of that than if you just get a skimpy sandwich and all that. You'll get up and you'll say, 'Shoooo, that was alright!'"

Everything I tried at Larry, Darrell & Darrell was more than alright.

Side Dish: What's Bad Barbecue?

Bad barbecue tastes like old meat.

Bad barbecue is sauced to death.

Bad barbecue tastes like baked meat—without distinctive smoke flavor.

Bad barbecue is tough and dry.

Bad barbecue tastes like it's been cooked in a crock-pot.

Still, on most days I'd probably prefer a bad barbecue sandwich to a fast-food hamburger. But why bother when we've so many good to excellent places to eat barbecue in Kentucky?

I think the Glass family—John, Kathryn, and their *six* children—better get ready to host me again soon, because I really want to get back there to sample more of Mr. Stovall's fabulous food.

Open: Monday–Wednesday, 7:00 a.m.–7:00 p.m.; Thursday-Saturday, 7:00 a.m.–8:00 p.m.

1106 Cuba Road; 270-251-0464

Pilot Oak

Southern Red's Bar-B-Que

Pilot Oak, a hamlet four miles north of the Tennessee line, has a feed mill, extensive cornfields, some big tobacco fields, a catfish farm, and the Pilot Oak Baptist Church, whose marquee said "Come in: We are prayer conditioned" when I passed by on a rainy August morning, traveling with friends John Glass and Todd "Asian Lad" Chappel. Southern Red's is a barbecue oasis in the middle of this sparsely populated southern section of Graves County, far enough south to support a good stand of kudzu. I'd have thought I was in southwestern Tennessee or Mississippi if I didn't know better.

A sign outside the cinderblock building says, "Hope y'all came hungry," and it's not lying. The food at Southern Red's is worth stuffing yourself over. Another sign closer to the road features a gruff-looking red pig wearing a Confederate gray hat and bandanna. But don't be scared away by the red-neck iconography; the folks inside are as sweet and hospitable as they come.

Southern Red's offers a fun dining atmosphere. Wooden pigs on the restroom doors are sex-marked "Boars" and "Sows." The cinderblock walls are painted a vibrant green and yellow. The towel rack in the boars' room is a pig. The wooden floor shows years of wear from when the building was the old Pilot Oak country store. A pig-shaped sign at the ordering counter says, "Eat Mor Possum." The menu is scribbled on a white board on the wall. Ceiling fans circulate the conditioned air, and it was plenty frigid.

We ordered a large barbecue platter with fried okra and fried green tomatoes and also a quarter rack of ribs. The platter came with three slices of fried tomatoes and over a dozen pieces of crispy okra. The tomatoes were particularly unctuous, so deeply fried you can feel the fat on your tongue, akin to the pleasure of eating a piece of bacon when the fat is crispy and seems to melt in the mouth. The pulled pork by itself has ample fat mixed in with the lean, good smoke, very tender and moist. It was piled high on a regular hamburger bun, with beautiful pink and browned pieces. All three of us loved the hot sauce, a medium-thick tomato sauce loaded with black pepper. The sweet sauce served on the ribs is thinner than the hot, also with a liberal amount of pepper. The quarter rack of ribs was four bones of meaty spareribs with the tips on and a gorgeous bark on the outside, glazed with sauce and a bit of sugar. They were cooked perfectly, tender while still retaining some texture and bone adhesion. We all thought these were some of the best ribs we'd ever eaten.

I guess we stood out like sore thumbs—three unfamiliar men snapping photos of food, sharing ribs and a sandwich, and talking into a digital voice recorder—because this hulking man walked over in an apron and stood by me. He said, "How y'all doing?" I looked up at his massiveness and told him how good the food was to allay his suspicions before telling him about our barbecue road trip. His name is Zach, and he's the steak cooker. Zach went back to the kitchen and sent out Micah "Red" Seavers, who along with his father, Fred, tends the barbecue. Red, an extremely gregarious fellow, came out and said, "You run everybody else off, guys." I looked around and sure enough, the half dozen men who'd been eating lunch had left while we were immersed in a daze of ribs and pulled pork.

Glass said, "That's terrible news—we didn't mean to," and Red laughed and said, "That's Saturday—that's the way it goes. How y'all doing today?" He agreed to sit with us a while and spin us a family history in barbecue.

Red runs the place with his dad, mother, wife, and "a bunch of yay-hoos." He's been smoking meats since he was twelve years old, for a total of fourteen years. His mom, Belinda, walked over while we were talking and said, "He could barely pick up the shoulders when he first started." The patriarch of the family, Fred, is a full-time preacher who used to live down from Hutchen's Bar-B-Que in Benton, and he'd go spend nights "preaching at" Mr. Hutch while he tended his barbecue pits. That gave Fred the know-how of barbecue, so that when he got injured drywalling and couldn't climb a ladder anymore, he decided to open Granddaddy's Barbecue near Berea, Kentucky. They sold their business in Berea to a man who "ruined it"—"You can never sell your family business and it stay the same way it's supposed to," Red said—and then they moved to West Virginia. Red graduated high school early (at age sixteen), and his father told him he needed to find something to do. So they opened a restaurant in Hinton, and then moved to Beckley.

I said, "There's not much barbecue in West Virginia—how did those folks take to it?"

Red said, "They didn't know what barbecue was—we threw a wrench in their cog. They had no idea. They was like, 'What is this?' and I was like, 'Eat it—it's good.'" They did well with the West Virginia restaurants but ended up selling them to move back to western Kentucky to take care of the grandparents. Red said his grandfather and father used to cure country hams and smoke meats outside.

"He's been doing this forever," Red said, "and you got to pass on a trade, I guess," and when I asked how long he intended to do barbecue, he said, "I got to make money, don't I? Everybody's got to do something, and I enjoy it. I don't have very many skills," he said with a grin.

Glass said, "This counts double."

I asked, "Y'all smoke whole shoulders or Boston butts?" and Red answered, "I cook anything." Glass mentioned a photo on the wall of Red holding up a giant beaver, and Red said he'd smoked it. They have a special smoker that he uses only for custom cooking wild game. "If you can kill it I can cook it," he said. "You know, everybody's known for a certain kind of meat and this and that; not everybody can cook every kind of meat, but western Kentucky as a whole, everybody's pretty open to eatin' a little bit of anything, and so everybody's learned to be pretty open to cooking a little bit of anything." And so Red smoked that eighty-three-pound beaver—the second biggest he's ever caught.

"I'm a federally licensed specialty nuisance trapper," he said. "That's my other skill set." Belinda said the beaver didn't taste half bad, and Red added, "Tastes like really sweet goat."

Red said the biggest problem with running a small family barbecue business these days is finding good workers. "Workers is the hardest thing. Even in western Kentucky," he said. "Used to be everybody was a good worker. Now it don't matter where you are. I think that's happened with all your family barbecue restaurants. I bet it's harder and harder to come by little barbecue places than you think."

I said it's getting harder to find places cooking with wood, and Red said, "Well, yeah! You know how much work is in that?" He said that luckily, the young woman who took our order is the daughter of a man who runs a sawmill, so they have a good source of fresh cut wood. "He got nine kids," Red said. "We trade him food for wood."

Red said they use two different kinds of wood. I asked if they use sassafras, and he said, "No, we don't use sassafras! That's a Yank wood!" Then he guffawed and said, "I'm sorry, but there you go." They actually use oak and hickory in measured amounts. "Oak is a dynamite wood," Red said, "but it's strong. Hickory pulls some of the harsh taste of oak out. *Hickory is the flu shot for curing the bitterness of the oak.*" That's one of my favorite barbecue lines ever.

Before leaving, we sampled a smoked quarter chicken and the brisket. About chicken, Red said, "Dark's always better. Not that my white-meat chicken ain't good, but dark's always better." When I expressed my surprise that they served brisket, he said, "We've been having it every Saturday and it's finally picking up. This isn't a beef-eatin' area. They're scared of it."

Belinda said, "We've kindly had to build it up." Now, people call ahead to reserve the brisket, and all but a taste had been sold before noon on that Saturday.

The taste of sliced brisket made me exclaim, "Lord, have mercy!"

Red said, "I try my best to put Texas to shame. That's what I shoot for. That's my beef brisket goal."

The brisket was juicy and flavorful throughout the entire piece. Glass foolishly asked, "What do you put on it?" and Red said, deadpan, "Stuff." We all laughed at that one.

They started cooking briskets in West Virginia. "We probably threw out the first dozen we cooked," Red said. "That's the hardest possible meat for me to figure out how to do right. It's either right or it's wrong."

Glass, who has a keen nose for food and drink, was attempting to figure out the special seasoning on the chicken, and he said, sniffing delicately, "Is that cinnamon?"

Belinda said, "That's very simple—just salt, pepper, and smoke."

The magnificent ribs come off the pit at 9:30, 12:30, and 3:30. Everything is cooked up fresh daily. They've been serving about thirteen hundred

---

Southern Red's Bar-B-Que's Quick Ribs

Fred Seavers of Southern Red's says, "Most of the time things work out pretty well at the pit; but sometimes things don't go as planned. One evening as we were running low on ribs, it seemed we just could not get the next batch done. Having remembered something I had watched a seasoned older barbecuer do to get his ribs done in an oddly short amount of time, I took a chance on it. It worked! This is not the way most slow smokers will make them because they will tend to be a little more firm than some like them, but many thought they were great."

The following cooking method is one you can use at home on your regular backyard grill. The ribs will not have quite as much of a smoky flavor, but they will have a great taste nonetheless.

You can use gas or charcoal. Put several hickory chips in a small pan with a little water on them, and lay over the fire. Put grill grate 8–12 inches off of flame. Rub ribs with salt, pepper, and brown sugar. Score back side of ribs with a sharp knife. Cook ribs bone side down over medium to high heat for 10 minutes. Flip ribs—cook meat side down for 10 minutes. Repeat up to 40 minutes. Do not allow ribs to burn. There is a difference between burned and charred. It may take you a few ribs to find out the difference. On last turn where you are putting the meat side down, glaze with your favorite sauce (preferably Southern Red's regular or sweet sauce).

---

to fifteen hundred people per week on the three days they are open. I'm not surprised that word has spread about this gem of a barbecue place located in "Podunk City" (to use Belinda's words). As Glass drove away, we couldn't stop raving about how good everything was.

Southern Red's is one of the rare barbecue places that I'd drive many miles to get to. Red told us, "There's two things to do in Pilot Oak. One is eat barbecue. The other is to watch the corn grow." The corn grows but for a season, but thankfully you can go year round to Southern Red's to feast on their magnificent meaty arts.

Open: Thursday–Saturday, 7:00 a.m.–9:00 p.m.

5085 State Route 94 West (in the old Pilot Oak Grocery); 270-376-2678

Benton

Manley's 4 Little Pigs Bar-B-Que

The masonry pits behind 4 Little Pigs are well used. They smoke whole shoulders over hot hickory coals for eighteen to twenty-four hours, depending on the season (longer cooking in the winter). Naked shoulders are cooked skin-side down until caramelized, about twelve hours, and then wrapped in foil for the rest of the smoking. The juice makes the exterior bark soft again.

Pit master Eric Binson said their barbecue pits had been there twenty years. Eric's grandmother used to own the restaurant, and he'd already been tending the pits for fifteen years (he was a mere twenty-nine years old when I met him in 2009). He said much of the skill of barbecuing you had to figure out on your own. "Of course, the nastier the pit looks, the better the flavor. If you've got a clean pit, you're doing something wrong."

The odor from the smoky pits was wonderful. My friend Dixon, visiting me from Mississippi, remarked, "That's a great smell."

Eric said he'd prepared over two thousand pounds of barbecue on Christmas Eve. During the holidays they smoke fifteen shoulders on all three pits (forty-five total), but on a normal working day they smoke only twelve because they want the meat to be fresh. "We want to pick 'em fresh every day, because people want fresh barbecue. People around here, you can't fool them about the quality of the barbecue."

The pork sandwich, chopped or pulled, is a generous portion of moist meat topped with a complementary mustardy sauce and served on a warmed hamburger bun. I got a "hot" sandwich, and it appears they sprinkle some cayenne pepper on the meat. Dixon got the mild sandwich, and it seemed there was a dry rub sprinkled on his meat.

This is a full-service place serving country ham, omelets, salads, burgers, catfish, and hot wings. They specialize in pulled and chopped pork with barbecue rib and chicken dinners on Friday and Saturday.

Open: Monday–Saturday, 6:00 a.m.–7:30 p.m.
100 Beach Wood Lane; 270-527-9471

Manley's 4 Little Pigs Bar-B-Que's Sweet Potato Casserole

This (recipe courtesy of Teresa Manley) is the most requested side dish at Manley's restaurant.

3 cups sweet potatoes, cooked and mashed
1 cup sugar
⅓ cup whole milk
2 eggs
1 teaspoon vanilla extract
½ cup butter

TOPPING
½ cup butter, melted
1 cup brown sugar
⅓ cup all-purpose flour
1 cup chopped pecans
2 cups cornflakes cereal

Preheat oven to 350°F. Rub a baking dish with butter. Mix the topping ingredients in a bowl. Whip together the sweet potatoes, sugar, milk, eggs, vanilla, and butter and pour into the baking dish, then crumble on the topping. Bake until golden brown and bubbly at the edges.

Hutchen's Bar-B-Que

Sitting in one of the red booths in this old-style diner, I got a flashback to the *Happy Days* era. Nostalgia is the best reason to visit this place. It's a full-service diner with an extensive menu, including breakfast items and a long list of sandwiches like burgers, BLTs, Philly steaks, chicken clubs, and catfish filets. I was prepared to like Hutchen's because it's such an established place, but I wasn't overwhelmed by their ribs or pork sandwich. But as I said, the menu is extensive, so maybe some of their other offerings hit the spot. The green beans sure were good.

My friend Dixon from Greenville, Mississippi, joined me at Hutchen's for lunch. The good pork sandwich was a decent quantity of tender, moist pulled pork with a moderate smoky flavor on a hamburger bun. The mild sauce is composed of vinegar, water, ketchup, sugar, mustard, garlic salt, pickling spice, onions, and lemons. I know because they list the ingredients on the bottles they sell. Dixon and I dug into a half rack of meaty spareribs. They weren't very smoky, and I'm pretty sure they boil or steam them (which pretty much guarantees "fall-apart tender"). They were lightly dry rubbed. I imagine there are people who would like these ribs a lot—those who favor very soft ribs with a light smoking that requires sauce to yield flavor. Dixon and I both rated them as mediocre. Dixon said, "The only mistake not made with the ribs is that they're not dry. They're moist but rather flavorless." I'd eat them over franchise fast food any day, but they didn't come close to ranking with my favorite ribs on my Kentucky barbecue safari.

Recommendation: get a pork sandwich and a side of fried okra, Cajun fries, or green beans and enjoy the old-school drive-in atmosphere. If you go there at night, the neon sign above the roof with "HUTCHENS" in green, a pig in orange, and "Drive-In" in hot pink will take you back to the 1950s.

Open: Monday–Saturday, 6:00 a.m.–8:00 p.m.
601 North Main Street; 270-527-9424

Murray

Coldwater Bar-B-Q & Catering

This barbecue joint with an intimate eat-in area stands across the road from the Coldwater Methodist Church and just down the road from the Coldwa-

ter Baptist Church on Highway 121 in a small rural community. It's primarily a catering operation, but Gary and Sandy Barnes keep the place open on
weekends because Gary is usually there cooking anyway. I noted a sign by the
menu on the wall saying, "This business is for sale," but Gary's barbecue is so
good that I have to feature Coldwater anyway, just in case they remain in business for several more years. They've been at the Coldwater location since 2004.

Gary does a lot of catering for Murray State University and churches
in the area. A huge stack of hickory wood lies out back of the small restaurant. Gary says he thinks western Kentucky has such fine barbecue because
the land provides so much hickory. On his huge custom-built unit he smokes
whole shoulders by shoveling burnt coals underneath, "basically the same way
they do at the Fancy Farm picnic," Gary said, "putting the shoulders on in the
morning and letting them cook that night and then taking them off early the
next morning. So it's twenty-four hours they're on there, but really the last six
to eight hours they're not doing much cooking." The St. Louis–cut spareribs,
ham, and turkey are smoked on a rotisserie unit—a big revolving drum with
shelves in it. The chopped pork has a sweet, smoky flavor, and the tomato/
vinegar sauce with cayenne flecks and a hint of mustard doesn't overwhelm
the meat. The meat is tender and moist with nice pieces of fat mixed in, on a
lightly toasted bun.

Gary said one key to a successful barbecue joint is knowing how to hold
the meat once it comes off the pit. "The one thing different I see in these places is if you get it when it comes right off the pit it's good, but they don't know
how to handle it after that. You can't throw it away, and if you serve it and it's
crap, then there you go. You just can't put 'em in the oven to warm 'em, and
that's what a lot of people try to do. You need to get moisture back into the
meat to reconstitute it."

Gary said the popular gas cookers have a tendency to dry the meat because people are cooking at 275–300° and it cooks the fat off. "When they
[the Boston butts or shoulders] come off the gas they're hot and warm and
juicy and really good," he said, "but you let 'em cool down overnight and next
day you try to fire them up again, there's no moisture there—they've lost it.
But people don't care, though. I've been in this business a long time. *People
don't care*. They're looking at the price of it, the convenience of it, and they
let the quality slide."

I said, "Some of us care."

He responded, "The vast majority don't. I could get a gas cooker and turn it out and probably do a lot better [financially]. But you are giving up the quality. Ours is the very intensive old-style barbecue."

Gary used to own a place called Coldwater Bar-B-Q Two closer to Murray, the very first place I ate at back in 2009 when I started my Kentucky barbecue tour. They've since closed. I was disappointed about this, because I ate some of the best brisket of my life there, thinly sliced and served with au jus, very different from Texas brisket I've tried. I asked why they closed, and Gary, echoing other barbecue folks, said, "I couldn't keep help. Me and Sandy just couldn't handle it. Nobody shows up for work. We just decided just to do only what we can do ourselves. Our catering business has grown. We served twelve hundred back in the summer in a catering job."

Coldwater will do catering at any time, and for now you can stop by there on weekends to get some real barbecue and homemade pies.

When I spoke with Gary in May 2012, he said they were considering moving their operation to Murray and getting that awesome brisket back on the menu.

Open: Thursday–Saturday, 10:00 a.m.–6:00 p.m.
8284 Highway 121 North; 270-489-2199

Bad Bob's BBQ & Grill #5

When I first ate at Bad Bob's, I didn't realize it was a franchise. The building is pretty small, and inside there was a lunch crowd eating at small tables with blue-and-white checkered tablecloths. The original Bad Bob's is in west Tennessee, and now they have over twenty restaurants in places as far as New York, Texas, and Florida. Bad Bob's franchises serve Memphis-style dry-rubbed ribs.

When I visited in 2009, Tony Baylis, head cook at Bad Bob's #5 in Murray, had been tending the meats for seven years. I met him out back of the restaurant, where he was tending baby back ribs. He puts glaze on the ribs and smokes them at 250–275° for four hours. He said, "When I take 'em off they just peel right off the bone." Tony says he's the only head cook at a Bad Bob's franchise who does ribs outside on a rotisserie smoker. All the other places use a "smoker oven" to cook the ribs inside the restaurant. "I like the outside cooker; it gives it more of an outside flavor," Tony said.

He cooks ribs over charcoal with added smoke from hickory chips. Inside the kitchen area, Tony loads Boston butts into a "Fast Eddy's by Cookshack" smoker oven, thirty-two butts per cooker, and gets a smoke flavor by adding wood chips to the bottom. He sets the temperature at 219° and cooks them for nine hours and forty-five minutes. The advantage, of course, is that the butts cook overnight and are ready in the morning. He then holds them at a temperature of 140° until serving time. The dry rub he uses on the meat comes from the company, as does the unusual sauce flavored with raspberry preserves.

When I asked Mr. Baylis what he recommended, he said ribs, so I got a plate of them. The ribs were real tender with a good smoke flavor. The sweet raspberry sauce is one of the odder barbecue flavors I've tried, right up there with the thin blackberry sauce served with ribs at Staxx in Frankfort. My friend John Glass, who tasted the leftover ribs later that evening, called the raspberry barbecue sauce "wrong." I think it's worth a try, this deviation from barbecue sauce orthodoxy.

Bad Bob's offers all-you-can-eat ribs on Tuesdays and all-you-can-eat pulled pork daily. They also smoke half chickens and bologna, and serve their barbecue on top of stuffed potatoes, nachos, and cheese fries.

Open: Monday–Saturday, 10:00 a.m.–8:00 p.m.
806 Chestnut Street; 270-767-0054
www.badbobs5.com

Brothers Barbecue ("Livin' High on the Hog")

I thought Brothers might be a franchise since there's a restaurant of the same name in Madisonville, but this Brothers has no affiliation with the other. The name isn't the most original, but the enthusiastic young men running this place have created unconventional versions of barbecue standards. You can eat in at Brothers, sitting at one of two tables (I took the one by the window looking out onto the street), but most customers get takeout. It's a pleasant shack atmosphere: concrete block walls painted clean white, laminate floors that look like wood planks, and a long ordering counter with used corrugated roofing tin as paneling, all of which gives the place a good funky feel. Daily specials and the regular menu are scribbled on white boards hanging from the ceiling. The Thursday-Friday special in September 2011 was a bacon-wrapped hot dog. Lucky for my cholesterol, I visited them on a Saturday when the special was smoked chicken wings (scrumptious). On Tuesdays and Thursdays they served up stuffed smoked cheeseburgers—two hamburger patties molded around a slice of American cheese (like the famous Jucy Lucy burger of Minneapolis), smoked on the bottom portion of the smoker to get a crust on the bottom side, topped with cheese that melts before being served. Can I get an amen?

Josh "Flash" Flaspoehler and Ron "Archie" Gladden are the brains behind Brothers. They chose the name because Josh's brother, Jon Flaspoehler, helped finance this barbecue venture. Josh and Ron practiced their craft for six months before opening up. They had contests with each other to see who could make the best ribs, brisket, and so forth. Ron's St. Louis–style ribs and spice rub got on the menu, and Josh's jazzy creations round it out. They currently smoke sixteen Boston butts every day of business. At the top of their takeout menu, they state: "In order to provide you with the freshest BBQ, Brothers smokes limited quantities of BBQ daily. All items are sold on a first come first serve, so come early or call ahead!" The butts smoke twelve hours the first day, then sit in pans with apple juice overnight in the refrigerator, and are finished the next day with four more hours of smoking. They don't use any rubs on the butts—just pure meat with the hint of apple juice. A "Big Bro" sandwich gets you one-third of a pound of this well-cared-for meat. It's very tender with a good smoke flavor. All the meats get indirect heat except for the chicken wings and leg quarters.

I tried their "beer butt" chicken—a whole chicken smoked indirectly with a can of beer inside the cavity for moisture and flavor, pulled for sandwiches. The sweet, malty flavor of the beer came through in the flesh, very pleasant even though I prefer chicken on the bone. They barbecued half chickens for a while, but quarter chickens sold better, so they've scratched the halves from the menu. They also custom cook deer and turkeys during hunting season and hams during the holidays. During Thanksgiving 2010, they served three hundred hungry people at Ron's banquet facility; local churches and the Salvation Army sponsored the meal, and Ron and Josh did the cooking and staffing.

I tried such barbecue standards as brisket, pulled pork, pulled chicken, and the less typical smoked wings—my favorite of these, as the odor of

Brothers Barbecue's Red Potato Salad

Josh "Flash" Flaspoehler explains, "We love the way the coolness of this dill potato salad goes perfectly with our 'Big Bro' sandwich with lots of our homemade hot barbecue sauce."

¼ cup white vinegar
½ cup sweet pickle juice
½ cup yellow mustard
3 cups mayonnaise
3 tablespoons dill weed
1 teaspoon onion powder
1 tablespoon ground black pepper
1 tablespoon celery salt
½ cup white sugar
5 pounds red potatoes, chopped and boiled
8–10 sweet gherkin pickles, chopped

Whisk first 9 ingredients together for the dressing. Add cooked potatoes and chopped pickles and mix well. Refrigerate a few hours for flavors to blend.

Brothers Barbecue's Mild Barbecue Sauce

Flash says, "Our mild is a very basic sauce, and that's what we love about it. It really lets the meat be the star. We especially love it smoked onto our burnt ends. I apply a glaze of the mild sauce during the last hour of smoking, and it creates a deeper, richer flavor."

64 ounces ketchup
1½ cups white sugar
4 tablespoons chili powder
2 tablespoons garlic powder
2 cups white wine
3 tablespoons black pepper

Whisk ingredients together until well blended. Refrigerate overnight for flavors to meld.

smoke was intense and the wings were glazed with a tasty peppery sauce. They must be popular, because while I was eating, a big man walked in and ordered wings, and I remarked, "These wings are gooooooood," and the man said, "Most of the times I get here they don't have 'em—they sell out before I get here." The rich, creamy potato casserole was a good accompaniment to the meats, and the brisket baked beans were also very good. The red potato salad contained big chunks of potato in a dill sauce, and the barbecue sauces were different from any I've had—very peppery, thin, and tangy with spices mixed in that I couldn't put my finger on. Josh told me one was his version of a North Carolina sauce, but because he hadn't been down to Tarheel country to try the real thing he created something that tastes peculiar—a twisted version of the original vinegar sauce. The cold, creamy dilled potato salad balanced nicely with the vinegar-peppery heat of Josh's hot sauce. In a world that's too easily standardized, I enjoyed these off-center tweaks on traditional flavors.

Most of the meats come without sauce except for the brisket sandwich, which is six ounces off the fattier end of a brisket chopped up (if you want your meat naked, order the sliced brisket sandwich, which they cut from the leaner part of the brisket). The sliced brisket was tender with a mild smoke flavor. They also sell the regional oddity of BBQ bologna, a four-hour smoked bologna roll served in a thick slice on a sandwich. The bacon-wrapped hot dog is a big hot dog with two thick-cut slices wrapped around and smoked for an hour and a half and glazed with their sweet heat sauce (Josh's creation—his homage to the Big Dipper, a burger joint in his hometown of Owensboro that deep-fries hot dogs). Josh says that smoking bacon makes the fat creamy, but you want to eat the dogs when they are fresh off the smoker.

The food was fun and very good, and I enjoyed talking with these young barbecue visionaries. I wonder what they'll come up with next. You should visit and find out.

Open: Tuesday–Saturday, 10:00 a.m.–7:00 p.m.
401 Sycamore Street; 270-761-PORK
1415½ Main Street; 270-761-7677

The Keg

I was taking a peek at the woodpile behind this restaurant around the lunch hour on a Saturday morning and was caught spying by two young fellows who happened to be the primary pitmen for this popular Murray State University hangout. So I parked the Ranger, jumped out, and struck up a conversation. Bundles of hickory slabs were stacked up behind a huge trailer holding two barrel smokers with several big smokestacks and a rusted firebox on the end for cooking down wood. The whole thing looked ominous, industrial and powerful, like the medieval ironclad dark knight of barbecue cookers. Or maybe the Darth Vader of cookers.

Hickman County native Darren Yates opened the Keg in Murray in 2002. There's an original Keg pub in Fulton, owned by Darren's business partner, that's been open longer. Craig Bagby smokes brisket and ribs, and Brandon Christopher—all of nineteen years old in fall 2011—barbecues whole pork shoulders and says he intends to do it until he can't do it any longer. Shoulders cook for twelve to fourteen hours, the ribs for three to four, and brisket for sixteen over hickory and mesquite. St. Louis–style ribs, ham, and turkey smoke on a rotisserie unit, and the shoulders cook on the flat pit. They burn down the wood to coals in the firebox and shovel them underneath the shoulders, and into the rotisserie they throw full chunks of wood for indirect smoking.

The restaurant has concrete floors in a sports-bar atmosphere, with several televisions mounted on the wall showing sporting events, Murray State athletic uniforms decorating the walls, many tables, and warm attractive wood paneling for walls. A big boar head hangs from a wall. The young woman who served me said it could get pretty rowdy on weekends with live bands and sports crowds. They have a full bar on one side of the restaurant with domestic beers on tap, and in a room off the side are three pool tables. So the restaurant can hold lots of people, and I expect it does get loud when the university crowd rolls in. One whole wall was decorated with fraternity paddles.

When I ate during the Saturday lunch hour, however, the place was peaceful. I ordered a brisket plate with slaw and beans and a side of pulled pork. Seven big pieces of brisket were piled onto the plate, steaming hot and smelling wonderful. The baked beans were piping hot, with lots of onion, green pepper, and chunks of pork inside, a little sweet and tangy at the same time. The brisket was rich and had grill marks on it. There was close to a pound of it on the platter. The meat was sauced with a sweet peppery concoction reminding me of A-1 steak sauce, very different from other sauces I've tried. The smoke and sweet sauce filled my mouth and nostrils at the same time—just a very different (but good) flavor experience. In a way, these pieces of fatty sliced brisket (the brisket here is served with plenty of fat marbled in, not just the lean meaty part) delivered a flavor a lot like grilled steak. I liked it, but it was much different from brisket I've had in Texas. Take this as a warning: if you expect Texas-styled naked brisket, you might be surprised. But if you want a mouthful of tender meat reminiscent of grilled steak and coated in a savory sweet sauce, then you'll probably enjoy this plenty.

The pulled pork had a deep smoky flavor, tender and moist, with a pleasant saltiness. It was some of the best I've ever had. The salty bark was delicious and the interior pieces were smoky and juicy. Several good sauces sit on the table, but no sauces are needed on this fabulous pork. In addition to pork and brisket, they offer the dry-rubbed spareribs, smoked half chickens, hickory-smoked turkey breast, and thick-sliced smoked ham. They even get a little wild, with their pulled-pork quesadilla, and there's a big list of side dishes, including fried okra and beer-battered onion rings. Sometimes they run a special of two-inch-thick pit-cooked pork chops, and the Keg also serves Cajun food. Darren's best friend in college went to Tulane's law school. Darren visited him frequently and was inspired by Louisiana cuisine.

So for a sports-bar atmosphere with great barbecue and an extensive menu of Cajun offerings (po' boys, étouffée, blackened fish and shrimp, oysters), come to the Keg. Look for the cartoon pig riding a horse painted under the banner "Go Racers" in the front window.

Open: Monday–Saturday, 11:00 a.m.–12:00 a.m.

1051 North Sixteenth Street (across the road from the Murray State University football stadium); 270-762-0040

Pit Stop BBQ ("Old Fashioned BBQ is Back")

Marc Hatcher takes pride in his barbecue, and he's a jack-of-all-trades, having welded together a quarter-inch steel smoker that holds a whopping 128 Boston butts. He also built his own barbecue shack south of Murray, in the area where he grew up. Marc said his building was strong, with hurricane straps on it, and when I said, "You're not expecting hurricanes here in Calloway County, are you?" he replied, "It's built like I build my barbecue. If you move it, it ain't going to wiggle."

Marc ran a lawn-care business for twenty-two years, so he's got a ready source of hickory for his all-wood cooking. A big pile of it lies out back of the double-smokestack cooker, which should be smoking about any time you drive by, since Marc is open 10:00 a.m.–10:00 p.m. every day of the week. "I come in at 8:00 and don't leave till 2:00 in the morning," he said.

Although Marc's been barbecuing as a hobby for years on weekends, Pit Stop just opened in the summer of 2011. I wonder how long he'll be able to handle those long daily hours, but hearing Marc's passion for his work makes me think it will be a long time before he burns out. He told me he'd keep barbecuing until "they turn me like this"—and he gave me two thumbs up to represent two feet sticking up in the dirt.

Marc was out of beef brisket when I stopped by on a Saturday afternoon. He said the brisket is a three-day process, and he's got people "coming around like crazy," some driving all the way from Illinois to get it. The St. Louis–style spareribs with cooked-on sauce were soft, tender, and very flavorful throughout—a little too soft for my preferences, but still delicious. My favorite, though, was the pulled-pork sandwich, a big pile of incredibly smoky pork on a hamburger bun with a golden buttery sheen on top. At present, Marc is selling fifteen cases of butts (at eights butts per case; you can do the math) and six to eight cases of ribs a week, and business is growing all the time. "We've been so busy here, you can't get away," he said.

Usually when I ask people what kind of wood they use, they say "hickory" but seldom specify the type. Marc was the first to say a particular species of hickory—"Only scalybark hickory," he said. "I've got tight-bark but I only use that as a bed of coals. Tight-bark isn't as sweet a wood as the scalybark. You've got more of a nuttier flavor—it's more of a sweeter hickory. A lot of people tell me there's no difference. Well, I've burnt a lot of wood—I've done a lot of ribs and stuff, and there's just a big difference."

I asked Marc how long he smoked the butts, and he said, "It all depends on your heat and moisture in the smoker. Anywhere between eight and eighteen hours." Marc ruined about fifteen to twenty briskets before "working the bugs out" and learning to cook them right. The sauce is the same way—trial and error. The hot sauce "doesn't kick you till the end." He buys fresh habaneros by the case and cooks them down with his sauce. The hot sauce is sweet and has great bite to it.

In September 2011, menu items included pulled pork, BBQ bologna, BBQ chicken, pork ribs, and brisket, but "coming soon" they'll have hamburgers because "people are begging us for them," Marc said. "My main thing is the barbecue, but you got people squealing for fries and burgers, so what are you going to do? We're about old-fashioned barbecue. A lot of older people are coming in because of that—not this ten-minute cooking. If it ain't right, it don't go out that [service] window."

Marc's firebox is four foot deep by eight foot long, with three doors for access. "I can throw in big chunks, logs, whatever I need," he said. He burns whole wood, going against conventional western Kentucky style, which burns the wood down to coals before shoveling them underneath the meat. "You gotta get that flavor off as soon as you throw that log in there. When you use your coals up, most of the flavor is already gone, because when the wood starts smokin', there's your flavor." He added, "I'd rather have a green piece of wood that's just been knocked down to a two-year-old stick. It's got more flavor to it."

When I bit into the pulled-pork sandwich and tasted that intense smokiness, especially of the barky pieces I requested, I knew what Marc was talking about. This is barbecue to make wood lovers swoon. Forgive the obscure reference, but Scotch whiskey lovers will understand this comparison: most pulled pork I've tried across the state is like a Highland whisky, good and smooth. Marc's Pit Stop pork is like Islay malt: pungent and extremely robust and smoky. I loved the meat on the buttery bun.

Marc is a big guy with a soft-spoken demeanor, and I watched him greet all his customers who stopped in. He takes a lot of pride in his work. "We're going to the top somewhere," he said.

Open: Monday–Sunday, 10:00 a.m.–10:00 p.m.

2393 State Route 121 South; 270-759-7001

Grand Rivers

Mr. BBQ & More ("Best Ribs by a Dam Site")

Oh, Lord. It's hard for me to restrain my enthusiasm for this place and the man who makes the magic happen. Mr. Cy Quarles, seventy-two years young

Side Dish: Poor Trigg County

I was driving in the Land between the Lakes area on the lookout for a barbecue joint, and I'd just crossed the bridge over Lake Barkley (an impoundment of Cumberland River) when I saw a sign for barbecue. I didn't see a woodpile, didn't smell smoke. I went around behind the place and saw a man readying his fishing boat for a day on the lake. I asked him about barbecue, and he said that Preacher's Barbecue in Cadiz had closed, and another place in Cadiz had closed. He said when he wanted good barbecue he drove over to Hopkinsville to eat at the Woodshed.

His wife came out of the house and said Bar B Que Shack on Pembroke Road was good. The man said he also drives down to Murray to eat at Coldwater Bar-B-Q. He also mentioned Knoth's over in Grand Rivers.

I started to feel sorry for this man for living in a barbecue-impoverished county, but the more I got to thinking, the more I thought, *Well, hellfire! At least he has several really good places within thirty minutes of his home.* When I lived in the upper Midwest for a spell, I couldn't find any excellent barbecue. So I felt less sorry for him then, but then thought what an oddity Trigg County is, near the eastern edge of this barbecue hotbed and yet lacking its own barbecue establishment.

Pork, pork everywhere, nor any bite to eat. At least locally. Poor Trigg County.

in September 2012, has been smoking the best pulled pork I've ever tasted for a good long time. He and his wife, Jan, happily married for fifty years, have been in business near Kentucky Lake for over a decade.

Mr. Quarles smokes whole pork shoulders for twenty-two to twenty-four hours—salting them down before putting them on old-fashioned masonry pits. Pre-salting gets the salt down into the meat and also works as a protective coating. Cy educated me on how to cook with wood without making the meat bitter. You cook slow, he said, and if you're cooking slow enough you'll get drippings about one and a half inches long and blunt at the end clinging to the grate underneath the meat.

I call these meatsicles. If the cooking is too hot, the meatsicles will burn off.

Cy shovels fresh coals under the meat every hour. He, or the man he's training to help him, tends the pits through the night.

I said, "When do you sleep?"

He smiled and said, "I didn't used to until I got this boy to help me."

The hoggy sandwich at Mr. BBQ takes the pork sandwich to a spiritual place. Cy loads a hoagie bun with a full half pound of his salty-smoky tender pulled pork. The bun is quality bread that he toasts after brushing with garlic butter. The sandwich is unbelievably fabulous. The meat by itself is all you need, but the garlicky bun actually complements this perfect pork. You bite into the sandwich and first the smoke and salt hit you, followed by the odor and taste of garlic. It's like the fine wine of barbecue sandwiches. For a change of pace you can drizzle on some of Cy's peppery vinegary sauce. When the ingredients settle in the clear glass bottles that hold the sauce, the various ingredients—oil, vinegar, spices—settle into pretty multicolored layers. The last time I ate this sandwich I said, "I'm so happy," and broke into giggles and started ooooohing and aaaaaahing and Oh Lording.

If you want to try Cy's ribs, you'll need to visit late on a Friday afternoon when he's taking them off the pit. To use Cy's language, "A hot rib off the pit is something to holler about." The tender ribs have a mahogany color and emit a smoky flavor similar to that of the pulled pork, because the ribs smoke for seven to seven and a half hours. Unlike some barbecue places that slather a thick tomato sauce onto ribs, Cy drizzles his with a thin vinegar sauce.

"Good fresh meat is the trick to barbecuing," he said. "And it's got to be fresh." He gets his meat from Smith Poultry in Hardin, about twenty-five miles away. Cy has meat special cut and wrapped in paper. "I won't cook anything that's wrapped in plastic," he said. "Plastic ruins barbecue. I can look at a piece of meat and tell you if it's been plastic wrapped. It looks like it's been frozen, and when the blood starts cooking out of it, it will be foamy and bubbly. The fresh meat won't. I rather just have it straight out of the cooler."

I love everything Mr. Quarles puts on the table. The side dishes are all homemade recipes, "pretty much what grandma used to cook," Cy said. The fried okra is crunchy and savory. The potato salad is creamy, with a distinct onion flavor, different than any I've had in my life. He smokes chickens for seven hours, and the meat plumb falls off the bones and remains moist after all those hours on the pit.

Mr. BBQ is located two hours west of my home, and I've stopped by there on five random occasions. The first time I ate there was on a Sunday late morning. I ate a hoggy sandwich for breakfast. Mr. Quarles has been there every time, watching over his place, and I've seen Jan there several times, too. She told me that although Cy has trained a younger man to tend the barbecue pits, Cy still does it 75 percent of the time. She said he's worked hard this past winter (2011–12) to fortify his woodpile. Cooking meats as he does on old masonry pits takes a lot of wood.

I encourage you to get to Mr. BBQ while you can, because Cy said he's ready to do some more fishing and less pit tending.

A note about ambience: after you load up on a hoggy sandwich and other delights from Mr. BBQ, you can drive down the road a short piece and look at the sailboats on Kentucky Lake—an impoundment of the Tennessee River—and in your post-barbecue glow gaze out at the water and know that, at least in this moment, the world is good. And if you have any interest in wooing someone, you might want to take them there after dining. The sailboats are a romantic sight, and when you got your Mr. BBQ goggles on, the possibility for love increases considerably.

Open: Monday-Thursday, Sunday, 6:00 a.m.–2:00 p.m.; Friday–Saturday, 6:00 a.m.–8:00 p.m.

Winter hours: Monday–Sunday, 6:00 a.m.–2:00 p.m. (depending on weather)

270 Dover Road; 270-362-4445

Knoth's Bar-B-Que

Knoth's has received plenty of acclaim over the years. On the wall in the restaurant hang various framed newspaper clippings with praising headlines: "Knoth's Barbecue Named 'Restaurant of the Year'"; "Knoth's Means Barbecue in a Big Way"; "Just the Best! Knoth's *Is Smokin* Pork All Summer Long."

When you walk in the side door at Knoth's, there's a small counter with barstools and a larger dining room beyond. In June 2009, I sat at the counter and ordered a pulled-pork sandwich. The meat was super tender and mildly smoky. The mild sauce was mustardy and sweet. The hot sauce had a lot of black pepper in it. The slaw was crispy and sweet with some mustard in it.

Mr. Hugh Knoth spoke with me about the history of the place. His parents started the restaurant in 1965. They have the same menu now as they did forty-five years ago. Hugh also emphasized the freshness of their meat and the old-fashioned cooking methods. He learned to cook from his father, who learned to cook from a man in "Old Kuttawa," a place that is now underneath the waters of Lake Barkley. Hugh has been doing barbecue since 1975.

"We haven't changed a thing," he said. "We have a limited menu, and it takes a lot of work." Mrs. Knoth added that they've lasted so long because they are closed during the cold winter months, giving them time to rest up before the next barbecue season.

Out back in the barbecue pits I spoke with Chris Espino, who had been cooking at Knoth's for eight years. He was born in Los Angeles but moved to Kentucky and started learning the craft of slow cooking from Hugh. He tended the pits as we talked, taking a long-handled shovel and scooping coals from where the wood burned down underneath an outdoor chimney and bringing the coals inside and opening a steel fire door and sliding the coals in the bottom, a few feet below the meat. Dozens of whole pork shoulders soaked up the smoke.

Chris said, "When I come here I don't know nothing of barbecue place."

I said, "I thought there's a tradition of *barbacoa* in Mexico."

"But it's different."

"Cooking the heads of cows and stuff like that?"

"Yeah, we eat all—the tail, the eyes, the tongue."

At Knoth's, whole pork shoulders smoke for twelve hours—first at 275° for two and a half hours, after which the shoulders are turned and cooked at 300° for an additional ten hours. The shoulders are held at 150° overnight until they are served the next day. Chris said trucks come in two times per week with fresh pork, and the meat goes directly from the delivery truck to the pits. They also smoke beef briskets.

It won't take you long to ponder the menu at Knoth's. You can get a pork or beef plate, pork or beef sandwich, fries and slaw, cold drinks and coffee. You can top it off with a milkshake or ice-cream cone.

Land between the Lakes Sweet and Tangy Pulled-Pork Sauce

Knoth's Bar-B-Que near Grand Rivers developed a sweet, yellow-orange-colored sauce that complements pulled pork (and ribs and chicken) well. A couple of other barbecue places with roots in the Land between the Lakes region—J. J. McBrewster's and Sarah's Corner Cafe, both in Lexington—have sauces that taste similar. I'd never ask the folks to give away their sauce secrets, but tinkering in the Berry test kitchen yielded a sauce that's a close cousin.

3 cups white vinegar
1 stick butter
1¼ cups ketchup
1 cup prepared mustard
½ cup water
1 tablespoon salt
2 cups white sugar
1 teaspoon black pepper
¼ teaspoon cayenne pepper

Heat wet ingredients over low heat, whisking to break up clumps of mustard. Add dry ingredients after well blended. Heat and stir until slightly thickened, 10–20 minutes. Adjust the pepper to taste. Yields about 1½ quarts.

Open: Monday–Thursday, 11:00 a.m.–7:00 p.m.; Friday–Saturday, 11:00 a.m.–8:00 p.m. (March–November only)
728 U.S. Highway 62 (west of Barkley dam); 270-362-8580

Marion

Hickory Heaven Bar-B-Q

Between Princeton and Marion on Highway 91, my love for Kentucky landscapes wells up in me as it often does when I'm passing through beautiful agricultural country. Newly cut corn and soybean fields and rolls of hay and grazing beef cattle and an old lady push mowing her yard on a sunny, cool fall day, a mixture of flat fields and long gradual hills, and the closer you get to the Ohio River the hillier it gets. I passed a sign for a community called Mexico and another for the Busted Knee Garage.

Marion, the seat of Crittenden County, has a cute town square with some businesses around it. A couple of miles northeast of Marion, Hickory Heaven, in business since October 2006, offers delicious beef brisket, good pork ribs, distinctive-tasting barbecued chicken, some awesome smoked peppered ham, and a good pork sandwich with mild smokiness. The hot sauce is thin, tangy, peppery, and sweet, and the mild sauce may even be more tangy than the hot. Both suited my personal tastes very well.

Rosa Orr, who runs the restaurant with her husband, Robert, and daughter Carmen, whips up several homemade side dishes and a wide selection of pies to round out your meal. Rosa said, "I make everything homemade but the fried food. Not too many people—not that I brag—make very good vinegar slaw. But people *love* my vinegar slaw. A doctor comes here every two weeks with his wife and mother-in-law and always gets chicken, vinegar slaw, and baked beans." Rosa also makes a family-recipe, mayo-based potato salad—and that's real mayonnaise, not salad dressing, which is the way I like it.

Rosa grew up in Lima, Peru, and even though she's lived in Kentucky for nearly forty years, since she was sixteen, she hasn't picked up much of the regional accent. She met Robert in South America when he played guitar and trombone with a navy show band. They came back to Kentucky to be close to the Orr family. Rosa and I talked about the tough economic times, and she said Robert drives a school bus to help pay for her health insurance.

A long wall of stacked wood runs in front of the big cylindrical tank cooker behind the restaurant. Robert barbecues only with hickory when it's available and sometimes adds a bit of white oak to extend the hickory supply. "We use only fresh meats. We pat out our own hamburgers. We don't freeze nothing," Rosa said.

The brisket was some of the best I've ever had. You get more than three-quarters of a pound on a plate. Rosa said a native Texan stopped by and said he couldn't believe how tender the brisket was. When I asked how long she cooked the brisket, Rosa laughed and said, "That's a secret."

The spareribs were very tender, with a good sweet flavor. A plate gets you more than three-quarters of a pound of ribs. I prefer ribs with a bit more chew, but lovers of fall-off-the-bone ribs will like these. They currently serve half chickens, but Rosa said she's considering quarter chickens in the future. The tender chicken had a far-out flavor. Rosa said, "We wanted something that wouldn't taste like ordinary chicken." She hinted that lemon pepper was part of the difference that lends to the slightly sour taste.

Rosa said they smoke whole pork shoulders because "the other ones [hams] are more stringy and the shoulders give more fat in it and give them more taste." The pork shoulders can be pulled or chopped to order. Rosa explained, "I usually pull it and chop some because I don't like long pieces on my plate and ladies, they usually don't like those big long pieces. So usually I chop it, but some people want it pulled, [so] I pull it for [them]. If they don't tell me anything, I just chop it. Sometime they like it little bitty." One woman who comes in regularly specifies, "I want burned and I want fat," and Rosa pulls to order. The large pork sandwich I ordered had about one-third of a pound of moist meat on a bun brushed with butter and toasted.

You'll also find regional items like smoked ham and smoked bologna on the menu. Rosa said she could custom-pull a whole ham in seven minutes. The smoked peppered ham was very good. "People order whole bunches for Christmas, Thanksgiving, and Fourth of July," she said. Rosa said smoking a sugar-cured ham is tricky because you have to know how much heat and smoke to add or you'll burn the thing. The ham soaked up lots of smoke, and I love the peppery flavor. Previously I'd eaten smoked city ham in Graves County and wasn't crazy about it, but I loved the taste of this tender, juicy, peppery ham at Hickory Heaven. It's the only place in Crittenden County where you can get ham like this.

For dessert, you can get lemon pie, coconut pie, cherry cheesecake, and many others. Rosa likes to cook and knows what makes food delicious. Hickory Heaven is a fine family-owned barbecue destination. If it were closer to my home, I'd patronize it regularly, especially for that excellent beef brisket and the homemade sides and pies.

Open: Wednesday–Saturday, 11:00 a.m.–7:00 p.m.; Sunday, 11:00 a.m.–6:00 p.m.

1890 U.S. Highway 60 East; 270-965-0200

Princeton

Heaton BBQ

Michael Redd was outside tending the pits when I visited one Friday morning in September 2009. If there were a barbecue comic book—and there should be—Michael Redd could be a superhero. First, there's his name, sounding like something out of a Quentin Tarantino flick (remember *Reservoir Dogs,* with Mr. Blue, Mr. Brown, Mr. Pink?). Second, he just looks badass—barbed wire tattooed around his right bicep and a black patch over one eye, buzz-cut hair and a shadowy reddish beard. The man left an impression on me, in part because he looks like he could kick butt in a fight, but also because he explained his meat-smoking methods so patiently and so well.

Mr. Redd, a lifelong resident of Caldwell County, has been smoking meats off and on his whole life. In big outdoor fireboxes, he was burning hickory slabs down to coals and bringing them inside the smoking garage to shovel them underneath the meat in the old-fashioned style. He prefers green wood because it has more moisture and the larger coals add steam to the meat. If the heat gets too hot, you lose meat because the outside of the shoulders will get too crusty, he said. Green wood helps prevent that. He puts whole pork shoulders on the pits between 10:00 and 11:00 a.m. and lets them cook until 7:00–9:00 a.m. the next morning—so, doing the math, shoulders smoke between twenty and twenty-three hours. Workers hand-pull the shoulders in the store. He smokes half chickens, slabs of ribs, and briskets. He browns the briskets an hour on each side and then wraps them in foil and lets them self-baste for several hours. Inside the store, they slice the briskets on request. Heaton purchases meat from Hampton Meat Processing down the road in Hopkinsville. Because of increasing customer demand, they've added some pits over the years. They get lots of traffic off I-24.

I asked Mr. Redd, "Any idea why barbecue's such a tradition in this part of the world?"

He answered, "I think it's because since we were a border state, we had slavery but we also had a lot of poor whites. It was the cuts of meats that you could get, the best and easiest way to do it. You could put it on in the morning, work your farm all day, and come in and have a pretty consistent cut of meat. That way you wouldn't have to be in a hurry. It'd be there waiting for you."

After talking with Michael a while, I felt comfortable enough to ask what happened with his eye. He said, "I had a cornea transplant. It was a 99 percent chance it would take and 1 percent it wouldn't. Welcome to the 1 percent. Too bad it wasn't the lottery."

Don't expect a frilly dining experience at Heaton BBQ, which is actually inside a Marathon gas station. You order barbecue at the same counter where you pay for gasoline. The menu has hamburgers and cheeseburgers in addition to the barbecue offerings. The real good pulled-pork shoulder was moist and tender, with a delicate smokiness, and the sauce tastes of ketchup, sweetness, and pepper. The barky pieces had a pronounced smokiness that I loved. More bark, please! They were sold out of ribs on the Sunday afternoon I ate there. The meat in the brisket sandwich was thinly sliced with a distinctive fat layer. They slice it up to order and heat it on a flat top. If you like fat, as I do, you'll probably be happy with the flavor, but it wasn't like Texas brisket, which is usually sliced thicker. The brisket had a rich, good aroma, but I couldn't get over how the steaming in foil and thin slicing and reheating gave it the texture and aroma of bacon. Not that there's anything wrong with bacon! I'm just saying that it was different from the "naked" briskets I've eaten down in Texas.

Patti and Russell Heaton have served barbecue here since 1996. Russell tended the pits for eight years before training others to do the labor-intensive work. They've been featured in *Garden & Gun* magazine. So get some meats, sit down in a plastic booth, and listen to the bell dinging whenever a car drives up to a fuel pump outside—and be thankful that Michael Redd and pit masters like him are still tending meats in those hot, smoking pits.

Open: Monday–Sunday, 6:00 a.m.–9:00 p.m.
495 Marion Road (in the Marathon gas station); 270-365-3102

Jewell's Open Pit

I was heading west on the Wendell H. Ford Western Kentucky Parkway bound for the Seventeenth Ever Barbecue on the River festivities in Paducah, when I pulled off at the Princeton exit in search of Jewell's, a place I'd learned about from Jane and Michael Stern's *Roadfood,* a coast-to-coast guide to local eateries. Accolades from such well-known food lovers are bound to bring in some customers such as myself who will drive a goodly piece off the interstate for fine barbecue. I'd been meaning to get there for a couple of years, ever since visiting Heaton's just up the road on an earlier trip. Jewell's was closed then, and this time around I wanted to get there for the lunch hour, since they close early on weekdays.

Highway 62 west of Princeton was busy during this Friday lunchtime, and cars riding my bumper pushed me forward at a quicker pace than I like when I'm looking around a new place. This caused me to pass right by Jewell's and drive on down the road a few miles before stopping at an automotive body shop to ask for directions. I backtracked and found the small, tan-colored cinderblock building just off the highway, on the left when you're headed east, just before you hit the commercial district. A couple of cars were parked outside. I saw the pits out back and whole slabs of hickory on a wagon bed.

Inside, I walked to the counter and a woman named Denise handed me a menu and told me to take a seat, so I chose one of three booths against the wall. The meats on offer were pork and bologna. I knew I'd be eating all day, so I chose "pork on garlic," pulled pork between buttered and toasted white bread with a hot sauce drizzled on top by request. Pickles and onions are optional. The sandwich came sliced in two triangles on a plastic plate. The pork was moderately smoky, and the overall affect of the meat, garlic toast, and sauce was delicious. I wished, though, that the sandwich had more meat. It was a smallish amount, probably about a quarter pound. The sauce tingled my lips and tongue with specks of cracked black pepper. The Sterns, in a story for *Gourmet,* describe this sauce as "rich and red, with a compelling citrus zest." The occasional barky pieces were superb, reminding me of the best pulled pork I'd eaten in western Kentucky at such places as Mr. BBQ, Carr's Barn, Prince's, and the Woodshed. I enjoyed the sandwich very much, but if I were hungry the $4 pork on garlic toast would put only a small dent in my appetite, whereas the whopper hoggy sandwich from Mr. BBQ gets you a full half pound of pork for a bit more money. I'd gladly pay a little extra for a larger sandwich.

Ten people were eating, relaxing, talking, and smoking in the one-room dining area. Farming implements—horseshoes, an old ax, a mule yoke, a pitchfork—hang from the brown paneling walls, along with other nostalgic items like a back scratcher made with a turkey leg and a weathered baseball bat and catcher's mitt. I enjoyed looking at tobacco-raising tools, like worn wooden pegs for setting tobacco back in the days before tractors and mechanical tobacco setters. My father and I used to "peg" tobacco in the springtime with such tools as these, which meant we walked down every row a week after planting the young tobacco seedlings in the earth with the machine setter and plunged that wooden peg into the soil, dropped in a plant, and closed the earth around it. It was the kind of work that gets adults down in the back. This homage to tobacco culture at Jewell's included long-handled tobacco knives for cutting the plants during late summer and also a twist of dried tobacco, just in case you missed the point of these tools.

After eating I went to the counter to pay and asked Denise how long they smoke the shoulders, and she said the owner was sitting over in the corner and I could talk to him. This was Lowell Jewell, the same fellow interviewed by the Sterns in *Roadfood*. They quote Lowell as saying, "I watch the food shows on TV when they go all over the place looking for barbecue. And I'm saying, 'Why don't you come to western Kentucky and eat the real thing?'"

True to form, Lowell was easygoing and open to talking in his thick Caldwell County twang. The Jewell family has been in Caldwell County all their lives. I complimented him on the use of garlic toast on the sandwich, noting how unusual that was, and he said, "We even have it on cornbread. More Yankees—or northerners—eat that than the local crew. We have a lot of people traveling through, that's the only reason we have it on the menu. We'd never heard of it, but we had a group come in and they want cornbread, so I saw that it was popular and put it on the menu. It does sell."

"But not with the local folks."

"Naw, naw. Course we eat cornbread every meal, so it's not as big a delicacy for us. But out-of-staters, they love it. And coleslaw. They want coleslaw on it. It's not bad. Ours is a mayonnaise slaw, not vinegar, so it goes pretty good."

I asked about the history of Jewell's barbecue, and Lowell motioned over at the man at the next table and said, "Dad started in the backyard at home with a little pit, and he was a coal miner at the time and the mine shut down, and everybody told us we should open this place, and we opened in 1984. Been going ever since. I been in *Food and Wine* magazine, *Gourmet* magazine, and of course up on the road trip." He gestured to the wall where Jane and Michael Stern's *Roadfood* review hangs. He then pointed to the near-by television and said, "I watch this all the time. They go to Texas. They go to North Carolina. They go everywhere but Kentucky for barbecue."

I said, "That's right. That's why I'm writing this book. We're neglected."

"Yeah, we're overlooked in every way," Lowell agreed. "The only recog-nition we get is Moonlite" (the famous restaurant in Owensboro). "Our bar-becue is cooked the old-fashioned way—no *gas,* no nuthin'. Hickory smoke only. That's it. We don't put any rubs. The only time the sauce hits it is when it comes through that ordering window. And if you don't want sauce, tell me, and you'll have nothing but pure barbecue."

Lowell puts the whole shoulders on the pits at 8:00–9:00 one morn-ing and they come off the next day. "It's a twenty-four-hour process," he said. "We start out skin side down and flip 'em two or three times throughout the day and keep the heat under 'em."

Lowell said all their side dishes are homemade: coleslaw, macaroni sal-ad, baked beans, white beans, cornbread—"all that's fresh made." Talking about the great variety of barbecue desires from county to county in west-ern Kentucky, Lowell said, "You can go to this county and everybody wants pork. You go to Lyon County, they want pork, chicken, ham, more variety. You go to Christian County, which is another joining county, they want mut-ton. Madisonville likes mutton, but we can't sell it here. This is pork terri-tory, Caldwell County." They sometimes smoke chickens for a change, and they sell well. I'd noted earlier that chicken was on the menu but crossed off with a black marker. Lowell spoke of chicken with a hint of derision in his voice: "It got to where everybody was like, chicken chicken, every day chick-en. And usually when you come to a barbecue place you like pork. Our pork is our staff."

We got into a discussion about gas-fired cookers, and Lowell asked me if I'd tasted gas on the meat at a particular restaurant, and when I said no, he observed, "They cover it up better than most." He added, "If you love barbe-cue—like when we clean our pits our regulars will say, 'You cleaned your pits,' 'cause they know. It don't have that great barbecue flavor—it's good, but it's not that great barbecue flavor that they're used to. It's like an iron skillet—better seasoned, the better it is."

Jewell's is a family affair. Lowell's mom opens for breakfast; his sister helps out when they need her; and his nieces wait tables.

When I asked him, "How long you intend to keep doing this?" Lowell smiled and said, "As long as the public keeps comin'."

Open: Monday–Friday, 5:30 a.m.–2:00 p.m.; Saturday, 5:30 a.m.–10:00 p.m.

1240 U.S. Highway 62 West; 270-365-5415

Hopkinsville

The Trail of Tears Intertribal Pow-Wow, happening each year the first full weekend after Labor Day—featuring Native American dancing and storytelling along with vendors selling foods, crafts, clothes, and music—is a good reason to make the drive to Hopkinsville. I enjoy sitting in the stands by the dancing circle, eating a piece of fry bread and watching colorfully clothed and feathered dancers compete in various styles—my favorite being the electrifying Fancy Dance performed mostly by young men and boys as they keep time with powerful war drums and fast drums and varied tempos, and the dancer must move according to the beat and strike a pose when the drum beats stop.

Hopkinsville was also home to the "psychic counselor and healer" (from a marker near his grave) Edgar Cayce. The Pennyroyal Area Museum, located in the old post office building downtown, displays Cayce's Bible along with other exhibits on the Black Patch Tobacco Wars, Jefferson Davis, pioneer home furnishings, old quilts, and old license plates.

And yes, Hoptowners love their barbecue, judging by the several great barbecue joints in Christian County, and it's one of the last places in southern Kentucky where you'll find mutton and burgoo as you head eastward.

Bar B Que Shack ("Real Pit Bar-B-Que")

Some barbecue places get all the press (Moonlite in Owensboro, for instance). Others languish in obscurity, often for good reason. And then you have places

Elisa Berry's Smoky Greens

I've been eating messes of greens since I was a knee-high rube and have never tired of them. My wife, Elisa, makes some of the best I've ever had. Of course I'm biased, but I also have good taste. This recipe was inspired by the "soul greens" of Smoketown USA in Louisville. Elisa took the vegetarian-friendly Smoketown greens and carnivored them up a bit, to the delight of my taste buds. I like adding the sliced boiled eggs, something my mama always did when we ate greens at home.

4 ounces dried black-eyed peas (you can use a 15-ounce can of them, or if you're lucky get them fresh)
1 smoked ham hock (or bacon or other smoked meat/bone)
3 bunches of greens, mixed (whatever you like—I often use collards, mustard greens, and kale)
1 can (15 ounces) diced stewed tomatoes
2 cubes chicken bouillon
Salt and pepper to taste
Hard-cooked eggs, sliced

Strip the leaves of greens, removing the largest, toughest stems. In a stockpot big enough to hold the fresh greens, add enough water to cover the ham hock. Bring to a boil and add dried peas and ham hock. Reduce heat to a slow boil and cook about 30 minutes, until peas are partially cooked but still firm. (If you use fresh or canned beans you may want to wait until later to add them, so they don't get too mushy.)

Add greens, the full can of stewed tomatoes with liquid, and enough water to just cover the greens. Bring to a boil. As the water gets hot, add bouillon and salt and pepper to taste. Cover and reduce to a simmer. Cook for 1 hour. When the greens are nearly ready, pull out the ham hock, let it cool, and then pull any meat off and put it in the pot. Serve with vinegar or Tabasco sauce. Garnish with slices of hard-cooked egg.

like Bar B Que Shack—a gem of a barbecue joint whose praises should be sung but that isn't well known outside its locality. The Shack took me by surprise with its high-quality long-smoked pork and mutton and delicious burgoo and hot slaw.

I walked into the Shack on a Friday afternoon and was greeted by one of several women who were running the place, mostly working the drive-through window at the back. The atmosphere is utilitarian, so the experience is like eating in a well-lit, open, clean garage. Walls and ceiling are corrugated metal, and floors are cement. Fluorescent lighting bathes the plastic-topped tables in a seating space that probably holds fifty to sixty customers. I was excited about the possibilities for great barbecue because I spied huge slabs of hickory piled up out back and smelled the smoke. The white board menu listed pulled pork, mutton, ribs, pork chops, and chicken; white beans, baked beans, green beans, potato salad, slaw, burgoo, and hot slaw; pies (pecan, chess, French coconut, and fudge) and peach cobbler. I chose a mutton sandwich on cornbread with hot slaw and burgoo for sides.

The hoecakes were hot, sweet, and fresh, and the chopped mutton has plenty of tasty fat mixed in and a deep smoky flavor from real pit cooking. The hot sauce is a tomato-vinegar-cayenne concoction, a nice complement to the mutton. I appreciated that the finely chopped mutton isn't sauced as it is in Owensboro when you get "chopped." This was simply meat, fat, and smoke. I loved it. The woman who rang up my bill said people wanted mutton and were willing to pay the higher price (compared to pork and chicken). Because the mutton was so good, I ordered a pound of pork pulled from their long-smoked whole shoulders to take home with me. The pork could use some salt, but the meat was very good: deeply smoked, extremely moist, and flaky tender. On hoecakes with the hot sauce, it would be mighty fine. I loved the crunchy hot slaw, which reminded me of Korean kimchee without the sourness of kimchee fermentation—finely chopped cabbage with a red hot sauce mixed in, leaving a nice afterglow of heat on the tongue. One of the workers told me that many locals get slaw on their pork sandwiches. The burgoo was a chunky stew of green beans, corn, cubed potatoes, black-eyed peas, green peas, meat, black pepper, and tomatoes—much thicker than burgoo I've eaten at Moonlite and Old Hickory Bar-B-Q in Owensboro, the burgoo capital.

Out back, I talked with James Baucum, who's worked the pits for a year, and Carlos from Chiapas, Mexico, the main cook for five years, as long as the Shack has been open in its current location. The pits are well-insulated, heavy-duty block rectangles with heavy lids weighed down by big rocks. Thick smoke hung in the garage, smelling wonderful. The whole shoulders cook at 200° for twenty-four hours or longer. They burn down hickory and oak slabs to coals in a huge steel barrel and shovel them underneath the meat. They cook spareribs in the mornings. James said if the temperature drops to 175°, they shovel more coals underneath to get the pit temperature back up to 200–225°, about every one and a half to two hours. When the mutton quarters are half done, they wrap them in foil to save the juices ("It dries out a lot quicker than pork does," James explained). Chickens and pork chops are cooked on a pellet cooker that feeds hickory pellets on it gradually. Pork chops cook for only one and a half to two hours.

I said, "You know, James, there aren't many people in Kentucky cooking whole shoulders for twenty-four hours."

"That right? You can taste that smoke all the way through, can't you?"

Carlos and I talked a while about the beauty of tongue tacos with cilantro and onion and good tortillas.

The skinny on the Shack: for my taste bud leanings, I favor the burgoo, the hot slaw, pulled pork on hoecakes with hot sauce, and a mutton sandwich on hoecakes with hot sauce. I wonder if the people of Hopkinsville realize how lucky they are.

Open: Wednesday–Saturday, 10:00 a.m.–varying closing times, like 4:00 p.m. on Wednesday

4687 Pembroke Road; 270-475-4844

Woodshed Pit BBQ

A little over twenty-four hours after I stopped at a barbecue joint in western Kentucky and paid $4 for a sandwich with a minimal amount of meat, I arrived at Woodshed and paid $3.50 for a sandwich that had serious loft, probably two inches of shredded pork heaped up on a regular hamburger bun. The meat was smoky and flaky with pieces of crispy bark. No sauce came on the sandwich, and I loved it.

I walked in and sat at the front counter and struck up a talk with two waitresses. I said I liked smoky flavor, and what did they recommend? One said she liked the chicken without the sauce because you could tell that it comes from the pit; the other said she liked the chicken with the sauce because it had more flavor. They said the chicken, mutton, and pork all come from the same pit. They serve baby back ribs on Saturday only. The ribs came with baked potato, salad, green beans, and a yeast roll. Homemade sides include the baked beans and burgoo. A plate comes with a meat and three sides. The green beans are doctored up with a bit of country ham.

Even though it was baby back Saturday, I opted for the pork sandwich, and it was wonderful. They smoke whole shoulders overnight. Pickle and onion are optional on the sandwich. The meat was tender and very smoky. This wasn't "wet" barbecue but rather dry in the best way possible—flaky but still moist meat. The sauce is a sweet, thin tomato sauce with some vinegar and flecks of pepper. The pork, with its salty-smoky flavor, reminded me of the best I've eaten in western Kentucky. Shoulders are cooked out back every day except Sunday. They put the whole shoulders and mutton quarters on the pits at 10:00 a.m.–noon and take them off early the next morning.

I sat in a little nook off the main dining room, a big, open area seating eighty people. There were twenty people eating there at 4:30 on a Saturday afternoon. A television on the wall played college football. People smoked inside. The floors are tile and the tables are simple laminated plastic with scoot-'em-up black chairs. Pies are on display at the counter in the front. Menus are located in slots underneath the table. The Woodshed has a drive-through window. As I ate that sandwich, several people drove up and got their orders. Later, the attentive server talked me into a piece of pie from their multiple options. I took her advice and got the coconut cream. The pork sandwich ranks high on my "best" list, and I also liked the sweet treat at $2 per slice. Other pies include raisin, caramel, chess, chocolate chess, lemon icebox, key lime, pecan, and apple.

Opened in 1984 on the western edge of Hopkinsville by the Mathis family, the Woodshed has a loyal clientele. (Their most famous customer was George W. Bush, who stopped by on the campaign trail back in May of 2000.) Jr. Mathis, the original owner, has retired and his sons run the place now. I told Phil Mathis, who stood at the drive-through window filling orders, that I really enjoyed that sandwich, and he said, "It's been a winning formula so far." They get their mutton and pork from Hampton Meat Processing in Hopkinsville, where they do "meat cut fresh daily on site." That ready source of fresh meat is surely a primary reason why that barbecued pork tasted so good.

"I guess you just call us a family-style restaurant," Phil said. "Mom and pop is about gone, you know?"

The Woodshed barbecues mutton quarters. Phil said mutton is so expensive, he didn't know why people didn't raise it around here. "I believe I'll start raising mutton—that's better than tobacco now." He noted that mutton is a drier meat but better for you than pork. "I take a pill for pork," he said. "I might have to start taking two!"

Give the Woodshed a try for their generous portions of that long-barbecued pork and mutton, extensive side dishes, and comfortable mom-and-pop atmosphere.

Open: Monday–Saturday, 10:30 a.m.–8:00 p.m.
1821 West Seventh Street; 270-885-8144

Herndon

Knockum Hill Bar-B-Q ("We do it the old fashioned way")

On a Friday in early November, I trekked over to Herndon, Kentucky, to tackle the Knockum Hill pork chop. Forget your fork and finicky eating—this is dig your hands in and pull the bones out and separate the fat with your fingers barbecue. This is as close to whole hog as I've found in Kentucky. Hillbillies say a snapping turtle has seven kinds of meat in it. This pork hunk is the snapping turtle of barbecue. After eating some of it, I brought it home and weighed it on my kitchen scale—and it *still* weighed in at two pounds, six ounces (bones and fat included). If you like real barbecue—deeply smoked meat that falls apart at the touch of your fingers and tastes rich and savory—and if you aren't afraid of bones and some natural fat, then don't visit the Hopkinsville area without trying this T. Rex of pork chops. It's baaaaaad (in the good way). I've never seen anything like it outside a pig picking.

Knockum Hill is just south of Herndon, a spot in the road with a market, a U.S. Post Office, a Methodist church, and a few houses, surrounded by sprawling cornfields. In the fall, the beauty of the changing leaves and fresh-cut fields and tobacco firing in the curing barns made for pleasant driving. The parking lot of Knockum Hill was full of pickup trucks at Friday noon. The tan metal building with a green roof is flanked by beautiful deciduous woods.

Mr. Oscar Hill, a healthy-looking seventy-five years old in 2011, has been barbecuing for over thirty years, doing it the old-timey western Kentucky way: burning down hickory wood to coals and shoveling those coals underneath meat propped on racks in well-insulated concrete and mortar pits. When I saw the rows of hickory slabs out back of his small restaurant and sniffed the rich aroma of smoke in the air, I anticipated something good. His monstrous pork chop exceeded my expectations; not only was it big, but it was cooked perfectly, with crispy bark on the outside and delicate tender meat on the inside and infused throughout with the sweet, savory hickory smoke. I loved it, wanted to eat the whole thing, but held back because I had to eat at several more places that day. I asked Oscar how long that pork chop had smoked, and he said it was a twenty-hour process. He said many people had tried to duplicate his big chop, but none successfully. The meat dries out quickly when you bust it open, so I recommend bringing a partner and eating it in one sitting. The pork chop costs $11, but two to three people could split it, although Mr. Hill said that some of his big eaters tackle the whole thing. He claims that you can eat the chop with a plastic fork. It's true, but I just dug in with my fingers, and the meat and fat melted in my mouth. I picked through a rib section and another part containing what appeared to be spinal bones. I'm pretty sure this chop is cut from the loin—it's like having four un-trimmed pork chops in one big hunk. Two table sauces complement the pork, both made from mostly white vinegar, red oil (chili oil?), and cayenne pepper, but this pork is so good that no sauce is necessary.

In addition to the miraculous pork chop (have I mentioned that this pork chop ranks in my top 5 percent of supreme barbecue experiences?), other offerings include pulled pork from Boston butts cooked over fifteen hours, whole and half chickens, and big spareribs. I didn't try the side dishes (burgoo, potato salad, and slaw), having enough on my plate with the pork chop. Delicious-looking slices of pie are also available, and you can view them inside a refrigerated case by the counter.

Four middle-aged gentlemen in business attire ate and talked at one table; at another table sat a group of six men in hunting camo and work boots; at another several African American guys wearing dungarees; at another, two Fort Campbell soldiers in army fatigues. You can eat inside the thirty-five-seat restaurant decorated with white and green checked plastic tablecloths and green window treatments, or, when the weather is good, outside at a picnic table underneath a big pavilion lit up by fluorescent lighting. Several porch swings hang from the pavilion. When I left that day, I heard what sounded like geese honking in the woods behind, and saw black cattle walking among the trees.

Knockum Hill was opened in 1980 by Oscar's brother-in-law Will, who still lives next door to the restaurant. Oscar bought the restaurant from Will in 1996. Because he's been at the business such a long time, Oscar said he'll sell the place if somebody gives him "the right price" for it. I heard something

Side Dish: The Gospel on Sauces

This I believe: Sauces are superfluous to great barbeque. My friend Bruce Bjorkman, host of the radio show *Cooking Outdoors with Mr. Barbecue* out of Portland, Oregon, wrote a whole book on barbecue dressings called *The Great Barbecue Companion: Mops, Sops, Sauces, and Rubs*. I respect Bruce's research and dedication to barbecue and enjoy reading the recipes in his book, especially the international flavors like *harissa* (Moroccan spiced red chili paste), Dominican sauce with mango and tamarind, Jamaican jerk rubs, and so forth. But after eating barbecue at 160 places all over Kentucky, I've become even more convinced that great barbecue doesn't need sauce, especially not heavy masking sauces. Two of my favorite joints—Mr. BBQ & More in Grand Rivers and Knockum Hill Bar-B-Q in Herndon—serve up finger-lickin' luscious pork seasoned simply with salt, wood smoke, and slow cooking. Both places offer very thin vinegar sauces at the table, and I'll shake a few drops on the pork as a kind of palate shifter to prevent taste bud fatigue, but the meat is just so good you don't want to overwhelm it with sauce. To me, that's what great barbecue is about—meat so good you don't even want a sauce.

similar from Cy Quarles at Mr. BBQ up in Grand Rivers. Both of these barbecue experts are near retirement. I'm just saying—get there while the sweet smoke rolls.

That pork chop was the best-tasting meat I've had in Kentucky from any cut of pig—which means the best meat, period.

Open: Friday, 9:00 a.m.–6:00 p.m.; Saturday, 9:00 a.m.–3:00 p.m. (doors close at closing hour, so get there sometime before 6:00 or 3:00)

11185 Highway 107 South; 270-271-2957

Bluegrass, Blues, and Barbecue Region

The folks at the Kentucky Tourism Council (or Chamber of Commerce or whoever did the naming) got it partly wrong when coining such a description for this eight-county region. Sure, Bill Monroe, father of bluegrass, hails from here. But the counties in the "Western Waterlands" region could as easily claim the barbecue title. Still, you can smack your lips on plenty of scrumptious smoked meats in this region, and I'm here to lead you to some of the best places.

Uniontown

Uniontown Food Mart

Several big steel cylindrical tanks sit outside of this grocery store/takeout barbecue joint near the banks of the Ohio River. Smoke puffed from chimneys rising out of the tanks as I talked with Dennis "Bubba" Girten, master smoker, while he pulled fat from whole smoked hams and tended beautiful racks of spareribs. It was mid-September, the sun blazed down on Uniontown, and when Bubba lifted the two hinged doors on one of the tanks, the juicy hams reflected the sunlight. I saw a halo around one of them.

Bubba wore black rubber gloves to pull off the already-smoked exterior fat and skin. He then shook black pepper on the hams liberally after the extra fat was removed, so that the pepper soaked into the meat as the hams

Side Dish: Ode to Catholic Church Fund-raisers

If you are lucky as I was, you'll roll into a community like Uniontown on a day when they are doing a church picnic. On a mid-September afternoon, I watched a few local fellers smoking seventy-eight hundred pounds of mutton on long cinderblock pits stacked three blocks high and topped with wire fencing.

When I expressed my surprise at the huge amount of meat, a man said, "It'll be gone by 8:00 tonight." They have a dining hall where you can have all-you-can-eat mutton for $9, or you can buy sandwiches or by the pound. In the morning early, they sell the ribs and the necks off the pit (since both cook up quicker than the thicker parts of the sheep).

I said, "Mutton ribs are pretty lean, ain't they?" and a fellow said, "Lean on the meat, but they're fatty as hell." The men guessed they lost 40 percent of the original weight during the cooking process by rendering the fat and through evaporation. The mutton cooks overnight for a total of about sixteen hours, the pit watchers basting the meats with dip to prevent dehydration during the long smoking. They treated me to a piece of mutton off the pit, and it was plumb wonderful.

"It's got a mineral, gamy flavor don't it?" said Raymond Hammond, one of the pit tenders. "It's a lot of work and a lot of fun. It's a homecoming thing. Mark your calendar—we do it every year, the Saturday after Labor Day."

And that evening I sat around on hay bales on the grounds of St. Agnes Catholic Church and ate mutton, watching people milling about, talking and sipping and sampling the scrumptious results of that long cooking. I know I'm going back. That mutton was so good as to reaffirm one's belief in the Fabulous Unknown.

Time: 4:30 p.m., first Saturday after Labor Day

Place: St. Agnes Catholic Church, 504 Mulberry Street, Uniontown; 270-822-4416

continued to smoke and the newly exposed fat browned. The hams smoke for about eight hours and are fully cooked when Bubba gets them from Farm Boy Foodservice in Evansville, Indiana. Ribs smoke for six to seven hours with a mixture of hickory, pecan, sassafras, and oak. Bubba said a friend flew in from Seattle with another fellow who'd never eaten mutton, and three days later they flew back to the Northwest with 150 pounds of mutton on the airplane.

I didn't get to try the ribs because they were sold out, and the racks on the smoker wouldn't be done until a couple hours later, so I settled for two sandwiches, pork and mutton, and ate them at a plastic picnic table underneath a small gazebo. I sipped a cold beverage, savored the sandwiches, and watched Bubba sweat out there in the intense afternoon heat. The pulled-pork sandwich was wet, tender, and intensely smoky. A thin "dip" was on the meat when the sandwich came to me. The wetness distinguished this style from the pork I found around Paducah and farther west. While I dislike a heavy sauce that disguises the meat, this thin dip tasted real good on the sandwich. The chipped mutton tasted like mutton is supposed to taste—gamy, tangy, and smoky.

One microregional specialty available at Uniontown Food Mart is chipped ham—what we call "city ham" (as opposed to salty country ham), smoked and chopped up with spices on it. Most ham consumed in the USA is city ham, so I'll bet folks from all around would enjoy this sandwich. I'm not sure if I'd call it barbecue, though, since the hams are already cooked when they hit the smoker. Let's just call it what it is: a smoked, chipped city ham sandwich. The Uniontown Food Mart barbecue menu also includes pork burgers, boneless pork chops, and whole chickens.

Bubba was born and raised in Uniontown. His sister married one of the Peak boys from the established Peak Bros. restaurant down the road. During high school he spent a summer with his sister and brother-in-law, and the latter, disapproving of Bubba lying around on the couch, said one day, "My dad's got something for you to do." He started a painting job for the Peaks, and three hours later they said, "You know how to chip mutton?" and Bubba said, "Naw," so an old black man took him inside and showed him how. Next thing Bubba knew, he was cooking and doing it all. Bubba does the smoking for Uniontown Food Mart seven days a week.

I said, "When do you rest?"

Chicken Dip

This delicious dip is courtesy of a pitman at St. Agnes, whose name I unfortunately failed to get.

2 46-ounce cans of tomato juice
2 sticks butter
1 cup apple cider vinegar
Black pepper and salt to taste
1 tablespoon of sugar
1 cup French's mustard
2 tablespoons cayenne pepper

Don't dip chicken until chicken is almost done, or you'll burn the dip.

He replied, "I go home at night."

Bubba said he'd do the smoking but wouldn't make a sauce, because "it would make the Peaks mad if I did." Family secrets and all. They trained him. He'd be stealing their recipe.

Bubba directed me to a big picnic down the road at St. Agnes Catholic Church, so instead of lingering around for the ribs, I went to check it out.

By the way, just a skip down the road from Uniontown Food Mart, you can park by the Ohio River and watch the water roll.

Open: Monday–Friday, 6:00 a.m.–9:00 p.m.; Saturday, 7:00 a.m.–9:00 p.m.; Sunday, 8:00 a.m.–8:00 p.m.

330 Mill Street; 270-822-5005

Waverly

Peak Bros. Bar-B-Que

I'm wary of alluding to pop technology—which is often about speed and trendiness—in a book about something as old-fashioned as barbecue, which is about taking your time and durability—but these are the times we live in. If you are on Facebook, you can look up Peak Bros. BBQ and see photos of people having a fabulous time there celebrating Derby Day, Mardi Gras, and University of Kentucky basketball games: women dancing on the bar Coyote

121

You Can Rely on Divine Providence to Help You Find a Church Picnic

But blessedly, the Diocese of Owensboro—the Catholic Church of Western Kentucky—makes it easier, publishing a schedule of the annual picnics in its monthly newsletter, the *Western Kentucky Catholic*. You can access it online— http://rcdok.org/ministries/communications /WKC_online.php—and search the archives electronically. The picnic schedule is published in the April edition.

The annual picnic weekends are pretty stable—Immaculate Conception in Hawesville, for instance, holds its picnic on the third Saturday in September. Most picnics occur on Saturday afternoons, a few on Sundays. To find out the precise day and time of a church's picnic, call the church office. They'll be glad to help you—and glad to have you come eat. As Bill Glenn told me at Owensboro's International Bar-B-Q Festival while stirring a vat of burgoo for Our Lady of Lourdes' cooking team: "God's on everybody's side, and he likes barbecue."

Ugly style; a bartender loaded down with Mardi Gras beads; women wearing elaborate Derby Day hats.

But Peak Bros. is also a family dining place. I'm reminded of pubs in Ireland, where all sorts gather. Men drink pints at the bar. Families—young kids, parents, grandparents—dine at the tables. A band plucks instruments in the corner.

When I ate at Peak Bros. on a Saturday afternoon around 3:00, the place was quiet—not the party atmosphere revealed in the photos. In short, if you desire a party atmosphere with your barbecue, venture into Peak Bros. in the evenings. They have a full bar. If you desire a "family atmosphere" and don't mind neon beer signs on the walls, go there for lunch or an early dinner. The bar/lounge area is separated from the restaurant.

The appetizer menu is extensive. They have "onion pedals" [*sic*] and cheddar cheese balls and deep-fried spicy dill pickles. Plates include mutton, pork, ham, and beef, sliced and chipped. A combo plate includes a bit of all of these meats, or you can get a sandwich. They also serve steaks and fried chicken. Sides include beans, slaw, spicy fried sweet potatoes, onion rings, and steak fries.

I started with burgoo: spicy and flavorful with chunks of corn, onion, potato, and meat. The spareribs were tender and wet, with a thin dip sauce on them. My personal preference is for less tender "naked" ribs that haven't been wrapped in foil or boiled, but they had a good smoky flavor. I tried a little bit of all the meats, which were coated in the same thin, vinegary Peak Bros. sauce that was on the ribs. The sauce worked better with the pork and mutton than with the other meats. The brisket had a thin smoke ring, was moderately tender, and tasted a bit like roast beef. It was good. The chopped mutton was real good, with the appropriate mutton whanginess. The chipped pork was smoky and very vinegary. If you like vinegar and smoke, get the chipped pork! The ham was tender city ham with some sauce on it. The sliced pork was lean, dry, and mildly smoky. It reminded me of a sliced pork loin, which lacks the fat of shoulders, and I found out later that they smoke fresh whole hams instead of fattier shoulders and butts—hence the leanness (and dryness).

In summary, my favorite meats were the mutton and chipped pork (loved it). Smoking fresh hams instead of shoulders makes pulling the pork difficult because of the lesser fat content. The "chipped" style comes out of necessity from the leaner hams. The sliced beef comes off the brisket. The sliced mutton comes from smoked mutton hams; chipped mutton comes from mutton ribs, shoulders, and necks. They use many different hardwoods for smoking.

Peak Bros. has burned twice, the first time in 1976. The current building is new, and nice quilts hang from ductwork along the ceilings. There's a letter on the wall from Ladybird Johnson, thanking the Peaks for a barbecue ham back in the 1960s. Earle C. Clements, who served as a senator and then governor of Kentucky, sent the Johnsons a Peak Bros. barbecue ham—a fully cooked, bone-in city ham.

The new restaurant has a huge brick and mortar pit in the kitchen, rising from the floor and disappearing into the ceiling, with big, sliding steel doors to access the meat. They keep the fires burning with chunks of hardwood from a big pile stacked near the pits.

I asked Irene Rich, whose father and uncle opened Peak Bros. back in 1948, if there was anything else memorable she could tell me about the restaurant. She thought a few moments and said, "We're a survivor," referring to how, like a phoenix from the ashes, they've bounced back from two devastating fires.

Open: Tuesday–Thursday, 10:00 a.m.–10:00 p.m.; Friday–Saturday, 8:00 a.m.–10:00 p.m.; Sunday, 8:00 a.m.–3:00 p.m.

6353 U.S. Highway 60 West; 270-389-0267

Henderson

In June, the W. C. Handy Blues and Barbecue Festival happens in the Ohio River town of Henderson. Blues music takes center stage, with local and national bands playing every night from Wednesday to Saturday. The free festival opens with a Taste of Henderson Barbecue, where you can sample smoked meats from local teams. If you plan well, you can get your music and barbecue on in Owensboro in May, in Henderson in June, and in Danville and Paducah in September. I love these small Kentucky towns and their joie de vivre.

www.handyblues.org

Thomason's Barbecue

Barbecue has been sold at Thomason's for over fifty years. When I visited in December 2011, I spoke with current owner Frank Gibson, who's been running the show for eighteen years. Frank said they've changed very little except for a few modern updates, like adding a steam table to hold the smoked meats in order to serve customers more quickly. "We've had days we've had three hundred customers in eight hours," he said, and serving the meat right off the pit "just takes forever." They've got one or two people pulling meat off the bones all day. The pulled pork comes from butts, and they cook the hams, shoulders, and ribs of whole sheep many hours before pulling the fat away to serve their lean pulled mutton.

"Just barbecue's all we do—you want a hamburger, don't come here!" Frank said, laughing. "Do what you do well, you know!" Frank said the beans are "one of our biggest-moving items," and that on some days, like holidays, "we've knocked over nine hundred pounds [of beans] in one day." They've

124

sold bean sandwiches at festivals. Frank said they're a good profitable item. "You need one of those," he said. These beans have been rated best in the South by one publication. The beans are baked in an oven with smoked meat and some of Frank's secret-recipe dip sauce mixed in.

Like several mom-and-pop barbecue joints with minimal indoor seating, Thomason's is a place where you can eat and listen in on conversations from many local folks coming in to get takeout orders—and they were really rolling in the door at 11:00 a.m. just a few days before Christmas. It's a cozy joint with just six booths, brown paneling on the walls, a display of loaf breads next to a little counter ordering area, and a cold-drink machine. Windows letting in natural light look out onto Atkinson Street.

This little joint has been reviewed in Jane and Michael Stern's *Roadfood* and in *Gourmet* magazine. The Sterns praised the delicious barbecue beans, calling them "rich and smoky, laced with shreds of meat and so vividly spiced you could make a meal of them," and the beans that came with my sampler plate were surely some of the best I've ever eaten—silky and savory, with smokiness from the added meat. Rounding out the plate was pulled pork, pulled mutton, a pork sparerib, slaw, two slices of rye bread (chosen from white, wheat, rye, or bun), and sliced dill pickles and onions. The meats were all swimming in a tangy thin dip that the Sterns call "sauce with natural, au jus character."

Frank said their vinegar dip doesn't have Worcestershire sauce in it. "Ours has got a lot more spices in it," he said. "I've seen customers get done with a sandwich and then drink the rest of the dip, you know what I mean?" he said, again laughing. "Soppin' it up."

The meats are cooked in an indoor masonry pit fired by hickory wood. Frank showed me the "warmer" behind the ordering counter: a steel door pulled upward by a cable to reveal the blackened doors of the interior pits. In the old days, the cooked meats were held in this warming area off the main fire pit and meats were taken from there and pulled to order. In the kitchen area, Frank opened the heavy door to the pit and, wearing heavy rubber gloves, fished deep inside the rectangular opening with the long pitchfork. He skewered a whole smoked turkey, beautifully browned, and pulled it out long enough for me to snap a photo. He showed me a hunk of mutton ribs and a mutton neck. "Some people just cook the mutton hams," he said. "We do the whole thing, buddy."

"See, there's hardly any fire in there at all," Frank said, looking into the narrow opening of the pit. "The firebricks get hot and you don't have to turn the meat." The coals are added from the outside and lay about four feet underneath the meat. "Grease is just raining in the pits all day," he said.

He said the EPA has complained about the smoke, but there's nothing they can do about it because it's food. I said that was good advertising. "Sometimes we just roll the smoke out of here, just fog the whole road out there."

I asked how long they cook the butts. "According to how big they are," Frank said. "Generally at least five hours. Usually five to eight hours." They cook at about 300–325°. "Usually the slower you cook 'em, the less shrinkage you have. Little ones sometimes take longer than a big one. You just don't know."

"How do you gauge when they're done?" I asked.

"We use a pitchfork on the pit, and we got an extra tine we cut off, and when it goes in like hot butter it's done. If it goes in there and tugs, it's not done."

Of the sample platter, my traveling companion Todd Chappel and I raved about the pulled mutton and the intense flavor of "chip"—the smoky bark of mutton and pork butts (mostly mutton), chopped fine and soaked in dip to soften the hard pieces. "We usually sell out of that," Frank said. The excellent rib meat pinched right off the bone. The first bite I tried was a chewy end piece, but the rest of the rib was tender with a good smokiness.

In addition to the lean pulled mutton, fabulous beans, and flavor-packed chipped mutton, you can try chopped beef brisket with the fat pulled out (listed on the menu as "beef"). "Twenty years ago people liked fat in their barbecue, but not anymore," Frank said. "The bulk of the people now don't want fat in it."

On the wall-mounted menu you'll also see ham and turkey. The turkey is a whole precooked turkey breast smoked about two hours, and the ham is a boneless Farmland pit ham. A turkey or ham plate will get you slices of these tasty smoked meats ladled with dip upon request. Frank said he sells a lot of turkey to women. The turkey was tender, juicy, and moderately smoky—very tasty. But we loved the pulled mutton and the "chip" the most.

Note: bring cash—no credit cards accepted.

Open: Tuesday–Friday, 10:00 a.m.–6:00 p.m.; Saturday, 10:00 a.m.–4:00 p.m.

701 Atkinson Street; 270-826-0654

J & B Barbecue ("Home of the Open Pit Chicken")

Located in a residential area, J & B blends in with the neighboring homes except for the sign out front. A house trailer sits across the road. J & B distinguishes itself from other barbecue places in this locality by grilling chickens and pork chops on an open pit—a style common to the south-central Kentucky counties of Barren, Monroe, and Cumberland, but a rare find in this closed-pit region that includes the cities of Henderson, Owensboro, and most of far-western Kentucky.

The J and the B are John Klein and Barry Burton, childhood friends, now middle-aged men, who cook and fish together. Barry's father was a fund-raiser for several Henderson charities—churches, schools, and sporting events—and the primary method of fund-raising was selling barbecued chickens. "We'd have five hundred to six hundred chickens every Saturday morning from the time I was twelve years old to twenty-five," Barry said. "If these groups didn't have enough help to work the pits, Dad would call me and my brother—get us out of bed—to go down and help. That's where we were taught the art of cooking chickens on an open pit—cooking over charcoal and wood, cooking slow, never getting in a hurry. I was thirteen to fourteen years old working a pit of 120 chickens every Saturday, every summer, of my childhood. So there was no watching *Tom and Jerry* and *Underdog*. It was all fund-raisers; Dad never took a penny for it."

Barry worked for Peabody Coal for twenty-three years before "retiring" into barbecue. John worked for twenty-seven years with the City of Henderson's gas department. "When I walked away from the mines, he retired," Barry said of John, noting that John's role as president of the booster club at Holy Name of Jesus Catholic Church in Henderson had given him plenty of opportunities to cook food for large numbers of people. They'd done some cooking contests together over the years. Barry told John, "I could always go back to coal mining—let's try it," and so the J & B Barbecue partnership was born. They first served carryout for two years from a little backroom of a hardware store and catered events for the coal mines, the Dana Corporation,

Alcan (an aluminum smelter), and the hospital. Then the corner lot came up for sale and Barry said to John, "Do you want to take it another step?" In 2005, they bought the lot, built the restaurant, and business has increased 15–20 percent each year.

"We kinda look at it as a team sport," Barry said. "I'm not the boss. Don't like nothin' that goes with that term and John doesn't either. If we keep the girls happy, we're thrilled. You want that peace-of-mind atmosphere when you're hustlin' and bustlin'." "The girls" includes Barry's sister, who runs the kitchen "and pretty much runs us," Barry said. "We try to keep our help happy. We pay 'em well. If they want to take their kids to Holiday World, we let 'em off. If they come in and don't want to be here, you're gonna have to pay for it."

Twenty chatty patrons occupied every table in the dining area at 11:30 a.m. The atmosphere is homey, with red checkered tablecloths and window treatments, a University of Kentucky flag in the corner, a flat-screened television mounted near the ceiling, and a quilt hanging on the wall with four squares displaying happy anthropomorphic pigs picnicking and barbecuing. One panel reminds me of *American Gothic,* except the pigs are holding meat instead of a pitchfork.

Meals come on Styrofoam plates, and sweet tea comes in a Styrofoam cup. I ordered the sampler plate with a quarter open-pit chicken, one meaty sparerib, and a serving of pulled pork. I also tried the pulled mutton, which is chopped into rough pieces and served swimming in a tangy dip. I *loved* the mutton. It was my favorite of the meats, packing the most intense flavor (it's also the item they smoke the longest). The chicken was a breast/wing portion, and even though it was white meat (which can dry out easily), the breast meat was tender and appropriately smoky. While cooking the chickens on the open pit, the J & B team bastes them with a dip of vinegar, butter, pickling spice, salt, and pepper. The pulled pork, already sauced, was very tender with a medium smoke flavor and a delicious sauce that didn't totally mask the flavor of pork. The big sparerib was nicely peppered, and the fattier top part was real good. The table sauce seems a bit thicker than other local dips, with a kiss of brown sugar and garlic. The potato salad was chunks of red-skinned potatoes, chopped celery, mayo, and mustard. The smoked baked beans were seasoned with onions, green pepper, and pieces of meat.

Overall, the sampler plate was a lot of food for a fair price and of high quality. I prefer more smokiness of meats and less sauce on pulled pork, but considering my personal dislike of heavily sauced meats, it's saying something that I actually liked this sauced pulled pork a lot. They also serve a charbroiled rib eye on a toasted hoagie bun, grilled burgers, and both ham and turkey smoked over wild cherry wood. When I return, I'll order the delectable spareribs and mutton and try to save some room for the banana pudding.

Out back, Barry showed me the two Backwoods Smokers—resembling industrial refrigerators—they use to cook ribs, Boston butts, hams, briskets, and John's award-winning smoked meatloaf (available as a catering item). The Backwoods Smokers hold a low temperature. "It'll take four and a half to five hours to cook twenty-seven slabs of ribs at 180–185," Barry explained. "We got a ten-gallon water pan we keep underneath the meat." They fuel the cookers with Kingsford charcoal and seasoned wild cherry. Mutton quarters are slow-cooked with hickory wood on a separate big barrel unit for twenty hours. No surprise that I favored the mutton over the other meats, as I, unlike John, prefer full smoke flavor. John can detect subtle changes in their sauce and doesn't like the strong flavors of intense wood smoke.

"If we run into a little bit of apple wood or peach wood, we'll use it," Barry said. "I don't know what it is about the fruit woods, but it allows the moisture to stay into the meats." Their friend David Alexander manages Cardinal Farms, a huge peach orchard in Henderson County that trims trees

---

J & B Barbecue's Basting Dip

1 gallon dark vinegar
2 gallons water
8 ounces salt
8 ounces black pepper
Pickling spice

Cover liquid mixture with a layer of mixed pickling spice and bring to a boil. Remove from heat and add one stick of butter. Good for basting open-pit chickens.

---

twice per year. J & B gets the wood trimmings in return for feeding the orchard crew. I love that tradition of swapping labor; it reminds me of how farmers harvested tobacco crops in years past. You help me and I'll help you. No money has to exchange hands.

The local underground coal mines are the staple of their catering business, Barry said. I watched two men cook some of the 650 rib eye steaks to be served to miners that afternoon. Barry said he was lucky to walk away from the mines, because after twenty-three years he'd already had one back surgery. "I was awful fortunate to have the job when I had it," Barry said. "Great benefits. I didn't realize I'd miss the benefits as much—it was a union mine—but I was just as thankful to walk away. I got a lot of friends my age and younger that are having trouble—knee replacements, shoulder surgeries. Lost quite a few to different types of cancers that I guess they picked up underground. I'm pretty fortunate to walk away from it and try something new. I can always go back."

I'd be real surprised if Barry ever works in mining again. They've got great help at the restaurant, fine food, and a loyal customer base. There's just a really good vibe at J & B. I understand why on their menu they include the motto "Where Friends Gather Round."

Open: Tuesday–Friday, 10:30 a.m.–6:00 p.m.; Saturday, 10:30 a.m.–1:00 p.m.

48 South Holloway Street; 270-830-0033

Slaughters

Good Ole Boys

Between Hanson and Slaughters on Highway 41, an old red caboose from the L & N railroad stands beside someone's house trailer. Good Ole Boys is a roadside shack just north of it. My friend Cristin and I arrived at noon on a Saturday and pulled into an empty gravel lot, but that changed soon after as dozens of locals came in for lunch. I saw lots of hamburgers and fries carried from the kitchen to seated customers.

Good Ole Boys epitomizes utilitarian dining: a big open room with wood-topped tables and pull-up chairs, old diner booths, and fluorescent lighting—very different from Hanson Market down the road, with its intentional cuteness. Good Ole Boys seems appropriately named—a place where local farmers and hunters gather to spin yarns. But I saw women and kids eating in, too.

We tried spareribs, shredded pork, sliced brisket, and mutton. Ham and smoked deli-style turkey breast are also on the menu, served as "trays" with bread, pickles, and onions, or as plates with two standard side dishes. The baked beans are the only homemade side. The pork, in the local style, comes heavily sauced. Pulled and chopped mutton come from whole sheep quarters. Spareribs cook for three hours and are then wrapped and put in the cooler to hold before serving. While I can't recommend the rubbery beef (from the brisket flat) or sauced pulled pork, I totally enjoyed the smokiness of the chopped mutton and the peppery dry rubbed ribs with their distinctive spices and well-smoked flavor. Cristin, a Simpson County gal, felt the same way. We both thought the mutton meat has a pungency that can shine through a sauce, but that the pork from Boston butts doesn't hold up to a heavy sauce. I'm sure locals feel differently or they wouldn't be serving pork this way.

I appreciated eating barbecue off a real glass plate—a rare find in barbecueland.

Owner Chuck Wells, a native of Hanson, has been running this country shack since 1991. He smokes on old-fashioned firebrick pits with split hickory and oak all day, then wraps the meats and lets the fire go out, for about fourteen to fifteen hours total smoking. The meats, sitting four to five feet above the flames, take on that distinctive real pit flavor. "I don't leave unless the fire is almost gone," Chuck said. "We wrap the meats and leave it in the firebrick and it stays warm for hours."

Way out in the country like it is, Good Ole Boys survives on local traffic —folks from Slaughters, Hanson, and sometimes people driving up from Madisonville. Chuck said he'll probably stick with it for another few years, but after twenty years he's about ready for something else.

I like the plain country style of Good Ole Boys—the gravel parking lot, the old dog who wandered up to me outside, the blackboard hanging on the wall with dessert names scribbled in chalk, the way customers talked to each other between tables like familiar friends—and I'd gladly return for the spicy ribs and mutton. Speaking of desserts, you might want to save some room for the homemade banana pudding and s'mores pie.

Open: Tuesday–Saturday, 6:00 a.m.–4:30 p.m.

9715 Hanson Road, Highway 41 (three miles north of Hanson); 270-322-8370

Hanson

Hanson Country Market

Drive into downtown Hanson (established 1873)—a strip of shops housed in old brick buildings near the train tracks—and you just might say, "Cuuuuuuute," as I did. There's an antique store, a bookstore, and an advertisement for Holsum Bread ("It's Batter Whipped") painted big as a billboard on the side of a building. Fans of quaint America come hither.

The Hanson Market is likewise cute, an old country-store atmosphere a block away from downtown that serves deli sandwiches, burgers, and barbecue. A sign near the road said:

CRAZY WEATHER

DON'T KNOW WHAT TO DO

TRY OUR BBQ

IT'S ALWAYS TRUE!

The barbecue offerings are pulled pork, ribs, half chickens, pork tenderloin, loaded baked potatoes topped with barbecue, and a barbecue burrito. I ate a pork sandwich, a slice of tenderloin, and a half chicken. Folks in Hopkins County seem to like their pork sauced. This sandwich will satisfy those who like saucy meats—shredded pork mixed with a tangy-sugary sauce, served with pickles and onions. I preferred the chicken, smoky and darkly colored from the caramelized sugars of the sauce.

While eating, you can feast your eyes on the knick-knacks hanging all around the walls. The whole market, outside and in, is built from pretty wood boards. A cathedral ceiling creates an open feel. Floors are red and white checked tile. Farming implements, like mule harnesses, tractor seats, and a rusty crosscut saw, decorate the walls. A great belt buckle collection is mounted in a frame; my traveling companion Cristin got a real kick out of that. One buckle, testifying to the importance of coal mining in this area, reads, "King Coal Knife Club, Madisonville, KY," and features a miner next to a pile of coal and an underground chute for hauling the ore out on train tracks. A mummified Harper's country ham hangs from a center post in the store under a sign stating, "I SPENT MOST OF MY MONEY ON BEER AND WOMEN—THE REST I JUST *WASTED!*"

Carlis Oakley, in business since 1999, cooks on a homemade natural gas unit made from a kerosene tank, using hickory and oak wood for smoke. Carlis likes using the bark of the wood. "You get a lot more smoke results out of the bark," he said.

The smoker is now enclosed in a building beside the restaurant. "We used to cook outside and that was a nightmare," Carlis said.

Carlis learned his sauce recipe from his mother, who used to work for two Hopkins County barbecue restaurants in the 1960s. Carlis said his spareribs are awesome, but he was out of them the Saturday morning we visited. The sauced pork from Boston butts is available every day. Tenderloins, ribs, and half chickens are cooked on Friday, and leftovers are served on Saturday—hence the shortage of ribs. He uses Swift pork from Hampton Meats in Hopkinsville.

Cristin said, "If you can make a day-old chicken taste that good, you're doin' somethin'." Amen to that.

I think my mama would like the homegrown cuteness of Hanson Market and the nostalgic feel of the old town. I can imagine weekend road trippers stopping by for a bite and then browsing in the bookshop or antique store down the road.

Open: Monday–Friday, 7:00 a.m.–5:00 p.m.; Saturday, 10:00 a.m.–4:00 p.m.

45 Veterans Drive; 270-322-8288

Madisonville

Brother's Bar-B-Que

Captain Kevin R. Cotton has two jobs involving fire. By day, he's a fire prevention officer at the Madisonville Fire Department. While off duty, he caters barbecue. His restaurant serves the public and does a whole lot of charity work, serving free meals to homeless folks in Madisonville and Nashville. I've noted elsewhere the connections between God and barbecue, having met several pit masters who also preach the gospel, and others who hold positions in a church. Brother's is located in a strip mall owned by the huge Covenant Community Church. Captain Cotton, a member of the church, spreads the spirit though his barbecue-focused charity work.

The inside of Brother's is about as slick as the outside, clean like a fast-food restaurant, with orange walls and modern ceiling fans and a well-lit ordering counter. Two Van Gogh prints decorate the walls, and the advertising —for instance, the photos on the ordering menu—has the airbrushed appearance of professional marketing. The advertising doesn't make me hungry for barbecue, because the photos look more like what I'd expect from a city deli.

"I think it's been proven that warm colors like red and orange increase the appetite, so painting a restaurant orange could possibly make people eat more. And that's pretty clever," Cristin Lanham said. She said the overall feeling of Brother's was "cute." I was glad Cristin could join me on this Saturday road trip. She's got opinions, and she ain't afeared of sharing them.

Cristin (a landscaper, Renaissance lady, and full-time mom) and I shared a combination plate with a half chicken, three big pork spareribs, smoked pork, baked beans, mac and cheese, and a roll. We also tried the brisket. Neither of us liked the mushy, sauced pulled pork from hams (instead of shoulders) cooked on a Southern Pride gas unit. The baked beans, Cristin said, "taste like Bush's baked beans from Southern Foods," and the macaroni was coated in a Velveeta-like cheese. Nothing distinctive about these side dishes. We did like the good ribs, however—full spareribs with the tips still on, tender with some smoke flavor and minimal doctoring (just ribs, salt, and smoke). The chicken, dusted with a tasty dry rub, was tender and mildly smoked. We also liked the thin-sliced, dry-rubbed brisket, which we rated as the best thing on the plate, proving yet again that chicken, ribs, and brisket are much more forgiving of gas cookers than are pork butts and shoulders. I also liked the sweet and tangy, black-peppery, tomato-based hot table sauce.

Talking about the bread, Cristin said, "Sister Schubert's, isn't it?"

I said, "I don't know what it is, but I do like the roll, which is better than most breads I've had at barbecue places."

"Sister Schubert's," she said with authority.

"What do you mean?"

"That's what it is—a Sister Schubert's roll. That's good. They're made in Horse Cave."

"That's my birthplace!" I said. "No wonder they're so good."

Later on, Cristin asked Ruth, the general manager, if they made the rolls, and Ruth said, "No, they're Sister Schubert's."

I said to Cristin, "You were right on, girl!"

"I get that from my daddy. I'm going to have to brag on myself when I get home."

The brisket is a new addition at Brother's, and I hope they keep it on the menu. If I return, that's what I'll get—a brisket sandwich, or a pile of brisket with one of those good rolls.

After we finished eating, we spoke with Captain Cotton, who pulled up in his catering van outside, just back from serving meals to some of the hungry people of Madisonville. He's also catered to bellies on the opposite side of the financial spectrum, driving his van all the way to the state capitol in Frankfort to feed state senators, representatives, and the governor's office. One of the senators, Jerry Rhoads (representing District 6 of Hopkins, Muhlenberg, and Ohio counties), pays for the catering. "Senator Rhoads wants to promote western Kentucky," Captain Cotton explained, "so that's how he does it."

Captain Cotton has also catered a wedding in Dallas, Texas. When I expressed surprise that someone living in Texas would order barbecue all the way from Kentucky, Kevin said, "They were here, they liked it, wanted it, called and asked if we would do it, so we did." People in Colorado also have him ship barbecue to them.

I asked, "What's the biggest item in demand?"

"Ribs. And this might shock you too, but Texas wants brisket."

I'm not surprised by these choices, since the ribs and brisket were my favorites at Brother's. But still—Texas? Listen up, Travel Channel and Food Network. Next time you do a show on "America's Best Barbecue," you know where to find us.

Open: Monday–Thursday, 10:00 a.m.–8:00 p.m.; Friday–Saturday, 10:00 a.m.–9:00 p.m.

1055 North Main Street; 270-821-1222

www.bbq.cc

Dave's Sticky Pig

Here it is, folks—my favorite place for barbecue in the Madisonville area. When I visited in January 2012, Dave Webb had only been open a few months. When I tried his great food, it was further confirmation that I'd done right by including places that have been in business for fewer than five years. Dave deserves your patronage. He serves creative homemade side dishes and some of the best dry-rubbed ribs I've ever eaten.

Sidekick Cristin Lanham and I arrived at Dave's Sticky Pig after a full day of barbecue tripping in the Madisonville area. We'd already tried Hanson Market, Good Ole Boys, and Brother's. First thing we noted when pulling into the parking lot was the real smoke and meat aroma enveloping the exterior of the restaurant, and out back we spied big chunks of barked hickory stacked up near some cool-looking cylindrical iron tank cookers with a firebox on the side. We entered the converted Baskin-Robbins with high hopes.

We weren't disappointed. I spoke with Dave, told him my business, and he made us a sampler with little tastes of many things on the menu. Here's the rundown. Cristin and I tried pork ribs, pulled pork, brisket, smoked ham, potato salad, mac and cheese, slaw, burgoo, banana pudding, and bread pudding. The pork (from whole shoulders cooked sixteen to eighteen hours on the smoker) was finely chopped and fluffy—and thankfully served without sauce (the other Madisonville-area barbecue places sauce pulled pork pretty heavily). It was a bit dry and not as smoky as I like, but it was still the best I had in the Madisonville-Hanson-Slaughters area. The brisket was thinly sliced with big ribbons of unrendered fat. While I like whole brisket (as opposed to the leaner flat), I wasn't so fond of this preparation, which made the fat far too visible. In my now-seasoned opinion, fat is great and palatable when it melts into the meat, but large hunks of it are a turn off, even for a fat lover like me. The leaner parts of the brisket were tasty, but I had to pick through lots of fat. The sliced ham was good, like much of the ham I've had in western Kentucky. Dave takes a fully cooked smoked ham and peels the skin off, applies dry-rub spices and wet mustard, and then smokes it. Sometimes they apply a maple syrup glaze near the end of the smoking.

And now to the excellent stuff! The St. Louis–style ribs. Ooooooh, the ribs. I've eaten some great dry-rubbed ribs in Memphis, the city that made them famous, and Dave Webb and company deliver something similar: fabulous, tender, dry-rubbed ribs that taste so good you don't need a sauce. Cristin and I both loved them. The side dishes are also excellent. The potato salad is creamy red-skinned potatoes mixed with diced green peppers and dill weed.

"That tater salad *is* right," Cristin said. (And yes, Dear Reader, she surely did say "tater." The word slides from my mouth, naturally enough, ever now and then as well.)

The mac and cheese was better than most because of the addition of chipped ham and lots of butter. I really liked the slaw, a crispy vinegar slaw with some sweetness and plenty of pepper. The burgoo was chunky, like a rich stew. The baked beans, Cristin said, "are about the best I've ever had." I liked them plenty as well. "They taste like smoked maple syrup," Cristin said. She then ordered a pint of beans to take home to her daddy.

About the banana pudding, Cristin, a savvy country girl, said, "I ain't had banana puddin' that good since church potluck. When church used to have potluck." Dave said it took him about two hours to make the banana pudding. We both liked the dense bread pudding, with some raisins in it, also. Only a bourbon sauce could make it better.

"We don't have gas anywhere in the restaurant," Dave said. "We use 80 percent hickory and about 20 percent oak. We try to get the bark off the wood, because bark will leave a bitter smoke taste." Dave found a stave mill that strips the bark from wood to make whiskey barrels, and he also saws large hickory trees into disks that, when split, become debarked.

"Cooking at home I've ruined a lot of meat by making it too bitter," Dave said. "Some people like a lot of strong smoke. It's very gender biased. Women do not approve of nearly as much smoke most of the time as men do."

Dave's son Ben, tending the smokers that day, said, "My wife won't eat much of anything we cook here. She says, 'I don't want to eat a camp fire.' A little bit of smoke is too much for her."

I said, "I'm a fan of smoke."

"Me too," Dave said, and Cristin agreed.

Dave retired from working fast food (Backyard Burgers) and fine dining (the #9 Steakhouse) for a whole three weeks. "I was bored to death. I was driving to Hopkinsville to the Woodshed for barbecue, and I thought, 'I can do better than that. I'm just going to find me a little place and open up.'"

I'm so glad he did.

Dave has traveled extensively and tried barbecue from all over the South, and he's concocted a sextet of sauces from different regions, including a Memphis Mild, a Carolina Pepper Sauce, a Texas Tomato, and an Auburn Orange, on the table for your sampling pleasure. My favorite by far was Dave's own Sticky Pig sauce, made with Sam Adams beer, labeled as "tart and spicy without being too hot or too sweet." I also liked Dave's Alabama White sauce (not on the table because its mayonnaise base requires refrigeration), a good accompaniment to chicken. Thanks to Big Bob Gibson's in Decatur for spreading that recipe around.

Dave's Sticky Pig's Sweet and Sour Slaw

Dave says, "I love to take motorcycle road trips. I started in Madison-ville and wanted to make it to Macon, Georgia, in two days but there were too many barbeque joints along the way. I'm usually not a fan of slaw on my pulled-pork sandwiches but I ate what the locals liked and discovered something similar to this slaw all along the way. They called it 'barbeque slaw' or 'hot slaw' and it tasted great on a sandwich. The original recipe came from a joint southeast of Atlanta, handwritten by a pit master with years of experience. I added some sugar and cut the spices a little to make it a little smoother when eaten without the meat. I don't usually put slaw on my sandwich but when I do, I love this version."

6½ ounces apple cider vinegar
5 teaspoons spicy brown mustard
3 tablespoons white sugar
6½ ounces brown sugar
1 tablespoon coarse black pepper
½ cup chopped celery
½ cup chopped onion
¼ cup diced green pepper
1-pound package slaw mix, either chopped or shredded.

Mix all ingredients except slaw mix together and refrigerate until well chilled. Add the slaw mix and stir well to blend. Serve with a slotted spoon to avoid getting too much vinegar.

I'm sorry Dave didn't have mutton when we visited, because he soaks it in a solution of cider vinegar, Worcestershire sauce, allspice, salt, 7UP, and lemon juice to rehydrate and tenderize it before smoking the front and back

Dave's Sticky Pig's Baked Beans

Dave Webb reports: "Baked beans are the most popular side dish in our restaurant because they're delicious! It's my recipe and I like simple recipes. We have cooked them in the oven in the past but cooking overnight on the smoker makes a big difference. I like baked beans but I can't deal with runny beans right out of a can. I don't want my beans to taste like barbeque sauce and I don't want them too sweet. We cook a lot of dried beans with a ham bone and smoked jowl at Dave's Sticky Pig, but this recipe works great with any canned baked bean or even pork and beans. There's enough flavor going into these beans to make any canned bean taste great."

1 cup onion, diced
½ cup green bell peppers, diced
6 cups beans
¼ cup prepared yellow mustard
¼ cup maple syrup
¼ cup light brown sugar
4 teaspoons granulated garlic
¼ cup of a sweet barbeque sauce
1 tablespoon lemon juice
2 cups smoked pork or beef brisket. Dice into ¼-inch pieces. Use bark from pork and briskets if available.

Preheat oven to 350º F. In a large casserole dish, mix onion, peppers, pork, beans, mustard, maple syrup, brown sugar, barbeque sauce, lemon juice, and garlic. Bake, covered, for 50 minutes. Stir and bake uncovered for 20 more minutes.

A preferred method is this: Place on smoker uncovered and cook about 12 hours at around 225º. We've experimented with liquid smoke but it isn't the same. These beans will come off the smoker with a crust of intense smoke flavor on top. Stir well and let it rest at least an hour, then stir again before serving.

quarters. Dave says the long marinating in the acidic liquid breaks down muscle stringiness. Young sheep you marinate three days; sheep over sixty pounds you marinate four days. After smoking mutton quarters for sixteen hours, Dave removes most of the fat and mixes all of the lean together for his pulled mutton.

I said, "Not much profit in mutton, is there?"

Dave's Sticky Pig's Banana Pudding

"My grandmother made great banana pudding from scratch. As she got older, she didn't cook very often but we still expected Granny's banana pudding on Sundays and holidays. She'd try to slip in the boxed pudding from time to time because custard is a little labor intensive for a senior citizen, but my older brother could always tell the difference. This isn't my grandmother's recipe. Like most older cooks, she never measured anything. This is the best my memory could do to match the taste of her custard. The cinnamon and nutmeg addition came from a customer's suggestion based on her grandmother's recipe. I saw her crying as she was leaving the restaurant after having our banana pudding and followed her out to see what was wrong. She said her grandmother had passed on a few years ago and she never expected to have pudding as good as her grandmother's pudding and ours brought back sweet memories of her grandmother."

2½ cups sugar
2½ cups whole milk
½ cup sifted cornstarch
4 eggs
1 ounce sifted flour
⅛ teaspoon cinnamon
¼ teaspoon nutmeg
1 ounce butter
1 ounce real vanilla extract
5 medium bananas, sliced
1 tablespoon lemon juice
1 (13.3-ounce bag) vanilla wafers

Use fully ripe bananas and refrigerate them before slicing to help them hold their shape. Slice the bananas into ¼-inch slices and toss with the

Dave said the cost of mutton is almost triple the cost of pork. He noted that while pork and beef are marbled, mutton is more likely to have big chunks of fat in it.

As we left, Cristin summed it up like this: "I'd take a special trip here to get ribs, baked beans, slaw, and tater salad. And that nanner puddin'." I agree with her 100 percent, and I'm betting that Dave's mutton is fabulous, too.

---

lemon juice to coat them completely. Refrigerate. Drain lemon juice before using bananas in pudding.

Make a double boiler, fitting a smaller saucepan snugly inside a large one. Place water in the large saucepan and set stove to medium-high heat. You will have to add water to the larger saucepan a few times during the cooking process.

In a saucepan, combine milk with sugar and cornstarch. Stir occasionally until sugar is fully dissolved and the custard seems to thicken slightly, about 20 minutes.

Measure the flour, cinnamon, and nutmeg into a sifter. Sifting these three items together before adding them to the milk helps mix them.

Using a whisk, lightly beat eggs in a mixing bowl. Temper the eggs with about a cup of the hot custard by stirring them briskly with the whisk while slowly pouring the custard into them. The outside of the mixing bowl should be warm to the touch before you add the contents to the saucepan of custard. Add the eggs, then add sifted cinnamon, nutmeg, and flour to custard pot and cook about 30 to 45 more minutes in the double boiler, stirring occasionally. The custard will really thicken up as it cooks. When it seems as thick as it's going to get, remove from heat and add vanilla and butter.

Pour a layer of pudding mixture in the bottom of a casserole dish large enough to hold the wet ingredients, and add a layer of whole vanilla wafers followed by a layer of half the bananas. Repeat as many times as necessary to use all the ingredients. Top with crumbled vanilla wafers.

Dave's Sticky Pig's Signature Sauce

Dave's confession: "My friend Roger and I used to stay up all night on summer holiday weekends, drinking, smoking meat, and experimenting with barbeque sauces and techniques. We made thin sauces, thick sauces, hot sauces, and sweet sauces. We used beer, whiskey, tequila, jelly, juice, applesauce, peanut butter—and pretty much anything we had around that we couldn't put on the smoker and didn't want to drink. It took a few years for us to decide that excessive alcohol ruins the chef, the meat, and the barbeque sauce, and we had a lot of misadventures together while feeding our friends and family. This is the sauce I settled on as my personal favorite, not too sweet or hot but spicy enough to complement the meat. Everyone seems to look for something different in a barbeque sauce, but this one was universally liked. I think it goes best with pulled pork."

8 cups tomato sauce
4 cups red wine vinegar
1 ounce Louisiana-style hot sauce, not Tabasco or anything super hot
4 teaspoons olive oil
1 tablespoon granulated garlic
1 tablespoon allspice
1 tablespoon onion powder
1 tablespoon coarse ground black pepper
1 tablespoon kosher salt
5⅓ cups sugar
1 bottle Sam Adams Boston lager
1½ teaspoons cornstarch

Mix the cornstarch in a splash of water to dissolve it. Place all the ingredients in a large stockpot and bring to a boil, stirring frequently. Reduce the heat and simmer, uncovered, for an hour or until sauce thickens. Do not start timing the hour until sauce has come to a full boil and you've turned the heat down! Keep stirring during the simmer step to prevent sticking and blend the flavors. Remove from the heat, cover, and allow to cool slowly to room temperature. Refrigerate after cooling.

Open: Monday, 11:00 a.m.–3:00 p.m.; Tuesday–Saturday, 11:00 a.m.–8:00 p.m.; Sunday, 11:00 a.m.–3:00 p.m.
206 Madison Square Drive; 270-326-5100

Owensboro

International Bar-B-Q Festival

Since 1979, on the second weekend in May, the streets of this river town look like an optimistic vision of hell on the Friday night of the barbecue fest, when cooking teams, most of them from regional churches, fire up their pits in the blocked-off streets, burning down hickory and sassafras to coals before loading wire grates with thousands of pounds of mutton, chickens, and pork. I say "optimistic" because you won't hear anguished cries erupting from tortured people, but rather good-natured talking and the popping of aluminum can tabs as the teams settle in for a long night of tending the meats that they'll serve to the populace the next afternoon. The City of Owensboro brings in sand for the teams to use as a pit base to protect the asphalt. Teams construct pre-made panels of steel poles and steel sheets (like the kind you'd put on a barn roof) to hold the heat in the pits, and they pile the sand eight inches high the entire length of the pits, which stretch up and down the streets. They fire up the wood on top of the sand, and when it burns down to coals load on the meat. I saw men flipping twenty dozen half chickens at a time, with one man on each side of the pits grabbing hold of a metal frame made from rebar and mesh fencing and, with a top and bottom frame, flipping the whole thing over to keep the cooking even. And there's lots of basting of meats with long-handled mops dipped into special sops, often a blend of water, Worcestershire sauce, vinegar, lemon juice, black pepper, brown sugar, and spices.

I get excited about the Owensboro festival every May. Just shutting down the streets of a town is reason enough to smile—blocking off traffic, allowing people to walk freely without fear of being run down by a car. The streets are lined with booth after booth of food vendors and barbecue teams. You can buy snacks from the vendors, but the main reason for coming, besides the pleasure of walking among the wonderful aroma of smoking meats, is to purchase the goods at the end of the long day of cooking. About 4:00

or so on Saturday afternoon, people start forming lines beside the setups of their favorite barbecue teams, and the early lucky ones—anyone who gets there before the food runs out—can purchase gallons of burgoo and pounds of mutton, smoked chickens, and pork. Folks take them home for eating and freezing for later eating. The monies paid go to support charities.

I've taken home a whole smoked mutton shoulder from the barbecue festival and left it in my freezer for a special occasion, and also a gallon of burgoo, that Kentucky version of the Brunswick stew—a concoction with lots of meats and vegetables cooked down for many hours to a rich, steaming, creamy brew, complex and tangy, with layered flavors. And I've hung out with the teams and watched them practicing their craft.

I spoke with Jerry Morris of Whitesville, the team chief of St. Mary's of the Woods cooking team. Coincidentally, the owner of Tony's Bar-B-Que Barn near Lawrenceburg is from Whitesville—a good chance he knows Mr. Morris, although I forgot to ask. Tony had told me he'd learned the barbecue trade by osmosis from growing up in Whitesville, where they barbecue "all the time." Meeting Jerry confirmed that.

Some teams decrease their pit-tending duties by boiling meats to tenderize them—which really is cheating, in my opinion—but St. Mary's of the Woods (my favorite team name, appealing to my inner tree hugger) doesn't boil. They put whole sheep on the pits at midnight and cook until done the next afternoon. They flip the meat every thirty minutes. Talk about labor intensive. When done, they take a meat saw to cut the mutton into half-inch slices and sell it by weight. St. Mary's of the Woods was grand champion in 2005. Every team appoints a judge who tastes and rates barbecue from all the teams in a blind judging process.

Many teams smoke with both hickory and sassafras. Owensboro is home to the world's largest sassafras tree—a three-hundred-year-old wonder. I love sassafras. I have several trees in my fencerows at home and often cut off a green branch to add to the smoker when cooking whole chickens and Boston butts. The spicy wood gives off a distinctive pungent smoke.

I asked Jerry if the big ice storm of 2009 gave them lots of sassafras, and he said, "No, I'd rather have it green, so I'd rather go out and cut it just before I get ready to use it." He pointed to his pit and said, "This pit here has being going since 8:30 yesterday morning. I put hickory logs that big around and they done burnt up on me. It's been burning for twenty-six hours." The caretakers of the pits keep vigilant watch through the many hours of cooking, standing by with water hoses ready to tame the flames that flare up when rendered fat drips down onto the coals.

In 2009, Jerry had been cooking at this festival for seventeen years. I asked him if all the cooking teams were Catholic, and he said, "No, sir. There's Crooked Creek and maybe one more that ain't Catholic, but they're good ole boys."

St. Mary's of the Woods cooked eleven hundred pounds of pork, one thousand pounds of mutton, three hundred chickens, and one kettle of burgoo; it was a two-day job. He said they'd gross about $11,000 for their charity, Trinity High School, to help students with tuition.

I also talked with Bob Newman from northern Kentucky, who'd moved to Owensboro and had been cooking with Blessed Mother Catholic Church's team for twenty-eight years. They actually mix some pork into their chopped mutton sandwich. These fellows have been cooking together since 1982, raising money for the church. He said sometimes a new guy or two would come on board, but mostly it was the same guys cooking year after year. I asked how different cooking styles were among teams, and Bob said a lot different, especially for the secretive dip recipes. Everyone has a job. One guy is in charge of chicken, another takes care of mutton, another burgoo, and they get their own crews together to prepare the food. They smoke with hickory and sassafras, the standard among the teams. The Blessed Mother team cooked four hundred chickens, twelve hundred pounds of mutton, five hundred pounds of Boston butts, and five hundred gallons of burgoo, and once the selling starts on Saturday afternoon "it will be gone in thirty minutes," Bob said. They were grand champion at the festival in 2008. The Blessed Mother church picnic is held in early August at 601 East Twenty-third Street in Owensboro.

Around the block, I spoke with Bill Glenn, who stirred a seventy-five-gallon vat of burgoo for Our Lady of Lourdes's cooking team. Bill is a Kansas City Barbecue Society master judge, a title that involves taking a course to become a judge, judging at thirty-five events, after which you have to get a score of at least 80 percent on a test. Bill scored 92 percent; his wife, who also judges, beat him with a score of 95 percent. Following their love of barbecue, they have judged at as many as thirteen contests in a year. Smoke from the wood-fired burgoo vats enveloped us as we talked, and my eyes watered, and Bill said, "You want to step back a bit? I'm used to the smoke by now." Lourdes has been cooking at the contest since it started about forty years ago. He said many teams mop mutton with a vinegar or lemon dip, enhancing mutton's earthy flavors.

Bill gave me a brief history of mutton cooking, which he said you only found around Owensboro and areas nearby. Back in the 1800s sheep were plentiful in the area, and hence the cheapest meat. Now their mutton comes from a packing plant in Indiana, and the animals are pastured in other states, so now mutton is the most expensive meat they buy. Mutton also has a lot of shrinkage. He said you put ten pounds of mutton on the pit and you'd probably get four pounds of cooked meat and bone after the fat cooks off; on the other hand, ten pounds of pork will yield about eight pounds of cooked meat. So if you have to pay more for mutton, that's a good part of the reason.

The Lourdes team cooks three to four times per year. Bill said there's a church picnic about every weekend from late May until September. He invited me to join them at any time to help with the cooking.

Dee's BBQ and Diner

Dee's Diner is proof that our Yankee cousins can cook barbecue. Dorothy "Dee" Harper and her brother Chuck Lemetti hail from southside Chicago near Comiskey Park, White Sox territory—a fact they don't try to hide, with their offerings of Chicago beef sandwiches. You also know as soon as you strike up a conversation with Dee, Chuck, or Denise (who's married to Chuck) that these folks lived for a long time in the upper Midwest. Their voices pack that Chicago punch I became familiar with when living up near there in the early years of the 2000s. They all moved down because Dee's husband was from Owensboro. "We moved here five years ago," Denise said. "It's laid back, kicked back, relaxed. I love it here."

Dee's occupies the building that was George's Bar-B-Q, an Owensboro establishment since 1955, and still serves barbecue using those recipes and the old pits. The original sign still stands out front. The atmosphere is old-school diner, with well-used cushioned booths, plastic tables, brown paneling harkening back to the 1970s, and a cathedral ceiling painted a shade of deep pink. The floor is brown tile. Low-volume country music filled the dining room. Fans dangle from the ceilings, and there's a salad bar. A sign on the wall advertises a fried Twinkie for $1.50.

Dee and Chuck took over the restaurant on March 10, 2010. I'd passed through Owensboro in August of that year and, because I had two dogs in the back of my Ranger, pulled up to the drive-through. I got a pound of mutton off the pits. Mike, the pit master who worked for George's for many years and now works for Dee's, saw the dogs and gave me two big mutton bones with meat clinging to them. I drove on up the highway, savoring slices of tender mutton, while the dogs tore into the bones in the bed of the truck. That was my first taste of Dee's after it changed hands from George's.

Dee's is famous for breakfasts, and Dee's motto is "If you leave hungry, it's your fault." They offer, for instance, a twelve-egg omelet that hardly fits on a plate. Denise told me, "The next time you're around here and you don't want barbecue, I suggest the Italian beef, da works. It's amazing. We even have a combo with the Italian sausage in it. My husband is Italian, so . . ." I asked Denise if she was a hunter, because she was sporting a hunting jacket in woodsy camo, and she said, "No, I just like it."

I said, "It gives you some kind of southern legitimacy, doesn't it? Until you open your mouth!"

And Denise laughed with me and said, "Yeah, right? And they're like, 'I like your accent,' and I look at southern people like, 'You're the one with the accent, you know?'" Denise's twelve-year-old granddaughter has picked up Kentucky talk quickly.

I like how Dee's extensive menu allows you to choose mutton parts from the whole sheep: chopped mutton, hindquarter, loin, shoulder, or ribs. Chopped pork, sliced pork, pork ribs, half chicken, whole chicken, sliced beef, and burgoo. To balance the meats, they have a diabetic or heart-healthy menu.

I cast aside the heart-healthy menu and chose fatty mutton ribs and a pulled mutton sandwich from the pit, with a side of fried okra. They came with George's traditional dip and also Dee Harper's own barbecue sauce creation. "Here a lot of people prefer that dip," Dee said, "but the younger generation prefers a barbecue sauce. So I just serve both."

Dee does all the cooking and recipes. She wants to segue into baby back ribs, prime rib, and smoked pot roasts eventually while retaining the traditional barbecue offerings. She said the first year of Dee's Diner she worked sixteen hours every day because she didn't want to relinquish food control to anyone else. "I sign it like an artist," she said. "Every plate that goes out has got my signature on it."

The mutton ribs were luscious, pure unadulterated musky flavor and plenty of melt-in-your-mouth fat to go along with the leaner parts. Beware: these ribs aren't for the fat-phobic. The crispy outsides delivered a good crunch and merged with the buttery-soft fat. The okra was perfectly fried, and the thin peppery dip was so good that my chum Todd said, "I could just drink it." Dee's special barbecue sauce—the one she made to satisfy those who don't like the traditional regional dip—has, I think, essences of fruit. The pulled mutton was a bit dry but had a good flavor, and the dip—which is different than any dip I've tried—added tasty moisture. A list of side dishes was scribbled on a white board on the wall, along with the daily specials. The Tuesday I visited, you could get—in addition to barbecue—a plate lunch of country-fried steak, meatloaf, or sausage and kraut with three sides and bread for $4.99 plus tax. Sides included mashed potatoes, peas, pinto beans, baked apples, okra, mixed greens, mac and cheese, and broccoli-rice casserole.

Dee keeps the mutton on the menu because people want it, even though she admitted that she's lucky if she breaks even on it. After losing the bones, fat, legs, and other nonmeaty parts of the whole sheep she buys, she ends up with only 30 percent servable mutton. Dee said mutton would be profitable only if you sold a lot of it, had a high turnover. At the end of the day, Dee takes the mutton she hasn't sold, bones it out, and grinds it into meat for her chopped mutton and burgoo. She also uses pork and beef brisket in her burgoo recipe.

"Burgoo sells," she said, especially in the summer months. Dee's burgoo is chunky and not as greasy as some I've tried. She tries keeping extra fat out of her chopped mutton and burgoo. "I like the taste of fat," she said, "but I don't want to eat it. I want to eat the meat next to the fat but not the fat itself. Maybe that's why I'm losing more [mutton weight] than everyone else, but I just won't do it."

I enjoyed Dee's business acumen and passion for food and compassion for her customers. Talking about the delicious mutton ribs—one of the most expensive menu items—Dee said, "Things are slow. People don't have that kind of money [to afford mutton ribs]. You can tell by their breakfasts, what they order versus what they normally order. It's going to take the economy a long time to bounce back. People are having to adjust. People are still going to enjoy themselves, going out to dinner, but they're not going to treat their whole family to mutton ribs, you know?"

I'm glad these Chicagoans have adopted Kentucky. They're offering good home-cooked food at very reasonable prices and keeping the mutton tradition going along with their uncommon (to the area) Chicago sandwiches and whopper breakfasts. They smoke with hickory and sassafras on the old pits. When Chuck showed me the pits, we walked though the kitchen, where a young man was peeling potatoes for the breakfast home fries. You got to respect the use of real potatoes. I'll get back there eventually for one of those Chicago beef sandwiches recommended by Denise, and when hungry for barbecue and feeling flush, I'll go for those great mutton ribs, the superb dip, and the burgoo.

Open: Monday–Wednesday, 5:00 a.m.–3:00 p.m.; Thursday–Saturday, 5:00 a.m.–8:00 p.m.; Sunday, 5:00 a.m.–3:00 p.m

1362 East Fourth Street; 270-686-0022

Moonlite Bar-B-Q Inn

Moonlite, one of the gutbustingest restaurants around, hardly needs an introduction. When I've wanted to pig out over the years—I mean really gorge myself on a ridiculous amount of food—this is where I've pilgrimaged. The most famous barbecue restaurant in Kentucky—certainly getting more press than all the others, having been written up in *Gourmet, Southern Living,* and *USA Today* (to name a few)—Moonlite has been serving up hickory-cooked meats since the 1950s. In 1963, Pappy and Catherine Bosley, a husband-wife team who'd been working for local distilleries, took over the restaurant, and Moonlite remains a Bosley family business, now employing over 120 people working in various departments. The restaurant seats 350 people, and they have a U.S.D.A.-inspected processing plant (the nine thousand pounds of mutton cooked up at the Fancy Farm picnic in 2011 came from Moonlite's plant). They have a catering department and a wholesale division for placing their barbecue and sauces in stores in a four-state region. Recently, when

149

in Leitchfield, Kentucky, looking for Bland's One Stop Barbecue (and not finding it), I stopped at a convenience store with a BBQ sign out front. The young woman at the counter told me they had Moonlite barbecue. So the long fingers of Moonlite's empire extended to this tiny berg over one hour's drive southeast. Impressive product placement. Sure, it's big and famous, but Moonlite is still a quality local establishment. It would be a mistake to lump it in with Famous Dave's and Smokey Bones.

Mutton—an adult sheep at least one year old, either a female or castrated male—is Owensboro's claim to barbecue fame. You just can't find barbecued mutton much outside this region, and Owensboro cooks up more mutton than any other city. Moonlite alone sells about ten thousand pounds of it weekly. Old sheep equals tough meat until you slow cook the stuff over hickory for a long time, tenderizing those muscles and rendering the fat. The cooks at Moonlite pour a thin vinegar-based dip on the meat several times during the long cooking to keep it from drying out. The beef brisket is sliced thickly and has a good bark on it. You can get "chopped" mutton, which is like a finely pulverized, rich and tangy meat paste, but I much prefer to taste the pure meat and fat of the pulled mutton. Thankfully, all the meats are served without sauce (except for the sauce-simmered chopped mutton). Moonlite's distinctive orange-colored regular sauce (I often spy it on grocery store shelves in Kentucky) is available in squirt bottles at the table.

The well-stocked buffet is the reason I went to Moonlite as a college student, and a few years back, when attending the barbecue festival in May, I ate there again with friends, including Keita Shinoda, a native of Chiba, Japan, who works in Kentucky and has a penchant for eating and blogging about eating. Keita loved Moonlite. I imagine I know why: Moonlite is like the wide-open frontier of America—just about everything about it is big, quite the opposite from Japanese restaurants with their small portions and immaculate presentation. At the Moonlite buffet, especially at dinner when they go all out, you'll see piles of mutton, pork, ribs, beef, and chicken, plus all kinds of southern side dishes like green beans, mac and cheese, broccoli casserole (very cheesy), beans and ham, mashed potatoes, and burgoo. They also have abundant sweetening, including pies (lemon icebox, peanut butter, pecan, coconut) and carrot cake. Keita's a man of modest dimensions, probably weighs 130 pounds wet, and I saw him polish off three plates of food during our hour of gorging. Oh, Moonlite also serves country ham on the buffet. Moonlite cooks their meats for up to twelve hours, and everything is good.

The buffet isn't the only thing going at Moonlite—you can also get sandwiches and plates, eat in or carry out, including a sampler plate of beef, mutton, and pork. But honestly, with the minimal price difference, you might as well experience the wide-open frontier of the buffet and try a bit of everything, loosen your belt, and let out a long sigh. You've reached the Land of Plenty.

Open: Monday–Thursday, 9:00 a.m.–9:00 p.m.; Friday–Saturday, 9:00 a.m.–9:30 p.m.; Sunday, 10:00 a.m.–3:00 p.m.

2840 West Parrish Avenue; 270-684-8143

www.moonlite.com

Old Hickory Bar-B-Q ("Five Generations of Quality Bar-B-Q")

I've stopped by Old Hickory many times over the years when traveling from south-central Kentucky to points north. Owensboro, like Henderson and Louisville, is one of those river towns you need to pass through if you want to cross into Hoosierland, where I lived for a while.

I'd heard of Old Hickory since the early 1990s, when I made road trips from Bowling Green to Owensboro to stuff myself—along with a carload of other young male college students—at Moonlite Bar-B-Q Inn's unlimited buffet (hard to resist for people on a tight budget). At the time, I could eat and eat without swelling in the midsection permanently, and Moonlite was *the* place to load up. Still is. But even while we gorged upon piles of meats at Moonlite, one big voice from a big man, Tommy Smith, told us we could get better barbecue nearby at Old Hickory. We told him to shut up and kept eating.

Now, as white hairs sprout from my cheekbones, Old Hickory is my go-to place when in Owensboro. I've gotten takeout from there more times than I can recall, and I've eaten in a couple of times. If you like mutton—and I *love* mutton, if cooked right—you'll be hard pressed to find any better than what Old Hickory serves.

This place has a family atmosphere, with country music playing, a hearth and fireplace in the dining room, and old black-and-white photos on the wall of people and town scenes. They proudly display their long history of fine barbecue in Owensboro, with family roots going back to 1918, when Charles "Pappy" Foreman started cooking mutton. In 1954 the family named the business Old Hickory.

I get mutton "off the pit." It costs a bit extra, but it's worth the pocket change to savor the texture and flavors of slow-smoked sheep—akin to the texture of prime rib, with a gamy, musky flavor. Chopped mutton is finely ground and heavily sauced, and while it tastes good, the pure essence of mutton is masked by the sauce. Order some mutton off the pit. If you don't like it, then you don't like mutton, because *this* is the way you can really taste the full-on flavor of the meat. It's an acquired taste for many.

Other than mutton, I've eaten the pork ribs at Old Hickory, and they are also some of the best I've ever had. During summer 2011, I stopped in with my friend Greg Brown, a native of Oklahoma. We arrived at 10:30 a.m. on a Wednesday, and the meats greeted us behind a glass case as we entered. Slabs of mahogany-colored pork ribs glistened under a lamp. Beautiful. I ordered one pound of mutton, sliced, and a woman took a whole fresh mutton shoulder and sliced it with a huge band saw, layering the pieces on an aluminum tray. I asked for it sauced, so she drizzled a thin brown mutton dip over the top of the steaming hot meat. We also got spareribs, which got the saw treatment like the mutton. The woman asked if we wanted them in half for easy road eating. I said, "Sure, why not?" And she did with that saw what's impossible to do with a knife or cleaver—slice across the bone to give us smaller portions of the thick meaty spareribs. The first bite from a meaty rib tip was a little dry, but then I bit into a piece with fat and it was juicy and full of smoky peppery flavor. The spicy sauce added a mild vinegar tang.

The mutton was sliced a quarter inch thick. Greg, a mutton virgin until this day, said it was spongy—a texture softer than pork or beef—and rich with ribbons of fat that melted quickly in the mouth. Greg's a picky eater. He'd just spent a weekend at my home, and I put him through the trials of Sichuan-style hot pot, sushi rolls, and cornbread salad. He's a meat-and-taters kind of guy—and not strange meat, either. Greg said that he'd eaten lamb before and didn't like it, but he did like the mutton. Despite the gaminess, the effect was delicate, he said. That mutton was tender and savory without smacking you with gamy funk (which I tend to like, being a fan of stinky bleu cheeses like Stilton, anchovies, and other funky flavors).

At other times at Old Hickory, I've had a mutton sandwich off the pit, which contains the same tender thick slices of meat, rich with a modest smokiness, with just a taste of sauce, heaped on a regular untoasted (and superfluous) bun. The mutton was less smoky than what I've eaten at Catholic church fund-raisers in the region, but it was still delicious. The sauce appears to be Worcestershire based and not as vinegary as other mutton sauces I've sampled.

My most recent trip to Old Hickory was in May 2012 when I was in town for the International Bar-B-Q Festival. I'd never interviewed anyone there, and knowing they'd be slammed that day I called ahead and scheduled a meeting with a young manager, Keith Cook, who gave me a tour of the kitchen area and detached main pit room. Inside the huge kitchen and prep area they cook chickens and ribs on a gas-fed Ole Hickory rotisserie cooker with an end firebox that burns hickory wood. Chickens cook at 275° for three and a half to four hours. Keith then took me outside and over to another building that houses two huge pits made from firebrick and steel (with sliding steel doors for accessing the meats). On these twenty-year-old pits, fired by hickory logs, the pit masters tend many pounds of mutton, Boston butts, beef briskets, boneless city hams, and boneless turkey breasts. A large band saw located near the pits is used to cut the whole sheep into manageable parts when they get a shipment. They load the pits with raw meat one morning and take it off the next morning. "We're cooking fourteen sheep and forty-eight butts today," Keith told me.

Pit master Gary Sandefur said he sops the meat every two hours with a dip of salt, pepper, vinegar, Worcestershire, and allspice. He has to rotate the meats, bringing the back to the front and moving the front to the back of the pits, to "get an even cook on everything." Gary fishes the meats from the back of the deep pits with long pitchforks. He said, "I tell you what—after you do so many of 'em, they start getting a little heavy. Some of 'em are pretty good-sized sheep coming in here." A big sheep might have a thirty-pound hindquarter. Gary looks strong as an ox, well muscled from all that lifting of heavy meats. He confirmed that his ancestry was Scots-Irish, and I joked that he'd fit in well at the strength competitions at Highland Games, like those held in Glasgow, Kentucky, every June.

I said, "The boneless ham thing is something I've only seen in western Kentucky. Any idea where that came from, this tradition of smoking up city hams?"

Keith said, "Anything smoked, everybody'll eat it. They want that barbecue ham. It's got that smoke flavor to it; it's better than sandwich meat you buy at a deli because it's got so much extra flavor. It's not full of water. Just add that flavor to it, that smoke."

Old Hickory offers custom cooking. Near the takeout counter, a menu hangs on the wall listing prices for various cuts of meat. Customers supply the meat, of course. If you want Old Hickory to smoke a ham, deer, or turkey weighing less than sixteen pounds, you'll pay $10. Over sixteen pounds costs $12. Whole chickens cost $2.50 each.

Gary said he's smoked a bit of everything. "I've done groundhog, coon, ducks, geese, goats, and possum."

"Did you try any of it?" I asked.

"I try everything that comes off these pits. That's why I got my carving knife over there."

I said, "Groundhog's really lean meat. I cooked one up when I was a kid. Of course I didn't know what I was doing so it chewed like rubber. How does a groundhog taste after you cook it low and slow?"

"Not as bad as I thought it would," Gary said. "I thought it'd be a little greasy, but actually it was really good. They eat a lot of tips of soybeans, so they're more or less like a grain-fed cow, or elk out in the West that are hay fed."

At Old Hickory, mutton necks, pork butts, and chicken are used to make burgoo. Gary said, "You know most of the people in eastern Kentucky, when they take up burgoo, their burgoo is a lot of squirrels, rabbits, and stuff like that."

Gary told me, "These pits are fired up every morning. There's no gas, no torches, no lighter fluid." He held up a piece of newspaper, rolled it up, and said, "That's our kindling right here."

After Old Hickory had a fire recently, they contemplated eliminating the old-fashioned masonry pits because of pressure from the insurance company. "In Indiana you can't cook over an open flame," Keith said. "In Kentucky you can. But insurance won't let us have the pit room attached to the main building. That's why we built this outside pit room. In order to keep the flavor and keep the name with the flavor, we built it separate instead of switching to rotisserie pits and gas." That sounds good and honest to me.

Keith said they use two kinds of dips: a vinegar-based cooking dip used to baste meats on the pits and a tomato paste–based finishing dip, which tastes, I think, similar to a thinned-down A-1 steak sauce. The sauce does contain vinegar and Worcestershire sauce.

After speaking with Keith and Gary, I sat down with friends and dug into a combination plate—customer's choice of any three meats plus two sides. Old Hickory recently switched from untrimmed spareribs to a St. Louis cut, and those ribs were wonderful, tender and smoky. The sliced mutton off the pit was the ultimate in mutton perfection. The brisket—oh, Lord—was tender slices of beef with a deep smoke ring. All meats were drizzled with the brown finishing sauce. I loved the bowl of complexly flavored savory burgoo. The baked beans carried the tangy flavor of barbecue sauce. The only thing that wasn't magnificent was the mac and cheese, which tasted like home-cooked elbow macaroni mixed with a mild cheese sauce.

I finished the meal with a bowl of decadent banana pudding. My friend George W. (Bill) Little Jr. also got the banana pudding, so I'll quote his assessment. George said it was "outrageous."

"What do you mean?"

"Couldn't be better," he said. George is over seventy years young. I'll bet he's eaten plenty of banana puddings during his life, so I'd call this high praise.

I agree. There was probably a half pound of pudding piled up in that bowl, with vanilla wafers on top—some of them crumbled, some of them whole—with whipped cream on top. Rich, creamy, crunchy.

Well done, Old Hickory, across the board. You deliver some of the best barbecue anywhere for people who relish the taste of meat and smoke.

Open: Monday–Thursday, 9:00 a.m.–9:00 p.m.; Friday–Saturday, 9:00 a.m.–10:00 p.m.

338 Washington Avenue; 270-926-9000

Ole South Barbecue

Collectable saucers with scenes from *Gone with the Wind* printed on them adorn the walls of Ole South, and in the corner—standing on high shelves—are dolls resembling the Butler family (Rhett, Scarlett, daughter) and the hoopskirted Melanie Wilkes with her husband, Ashley, in military uniform. Big lifelike paintings hang on the walls displaying Confederate soldiers in a nostalgic light: men in gray on horseback riding through a snowy landscape above the caption "Onward Christian Soldiers, Fredericksburg, Virginia"; General Robert E. Lee well dressed and noble upon his white horse; and then there's Vivien Leigh—our favorite Englishwoman southern belle—sitting on the velvet-red steps of her mansion. The Ole South logo models the intermission and closing scene of *Gone with the Wind*—a lone mature tree in the foreground, a plantation home in the background—conjuring up loyalty to terra (or Tara) and the "good old days" of Dixieland past. There's even a display of Golden Flake potato chips ("The South's Original Potato Chip since 1923"). The whole effect of the decor is kitschy and amusing—and yes, potentially insulting to the politically correct.

Jason Shuler, the new owner of Ole South, told me the name of the restaurant came with the purchase—indeed, that the original owner put it into the purchase contract that the restaurant has to keep the name "Ole South" for years before it can be changed. The original owner, Tommy Osborne, catered to Confederate reunions and really played up his fondness for Civil War history and southern mythology. Jason just seems to take it in stride as part of the restaurant package he bought into.

Located on the southeast side of Owensboro since the 1990s, Ole South is a full-service restaurant with a large open dining room. I can imagine that years ago this place was "out in the country," as new businesses—a strip-mall atmosphere—have grown up all around it. The exterior resembles a brick ranch-style home—the building was once a food pantry—and the interior, with the big salad bar and buffet, is designed for family dining. The extensive menu includes sandwiches like sliced or chopped mutton and pork, a turkey club, chicken, and barbecue ham. They also smoke whole (untrimmed) pork spareribs and half and quarter chickens. The chopped mutton—which looks pretty much like meat paste—is leftovers from the mutton pulling, pressed through a sausage grinder and sauced. I wasn't prepared to like it, but I did, especially when I tried it with bread and raw onions. The texture takes some getting used to, but the chopped mutton packs a wallop of flavor. You can get a combo plate with three meats for variety.

The sliced mutton wasn't ready for serving when I visited at 2:00 p.m.—it was on the masonry pits, smoking with indirect heat for the dinner crowd—so I ordered instead the sliced ham, sliced pork (from Boston butts) drizzled in dip sauce, smoked chicken, potato salad, and barbecue beans. And yes, the chopped mutton.

The hostess with the mostest Tammy—wearing a green elfin hat to celebrate the Christmas season—brought us fresh cups of coffee and plenty of creamers, and on a cold December afternoon Todd Chappel and I tucked in. The ham—which smokes for eight hours—is sliced and served with the brownish-red vinegary dip. The potato salad was a bit sour with dill pickles and onions—one of the best I've tried—and the thick beans had mustard undertones; both sides were very satisfying. The half chicken was tender with a medium smoke flavor, complemented by the wonderful dip. The thick-sliced pork was juicy and tender but not fall-apart tender, because these butts are cooked to a lesser internal temperature than pork butts that just flake apart. I loved the barky pieces. All the meats were delicious. It would be hard to pick a favorite. But because this is mutton country, and because I love mutton, I'd tip my hat to the chopped mutton and try the sliced if it were available. The sliced smoked ham with dip is also worth trying—something you won't find much outside of Owensboro.

"We use hickory and cook all our meats from twenty-four to thirty hours at about 220°," Jason said. "Our new motto and advertising campaign is 'We do it longer and better than everybody else.'"

Jason has owned Ole South since 2008; he managed it for six years before that. Jason and pit master Jamie Cook fire the long pits with chunks of hickory loaded into the pit area closest to the exterior door (and the woodpile). They cook chickens and ribs closer to the fire and pork butts and mutton on the farthest end of the pits for long indirect cooking.

Back in the pit area, Jason stirred a forty-gallon drum of dip with a huge ladle. Todd and I found the dip a wonderful accompaniment to the meats, especially the slices of smoked city ham.

Ole South Barbeque's Mutton Dip

When I visited the pit area of Ole South, I saw Jason Shuler stirring a forty-gallon flame-fired cauldron of mutton dip with a three-foot-long paddle. This dip recipe also requires a big kettle, like a sixteen-quart stockpot. Thanks to Jason for providing this high-volume recipe for Owensboro's distinctive mutton dip.

1 gallon Worcestershire sauce
1 gallon water
2 tablespoons salt
1 tablespoon black pepper
2 cups white vinegar
1 cup lemon juice
2 pounds brown sugar
5 pounds tomato paste

In a large pot, cook all ingredients until paste dissolves. Use it to baste meats, preferably mutton, periodically throughout the many hours of cooking required to tenderize the muscle tissues. When serving mutton, offer this dip in a bowl on the side for the dipping of individual pieces. Yields about 2½ gallons.

Ole South delivers quirky kitsch, quality barbecue, ample seating in a family-dining atmosphere, and friendly service. They cook old school on those long masonry pits. They also have a barbecue buffet in more intimate surroundings than you'll find at Moonlite across town, plus banana pudding, peach cobbler, and bread pudding to send you home waddling.

Open: Monday, 6:00 a.m.–2:00 p.m.; Tuesday–Thursday, 6:00 a.m.–8:00 p.m.; Friday–Saturday, 6:00 a.m.–9:00 p.m.; Sunday, 6:00 a.m.–2:00 p.m. 3523 Highway 54 East; 270-926-6464

Central City

KP's Smokehouse

Suuuuuuuuuu-weeeeeeee! This barbecue joint exudes cuteness, from the funky cartoon pigs painted on the walls to the Polynesian-style grass dangling here and there to the plastic palm tree in the corner of the water closet, right next to a cartoon pig in blue jeans holding its crotch next to the words "Gotta Go!!"

The ladies who run KP's nailed the fun factor. You can see their sense of humor in the multiple-colored tie-dyed shirts they sell, designed by the same Bowling Green artist, Lori James, who painted the numerous pig scenes on the walls. The front of the 2011 T-shirt design features a big-haired (as in bouffant) pig in tiger-striped bikini and knee boots sitting in a tire swing, above the words "Leave Your Attitude at Home." The back design shows three female pigs dancing around a table, above the words "Babes Gone WILD!" A mug of beer and mug of coffee are falling from the table, displaced by the pig babes' wild dancing. The pigs have hourglass figures and wear bikinis, pink lipstick, earrings, high heels, and big hair. Carol Adams, the vegan-feminist author of *The Sexual Politics of Meat* and *The Pornography of Meat,* would have a field day with this place.

I visited KP's with a group of buddies. As soon as we walked in the door, the front lady, Dana, said, "We're out of brisket." They were also out of Shock Top ale—it had been a big Friday night, apparently. We shared a sampler platter, which came with a full slab of spareribs, two pork sandwiches, a half chicken, four side dishes, and two dinner rolls. We also got a smoked turkey sandwich, a bologna burger, and a basket of smoked jumbo wings, which come "hot," "BBQ," or "naked." While waiting for the food, my friends watched a Saturday football game on the big-screen television in the large room in the back of the house (KP's is located in a ranch-style house). The floors are laminate that looks like wood. Tables are thick lacquered wood. Colorful beer signs glow on the walls of this room, which feels like a homey sports bar. On tap they had Miller Light, Bud Light, Shock Top, and Amber Bock. It's a rare find in Kentucky, especially in a small town—a barbecue place with a beer license.

The meats are all lightly smoked on an Ole Hickory cooker, which Patti Pryor, the owner, keeps in a garage beside the house. Patti opened the doors of the cooker to reveal a rotisserie with racks filled with baby back ribs and rolls of bologna. On the other side of the stainless steel unit is a firebox that holds a blasting flame from natural gas. The flame licked a piece of hickory inside to give the subtle smoke flavor of the meats.

As a lover of smoke, my favorites of the meats were the chicken wings and tender half chicken. The juicy chicken wings, glazed with barbecue sauce or topped with typical buffalo wing hot sauce (or served "naked"), packed the most flavor. Fouad Atalla, one of the guys, said he'd be happy making a meal of a basket of smoked wings. I agree, and I'd add on the tasty side dishes and a piece of pie, all homemade.

Everyone agreed that the "deluxe baked beans," hash brown casserole, and "tangy coleslaw" were delicious. The beans—a four-bean mixture cooked down in a savory sauce—were as good as I've had anywhere. The slaw was crispy slices of cabbage hinting of sweetened vinegar. The hash brown casserole was hot and cheesy. The pork loin sandwich was thinly sliced with very little smoke flavor. The pulled-pork sandwich was similar, except the meat is moister than the loin. The turkey sandwich was moist sliced turkey breast, slightly smoked and served with Jezebel sauce (a tangy sauce of fruit preserves, usually apple, and horseradish). The "bologna burger" was a half-inch-thick slice of smoked bologna served with a hot horseradish mustard sauce. "It'll clean out your sinuses," Patti said.

The fellows enjoyed the bologna—I think because most of them hadn't eaten it in years. Fouad, a plastic surgeon, sliced the sandwich into ten even pieces with a plastic knife. The bologna was tasty. The big spareribs that come with the combo can be ordered naked, wet, or dry rubbed (our choice). The ribs were good. The meat still clung to the bone, and the smoke flavor was second to the chicken. All the food was served on paper in plastic baskets. Sandwiches came on regular untoasted hamburger buns. Tangy, sweet, and hot sauces are on the table—needed to add flavor to the pork sandwiches.

Born and raised in Central City (whose claim to fame is the Everly Brothers), Patti opened KP's in 1994 as a carryout business two days a week, but the business has grown into its current full sit-down restaurant with televisions and draft beer and party room capacity. Patti said all their sides are "Granny's recipes," which doesn't surprise me (they were *really* good). During the destructive ice storm of 2009, which knocked out power in communities across the state, Kentucky Utilities set up a big generator at KP's, and they served sixteen hundred meals daily from two regular home ranges and their barbecue pit. Patti said their pit is now on wheels, ready to meet the needs of people during disasters.

Patti said she's having fun at the business. "Besides being the Pit Queen, I do all the cookin'." Her "right hand" is Dana Haney, the public face of KP's, who takes care of the restaurant management, taking orders, answering phones, and so on. Patti said they laugh a lot when working, and that doesn't surprise me either. KP's just has the feeling of a good-time place, a real relaxing atmosphere to meet with friends, maybe watch some sports, and eat some of the tasty food.

I noticed some barbecue oddities on the menu, like "smokehouse quesadillas" (floured tortillas, cheese, and Southwest spices with pork, turkey, or pulled chicken) and "barbeque salad," which could satisfy dining companions not wanting a full-on meat fest. A sign by the ordering counter also listed Derby pie, key lime pie, fudge nut pie, and blackberry cobbler.

I asked Patti about the fat painted pigs adorning the walls and the skinny female pigs on the T-shirts, and she said, "Babes gone wild! These are the new ones since my divorce. Those are fat pigs on the wall. These are skinny pigs on the T-shirts because we're down to running weight now." We all laughed at that.

I said, "Because you're back on the market now!"

She said, "There you go."

KP's is a very short drive off of the Western Kentucky Parkway. Travelers looking for a clean, well-lit, colorful restaurant run by nice ladies who cook up quality homemade side dishes, mildly smoked tender meats, and decadent desserts—and maybe even a salad—should be happy here. We were even lucky enough to be served by a young woman in a cheerleading outfit. How often does that happen?

Lovers of old-fashioned deeply smoked barbecue take note: you won't find that here. You'll find fun and some good food. I'd go for a bunch of those chicken wings and several of the side dishes. Oh, and if you're thirsty for a brew with your barbecue, know that KP's is one of the few barbecue joints where you can have it.

Open: Thursday–Saturday, 11:00 a.m.–8:00 p.m.
902 West Everly Brothers Blvd.; 270-754-3400

Caves, Lakes, and Corvettes Region

Guthrie

A railroad town nudging the border of Tennessee, Guthrie was the boyhood home of Robert Penn Warren, the first poet laureate of the United States and winner of Pulitzer prizes in both fiction and poetry. Warren left Guthrie to attend high school in Tennessee and never came back to live. Maybe he'd have stuck around longer if these two barbecue places—less than a mile apart from each other—had been in business back then.

Mike's Pit Bar-B-Cue

Mike and Nancy Reeves made me feel right at home when I waddled into their cozy restaurant on a Friday afternoon, having already visited five barbecue places that day. Nancy tried coaxing an order out of me as I stared at the abundant choices—pulled pork, pork chops, boneless pork loin, whole or half chickens, pork spareribs, brisket, turkey; fried corn, hash brown casserole, turnip greens, burgoo, green beans, and more—and, unable to decide, I asked, "What do you think the person who does the smoking thinks he or she does best?"

"Ask him," Nancy said, motioning to a table where a white-haired and mustached man sat, wearing a shirt that said MIKE above the breast pocket.

I said, "Hidee, Mr. Mike" and shook his hand, and that's about all I had to say, because when Mike opened his mouth the words flowed like a warm river of sweetened molasses, and kept flowing all through my meal. Mike decided I needed a combo plate, which comes with four meats and two sides. I chose burgoo and hash brown casserole. "Barbecue place, you need burgoo," Mike said. "This recipe came, I think, from the Golden Pond area of Land between the Lakes."

Mike's been serving barbecue in Guthrie many years. Nancy pointed to a photo of Kentucky governor Steve Beshear on the wall and said they catered a meal at the Guthrie water plant when Beshear visited. "His security detail sure likes our barbecue. He does too," she said. "They called here a while back, they's going to be in Russellville, wanted to know if the hog was dead. They wanted some sandwiches. So one of our local politicians took it to 'em!"

I asked Nancy about the fried corn, and she said it's cream-style corn fried in bacon grease. I also saw several pies on the menu, including buttermilk pie made by Mike.

"We make everything here but the potato salad," Nancy said. "We don't have time to do the potato salad, we go through so much of it. I sent five gallons out this morning."

While Mike prepared my combo plate, I asked, "You think he has time to talk with me?" and Nancy answered, "Oh, he'll talk to you, I guarantee you that. If he doesn't, I'm calling the mortician!"

And so the food came, and the words flowed. Mike was born in Hickman County, Tennessee, but moved to Guthrie at age nine. He came out of the Marine Corps and started cooking barbecue. "It was in me to learn how," he said. "I found I have a gift to cook. I've got a school-trained chef in here that knows more than I do, but when it comes down to actual cooking I can cook circles around her."

I tasted a similar moderate smokiness in all of the meats, with chicken and pulled pork winning on the flavor scale. The St. Louis–style rib was tender. Mike said he didn't like baby back ribs and almost refused to cook them. I asked why. "I just don't like 'em," he said. "There's something missing."

He cooks the chickens for three and a half hours. Ribs cook six to eight hours. The half-inch-thick pork loin and pulled pork from Boston butts were both moist and tender. The burgoo was chunky and delicious. Of the table sauce, a nationally registered trademark, Mike said, "That's a true sauce. It puts the flavor in the burgoo and the barbecue beans. It's good in chili. My buddy puts it in spaghetti sauce. Somebody said it's really good on broccoli."

Customers, mostly men, steadily walked in to place takeout orders, and Mike greeted them as we spoke. He told me, "I've had people as far away as Atlanta up here try to figure out what I'm doing."

A man in line said, "So is everybody else up here."

Mike and the man laughed, and Mike said, "As long as I do it right, that's what counts, isn't it, Garth? Garth's been eating my barbecue for about thirty-eight years."

"It hasn't hurt me yet," Garth said.

Mike almost learned to cook barbecue from a Guthrie woman with a bad reputation. "She was a super lady. But she just didn't fit in most folks' box. My mother threw such a fit 'cause I was going to be staying down there all night watching barbecue cook with this lady with a reputation, and all I wanted to do was learn to cook barbecue. That was in '63. In '74, Donald Starnes at Starnes Barbecue in Paducah let me come up there and watch him one day. I watched, looked, and learned the basics. I've been building on that for thirty-nine years now. The first barbecue I cooked was the first week of January 1975."

I noted that Mike was reading a Bible when I walked in, and he said he was reading up for a Sunday sermon—he was filling in for an absent pastor at a local church—yet another confirmation of the relationship between barbecue and higher powers. "I try to edify and exhort and encourage and build people up," Mike said. "My primary gift is mercy. In spite of everything we've got, all the material things, we have a generation of broken, hurt, and disillusioned people."

I said amen to that.

Mike said he's seventy years old and putting in seventy to eighty hours per week at the restaurant. He's got the place up for sale. When it sells, he wants to set up a concession stand to barbecue a couple days per week. "And I want to preach more."

About the barbecue business, Mike said, "You got to keep it simple. You cannot commercially sell whole-hog barbecue, backyard barbecue, or competition barbecue. It's not feasible. I can cook better barbecue than this. But I can't do it every day, five to six days a week. That's word for you right there." He added, "I'm tired. I want to go fishin' sometime."

By the time I left Mike's at 5:40 on a Friday afternoon, business was hopping. Well, I hate to sound like a broken record, but here's another long-established barbecue man ready to swap his pits for a fishing pole. You better call ahead to see if Mike, or his successor, is still smoking.

Open: Tuesday–Friday, 6:00 a.m.–7:00 p.m.; Saturday, 6:00 a.m.–8:00 p.m.

9926 Russellville Road; 270-483-8001

www.mikesbbqllc.com

Red Top Bar B Que

I was amazed by how busy this little joint was at 4:00 on a Friday afternoon. Many people must commute between Kentucky and Clarksville, Tennessee, because traffic flowed steadily on Highway 79, which runs by Red Top. The parking lot was full of cars by 5:00 after I finished my great meal. An SUV with POLICE printed on the side was sandwiched between two mammoth Ford trucks, in addition to a minivan, two midsize sedans, and my old beat-up Ford Ranger. I saw white folks and black folks filing in through the front doors of the restaurant, which is decorated on the exterior to look like a log cabin. Red is the primary motif: red metal roof, red tank smoker with the engine of an old tractor attached to one end and the seat and steering wheel of the tractor attached to the back to make it look like one big long tractor. It was a good scene on the outside.

Inside, I waited in line a while, which gave me time to ponder the extensive menu scribbled on a white board behind the counter. The eating area holds just a few tables. Most people were getting orders to go. If you do eat in on a busy afternoon like this one, you'll have plenty to watch, as the ordering area and eating area are part of one room. In business "off and on for about twenty years" (according to the young woman running the counter), Red Top in "Tiny Town, Kentucky," is currently owned by Follis and Shane Moore, who also do the meat smoking.

I got a three-meat sampler with smoked kielbasa, a meaty sparerib, brisket, hash brown casserole, and burgoo. Actually, I ordered broccoli-rice casserole at the recommendation of a young fellow who said, "It will knock you off your feet!" but they were out of it. While ordering I heard meat being chopped in the background. The young woman who took my order said all dishes are homemade except the potato salad and slaw.

I took the Styrofoam plate outside and sat at one of the picnic tables underneath a pole garage. The huge, meaty sparerib had a beautiful smoke ring and was extremely tender and flavorful. The cornbread was crispy and tasted like hush puppy batter, firm and not sweet. The brisket was finely chopped— I should have asked for more bark—tender, and very salty (and I'm a lover of salt). Three pieces of kielbasa—something you don't find much on menus in Kentucky—turned a dark shade of red from the smoke, a crispy snap on the skin, and juicy within. Sauces, which aren't needed, include hot and mild tomato-based blends tasting of vinegar, sweetening (maybe molasses?), cayenne, and perhaps a touch of liquid smoke—akin to a Kansas City sauce. The pile of hash brown casserole was cheesy and oniony, and the hot, chunky burgoo contained corn, black-eyed peas, green peas, potatoes, tomatoes, kielbasa, and pork. Everything on the plate was fabulous except for the over-salted brisket and slightly dry cornbread.

Still hungry at the end of your meal? At the counter they tantalize you with pies: chess, apple, fudge, pecan, and coconut cream.

ADDENDUM: I returned again to Red Top for lunch on June 6, 2012. Elisa and I had driven to Cumberland Furnace, Tennessee, to pick up a New Zealand White rabbit buck named Walloping Wabbit Geronimo (no kidding). Elisa's developing meat-rabbit breeding stock for home consumption. We heard that domestic rabbit barbecued low and slow tastes really good. (When we tried it later, we found the meat to be mushy, however. Better stick to frying these tender rabbits.) Our return journey took us right by Red Top, a few steps north of the Tennessee line, at noon. The place was plenty busy, with all the inside tables occupied and others getting takeout. We got another three-meat sampler for the road, along with a piece of chocolate pie.

Here's the rundown. This time around I ordered pulled pork, smoked chicken wings, and ribs, plus broccoli-rice casserole and sweet potato casserole. We chose rolls over cornbread. The pulled pork was excellent—highly seasoned, moist, and deeply smoked. We both thought it was some of the best we'd eaten anywhere. The chicken wings were salty, spicy, and smoked. I liked them, although Elisa thought they were a little soft. I was struck this time around by the dry rub used on the ribs, something reminding me of Cajun spices, like pulverized sassafras leaves used to thicken gumbo or perhaps ground sage. The ribs were nicely flavored but not as tender this time around. I was glad I didn't get a plate of them. But the awesome pulled pork made up for it. All the meats were salty and well seasoned and served without sauce. The casseroles were both real good, our favorite being the whipped sweet potatoes with spices and nuts. The broccoli casserole was creamy and heavy on the rice. We both liked it. The store-bought rolls were superfluous. The chocolate (or fudge?) pie had a pudding filling with a big meringue, and we tasted lemon in the crust. It reminded me of the pies made by many southern Kentucky homemakers, like my maw maw (grandmother) Gladys Berry's pies. Elisa hadn't had this kind before. She grew up in Florida. It tasted like homemade chocolate pie is supposed to, but we agreed that it was too sweet for our tastes and we wouldn't get it again.

In summary, it was a lot of food for the price, and the quality was, like the first time around months before, high. Now that I've tried a bit of everything, I'd get a three-meat sampler with pulled pork, sausage, and ribs (hoping that the ribs were fresh and stellar like the first time I ate there, because I really dig the dry rub), along with hash brown casserole, sweet potato casserole, with extra sides of burgoo and fried okra. I'd get the cornbread over the forgettable rolls. That meal could feed two people with moderate appetites.

Open: Monday, 10:00 a.m.–2:00 p.m.; Tuesday–Saturday, 10: a.m.– 7:00 p.m.

10388 Russellville Road; 270-483-1328

Side Dish: Mapping the Burgoo Belt

Just what is burgoo? Simply, a stew with a slew of ingredients that, in the best versions, includes lamb or mutton—the primary ingredient that sets Kentucky's burgoo apart from Georgia's and Virginia's Brunswick stew. A recipe for Kentucky burgoo published in John Finley's *The Courier-Journal Kentucky Cookbook* includes pork shank, veal shank, beef shank, lamb breast, a four-pound hen, potatoes, onions, carrots, peppers, cabbage, corn, tomatoes, okra, lima beans, celery, and seasonings (including Worcestershire sauce, a common ingredient in the thin dips used to baste mutton at Owensboro-area barbecue restaurants).

Burgoo can be thick and chunky or ground into slurry. I like both styles. What sets the best burgoos apart from run-of-the-mill beef stews, though, is the gaminess of the mutton. Matt and Ted Lee call this flavor "deep holler," a fun and fitting label. In *The Lee Bros. Southern Cookbook*, they explain that "the origins of Kentucky burgoo are even murkier than those of Brunswick stew. According to legend, the town of Bergoo [*sic*], West Virginia, played host to a large hunting party, and at the end of a successful week of hunting bear, deer, and squirrel, the participants dined on a stew that included everything they'd shot. . . . Others claim that the word 'burgoo' was a common term for the oatmeal-like gruel cooked as sailors' rations in the eighteenth century, and that it was adapted by some witty Kentuckian to describe a very different dish."

During Owensboro's annual barbecue festival, you can watch men from the cooking teams stirring wood-fired seventy-five-gallon cauldrons of burgoo with giant paddles. Get close enough and the smoke from the fires stings the eyeballs.

The rest of the year you can order burgoo from 18 different barbecue places. Perhaps I missed one or two, but this is pretty much it: 18 places out of the 160 I've visited, just over 10 percent. Follow Highway 41 down from Henderson to Hopkinsville to Guthrie, then draw a line straight up to Owensboro, and you've pretty much mapped the Burgoo Belt. Three Hopkinsville-area restaurants serve it; one in Madisonville; two in Guthrie; four in Owensboro (the burgoo capital). Outside of this Burgoo Belt, you can sup on it at Ruby Faye's Bar-B-Que in Clinton; Peak Bros. in Waverly; Mark's Feed Store, Ole Hickory Pit, and Shack in the Back BBQ in Louisville; Tony's Bar-B-Que Barn near Lawrenceburg; and at Billy's Bar-B-Q and Ky. Butt Rubb'in BBQ in Lexington. Turf Catering Company also serves up burgoo at Keeneland, the famous thoroughbred racetrack in Lexington. Their recipe, which calls for stew meat (not mutton), is available on the Keeneland website, or you can watch Keeneland's Chef Ed prepare a drunken version of it on YouTube under the title "Chef Ed Prepares Burgoo." Well, I'm pretty sure Chef Ed isn't drunk, but his burgoo, containing both red wine and sherry, sure is.

Russellville

Roy's Bar B Q

I've eaten Roy's chopped pork between two hoecakes several times when passing through Russellville. The texture of the meat is a bit soft for my liking, but the flavor is outstanding—smoky, tangy, magically seasoned, and the hot sauce, which I prefer, is vinegary with a hint of tomato and some pepper. The sweet sauce is a mustard-vinegar-pepper concoction. The hoecakes are nice and sweet. They also serve pork ribs, half and whole chickens, and sliced beef cooked in sauce. Roy's has two locations, the original big restaurant west of Russellville and a smaller shack across town on the east side. The meats are smoked with hickory wood at the original location.

I ate at the big restaurant on a Sunday in March, and local patrons were glued to the television watching University of Kentucky basketball, not surprising considering the abundant UK sports stuff covering the walls. I ordered the dill pickle appetizer, expecting fried pickle chips but getting instead pickle spears battered and fried and served with ranch dressing. They were good. The ribs on this day, however, were not good; they were overcooked and caked in sauce, reminding me of baked ribs, and they seemed old. The macaroni salad had pickles in it, blended with a creamy dressing, and the breaded okra was fried to a nice crispiness. The potato wedges I saw at another table looked good, but I didn't try one. The mashed potatoes were nothing special. Which brings me back to my original point: Roy's has delicious chopped pork, and I love getting it between the hoecakes. Maybe the restaurant just had a bad day on the ribs, but they didn't suit my rib tastes at all. I recommend the chopped pork between hoecakes, fried okra, macaroni salad, and a piece of peanut butter pie.

Open: Monday–Saturday, 10:00 a.m.–8:00 p.m.; Sunday, 9:00 a.m.–2:00 p.m.

101 Sarah Lane; 270-726-8057

Franklin

Dunn's B-B-Q

The menu at Horace Dunn's gray-painted cinderblock shack is delightfully simple: ribs and shredded pork, as a sandwich or a plate. (How do you eat a rib sandwich? Suck the meat off the bones and use the bread to sop up the sauce.) A plate gets you a meat and two of these: potato salad, coleslaw, baked beans, chips. You can also get "BBQ on cornbread"—that was my choice— a good heap of tender, juicy, lightly smoked shredded pork over thick crispy hoecakes, topped with a tangy tomato sauce. A scoop of eggy potato salad and piping-hot barbecue beans rounded out the meal. The potato salad had sweet pickle relish mixed in. The shredded pork reminds me of what I've had in some north Mississippi and middle Georgia barbecue joints, where the meat is chopped finely, with a minimum of smoky bark, and served with sauce of more tomato than vinegar. I liked it plenty.

I arrived at Dunn's on a Thursday afternoon at 1:00. You probably wouldn't stumble upon this little shack if just passing through Franklin, as it's located in a residential neighborhood a few blocks off the town square and nearby the Elevated Baptist Church. There was no wood smoke luring me into the place, and except for a small "Open" sign in the window above the air-conditioning unit and a pickup truck parked behind the building, I would have assumed the place was closed. When I walked in, Mr. Dunn was on the telephone, talking with someone about getting a new microwave oven.

The atmosphere is intensely intimate. I sat at one of two tables and looked around. Signed photos decorate the place: Joker Phillips, head football coach at the University of Kentucky, looks out from the photo frame sitting on the tabletop, and Kentucky Supreme Court chief justice Joseph E. Lambert thanks Mr. Dunn for his excellent barbecue. A television played in the corner by the window. Dunn got off the phone and made my order, and while I ate he told me some of his barbecue history. When I inquired about the photos on the wall, he showed me a jar of pickled tomatoes Chief Justice Lambert's wife sent him back in 2000. The retired lawmaker has eaten at Dunn's twice.

Dunn got into barbecue after working for Rudy's Farm and Tennessee

Pride packing companies in Nashville for twenty years, where he learned how to handle meat. I recalled a television commercial jingle from my childhood:

Foooooooooor real country sausage
The best you ever tried
Pick up a pound or two
Of Tennessee Pride!

In January 2010, Dunn was featured on the "Hometown Hero" segment of Bowling Green, Kentucky's television station. They filmed him making up a barbecue plate and told about Dunn's charity work in the community. He's a member of the Gentlemen's Unlimited Club, which has been helping local people for thirty years: delivering toys for needy children at Christmas and preparing and delivering food for 150–200 people at Thanksgiving. "It was real cool," he said. "I be in Sam's [Club] and a guy walked up to me and say, 'Man, I saw you on TV—Hometown Hero.' You know, it kinda made me feel good." During the Hometown Hero television segment, Dunn said, "I get a thrill out of helping someone less fortunate than I, and that's just what we do. We enjoy doing it."

The phone rang, and Dunn talked with a woman about reheating her barbecue in a microwave. "If you don't know what you're doin', you can ruin the meat," he said.

Because his microwave was busted, Dunn couldn't heat up his barbe-cued ribs, but he wanted me to try one anyway. "They cold," he said. "But I just want you to taste it." The sparerib was tender, even without being warmed up. He smokes primarily with hickory, sometimes a little oak, using indirect heat, but he's careful not to put too much smoke in the meat.

I said, "I'd be real happy coming in here getting a rib plate," and Dunn said, "I took me about three bones home last night, and I really did enjoy it. I don't try to brag on it or anything. I just do what I do." A rib plates gets you four bones of these tasty and tender (even when cold) spareribs.

About that time a middle-aged woman walked in and wanted ribs, and Dunn explained that the microwave was busted and he only had shredded pork.

"I'm hungry," she said. "That's what I want" (meaning ribs). She took a seat and waited for the new microwave to show up.

We got into a discussion about barbecue styles in the state, and I mentioned that I liked getting mutton off the pit instead of chopped and sauced, and Dunn said, "I like mutton," and he looked over at the woman waiting on her ribs and said, "Hazel, you like mutton?" and she said, "Yeah, I like goat too."

Dunn said, "I like goat too! But I don't want sauce on my goat. Boyyyyyy, I love goat! My mother used to cook it for us. Goat and sheep are brothers and sisters."

Dunn has been smoking meats for twenty-something years. "I like what I do," he said, "and when you like what you do you try to do a good job, know what I'm saying? I don't know how much longer though. I'm gettin' over the hill. It's a lotta work."

Open: Wednesday–Friday, 10:30 a.m.–5:00 p.m.; Saturday, 10:30 a.m.–3:00 p.m.

410 Jefferson Street; 270-586-5115

Wildfire BBQ and Grill

Jeff Lewis cooks a whole beef brisket because he likes the way the fat renders in with the leaner meat, and I concur. Whole-cooked brisket generally suits my tastes better than one that's been trimmed of fat. Jeff's brisket is sliced a quarter inch thick and is appropriately tender (but not overcooked). Wildfire also offers up tender, flaky pulled (more like shredded) pork, sliced pork shoulder, smoked bologna, baby back ribs, and half chickens. "We do a world of chicken here," Jeff said. They also do loaded potatoes, barbecue nachos, and a "smoke stack": cornbread topped with barbecue beans, pork, cheese, onion, and pickle.

A safety environmental engineer by education and training, Jeff has "always done barbecue." He bought a vending trailer about ten years ago and served barbecue as a hobby while working full-time for a utility company, when his wife said, "Why don't you do what you really love?" So Jeff opened Wildfire in 2004.

Raised in Muhlenberg County and schooled at Murray State in western Kentucky, Jeff moved to Houston after college and "didn't have a clue what brisket was." But he found out in Texas, and he brought this knowledge back to his pleasant eat-in joint south of Franklin, a couple hundred yards off the main highway. Because of its slightly off-the-road location, Wildfire BBQ may not catch the eye of the casual traveler, but Jeff said he likes his nonprime real estate because, in his words, "I go to bed at night knowing I'm going to pay my bills. I don't want a $5,000 a month lease over my head." Jeff noted that they have good customer support, even during this downed economy, because they do a lot of work for churches, schools, and industries in Franklin.

I ordered a "pit combo," which came with brisket, shredded pork, and one piece of sliced shoulder, plus turnip greens and BBQ beans, two of their best-selling sides. I also tried white beans, fried corn on the cob (half an ear of corn soaked in a saline solution and then deep fried), and fabulous home-fried potato chips—thinly sliced potatoes fried till crispy and salted. Sauces are a medium-hot tomato-based table sauce and a "way-way kick-you-like-a-mule hot one that I keep in the back" (Jeff's words). They also have a thin vin-egary pepper sauce that's good on the shredded pork. The hot sauce is sweet but finishes with a substantial tongue burn and tingles the back of the throat. I liked it.

For indoor eating, there's an intimate dining area with black and white checkered tables in booths, some freestanding tables, a couple of televisions mounted on the walls, ceiling fans, and wood-paneled walls, with corrugated roofing tin for wallpaper. Because it was a pretty fall day, I joined my trav-eling companions Shane Wood and Cooper Burton, young journalists from Western Kentucky University, at a picnic table in a screened porch area off the dining room. Shane was digging the country music that played from speak-ers in the porch area. "I'm not a country music fan, but it works in this envi-ronment," he said.

Jeff's had some steady help over the past few years, and that keeps him satisfied with his current location. About the difficulty of keeping good help—a recurring subject in my interviews with barbecue people—Jeff said, "You got people who will steal money; you got people who will steal food; and you got people who will sling anything out there. The girls here know that if it doesn't look good to them, *do not serve it.* I'd rather you throw it away and waste that food than ruin a relationship with a customer. We do make mistakes—but if you tell me about it I'm going to fix it."

While finishing my meal, I saw a fellow wearing overalls and sporting a foot-long goatee walk in and give Jeff a hug. Originally from the barbecue Mecca of Graves County, motorcyclist Robert Thornton now lives in Elizabethtown but drives one hour south to Franklin to get barbecue. He said that up there in E-town their idea of barbecue is "meat puddin'"—pork butt cooked in a crock pot with barbecue sauce dumped on top. He said, "Up there they don't smoke meat, and I kid around with 'em that their meat puddin' could be possum or any kind of roadkill. You can't tell what kind of meat it is!"

You won't get any meat puddin' at Wildfire. The meat comes unsauced, and you can taste the smoke from the scaly bark hickory Jeff uses. Next time I'm down there, I'll try the half chicken—Jeff does one plain and one with a dry rub that outsells plain ten to one—and I'd gladly order the tasty brisket and moist pulled pork again, along with some of those crispy home-fried potato chips. Also, the tangy BBQ beans were much better than most I've had, with rich barbecue sauce and meat mixed in with them. For lighter appetites, try the peppery beef brisket sandwich. Jeff sells a lot of brisket, and for the record, Wildfire is one of the only places in this part of Kentucky that serves smoked bologna and the only local place to get sliced shoulder. Before serving the thin pieces of cooked shoulder, Jeff takes tongs and dunks the shoulder into a finishing sauce of water, rendered brisket fat, and brisket seasonings. Jeff said he'd tried serving sliced pork shoulder with a Monroe County vinegar dip at first, but locals didn't like it. "It's strange," he said. "I could almost throw a rock and hit the county that serves it, but the people here don't like it."

We agreed that intense local taste preferences are fascinating. Twenty-five road miles to the east of Franklin, Smoke Shack BBQ in the town of Scottsville sells a load of grilled shoulder sopped with vinegar dip. Twenty-five miles north, Smokey Pig in Bowling Green specializes in shoulder sopped with a fiery-tangy dip. But here in Franklin, Jeff couldn't give it away when he applied the vinegar sop, so he's made modifications to suit the local tastes.

Open: Monday, 11:00 a.m.–2:00 p.m.; Tuesday–Friday, 11:00 a.m.–7:00 p.m.; Saturday, 11:00 a.m.–2:00 p.m.

105 State Street (Highway 31 behind Bowen Tire); 270-586-5227

Pork Shoulder, "Monroe County Style"

It's hard to know where to place this note on the favored barbecue style of south-central Kentucky, but I'm choosing here since Bowling Green is the westernmost place where you can find it (with the exception of Wildfire BBQ and Grill's modified version of it), and by the time this book is published someone else might be serving it, because shoulder has moved from its home base in Monroe County and, like the little island of England, has slowly but surely colonized the surrounding counties.

"Shoulder" means something different in Allen, Barren, Monroe, and Cumberland counties than it does in the far western part of the state. Way over there in the Mayfield-Paducah–Land between the Lakes area, "shoulder" means whole pork shoulders cooked slowly for twelve to twenty-four hours (a few places cook longer, but the twelve-hour mark seems the minimum time for whole-shoulder cooking). In south-central Kentucky, "shoulder" means thinly sliced pieces of Boston butt grilled over coals (usually cooked-down hickory, but some use charcoal) until done. The meat is often seasoned with pepper and salt and sopped with a thin sauce of vinegar, black and red pepper, and fat (either butter, lard, or a combination of these), akin to the old-fashioned sauces of eastern North Carolina. If you like your barbecue hot, then get it "dipped," which means your slices of peppery pork shoulder will be coated, either by dunking into the sauce pot with tongs or by drizzling on the thin sauce with a ladle.

Shoulder tastes similar at the different places, with variations based on thickness of the slice, length of cooking, and sauce modifications. Some of my fondest high school memories are of road trips taken to Tompkinsville (T-ville) for a barbecue run: getting it to go, getting it dipped super hot, and sweating along with friends as we gnawed the meat off bones and drank cold drinks at home-construction sites or down by Salt Peter Cave in Barren County. I like the peppery dip sauce so much that I asked for a side of it to pour into my mashed potatoes and beans, and the white bread that comes with shoulder plates is good for sopping dip sauce. I usually "just say no" to white bread, but this is one time when I eat it. You need something to balance the rich greasiness of the shoulder and dip.

To get good uniform slices, the shoulder must be sliced frozen with a meat saw. Ross and Ross meat market in Tompkinsville furnishes the shoulder for forty-one barbecue places in southern Kentucky and northern Tennessee. They custom slice the Boston butts per request of thickness, which ranges from one-fourth to three-eighths of an inch thick. Frances' Bar-B-Que in Tompkinsville serves shoulder sliced thinner than most, and Hamilton's in Burkesville serves a thicker slice—more like a pork steak.

Don't visit the area without trying some of this distinctive regional style of smoked meat. Barbecue purists—you might call them snobs—say this isn't barbecue but grilling, because the meat doesn't sit on the pit for a dozen hours. But where do you draw the line? How long must a piece of meat cook over coals before it's officially "barbecue"? Hell, you can smoke a tasty chicken in three hours at 325°F. A rack of St. Louis–style ribs might take five hours at 230º. Slices of shoulder grill for fifteen to forty-five minutes. So what? It still tastes like smoke and pork, and people around here love it. Ultimately it doesn't matter what you call it—grilled pork steak, shoulder, or barbecue—because the stuff is good. Eat it.

Monroe County Barbecue Dip

R. J. Howard, who has roots in Monroe County but lived down the country road from me in Barren County during my childhood, shared this recipe. R. J.'s wife, Sue, was one of my "second moms" when I was growing up—no telling how much of her food I ate when playing down at their house.

Her father, Leon Nuckols, was supposed to cook chickens for a huge political rally during the Kentucky gubernatorial race of 1963 between Republican Louie B. Nunn and Democrat Edward T. Breathitt (who became Kentucky's fifty-first governor). Leon asked his son-in-law R. J. to help him barbecue, and R. J. went to Monroe County and got Hess Evans, a patriarch of Monroe County barbecue who'd cooked chickens for years, to lend his expertise. Hess wouldn't give his dip recipe away, but he needed to go to the grocery store to get the ingredients. R. J. took him to the store, paid attention to what Hess bought, and that's how he came to have this original Monroe County dip recipe.

This is a chicken-sopping dip, but it's also used at barbecue joints to sop tenderloins, sliced pork shoulder, and hamburgers. Pit masters tweak this basic recipe, adding a little yellow mustard, tomato sauce, or salt. Play with the recipe. But Sue would probably prefer you to leave it alone. She thinks it's just right.

3 gallons 40-grain colored distilled vinegar (not apple cider vinegar)
3 pounds lard
3 pounds butter
4 ounces (or more) black pepper
4 ounces (or more) cayenne pepper

This mix should be enough to cook 50 chickens (100 halves). Melt ingredients together in a metal pan. Once melted, stir sauce frequently and keep hot by allowing the saucepan to sit on wire rack with chickens. Chickens should be cooked on a wire rack over hot hickory coals. Cooking time approximately 4 hours. Turn chicken halves every 30 minutes and apply sauce generously every turn.

Monroe County Barbecue Dip for a Smaller Crowd

For those times when you aren't cooking for big political rallies and family gatherings of seventy people, you might want to pare down the dip. Here's a modified version for the home cook, one-third of the original quantity.

1 gallon 40-grain colored distilled vinegar (not apple cider vinegar)
2 cups lard
4 sticks butter
⅓–½ cup black pepper
⅓–½ cup cayenne pepper

Melt ingredients together in a metal pan. Keep warm to keep dip liquefied. Sop meats every time you flip them.

Bowling Green

Smokey Pig Bar-B-Q ("Monroe Co. Style")

"A Lunch with a View," I thought as I sat in the off-dining room and gazed out the window looking down on Barren River one March afternoon, my fingers greasy from slices of porky peppery sliced shoulder. The restaurant perches high on a bluff and you might not know you were eating so close to a river if you didn't go into the back room. It's the loveliest view I've seen from inside a barbecue place. You look down the bluff at a bonelike sycamore standing by the water. Visit in spring and you can watch leaf buds sprouting on the trees.

Bowling Green is my home base, and Smokey Pig has been a mainstay in my life over the years. As a college student longing for the thinly sliced shoulder cooked over hickory coals I had eaten so often at my uncle Roy's and at a few shacks in my native Barren County just one county over, Smokey Pig was the one place in this college town that provided that fix. That was the late 1980s, and Smokey Pig is still doing good business, judging by the bustling crowds of locals who cram into the place at lunchtime. When I lived away from Kentucky, I often daydreamed of the exterior of Smokey Pig, how when you pass by on the highway you can see billowing clouds of hickory smoke, and if the wind is right you smell it, too.

My #1 meal at Smokey Pig is the "dipped" shoulder plate with redskinned mashed potatoes, mac and cheese, and vinegar slaw (plates come with two sides), along with the real reason for the meal: the three beautiful slices of deep-brown-colored pork shoulder that come with a plate. When ordering I tell them to "dip the hell out of it" because I love the vinegar-based sauce studded with flecks of black and cayenne pepper that complements the smoky pork. The sauce settles to the bottom of the partitioned Styrofoam box that all "plates" are served in, and I eat the bottom piece first because it has more sauce on it. The "Monroe County style" calls for pork shoulder sliced thinly with bone in. I eat everything but the bone, especially the delicious fat that's marbled in with the meat and that melts in the mouth with minimal chewing—sort of like fresh pork cracklings, if you've been fortunate enough to eat them directly out of the kettle at hog killings. You should eat the fat— all of it. Everything but that little bone should be consumed, and the bone is so thin I'm tempted to eat it too, especially when dipped in that savory sauce. Plates come with two slices of spongy white bread—pretty lame for general eating, but perfect for sopping up the dip that remains in the bottom of the tray.

The thin slices of meat soak up a lot of smoke in a short amount of time. They cook it over live hickory coals. The dip sauce might be too hot for some folks. Before the young man who fixes my plate got to know me, he said, "You sure you want this much dip? This ain't Taco Bell." Now he just ladles it on and gives me an extra cup of dip to mix in with my vinegar slaw. You like pepper and vinegar? Try it.

Open: Tuesday–Saturday, 10:30 a.m.–7:00 p.m.
2520 Louisville Road; 270-781-1712

Jimmy D's Real Pitt Bar-B-Que

Jimmy Diemer opened his brightly colored takeout barbecue and regional foods shop on November 1, 2007, but he's been in the food business for a long time, ever since he was an army cook in the 1960s. "That's where I got my primary training," he told me, chuckling. "Uncle Sam did that."

I sat with Jimmy outside the shop at one of four picnic tables (the only seating available on the premises). Fall sunshine lit up my Styrofoam container of pork ribs and beef brisket, and occasionally a gentle warm breeze puffed smoke our way from the covered cooking area beside the store, making me even hungrier. Jimmy stopped his story a moment to say good-bye to two men eating at another table. "Thank you boys. Y'all take care!" Jimmy has a real easygoing way about him, greeting customers like old friends and saying good-bye to them when they depart.

I asked Jimmy how he got into the barbecue business. "I'd say that me being here is the good Lord inspired," he said. A longtime grocery store owner in Bowling Green, Jimmy had been thinking about the barbecue business for a while. Then one day a man who worked at Lowe's garden department came into his market and said, "Jimmy, I got out there what you need. We got some steel Brinkman smokers to make barbecue. Come out there and I'll show them to you."

So Jimmy went to Lowe's, and he liked what he saw, but the asking price of $599 took him aback. He said, "Shoooo, Lord man! I don't know that I need one that bad." He left without buying one. A few days later the man returned to Diemer's market and said, "Jimmy, my manager told me to sell some of them smokers at half price because people want gas and electric now, they don't want that."

Jimmy said, "Well, I tell you what, now we're talking. You put me one back."

It was December when Jimmy took the smoker home with him. He cooked Boston butts on it in zero weather. "I was getting up every three hours and firing that thing," he said. He took the meats to his market and gave samples away, testing his recipes.

"I did that for I don't know how long," Jimmy said. "Then one morning I said, 'You know, I believe I got it this morning.' I pulled into the store and there's a fellow named Bobby Shoefelt who liked to smoke meat, good cook. He coming down the aisle and I said, 'Bobby, come over here a minute, I want to show you something.' He come over there and I said, 'Bobby, taste this.' He ate that barbecue, he smiled, he raised both hands and looked to heaven and he says, 'Gimme five pounds!' I knew right then we was on the road to the barbecue business. After that, we haven't looked back."

Jimmy still has that original smoker from Lowe's, but he's now upscaled to the biggest tank unit Brinkman makes. He cooks with indirect heat, using only hickory, oak, and sassafras. Split wood is stacked up beside the long barrel-type smoker. Jimmy uses various woods because hickory burns too hot to use only hickory. "You'll burn your meat up."

Jimmy D's is a wonderful little meat emporium. In addition to the barbecue offerings (ribs, brisket, pulled pork, pulled chicken, sliced grilled shoulder, smoked bologna and wieners), the store sells Penn country hams from Campbellsville and smoked bacon and sausage from the Scott Hams company in Greenville.

The signage inside the store is enough to make your head swim. White paper signs scribbled with magic marker announce

Try our new pulled beef sandwich—it's good!

Everything is real homemade—it's good!

Let us slice this slab bacon at no charge

Jimmy D's Smoked Sliced Bacon—Real Smoke Flavor

COUNTRY HAM   **FRESH PORK SAUSAGE**

Refrigerator units stretch the length of the store. You can get any of Jimmy D's side dishes in quart containers to take home, as well as meatloaf cooked and ready to heat up. Shelves are well stocked with sorghum, honeys, jams and jellies, and tomato juice from Spring Valley Farms in Holland, Kentucky.

Ricky Prince receives a whole shoulder for custom cooking, Prince Pit BBQ, Bardwell.

Wes Berry beholds the barbecue potato at Hardware Cafe, Cunningham. (Photo by Andrew Coiner)

Lisa Powell, Red Grogan's Bar-B-Q, Clinton

Valerie Minor,
Deno's BBQ, Fulton

Pulled pork on toast,
Harned's Drive In,
Paducah

Boudin Man BBQ
Team prepares whole
hog at Barbecue on the
River, Paducah.

(*Above*) Sign near picnic grounds, Fancy Farm.
(*Left*) Wheeling shoulders to be chopped, weighed, and sold at the Fancy Farm picnic.
(*Below left*) Protesting at the Fancy Farm picnic and barbecue.
(*Below right*) Taking pork shoulders off the pits at the Fancy Farm picnic.

Suzanne Flint, Carr's Barn, Mayfield

Jan Quarles delivers the magnificent hoggy sandwich at Mr. BBQ & More, Grand Rivers. (Photo by Jeanie Adams-Smith)

Cy Quarles and his long-smoked pork shoulders, Mr. BBQ and More, Grand Rivers

(*Left*) Michael Redd harvests pork shoulders at Heaton BBQ, Princeton. (*Below left*) Kenneth and Lowell Jewell saw hickory slabs at Jewell's Open Pit, Princeton. (*Below right*) Chris Espino, Knoth's Bar-B-Que, Grand Rivers.

Hickory slabs burning to coals, Jewell's Open Pit, Princeton

Chopped mutton with cornbread, Bar B Que Shack, Hopkinsville

Mutton on the pits, St. Agnes Catholic Church picnic, Uniontown

Oscar Hill and the "Big Chop," Knockum Hill Bar-B-Q, Herndon
(Photo by Jeanie Adams-Smith)

(*Above left*) Bar B Que Shack, Hopkinsville
(*Above right*) Highway 107 south of Herndon, early November

Slicing mutton at St. Agnes Catholic Church picnic, Uniontown

(*Above left*) Frank Gibson, Thomason's Barbecue, Henderson.
(*Above right*) Blessed Mother Catholic Church's Cooking Team stirs burgoo at
the International Barbecue Festival, Owensboro.

(*Above left*) St. Mary Magdalene Catholic Church's Cooking Team at the
International Barbecue Festival, Owensboro.
(*Above right*) John Klein and Barry Burton, J & B Barbecue, Henderson.

Saint Pius X Catholic Church's Cooking Team member flips mutton
quarters at the International Barbecue Festival, Owensboro.

St. Louis–style pork ribs, sliced mutton, beef brisket, burgoo, and sides at Old Hickory Bar-B-Q, Owensboro

Jimmy Diemer, Jimmy D's Real Pitt Bar-B-Que, Bowling Green

Gary Sandefur skewers a mutton quarter at Old Hickory Bar-B-Q, Owensboro.

(*Above*) Big Bubba Buck's Belly Bustin BBQ Bliss, Munfordville. (*Right*) Grilling shoulder at South Fork Grill, Glasgow.

Shoulder plate "dipped," Backyard BBQ, Tompkinsville (Photo by Jeanie Adams-Smith)

Anita Hamilton,
R & S Bar-B-Q,
Tompkinsville
(Photo by Jeanie
Adams-Smith)

Frances'
Bar-B-Que,
Tompkinsville
(Photo by Jeanie
Adams-Smith)

David Arms,
owner of
Frances'
Bar-B-Que,
"dips and flips"
sliced ham.
(Photo by Jeanie
Adams-Smith)

Wormie carries coals, Collins Barbecue, Gamaliel (Photos by Jeanie Adams-Smith)

Sliced shoulder on the pit, Collins Barbecue, Gamaliel

Wormie watches Wes Berry sample his quarter-pound "double dipped" hot dog to see if Berry can handle the heat, Collins Barbecue, Gamaliel.

Pat and Norman,
Hamilton's Bar-B-Q,
Burkesville

Beef brisket,
mac and cheese,
and green
beans, Doc
Crow's,
Louisville

Rite Way Bar-B-Cue,
Louisville

(*Above*) PBLT (smoked pork belly, lettuce, and tomato) sandwich, Hammerheads, Louisville. (*Right*) Chefs Adam Burress and Chase Mucerino, Hammerheads, Louisville.

BBQ lamb ribs, Hammerheads, Louisville

Pitmaster
Richard Tucker,
Ole Hickory Pit,
Louisville

Flintstones (beef) ribs,
mac and cheese, soul
greens, and cornbread,
Smoketown USA,
Louisville

Roy Scott stokes his
custom dumpster
smoker at Scotty's Ribs
and More,
Louisville

Beef briskets Boston butts and photojournalist Domin Fuhrmann at Texican's BBQ Pitt, Crestwood

Pork ribs, beef brisket, and pulled pork, Sarah's Corner Cafe BBQ, Lexington

Christian Clark, Pit Stop BBQ, East Point

Jimmy D's spareribs and baby back ribs are delicious—the meat is tender but still clings to the bone, with a good smokiness—and from the extensive side dishes I favor the flavorful rich turnip greens, pinto beans, and mashed potatoes. How rare to get real mashed potatoes outside the home. Jimmy said, "We use Idaho bakers—that's the only thing we use. And we use fresh green cabbage, not the white New York dried." The tasty, tender pulled pork comes from smoked Boston butts. The beef brisket is marinated before smoking, so the flavor is full throughout. Jimmy said the brisket is a very popular item, and he's received the desired accolades from Texans who drop by off Interstate 65.

If you've got a sweet tooth, save some belly room for Jimmy's banana or chocolate pudding. It's real good!

"This is my retirement," Jimmy said. "This is fun. I love it. It's work, don't misunderstand me. But it's sort of a passion, and it's really grown." He said he plans to barbecue "as long as the good Lord will let me."

I'd like to think the good Lord favors Jimmy's good-natured generous spirit and will grant him—and his loyal customers—many more years of barbecue pleasures.

Open: Tuesday–Saturday, 10:00 a.m.–6:00 p.m.
5449 Scottsville Road; 270-781-2234

Alvaton

Split Tree Barbecue

On a sultry late morning in early July, I rode passenger in the car of Shane Wood, one of my students who'd shown a great enthusiasm for barbecue when I confessed to a class of students how I'd spent my summer vacation traveling Kentucky in search of the best smoked meats. Shane approaches life with eyes open wide. He was about to work on a dude ranch in Colorado, and he wanted to fill his belly with some good barbecue before heading off.

We left the traffic jam that's Scottsville Road and headed south of Bowling Green, and not far past the I-65 interchange the landscape shifts from concrete to greenery and you can breathe again. The humidity hovered over the treetops and cornfields as we drove the four-lane divided highway to our lunch at Split Tree Barbecue.

When I was a college student at Western Kentucky University in Bowling Green in the late 1980s, I used to pass Split Tree regularly on the way to visit friends in Tennessee. Back then Highway 231 was a two-lane road that wrapped and slithered over the knobs, and Split Tree was a small barbecue shack sitting by the road. When the state claimed the land for the road expansion, Jerome Wilson, proprietor, rebuilt in a grander style reminiscent of a hunting lodge. Animal parts, like the head of a wild boar, hang on the wood-paneled walls, and sturdy wooden-topped picnic tables fill two dining rooms with plenty of space in between, reminding me of German beer halls—groups of people sitting six to eight to a table with line after line of tables in an open space, creating a sense of community. When my brother Drew graduated from college, we had a family lunch at Split Tree after the ceremony, and I liked how the picnic table seating encouraged talking among tables.

Jerome Wilson opened Split Tree in 1981. He ran the original Split Tree shack for twenty years until the new road forced him to relocate. He learned to cook at an early age because he came from a family who shared cooking duties at home. His dad taught agriculture classes, and his mom worked in a factory, and every afternoon his mother came home from work and they hand-milked cows. Jerome and his siblings had to milk, too. But then his sister, who now works with him at the restaurant, "complained about having to fix the supper meal every night while mom was at the barn." Their mother listened to this complaining for a while, and then she devised a new system and sent Jerome's sister to the barn to milk cows and sent Jerome to the kitchen to cook supper. They had a three-week rotation of work duties. "We could all cook," Jerome said. "Whatever was in the freezer, it was open season."

Earlier in life, Jerome traveled the country a lot working construction and tried different barbecue styles. He learned the delicate art of smoking while working construction in Alaska. "An old feller up there taught me how to make squaw candy."

"Squaw candy?"

"It's made out of salmon. You smoke it for fifteen days, cold smoke, and you just keep enough smoke in there to keep the flies off. We converted an old outhouse into a smoker."

The old man also taught Jerome how to make a perfect brine using a sixteen-penny nail stuck into a potato. You add enough salt and stir it, and when the potato floats you put the fish in the brine and let it soak for three days, and then you hang the fish and cold-smoke it. The smoke pit was buried in the ground about fifteen feet away from the outhouse, and they ran a pipe from the pit to the outhouse, and by the time the smoke reached the outhouse it was "cold." They took shifts keeping the smoke rolling. The old man, who grew up in Sand Point, Alaska, said that if you didn't take the mother of the girl you wanted to court some squaw candy, then you didn't get a date.

Jerome designed his barbecue pit at Split Tree based on his Alaska salmon-smoking experience, although "Mine runs a lot hotter." He smokes Boston butts for eighteen hours. He loads the masonry pits at night and cooks every day. The fire gets up to 300° at night when he fires up the pits, and then it dies down through the night, but there are always coals in the pit. The masonry pit is so thick it never cools down totally.

I reminded Jerome that over twenty years ago I stopped by his shack and ordered a shoulder plate—thin-sliced shoulder in the "Monroe County" style cooked over hickory and dipped in vinegar-pepper sauce that I grew up eating—my primary idea of barbecue at the time—and he'd said curtly, "We don't *do* that." When I told this story now, Jerome grinned and said, "Every section of Kentucky it's cooked a little different. You get over around Tompkinsville and it's nothing but shoulder, and I personally don't consider that barbecue. That's *grilling*. Barbecue is slow, and you add a lot of flavor by using nothing but green hickory wood." He gets plenty of hickory from local loggers and uses about one and a half ricks weekly. He cooks only with wood, and cooks only spareribs, Boston butts, and whole chickens. "Boston butts are the best cut of meat, bar none," Jerome said. "It's just the right size, doesn't have any bone in it, and the flavor is better than ham or tenderloin."

This stripped-down approach to barbecuing yields some fine results, especially the barbecued chicken, which is seasoned with nothing but smoke. I normally avoid chicken at barbecue places, but I was tempted to taste this bird since it was one of only three meats on the menu. Shane and I made ourselves at home at one of those large picnic tables in the big open eating area off the main room where you place your order at the counter, and we shared a rib plate, chopped pork on hoecakes, and a half chicken. The side dishes at

Split Tree are simplified like the meat menu: baked beans, slaw, and potato salad. They also offer Golden Flake chips and fat whole dill pickles (contained in a jar on the counter). We chose to wash down our lunches with Styrofoam cups filled with crushed ice and delicious sweet tea.

Shane and I both loved the chicken. The skin during the five to six hours' smoking turned golden brown, and the flavor of that smoky skin, combined with the lush tenderness of the flesh, made us grunt and ooh and ahh and smack our lips with pleasure. Jerome smokes the birds whole and then cuts them after, so with a half chicken you get both white and dark meat—a drumstick, half breast, and wing. I went for the wing first to increase the crispy skin (read: tasty fat) to meat ratio, before Shane could get his greedy hands on it. Just kidding, Shane. You are a courteous, well-mannered young man. Ole Doc Berry was the greedy one at this table.

The spareribs had a deep smoky color and came steaming hot on the plate. Their smoke flavor was great, and the ribs in the meatier/fattier center part were tender, but the thin end pieces were tough and chewy. Because of this, the ribs weren't my favorite. But that just might be because these ribs were thinner than others. The chopped pork on hoecakes was also good, with chunks of well-cooked pork—about a cup of it—piled on a thin hoecake and drizzled with sauce, topped with another hoecake, best eaten in pieces with fingers (instead of trying to eat as a sandwich). The Split Tree "house special" is this same concoction smothered in their pork-infused barbecue beans. I reckon you might have to use a fork for that dish.

Split Tree has a one-size-fits-all sauce, a tangy and sweet tomato-based sauce with a considerable vinegar tang, reminding me of Memphis sauces. Jerome, who prepared each meal ordered, drizzled a modest amount of sauce on the chicken, ribs, and chopped pork. Plastic bottles of the sauce sit on the table if you want more. Jerome's sister, who took my order, said she made up gallons of sauce weekly. I also watched her flipping hoecakes on a flat iron behind the ordering counter.

At the end of our interview, I asked Mr. Wilson if I could see the custom salmon-smoking-inspired barbecue pits he'd designed, and he smiled and said, "Naw, I ain't gonna let that happen." Perhaps he thought I might steal his secrets.

Shifting gears away from the pit talk, Jerome told me that over twenty years ago Charles Kuralt, the traveling foodie, did a Thanksgiving special and chose Split Tree as one of the thirteen best places in the country to eat at.

And you should eat there, too, and when you do, give that chicken a try. A half bird set me back a reasonable $3.95 in the summer of 2011.

Open: Monday–Saturday, 10:00 a.m.–9:00 p.m.; Sunday, 11:00 a.m.–9:00 p.m.

115 Wilson Road; 270-842-2268

Scottsville

Hickory Hill Barbecue

Here's yet another reason why I've decided to feature barbecue places that have been open for only a short time. Ron Keen, who along with his wife, Sue, runs this small barbecue shack three miles west of Scottsville, serves up some of the best deeply smoked ribs I've ever had, and his pork pulled from butts smoked low and slow over hickory is hands down some of the best you'll eat in south-central Kentucky.

I visited during a blistering one-hundred-degree-plus Saturday noon on Labor Day weekend. I'd just filled my little Ford Ranger with eleven hundred pounds of pig and chicken feed from Hoover's feed mill nearby on Shores Road off Highway 585, where a big community of Amish folks lives, and the Ranger was sagging as I pulled up the hill into the gravel parking lot of Hickory Hill. Most people with sense were getting their barbecue to go and eating it in an air-conditioned room somewhere, but I ordered a quarter rib plate with barbecue beans and potato salad, plus an "island BBQ" sandwich, and carried these treasures over to one of three picnic tables shaded by big umbrellas arranged in front of the small trailer that serves as the kitchen.

I just had to try the island BBQ, because I had read on Ron's website (which he developed himself) that he actually puts a slice of pineapple on this pulled-pork sandwich, along with a special sauce. Hard to pass up something as quirky as that in south-central Kentucky. I was reminded of Big Kahuna Bar-B-Q in Leitchfield and owner Frank Hewes's Polynesian-influenced beef and sauces, and felt it oddly coincidental that two barbecue upstarts in this region tinkered with flavors of the tropics, using fruits like mango in sauces, adding pineapple, and so forth.

I sat at that picnic table, the dry heat blazing down, and popped the top of the Styrofoam box of the rib plate. Inside, hallelujah! Three bones of thick meaty ribs, dark bark on the outside, glazed with a medium-thick hot sauce of a color leaning toward red wine and studded with red pepper flakes. I had requested the hot, but they also offer a mild, a sweet, and a hickory bourbon sauce that's not on the menu (I found out about this later when I talked with Ron after eating the ribs and sandwich and finding them wonderful). The ribs were super smoky. Ron smokes only with hickory, and whatever he does to his "voodoo" ribs, well, let's just say the clichéd thing—it's magic. The meat of these thick ribs was flavored throughout—not just on the surface—and that smoky pungency was just what I want in a rib. It might be too much for some folks, but I knew when biting into them that I was eating a rib cooked over real wood and tenderized by time and slow cooking. The meat clung to the bone and had some chewability. Barbecue is finger food, so when pulling a rib bone away from the quarter slab (Ron sliced them partly through to aid the pulling but didn't separate them totally, which made for a pretty presentation), I got sauce all over my fingers and palms. Fortunately, there was a wet nap included with the plastic fork and napkin packet that came with the meal.

The pork sandwich was one of the strangest concoctions I've had in my barbecue travels, but it was real good: a heap of very smoky pulled and chopped pork on a regular white-bread bun topped with an ample but not overwhelming amount of a sweet and tangy yellow sauce tasting of pureed fruit and crowned by a heated ring of pineapple. The sandwich was sweet, and the deliciousness of the pork showed through. The pineapple complemented the smokiness of the pork. It was a lot of sandwich—a big heavy hunk in my hand.

When I ordered, I said, regarding the island BBQ sandwich, "I'm fond of bark, so if you want to work some of that in there when he pulls it, that'd be good." I was noting the lack of bark on the sandwich when I spied an extra Styrofoam container setting off to the side, and I said, "Oh, that must be sauce." I opened it up and found a nice little prize—barky pork pulled from the exterior of the butts. When I ordered and said I liked bark, I expected it on the sandwich, but I was really glad to get it this way, unadulterated by sauce, because that pork was as tender and smoky as any I've eaten. I savored these tasty morsels and said, "Oooh, Lord," and licked grease from my fingers. Really, it tasted much like what I prefer when I smoke up butts at my home—an intense hickory smoke flavor with seasonings throughout the meat (I often use injections of apple juice and other spices), tender and moist. The scoop of potato salad was also good, with a flavor more sour (from chopped dill pickles) than sweet, and the BBQ beans were pork and beans pepped up with barbecue sauce and shreds of smoked pork. In addition to the pulled pork and ribs, you can get (if the cholesterol police are on your trail) pulled smoked chicken or a barbecued chicken breast.

A hot breeze blew across the property and flapped the American flags hanging from the barbecue trailer. People pulled into the gravel parking lot and walked up to the ordering window. A couple on a Harley blasted down the highway, the woman's headband flapping behind her. One man ate a pork sandwich on the covered porch of the trailer because he didn't want to get sauce inside his new car; his wife waited in the air-conditioned car. Country music played out of speakers mounted high on the trailer.

While I was eating the island BBQ sandwich, Ron came out of his trailer and asked me, "Everything okay?" and I said, "Yeah, everything's great. Can I talk to you a second?"

That second turned into a half hour. We talked barbecue. Ron admitted that the ribs weren't baby back (what's listed on the menu) because his supplier from Nashville didn't have any, so he cooked spareribs instead. But the spareribs had been cut short so they could have fooled someone into believing they were baby backs. I actually thought they might have been the "extra meat" baby backs available these days.

Ron has cooked for family and friends all his life. In 2008 he semi-retired from his day job and decided with his wife, Sue, that they'd try serving to the public. They have a good location, being so close to the big Amish community, which sees a lot of traffic passing by, especially during the produce season of summer. He's developed a following of repeat customers from as far away as Nashville and Louisville and has even shipped barbecue to Memphis. "People come back and I recognize 'em, and I say, 'Are you back visiting the Amish?' and they said they came back to get barbecue." He said his work is a "labor of love."

I asked Ron how he got the idea for the island sandwich, and he said, "Well, I love the islands. I used to vacation near Hilton Head and Savannah. It's kind of the pork and pineapple thing that you'd see at a luau sometimes, that type thing. I tell people I can't get 'em on the beach, but I get 'em as close to it as I can."

A buggy driven by a young Amish woman passed out on Highway 100, and the clip clop of horseshoes pounding the pavement mixed in with the country music. I told Ron I got my produce from the local Brubaker family and my pig and chicken feed from Hoover's feed mill over on Shores Road, and he said the Amish folks stop by all the time to get the pork. Earlier, talking with the young man at the feed mill (who muscled hundred-pound sacks of feed into my pickup like nobody's business), I asked if he'd eaten the barbecue at Hickory Hill, and he said, "Yeah, I like it, but my little brother can't handle the spice in the dressing they put on it." I smiled at that—never heard of barbecue sauce called dressing before.

I asked Ron how business had been with the slow economy, and he said, "It's been great. A lot of times this parking lot is full and the field is full. You can't move." Hickory Hill is in the country, and Ron said that when people ate out there in the spring when everything was lush and green after all the rains, they said, "This looks like being in the Smoky Mountains somewhere."

Ron had to go tend his smokers, so I thanked him for his good work and looked around at the beauty of the place—the big dry field stretching out to a treed horizon—and watched the smoke billowing from the stack of an iron cooker out back. And I called it good.

Hickory Hill is open only two days per week, seasonally. The Keens are operating on the premise that if you starve people of barbecue for five days per week, then they'll come running when it's available. It looks to be working for them.

Open: Friday–Saturday, 10:00 a.m.–6:00 p.m. (closes for winter in October or November—call ahead)

2791 Franklin Road (west of Scottsville on Highway 100); 270-622-0508

www.hhbarbeque.com

Hickory Hill Barbecue's Kentucky Bourbon Barbecue Sauce

I asked Ron Keen to share a recipe with us, perhaps his far-out "island" barbecue sauce, and here's his response: "I think I choose not to disclose my island sauce recipe, as it is quite an exclusive for us. However, I will submit for your use my recipe for our Kentucky bourbon barbecue sauce. Our baby back ribs with Kentucky bourbon sauce have gained a reputation I'm proud of!" Thank you, Ron and Sue Keen.

¾ cup of your favorite Kentucky bourbon
½ onion, minced
4 cloves garlic, minced
⅓ cup apple cider vinegar
⅓ cup red wine vinegar
2 cups ketchup
¼ cup tomato paste
½ cup brown sugar
½ teaspoon ground black pepper
½ teaspoon salt
2 tablespoons liquid smoke
¼ cup Worcestershire sauce
⅓ teaspoon hot pepper sauce
⅓ teaspoon ground cayenne pepper
2 teaspoons vegetable oil

Heat vegetable oil in a skillet over medium heat. Add the onion, garlic, and bourbon. Simmer for 10 minutes or until onion is translucent. Mix in the remaining ingredients and bring to a boil. Reduce heat to medium low and simmer for about 20 minutes. Run through a strainer and enjoy!

Smoke Shack BBQ

If you want good barbecue in Scottsville, unbuckle your kilt (you'll need the extra space at the waistline) and visit this true takeout shack, where you can smack your lips on the best hickory-cooked chicken and sliced pork shoulder within the city limits of Scottsville. They also serve shredded pork from Boston butts, pork spareribs, pork tenderloin, and hickory-grilled hamburgers and hotdogs.

My anticipation was high as I pulled in at 10:50 on a Thursday morning and saw smoke billowing out the back of the small, brick, ranch-style building, which looks like a converted duplex, next door to the Redemption Worship Center. Across the road stretched an open field full of rolled hay and a line of mature trees. I sneaked a peak out back and saw a huge pile of split hickory and several dozen huge bundles of hickory boards and a dumpster-sized firebox for firing this wood down to coals. The wood and smoke—and probably the fact that I'd eaten only a small bowl of granola for breakfast—stirred my stomach.

I walked inside a small air-conditioned room furnished with a small table and three chairs, another table with two chairs, a standup cooler stocked with Coca-Cola products, and a counter for ordering. The menu hangs on the wall. Cinderblock walls are painted white. The shack was sparsely decorated except for a calendar photo of the Scottsville Police Department, a rack of Lay's potato chips, and Smoke Shack T-shirts (for sale). A young woman asked me what I wanted, and I said I needed a little time. Only one other customer stood at the counter. I stood back and pondered the choices, and then a bell went off and the door opened and four men wearing yellow safety vests, like from a road construction job, walked in, followed by a big man in overalls.

I'd missed my chance for quick ordering, so I took a chair and looked over the menu, and the door chime kept dinging as more and more men filed into the place and stood in line to order. The men all talked in the thick Allen County drawl, and their orders sounded something like this: "Give me a half chicken plate sprinkled," or "I want a shoulder plate dipped." In the local lingo—and you find the same thing next door in Monroe County, where the owners are from—"sprinkled" means that your meat will be drizzled with a vinegar-pepper sauce, "dipped" means they dunk or ladle sauce over your meat, for a hotter peppery flavor. I noted that most of these men ordered shoulder plates and chicken plates. That should have told me something. Pay attention to the locals.

Finally the swarm of men left and I was able to order. The menu says that ribs aren't ready until 11:00 a.m., and since it was right then 11:00, and because I'm a sucker for ribs, I ordered a rib plate with vinegar slaw and potato salad—despite my hearing the locals ordering chicken and shoulder. The rib plate set me back $7.50, very reasonable. I sat at the unoccupied table in front of the ordering counter, by a window looking out onto the blacktop driveway. From the window you can see the Dairy Queen and the U.S. Bank up on Highway 100. Smoke Shack sits down an incline from the highway. I imagine that many folks driving by on that busy highway are beckoned down the hill by that beautiful smoke rolling out the back.

You can get all the meats—even the ribs—as a sandwich or a plate. A sandwich just comes with two slices of white bread. A plate comes with a choice of two of the following barbecue standards: baked beans, vinegar slaw, mayo slaw, or potato salad. I opened the Styrofoam lid and discovered a steaming hunk of spareribs covered with a piece of aluminum foil (apparently to keep the white bread from getting wet). About bread: I don't eat white bread often—certainly not if I have to save belly space for food much better than white bread—and I noticed that you can get two hoecakes added to your order for a mere 25¢. The hoecakes looked good. If I wanted bread, I'd go that way. They smoke Boston butts for eight hours for their shredded pork sandwich, which you can get on a bun or cornbread.

The ribs were darkened nicely by the smoke. I lifted a bone and it pulled right out, telling me that the ribs were probably wrapped in foil. But the flavor was really good—the smoky rich taste of pork rib mixed with a tomato paste–like sauce. The helping was a generous five bones plus a hunk of flap meat (if you've cooked spareribs at home, you know what I'm talking about). The flap meat was tasty but tough. I liked the ribs. The texture was too soft for my liking, but the meat tasted rich, salty, and smoky. I licked the sauce from my fingers and was happy. As for sides, the potato salad was creamy with chunks of potato and the distinctive sour flavor of pickle juice, and the vinegar slaw was finely chopped crispy cabbage and carrots, appropriately tangy.

After the satisfaction of the rib plate, I tried the shoulder, tenderloin, and half chicken, and then I understood why the local men were ordering so much chicken and shoulder. The half chicken worked like a sponge to soak up the hickory smoke and vinegary pepper sop that Cliff Smith, the pit master, mops on during three hours of cooking over hickory coals. Cliff also sprinkles a seasoning salt onto the chicken from a shaker jar, which works well with the smoke and vinegar. The result is truly outstanding smoked chicken. The slices of shoulder are just what I want from Monroe County–style barbecue: thinly sliced ovals of pork with a band of fat ringing the leaner meat, cooked over hickory to the point of being tender but not dry, and the flesh takes on a darker hue. I like it dipped with sauce on the side. Smoke Shack's sauce tingles on the lips; I know because it's tingling mine right now, as I brought some home with me for additional "research." I love my hobby.

As for the pork tenderloin, I have mixed feelings about it. First, I think tenderloin isn't the best meat for barbecue, as it's too lean, and this shows, because the pretty strips of white tenderloin meat were dry, especially when not wetted with dip sauce. But—and this surprised me—some pieces of the tenderloin were darker than others, like getting both white and dark meat on a chicken, and like a chicken's fattier thigh and leg meat, there were pieces of darker meat in the tenderloin that were moister. These darker pieces soaked up more of the vinegar sauce and raised my assessment of it, but you have to love the vinegar sauce to enjoy a piece of meat soaking in it. I wouldn't want well-smoked meat smothered in a thick tomato sauce, but I'm more tolerant of a liberal dousing of vinegar sauce, at least when the meat is smoked sliced shoulder in the Monroe County style and the less fatty tenderloin.

Back at the grill, Cliff flipped pieces of shoulder and big three-quarter-pound hamburgers and drizzled them with vinegar sop. The meat cooks about one foot off the smoldering hot coals that Cliff brings in from outside with a shovel. Cliff said that shoulder is the biggest seller. He'd been tending the meats for five years in 2011—but apprenticed a lot longer than that—and Smoke Shack has been open since 1995.

It's a family business that first started in Gamaliel in Monroe County under the name of Uncle Bo's. They operated there for five years before moving to their current location because there was a desperate lack of barbecue in Allen County. Now they are the only deal in town, which seems good for business, judging by the healthy customer flow on this Thursday lunch hour.

Cliff said they used to be even busier before several factories left town for cheaper labor in Mexico. They used to have a G.E. plant and a Sumitomo factory, but both closed their Scottsville operations. Still, the place seemed well patronized, and Misty Dodson, who took my order and has worked at Smoke Shack for thirteen years, confirmed that, yes, business had been good on this

Side Dish: Allen County Amish Country

Smoke Shack BBQ is located just south of Scottsville, and if you continue west on Highway 100, which splits into Highway 585, you'll find yourself in the thick of beautiful agricultural country where many Amish folks have settled. One August afternoon I drove to Hoover's Feed Mill at 1013 Shores Road to buy feed for my two Duroc hogs, the roads twisting through some of the most beautiful land I've seen, and saw roadside wagons filled with watermelons and cantaloupes with signs posted on them—"2 cantaloupes for $1"; "Watermelons $1 each"—but nobody was around selling: it was the honor system. Mimosa trees lined both sides of the road, and I passed fields of corn and some tobacco patches, a rare sight in Kentucky these days. The country is populated with modest homes, with stacks of wood standing outside.

After getting my load of feed, I visited the Thomas Brubaker family down the road, who live a *Little House on the Prairie* life in the twenty-first century. I've subscribed to the Brubakers' CSA (Community Supported Agriculture) for the past three years, writing them a check in early spring for the promise of organic fresh vegetables and some fruit weekly for twenty-eight weeks, and I just wanted to stop in and say howdy. The whole family was there, children all over the place. Thomas's son packed me a box full of red and white potatoes, a big bag of fresh corn, and a gallon of goat's milk. And then I drove on down the road, where I met a horse-drawn buggy. A teenage girl held the reins, and she was pulling a wagon filled with cantaloupes. I passed a small sign advertising "Shoe repair" hanging from a mailbox at the end of a gravel drive, and another saying "Harness shop." Horse droppings lay in the road. It's a peaceful country, as close to a bygone era as you're likely to find in this fast-paced world. It makes for a real pleasurable Sunday drive. But if you want animal feed at Hoover's Feed Mill or produce from the Amish folks, come Monday through Saturday, because they take resting on the Lord's Day seriously.

sultry August Thursday. Misty was a real ambassador for the shoulder and chicken and vinegar sauce, and she said all their side dishes are homemade.

Cliff has been working there since 1999, since he was fourteen years old. His sister and brother-in-law, Chasity and Matthew Wilson, are the owners. Misty is his brother-in-law's cousin. And Cliff's wife works the counter. Confused yet? I sure was. I said, "Sounds like a real family affair," and Cliff said, "Most are family. A couple of girls who work here ain't," and Misty added, "We treat 'em like family though."

By the time I left Smoke Shack, I felt like I'd been treated like family, too.

Open: Wednesday–Saturday, 10:00 a.m.–7:00 p.m.
100 Holt Drive; 270-237-5629

Pig

Porky Pig Diner

An eatery in a community named Pig that calls itself the Porky Pig Diner must have barbecue, right?

Well, yes, it does, but one kind only: pulled pork from Boston butts cooked seven to eight hours with indirect heat on a steel smoker beside the store. Calvin Durham, who along with his wife, Ramona, runs the diner, can smoke two hundred pounds (about twenty-four butts weighing eight pounds each) at a time. The smoker was cold when I visited, and I asked Calvin how often he fired it up. He said in the fall, maybe once per week; in the summer, two to three times per week. Fortunately, pork butts are a cut of meat that holds well after cooking; it's pretty forgiving about reheating. Calvin uses hickory wood to smoke the butts for three and a half hours, then double wraps them in foil for another four hours of cooking. "You're done smoking after three hours," Calvin said. "It's absorbed all it's going to take." Sometimes they use a little apple wood, sometimes wild cherry. "There's a lot of hickory in Edmonson County," Calvin said.

And the pulled-pork sandwich I ate (along with big, crispy, seasoned, beer-battered fries and baked beans) was good: big pieces of tender, smoky, salted meat layered on a bun lightly toasted on the inner sides. The sauce is—in Calvin's words—"a sweet, zesty hickory-mesquite flavor."

People travel all the way from Elizabethtown (about one hour north) to get the catfish at Porky Pig. "That's my #1 seller," Calvin said. "My barbecue is second in line." Sometimes they run specials of other smoked meats, like smoked chicken and a two-inch-thick pork chop on Saturdays if the weather is good for outdoor smoking. There's indoor smoking as well—of the tobacco kind. These rural eateries and markets resist the indoor smoke ban of cities.

The dining room is decorated with plentiful pig art, including a sparkling golden pig a Western Kentucky University professor just sent them back from a trip to China. The professor stops at the diner when taking students on field trips to Mammoth Cave—and has even given them extra credit for eating at Porky Pig. There's a small gift shop off the main dining room.

I asked Calvin what got him into the restaurant business. "Stupidity," he said, laughing. Actually, he had been driving a truck for years and in 1995 decided to open a place that "served food like I wanted to eat instead of what I'd been eating for the last twenty years [on the road]. So we went to serving home-style cooking."

Calvin and Ramona have received some good press over the years. "We've probably had 2 million pictures took here from tourists," he said, "and we had a newspaper out of Cincinnati here, and one from New York here, and we're in two or three different books. One is called *Passing Gas*." (That's a cross-country photo book featuring towns with quirky place-names.) He added that Western Kentucky University has probably had a hundred students do projects on Pig. The university has one of the strongest photojournalism programs in the USA, and they send students out on shoots. Pig (both the community and the diner) offers the kind of rural Kentucky charm that can make good stuff for photos.

An endearing feature of the Pig diner is Pound Hound, a chunky basset hound that lounges on the porch. "He showed up at someone's house down the road," Calvin said, "then he wandered up here. So we took him back, and he came back, and we took him back again, and he came back, and one of the boys who comes in here took him home with him, and forty-five minutes later he was back. Timmy said, 'Well, he's not going to stay here [at his house] so leave him up there,' and he's been here ever since." Pound Hound has good instincts. He gets well fed at the diner and also receives plenty of attention from customers.

You can get well fed there, too.

Open: Monday–Thursday, 6:00 a.m.–7:00 p.m.; Friday–Saturday, 6:00 a.m.–8:00 p.m.; Sunday, 7:00 a.m.–3:00 p.m.

125 Park Boundary Road; 270-597-2422

Munfordville

Big Bubba Buck's Belly Bustin BBQ Bliss

And the award for the best-named barbecue shack goes to . . .

This shack just east of I-65 cracks me up, blowing the Kitsch-O-Meter sky high. A hand-painted sign out front reads, "BBQ OPNE," with the N painted backward. The sign leans against a rusted old farm tractor, above which flies Old Glory. Various smokers clutter the property, including a large one made from a natural-gas tank with bits of metal welded to it to make it look like a pig, with a snout (from a baked bean can) and a tail (a shock spring from a 1948 fire engine), eyes painted on, and eyelashes made from the tongs of a concrete rake.

Inside are some small folding tables with assorted nonmatching chairs. Two large American flags hang from one wall, and a cross hangs between them, along with the Ten Commandments mounted behind the ordering counter. Pig art lines a shelf high up on the wall and decorates the top of a refrigerator. A piggy clock keeps the time. A flat-screened television plays loudly. Blue carpet covers the floor, and pine paneling covers the ceiling. A sign says, "Sorry, this is not fast food. We cook to order. Thanks. Signed, Big Bubba."

And yes, there's that wonderfully alliterative name.

They sell T-shirts, pies, jellies, and butter. They've shipped barbecue sauce all the way to Puerto Rico and T-shirts to Australia. The menu includes ribs, pork sandwiches, sliced shoulder, fried pork chops, fried bologna, and a barbecue taco. Side dishes are extensive: potato salad, pinto beans, collard greens, fried corn, fried okra, fried green tomatoes, sweet potato fries, fried squash and zucchini.

I waited for my meal as Rocky Balboa fought Mr. T. on the television. Big Bubba's has been written up in the *Trucking Times,* a newsletter for truck drivers. Being so close to I-65, a busy trucking route linking the North with the South, Bubba's gets 95 percent of their business from truck drivers.

The chopped brisket sandwich came without sauce on a regular hamburger bun. The meat was tender with a lot of fat mixed in and good bark on the outside. The flavor was smoky and fatty—real good. The pork sandwich was sauced lightly, heaped on the bun. I wasn't a big fan of the sandwich, as it wasn't very smoky and had a sloppy joe flavor, and I'm just not into that. The richly flavored collard greens were salty, with meat cooked in, and the sweet "tater" fries were crunchy and sweet. I liked both side dishes a lot.

"We cook all year long," Amanda (who goes by "Dixie Darling" on the CB radio), explained. "Blizzards, tornados, ice. We chiseled ice off the grill doors just to get in to cook." Ribs are the #1 seller, followed by the sliced shoulder and shredded pork sandwich. I asked Amanda what she likes best, and she said, "The hickory-smoked Cornish hen."

"That's not on the menu," I said.

"Naw, it's a specialty. I like that and the beef brisket. And the banana pudding. If we don't have banana pudding, they will not come in and eat." Meaning the truckers.

Briskets smoke eighteen to twenty-four hours. Boston butts—she said, "I put them on this morning and they'll be ready about this time tomorrow afternoon." In other words, a long time. They cook everything on homemade smokers—that outdoor pig art fashioned from steel cylindrical tanks—keeping the heat going through the night with charcoal and adding slow-burning hickory for additional heat and smoke. The baby back ribs go right on the pit with no rubs or sauces. Just meat and hickory smoke. The ribs I tried were very tender and went well with their super-hot sauce. While the sweet potato fries come from a food-service company, the zucchini, green tomatoes, and corn come from their own garden.

When they first started, Robert "Bubba" Chapman had $200 in his pocket. He bought a case of Boston butts, and they set up for the annual Civil War Days. Locals loved it and asked for more. So they built a trailer and rented a lot near McDonald's and sold out of the trailer for three years. They made enough money to move the trailer to the current location, and a year later they built the dining room on. Then they added bathrooms.

It's a family business. Amanda is Bubba's sister-in-law, having married "Little Bubba." Additionally, there's Bubba, his mom, his wife, and the babysitter—the original working crew. Their truck-driving customers are loyal. Amanda said, "If they know they are going on vacation or getting laid off, they'll call and tell us, 'Hey, I won't be in next week,' or 'I won't be in for two weeks,' because we're pretty much family, and if they don't come in on their regular time then we don't know what happened to them."

In one such case, a regular trucking customer who came in often to get a catfish taco with hot barbecue sauce on it had a wreck near his home near Atlanta. The wreck shattered both of the man's knees and broke his neck. The man's wife got up in the truck looking for numbers for the trucking company so she could tell them what happened for insurance purposes, and the only number she could find in the truck was the one for Bubba's. Well, she called. Bubba answered.

She said, "Who is this?"

"This is Robert Chapman. I own Big Bubba's barbecue in Munfordville, Kentucky."

"Well, my husband is a regular customer of yours. He gets the catfish taco. With the hot sauce."

Amanda, telling this story, said, "Well, we knew exactly who she was talking about."

The woman said, "My husband's been in an accident and this is the only number I could find in his list of important numbers."

So, the folks at Bubba's went and bought a card, and they all signed it, and Bubba shipped the man a bottle of sweet and hot sauce, and the man's wife bought a case of catfish and some taco shells so she could make him catfish tacos.

I love that story.

On a return trip to Big Bubba's, I ordered ribs during a weekday lunch hour. This time they were spareribs instead of baby backs. I got them to go and ate them down by the Green River at a park in Munfordville. These ribs were a bit tough, as spareribs tend to be if not cooked long enough. And they didn't have the super-hot sauce I tried (and loved) on my first visit. This gives me reason to return, to see if the chewy spareribs were a fluke.

Whatever the case, I recall fondly that initial meal I had at Bubba's, and Amanda's great storytelling, and the homemade side items, and the flavorful brisket and very good baby back ribs. We'll just have to give them another try. You should, too. The place and people are pretty unforgettable.

Open: Monday–Friday, 10:00 a.m.–10:00 p.m.; Saturday–Sunday, 10:00 a.m.–8:00 p.m.

U.S. 31 West; 270-307-8309

Uno

Mama Lou's Bar-B-Que and Gifts

The commercial district of Uno has seen better days. The few buildings that once held businesses now stand quietly closed, home to spiders, except for one wonderful exception—Gerald and Wanda Judd's conversion of the old Uno general store into one of the best home-cooking little barbecue joints around, in business since March 10, 2010, and going strong.

My companion (now wife) Elisa and I arrived at Mama Lou's at 1:00 p.m. on a Thursday. We were impressed by the number of vehicles parked up and down the highway. Across the road, a healthy field of August corn stretched to the horizon. The Clear Point Cumberland Presbyterian Church stands next door, and a weathered tin-roofed tobacco barn behind the store adds to its rural rusticity. I'm glad we arrived when we did, because we got the last of six tables, and then some other folks came in and had to wait for a table, and the front door kept donging as others walked in to get carryout orders, including a group of young Amish fellows who occupied a vacant table and played the triangular "I.Q." game with the golf tees while they waited on their to-go food. An extensive mug collection (not for sale) lines the shelves along the walls. Some of the gifts for sale include handmade soaps and "goat milk products." At a nearby table, a woman smoked a cheap cigarillo. I guess Uno doesn't cotton to smoking bans like some larger fancier towns. Kentucky does rank near the top of the list of states in tobacco usage—and we use all

Side Dish: Kentucky's Curiously Spoken Place-names

I was eating at Mama Lou's in Uno and talking with owner Gerald Judd when I asked him a question about the history of the little rural berg, pronouncing it *OOO-no*, and he smiled and answered my question by calling it *YOU-no*.

Kentucky offers a wonder of creative takes on the English language. We especially love twisting European names into our own Kentucky brand of English. I grew up near the rural community of Etoile in southern Barren County. *Etoile* is a French word meaning star, pronounced by the French as *e-TWA* (or something like that). Locals, of course, pronounce it *EE-tull*. I've heard some call it *EE-toil*, but that final syllable comes out more like *ull* than *oil*.

Speaking of which, my uncle Terry once had car trouble in New England. He walked into an auto parts store and asked for a *kortuhvull* as in "I need a kortuhvull." The guy behind the counter just looked at him quizzically. Uncle T. tried again. No luck. He tried slowing down, saying, "Kort-uh-vull," but the New Englander still didn't get it. About that time, someone else walked up to the counter and ordered *OY-yull*, and my uncle caught on and asked for a kwart of oy-yull, thus completing the transaction.

No surprise, but Kentuckians refer to Versailles, the French-named town west of Lexington, as *ver-SAILS*. There's a spot in the road in southern Grayson County named Moutardier. Locals call it *MOODY-deer*. In Hart County, there's a place on Green River spelled Rio, as in Rio Grande. What do locals call it? *RYE-o*. Seriously.

I love these revisions of proper pronunciations. In all fairness, it's the devilish French words that cause the most trouble. Sometimes Kentuckians do get it right, however. In Edmonson County you'll find the community of Chalybeate. For the life of me, I figured people would call this place *chally-beet*, but they don't. They pronounce it *kuh-LIB-e-it*, real close to the dictionary's directions.

kinds of it. Twist, plug, and shredded tobacco for chewing; various cuts of "dip," smokeless tobacco for tucking into the lip; pulverized tobacco called "snuff" for snorting through the nostrils; and of course various smokeable forms. The high ceilings of Mama Lou's, along with the air-conditioning and ceiling fans, helped filter the smoke.

We ordered a brisket platter with slaw and baked beans and a rib platter with green beans and fried potatoes. The food was served on heavy-duty paper plates, along with real (not plastic) forks and knives. I'm glad we chose the cornbread, because the perfectly browned huge wheels—about the size of a Frisbee golf disc—were as sweet and good as I've ever had. The green beans were just like Mama makes—and I mean my own mama, Linda Berry, who can cook up country grub as good as anybody. These aren't your health-conscious steamed skinny green beans but rather the broad kind stewed along with fatty pork until soft and rich. The fried potatoes were diced and peppered and cooked in oil until soft, reminding me of my grandmother's version. The baked beans are cooked with country-style crumbled sausage and have a pleasant mustardy taste. Five bones of extra-meaty baby back ribs with a sweet tomato-based glaze rounded out the rib platter, and the brisket platter came with six thinly sliced strips of brisket, also moderately sauced.

The sauces here are less vinegary than what I've found in far-western Kentucky, but also thinner than I've had in Kansas City and Chicago. Elisa, who'd eaten brisket down at two famous places in Lockhart, Texas, several months before, said that Mama Lou's brisket was exceptional. She even favored it over the brisket at Black's, one of the Lockhart restaurants, noting that Mama Lou's meat was moister. I also loved the brisket. It was smoky, tender, well seasoned, and juicy—just everything you expect from an exceptionally prepared brisket. The meat and fat pretty much melted in the mouth. A couple of the rib pieces—the very meaty outer portions—were on the dry side, but when I dug deeper into the fat closer to the bone, the meat was delectable. And some of the ribs were all-over tender, even the outer bark, which soaked up plenty of sweet hickory smoke. We loved all the side dishes and the brisket, and the ribs were also very good. There was nothing but bone left when we got done with them.

After eating we spoke with the Judds, who were sweet as can be. Wanda was our server, and she kept checking on us throughout the meal. She said they'd been serving five hundred to six hundred people weekly from Tuesday to Saturday, which is a lot for a small place that seats only twenty to thirty. They get Mammoth Cave traffic and have developed a following of local regulars who eat out on the deck on Friday and Saturday evenings when the weather is nice. One customer drives all the way from Mount Washington, up near Louisville, once each week to get hamburgers. I could see why when I saw the burgers being served nearby—real hand-shaped burgers smoked and served on Texas toast. The Papa Lou burger weighs in at twelve ounces, and a beautiful slice of red tomato was balanced on top of the one served at the adjacent table. They've had people driving up from Nashville and down from Bardstown and E-town (regional name for Elizabethtown). "We're really happy and blessed," Wanda said about their success during their first sixteen months of business.

The "daily special" is a one-pound potato loaded with sour cream, butter, shredded cheddar, *real* bacon bits (from thick-cut slab bacon they fry themselves), topped with six ounces of their pulled pork. It's a big seller. "Everybody loves it around here," Wanda said. "It's a meal in itself," Gerald added.

Wanda and Gerald put much thought into the menu when they opened in February 2010. "We're out in the boonies," Gerald said. "If you can't get the biggest attraction you can—if you just come out here and sell barbecue alone—then you're done. Because a lot of women don't like barbecue. They want breast of chicken. I can't sell salads simply because I don't have space for refrigeration. So we at least tell everybody, "If you're on a diet, you're probably in the wrong restaurant."

We all laughed at that one.

I said, "Thank goodness. And you can taste it in those green beans."

"We chop our own ham. We even make our own bacon bits—we fry our own bacon. I buy thick-cut hickory smoked bacon and fry it up two or three pounds at a time and I chop it by hand."

I complimented Gerald on the homemade sides, and he said, "Well, this area's raised on beans and potatoes and cornbread. So when we designed our menu, I told Wanda, 'We're not gonna do the little hash brown squares, we're gonna fix real live potatoes we peel and dice ourselves and fry 'em in a skillet like Mama did.'" He added, "In our beans we use fresh home-ground sausage; we don't use store-bought sausage."

I told him I loved the cornbread, and he said they'd gone through six pounds of cornmeal already that day. I said, "That was a healthy round of cornbread," and Gerald responded, "Well that's another thing—our philosophy here is that when you leave we want you to feel like you got your money's worth. If you still hungry, you tell us and we'll put some more on your plate. We have good food and we have service. If we don't stay on top of those two games out in the boonies, we're done."

At the end of our meal, Mrs. Judd asked if we wanted dessert—a slice of pecan or peanut butter pie, perhaps?—and Elisa and I just laughed and said, "Are you kidding?" We were stuffed to the gills with the big portions of meats and sides. Wanda joked that there's some dessert called a holy cow cake that she's thinking about revising into a holy pig cake. I thought about the pig-smoking Catholics of western Kentucky—about the long-smoked pork and mutton they serve up at their church fund-raisers—and thought Mrs. Judd was right on track with that name.

Gerald said they want people to come to their place and lay back. "Our employees sometimes just sit around in the dining room with customers," he said. "Life is extremely stressful. People need forty-five minutes off ever once in a while. So we want 'em to come out here and sit around and laugh and cackle and just have a big ole time. And we do. We look out here at one guy he might be sitting here one minute and over there the next, trading tables and seeing old friends. We got lawyers, executives, country folk, housewives, kids—you name it, they come here. And that's exactly what we wanted."

"We cook all our meats daily," Gerald said. "We don't freeze meat. We just don't take any short cuts at all. I got it ingrained in all my girls in the kitchen. *We don't take short cuts.* Period. Don't even let the thought cross your mind—if it does, go to the bathroom and smack yourself."

In addition to pulled pork, ribs, and brisket, you can get sliced shoulder cut three-eighths of an inch thick. "We sell a ton of shoulder," Gerald said. "I sell a couple of hundred pounds a week." You get two to three slices of shoulder on a plate, depending on the size. "I make a vinegar-based sauce just for the shoulder. They call it a Monroe sauce. I've got a variation of it, my own recipe."

Gerald won the best barbecue chicken award in 2010 at the Hart County fair. He's been selling chicken halves on Friday nights as a special. He's now thinking about smoking whole prime ribs for three hours and then cutting them and grilling the rib eye steaks. When we left that day at 2:30, Gerald was putting Boston butts on his big steel smoker for the next day's lunch.

Mama Lou's is right off Highway 31 East, due east of Horse Cave (my birthplace) as the crow flies. This is a gorgeous part of Kentucky. Just south of Mama Lou's is a produce stand called Dennison's Roadside Market, a big barn with two big greenhouses. Everything was lush this early August—tobacco in the fields and hanging in barns from the recent harvests, lots of field corn rolling through the hills. We drove by dairy farms and a livestock market. Come for the beautiful country and the excellent food.

Open: Tuesday–Saturday, 10:30 a.m.–7:00 p.m.
5112 South Jackson Highway; 270-786-4198

Glasgow

The Bar-B-Q Place

Some barbecue places are the kind of places you'd like to take your mama. The Bar-B-Q Place isn't one of these—unless your mama happens to ride motorcycles and enjoy stripped-down barbecue shack decor with cement floors and old refrigerators where they pop ice cubes from freezer trays and pour the sweet tea right from plastic gallon jugs into a plastic cup that says

CASH

EXPRESS

Loans

Checks Cashed

The Bar-B-Q Place serves mostly a takeout clientele, judging by my brief time sitting inside the one small eating area off to the side of the ordering window. Outside, a long wooden wagon full of hickory and oak blocks from a local sawmill serves as the best advertisement for the Place. Right next door, sharing the same red metal building, is Backcountry Archery Hunting Supplies. A covered tin garage houses a huge cast-iron cooking unit with two smoke pipes, made in Houston by Dave Klose's custom barbecue pit company. Several wooden picnic tables sit under a covered area by the front door, shaded in the afternoon sun.

Entering the Place, I approached a counter that lets you see right back into the kitchen. The menu above the counter is real simple. You can get plates or sandwiches of shoulder (sliced thinly and grilled in the local style), pork chop, shredded pork, chicken, and hamburger. The sides were written in marker on a white board: baked beans, green beans, turnip greens, fried taters, mayo slaw, vinegar slaw, tater salad, potato chips, or hash brown casserole. A plate gets you a meat and two sides. One of the side dishes, pinto beans, had been smudged off the white board when they ran out of them. The soft fried potatoes—steam fried in an old cast-iron skillet—are very popular, as are the baked beans and slaws. Photos of bands like Burly Cruz—country musicians with roots in Glasgow—hang on the wall. I'm guessing their name is a nod to the tobacco-raising culture of Barren County.

A gregarious big man wearing a headband greeted me when I walked in, "How ya doin' today?" in a booming, low-pitched, country-twanged voice. This is Kenneth Hawkins, owner and pit master. He whistled while he worked. I got a shoulder plate with hash brown casserole and turnip greens and took a table in the window-unit-air-conditioned seating area. The thinly sliced shoulder, dipped in a peppery vinegar sauce with more tomato and sweetness than I usually see in this area, was really tender and fresh, and the piping-hot hash brown casserole was very cheesy. The turnip greens were pungent and finely chopped. The hot dip sauce wasn't as spicy as dips at other places in town, like South Fork Grill, whose hot sauce catches in the back of the throat. People averse to spiciness could really get into this tasty sauce at the Bar-B-Q Place. Without the sauce, the shoulder reminded me of the rich taste of bratwurst, and three hefty pieces came on the plate. I could hardly stop eating it. The cold sweet tea was a perfect drink with the meal on this hot afternoon. I got two free refills of it—and I've more or less weaned myself from sweet tea except when I visit my parents, who always serve it with family meals.

I sat at one of four plastic card tables seating two each and was the only eat-in customer, but during my meal three other men came in to order take-out. One was greeted with a boisterous "Rustyyyyyyyyyyyyy!" by both Mr.

Hawkins and Michelle, the woman who cooked up and served the sides and made the sweet tea.

"It's home brewed," she said when I complimented the tea. "I boil 'em [the tea bags] in a little pan, like they did it way back when." A *Thunder Roads* motorcycle magazine is propped between the napkin holders and white-paneled walls, and framed sketches of different Harley-Davidson motors hang by each table. The ceiling is rough particle board that's been painted gray. Truly, the Place exudes *l'essence de barbeque shack*. Your mama may indeed like it if she has a penchant for shackiness.

I asked Mr. Hawkins for some information about his particular place (as opposed to the history of barbecue in the region), and he said, "*Particular* place? Why?" and burst out laughing. Then he said, "Dude, I can come up with a story," and laughed again.

Michelle said, "Once you get him goin' he won't shut up. He is a storyteller. He is a singer also, and so some nights you might come in and he be singing." At this, Mr. Hawkins cackled out laughing again.

As a young fellow, Hawkins worked at a garden center in Glasgow for ten years before deciding to open his own in Tompkinsville. "I got over there and there's barbecues on ever corner there is," he said. "Glasgow at the time had *one.*" That was in 1989. "In '92ish, I's thinking, *Well, the garden center isn't making me rich. Surely Glasgow can do with another barbecue*, so in spring of '93 I opened this up." He sold the garden center two years later and has been doing barbecue full-time in the same place since. "Not very exciting, is it?" he laughed.

Hawkins smokes Boston butts for ten to twelve hours. You can also get a half chicken or a boneless skinless breast. "They're not popular, but I still do 'em," he said, adding, "Round here, 90 percent is shoulder or shredded." The shredded, in the local style, is pulled pork with sauce already mixed in. On the wall I saw a handwritten sign that said

Going Home Special
feed a family of 4 for only
$12.99
8 pc. of shoulder or 1 pound of shred pork
2 large side orders of beans and slaw and
SUPPER'S DONE!

I said, foolishly (as if the sign didn't explain it well enough), "What's your going-home special about?" and Hawkins said, "Meat, couple of large sides, just for your small family. I mean, if you got four people my size that ain't ever going to feed 'em. But if you got your average American father and mother with one whole child and half of another, then"—and he burst out laughing again—"that'll cure 'em just fine!"

I asked Hawkins how long he intended to do this. "I've no intention of retiring. I mean, everybody needs to do somethin'. If you set around with nothin' to do, then you just wither away." At age fifty-two—and already having been in business in the same location for nearly twenty years—Mr. Hawkins is on the road to someday having one of the longest-running single-owner barbecue shacks in the region. He already holds that title in Barren County. Considering the great quality of the food and the friendly service, I expect the Bar-B-Que Place to be around as long as Mr. Hawkins wants to stay in the business.

As I left the shack, I noticed a wooden sign outside that said, "The best BBQ . . . in this *whole* building!" I smiled at that touch of modesty and humor. It seemed to tie in well with Kenneth Hawkins's down-to-earth hospitality and low-maintenance approach to restaurant decor. Nothing fancy—just good food at very reasonable prices.

Open: summer hours: Monday–Sunday, 11:00 a.m.–5:00 p.m.; winter hours: Monday–Saturday, 11:00 a.m.–5:00 p.m. (or until the meat runs out)

1499 Burkesville Road; 270-651-6266

Bar-B-Q Hut

In the late 1980s, a place called Granny's served up the first Monroe County–style shoulder I'd eaten outside of Tompkinsville. Located close to two major factories—Eaton Axle and R. R. Donnelley and Sons, a commercial printer—Granny's saw a lot of lunch business. I worked in the pressroom at Donnelley's right out of high school, and back then I often washed my ink-stained hands and rushed over to Granny's during the lunch hour, getting a sliced shoulder plate dipped hot. It was wonderful, this easy access to Monroe County–style barbecue—the only kind of barbecue I knew other than my Uncle Roy's slow-grilled kielbasas, tenderloins, half chickens, and sliced pork shoulder. But then the Dark Ages came to Barren County when Granny's closed and sat empty for three years, my source of regular barbecue fixes gone, like a thief in the night.

I'd already left my hometown for college when Granny's was reopened by Glenda and Betty Poynter, who changed the name to Bar-B-Q Hut. The newest owners, the Wilsons, have kept the Hut name and continue to serve up pork shoulder cooked on an open pit. They have a very comfortable seating area inside and also a drive-up window. Out back, slabs of hickory and a huge iron kettle for burning down wood to coals let you know you are in a good place. There's a sawmill nearby on Industrial Drive, right in town. No shortage of good-smoking hardwoods in this town settled by Celts. Glasgow hosted the International Highland Games in 2001, and each year kilt-wearing Scots and long-lost American cousins of kilt-wearing Scots converge at Barren River State Park to toss telephone poles, dance, and listen to good music.

I arrived around 3:00 on a Thursday afternoon, and Mrs. Jenny Wilson, who took my order, said she was hungry. They'd had a big lunch crowd and she hadn't yet eaten anything for herself. "Imagine," she said, "working in a barbecue restaurant and being hungry!"

On my way to the Hut, I passed First Church of the Nazarene, east of the town square in Glasgow, which had a sign by the road that read, "If you think it's hot now, die without Jesus," which really had me hankering for air-conditioning. I found it inside the Hut, along with nostalgic decor from old television shows like *I Love Lucy, The Andy Griffith Show,* and *The Three Stooges,* and a picture of two dancing pigs. Photos of Humphrey Bogart show just how cosmopolitan a barbecue place can be in Glasgow, Kentucky. You can bring your family to dine at the Hut, as the seating is ample—space for probably fifty people—and the atmosphere is super clean. Ceiling fans and air-conditioning keep things cool. Every time someone goes through the drive-through, a doorbell ding-dong goes off.

You order at one counter and pick up at another, but I went to the restroom and when I returned my shoulder plate was waiting for me at the table I'd chosen by a window. The shoulder with hash brown casserole and cowboy beans was served on a Styrofoam plate with plastic fork and two slices of white bread. Everything tasted fresh and homemade. I loved the cowboy beans, which had green pepper and hamburger meat mixed into sauced baked beans. The hash brown casserole (available on Wednesday, Thursday, and Friday) was salty but, if you like salt as I do, very flavorful and good. The shoulder tasted of mild smokiness and came without sauce; you add the hot or mild sauce as you wish from bottles on the table, but the meat tasted good without sauce. A normal plate gets you two pieces of shoulder, or you can get three pieces for an extra charge (a mere 50¢ when I visited). It was a real pile of food for the price ($6 in August 2011). The fat on the shoulder was softer than at other local places, like South Fork Grill, telling me it isn't cooked as long. The mild sauce was thicker than most local dip sauces and less buttery, with a lot of vinegar and pepper. The sweet sauce is a thicker tomato-based sauce with a liquid-smoke flavor. The hot sauce, my favorite, was strong on vinegar and pepper. It had a nice after bite and went well with the shoulder.

Regular side items are potato salad, baked beans, mayo and vinegar slaws, and French fries. Special sides, written on a white board, included the two I got plus white beans. Shredded chicken and chicken breasts were also listed on the white board as specials. Regular meats are shoulder, pork chop, shredded (pork), a "hossburger," half chickens, Polish sausages, and hot dogs. Meats come as sandwiches or with plates. From 4:00–7:00 on Fridays, they add fried catfish and rib eye steaks to the regular menu offerings. Catfish sales are really picking up through community word-of-mouth advertising.

As I ate, the drive-through stayed busy, keeping Mrs. Wilson from eating her lunch. Brother Jimmy Wilson, originally from Scottsville, runs the Hut along with his wife, Jenny. Brother Wilson pastors the Shepherd's House, a nondenominational church. He gets his smoking wood delivered by the Charles Watkins Lumber Company. Brother Wilson saws it up and they burn the wood on little racks in the firebox until the coals fall down into the bottom, and they shovel the coals up, bring them inside, and shovel them into the pits. The meats stand about seven to eight inches off the coals. "All of our food is open pit cooked," he said. "The grease drops down on the coals and goes *sssspppzzzzzzzzzz!* and smokes and the fans blows it right back up through it, and there's really never a flame under it."

When Brother Wilson told me he was a preacher, I said, "Well, looks like the good Lord has blessed your shoulder"—a line I'm pretty sure I've spoken before when talking with religious barbecue men—and he had sense of humor enough to laugh. He bastes and seasons the chickens as they cook. The hamburgers are fresh ground and hand patted daily, cooked on the same open pit as the shoulder. The smoked Polish sausage is served on a regular hot dog bun, and its popularity is picking up, but shoulder remains the #1 seller. The "pig pie" is cornbread topped with shredded pork and smothered in baked beans. Sandwiches are usually served on a bun, but you can get cornbread instead for no extra charge. Friday is the best day to get special side items not regularly on the menu, like the cowboy beans, white beans, green beans, and occasionally—"When I get my wife to do it," Brother Wilson said—homemade peach cobbler. He added, "We do good on Monday and Tuesday, but seems like everybody's taste buds start leaning towards the barbecue near the weekend."

A note on the "shredded" you see on the menu in these parts: beware. This isn't the same kind of shredded you'll find in the western counties of Kentucky. The "shredded" at the Bar-B-Q Hut is boiled Boston butts, pulled and mixed with a sweet sauce and served on a bun or cornbread. I'm not a fan of this style of shredded pork, as it's not barbecue. That's where I draw the line; meat that isn't smoked isn't barbecue. Addition of sauces does not barbecue make (stylistic shout-out to southern food expert John T. Edge's favorite syntactical habit). But locals prefer this stuff called "shredded" because they grew up with it, I reckon. I'm dissing my homeland here, but I think Barren County shredded pork doesn't hold a candle to the long-smoked whole shoulders of far-western Kentucky. Of course there may be places in Barren County that serve unsauced pork pulled from slow-smoked butts or shoulders. I haven't tried the shredded pork at every place in the county, as I usually go for the shoulder—the slices of butt that are actually grilled over coals, not boiled, for heaven's sake.

The Wilsons plan on staying in the barbecue business a good while. It's truly a family business—just Jenny and Jimmy, their son and daughter-and-law, plus one nonfamily employee. "It's hard work, long hours, greasy work, dirty work," Brother Wilson said. "You make money, but you don't make big money. You pay your bills, you have a little bit left over, and you live off that and get by. You can expect to survive and that's about all you can expect. It's kind of like preachin'—you got chicken one week and feathers the next," he said, and laughed.

While I was talking with Brother Wilson, a familiar-looking man walked in, and Brother Wilson said, "Well there's Mr. Tompkinsville himself!" and the man said, "Yeah! They rolled the doors open and let me out one more time."

"This is one of our faithful customers," Brother Wilson told me. "He says he lives in Tompkinsville but gets his barbecue in Glasgow here."

The man said, "They always say T-ville's got two main industries—car washes and barbecue. But, for the best-tasting barbecue, guess where I stop and take my food back home with? If you want barbecue that's addictive, stop here."

I asked what made this barbecue so addictive.

He answered, "You can't find potato salad like this anywhere. The mayonnaise slaw has a flavor that you'll not find duplicated. Then you get into the chickens. It's not hard on the outside, but tender all the way through."

I said, "You sound like his best salesman."

He said, "I'm a chemist—by nature. That's my job. I work out here at Donnelley's doing tests on ink and paper and other chemicals."

I said, "That's where I recognize you from. I'm Ken Berry's son, by the way. I worked at Donnelley's for a while."

The man then introduced himself as Ben Robertson. He said he was the oldest person working in the lab at the magazine factory, and he chalked up his longevity in the printing business to eating barbecue and drinking Monroe County water. "You live forever," he said. "The Lord's been good to me."

Before leaving, I tried the potato salad, which was truly superb—a creamy, rich salad of real potatoes, almost like mashed potatoes, with plenty of boiled eggs whipped in with something unctuous, probably butter. The vinegar slaw was really fresh and crunchy with sugar to balance the tart. And yes, the cowboy beans were as good as I've ever had in the baked bean department.

When I return to the Hut, I'm getting another shoulder plate with potato salad and cowboy beans and one of those Polish sausages. And I surely won't pass on the peach cobbler if Mrs. Jenny decides to make one.

Open: Monday–Tuesday, 10:00 a.m.–2:00 p.m.; Wednesday–Thursday, 10:00 a.m.–5:00 p.m.; Friday, 10:00 a.m.–7:00 p.m.
594 Reynolds Road; 270-659-2933

South Fork Grill

The shoulder at this roadside shack off Highway 31E is cooked over manufactured charcoal instead of cooked-down coals from hickory slabs, but it's still some of the best I've tasted. When I ordered at the little walk-up window, the woman who took my order asked if I like it hot, and I said, "Oh, yeah, very." Mr. Danny Spencer, the owner, fixed my plate, and he didn't disappoint, as the first bite of shoulder hit the back of my throat with an intense pepper pungency that made me cough.

I ate at one of two picnic tables underneath a covered awning outside this takeout shack. Flies buzzed around me. My shoulder plate was served in a Styrofoam container filled with three pieces of spicy sliced pork and a scoop of potato salad, a small Styrofoam container of baked beans, and two slices of white bread, with some hot dip sauce on the side. The walk-up window remained busy while I ate my meal, as did the drive-up window. The smoke from the roadside pits works as an appetizer, exciting the senses before even tasting the meats. This shoulder had a lot of black pepper on it, was really tender and pretty smoky. The meat dipped in the vinegary-pepper-fat sauce was wonderful, and like I said, it about took my breath away. The beans were sweet baked beans with bacon and onion mixed in. Really good. The potato salad was creamy with chunks of potato and sweet pickle and egg. The winner, though, was the pieces of shoulder, nicely browned and peppery with delicious fat. The meat had great flavor, even without the dip. And I loved the spicy dip sauce. I dunked my white bread into it.

Danny's shoulder and chicken grill is a heavy custom-built pit made out of a pontoon trailer. About two-thirds of it is a covered grill with welded iron for a roof. A sign on the back says, "Bar-B-Q Buggy," with a red stop sign announcing, PIG X-ING. The buggy makes me smile because we have lots of Amish folks in this area who mount caution triangles on the back of their black-painted horse-drawn buggies to help motorists see them at night. Danny's buggy, parked out by the highway and sending clouds of smoke into the sky, makes people brake for pork.

The traffic on 31E was heavy, and I watched the heat radiating from the smoker. The man tending it was sweating. Truck after truck pulled in as I ate, and it was an all-male clientele. A lot of men, pickup trucks, baseball caps, ningng.

and blue jeans. A young Barren County guy took a bench across from me and said this shoulder was his favorite around. He didn't like Honey's down the road. When I asked why, he said, "Don't know. Got a whang to it." He explained how he barbecues deer hams by cooking them in an underground pit in a big pan with seasonings.

Danny has been barbecuing on the local scene since 1995. His business used to be out closer to Barren River reservoir in the community of Haywood. He'd been at his current location for "about three and a half years" in 2011. He smokes Boston butts for twelve to fourteen hours over wood in a six-hundred-pound smoker behind the shack and cooks half chickens over coals, as he does with the shoulder. Thankfully, Danny offers both pulled (without sauce) and shredded (with sauce), so if you don't want your meat drowned in sauce, ask for pulled without. He does country-style ribs on Fridays only. Danny learned to barbecue from Wayne Chisolm, one of his old fishing buddies who owned one of the first barbecue joints in Glasgow about forty years ago. One Memorial Day weekend, they bought butts and cooked them up, and the business grew from there.

Danny told me he's the second person in Barren County to start serving shoulder to the public. Granny's was first. Ken Hawkins's Bar-B-Q Place came along next, followed by newer places like Moose's. For a brief time Danny tried selling north Alabama–style smoked chicken with a mayonnaise-

---

South Fork Grill's Vinegar Coleslaw

4 cups distilled vinegar
5 cups sugar
Pinch of salt and pepper
2 heads large cabbage, chopped
1 carrot stick, chopped
½ medium onion, chopped
¼ green pepper, chopped

Heat vinegar, sugar, salt, and pepper. Set aside and let cool. Add 7 cups cabbage mix to the cooled vinegar. Stir well and refrigerate. Makes 10–12 servings.

lemon white sauce, but it didn't take in Barren County. "You get away from shoulder, you in trouble," he said, testifying to the locals' devotion to the Monroe County style.

In addition to shoulder, South Fork offers deep-fried hot dogs, which curls my toes just thinking about it, and serves a United States' greatest hits of hot dog styles: Coneys with chili and cheese, Chicago style (my favorite), and New York style with kraut and mustard. Rounding out the menu are hamburgers, pork tenderloin, and what my father says is some of the best fried catfish around.

Open: Tuesday–Thursday, 10:00 a.m.–2:00 p.m.; Friday, 10:00 a.m.–"until we run out"; Saturday, 10:00 a.m.–2:00 p.m

2224 Scottsville Road; 270-659-4227

Monroe County / Tompkinsville / Gamaliel

Growing up in the agricultural and manufacturing county of Barren—designated in February 2007 by the *Progressive Farmer* magazine as the "best place to live in rural America"—I viewed eastern Kentucky as a place of outlaws, a rough-and-tumble culture of moonshiners, coal miners, banjo pickers, and subsistence farmers. I learned these hillbilly stereotypes from television, comic strips, and the movies. The stereotypes are partly rooted in reality. Eastern Kentuckians *have* done the backbreaking work of coal mining, and there's been plenty of moonshining in Appalachia as well. The book *More Mountain Spirits: The Continuing Chronicle of Moonshine Life and Corn Whiskey, Wines, Ciders and Beers in America's Appalachians,* by Joseph Earl Dabney, documents it.

This is a long-winded way of introducing Monroe County, which in ways feels like an eastern Kentucky county. It's a liminal space or hinge between central Kentucky and Appalachia. For instance, the town of Gamaliel lies near the Tennessee line—a stone's throw from the dinky beer shacks that serve the thirsty Kentuckians living in dry counties just across the border. When I was in high school, I heard stories of these joints: how Todd Clemmons, a wild classmate a couple of years older, drove down there to shoot pool for money stakes at Dink's, one of these beer dives. Southern Monroe County is a beautiful land of green rolling hills and weathered tobacco barns, cattle in the fields, and one-room country churches. It's also full of pickup trucks and a roughneck leave-me-be attitude, reminding me of how I imagined eastern Kentucky after hearing stories of Appalachia when I was young. David Arms, owner of Tompkinsville's Frances' Bar-B-Que, told me his father, a Monroe County dweller, was recently featured in a publication called *Cures What Ails Ye: Memories of Moonshining in Clay County, Tennessee,* compiled and edited by Friends of the Clay County, Tennessee Library, just down the road from Tompkinsville. The book tells the history of the region's illicit spirit makers. Quite a few of the old moonshiners, including David's father, are still living.

I've been "driving down to T-ville" since I was a boy. Well, I didn't drive then, but I rode with my parents over the roller-coaster hills that slither through Monroe County, which, along with Owensboro and Paducah, considers itself to be a "barbecue capital." Tompkinsville, the county seat, must have one of the highest per capita barbecue joint ratios in the USA: at present four regularly open places serve a town population of about twenty-six hundred. Of course they serve the county as well, and including Collins Barbecue in Gamaliel, the ratio is five barbecue places in a county of twelve thousand people. We drove down to T-ville to visit the Old Mulkey Meeting House, a log church built in 1804, and to eat the thinly sliced pieces of Boston butt grilled over hickory coals, "shoulder" in local parlance.

All the Monroe County joints serve similar items—some places just have more extensive menus. Your best bets are half chickens, thin-sliced ovals of Boston butt (listed as "shoulder" on the menu), and pork tenderloin. I've come around to tenderloin. It's leaner than I like, but the meat flippers in Monroe County (and in Cumberland County to the east) grill the tenderloins longer than the slices of shoulder, so the outside gets smoky—the closest thing to the long-smoked western Kentucky–style pulled pork I prefer. The vinegar dip adds needed moisture to the tenderloin. Also, the chickens cook for a few hours on the open pit, soaking up a good bit of smoke from the coals. All the places burn down hickory slabs to coals and shovel the coals underneath the grates that the meat sits on, except for Frances', which uses charcoal. The dip sauces are very similar at each place—a combination of vinegar, lard, black pepper, cayenne pepper, and salt—but each place tweaks these ingredients slightly for subtle differences in flavor.

A word of warning: Monroe County folk must love salt (as I do), because several items I tried, from side dishes to meats, were incredibly salty, even for me. One example was the smoked chicken at Frances'—a half chicken smoked slowly on a gas-wood hybrid cooker. The pork spareribs at Collins Barbecue were also really salty.

Vinegar also reigns supreme in this grilled-meats country, forming the base for the ubiquitous oily-peppery sops basted on meats during grilling and showing up in surprising places, like in the super-vinegary "barbecued eggs" (David Arms at Frances' claims to have originated this local oddity) and in the tart French-style green beans at Red Barn Bar-B-Q. So, if you like salt and vinegar, come to Monroe County and dig in.

I didn't eat every meat on every menu in Monroe County, but I did go wild at Frances' and selected brisket as one of three meats on the "mix plate," and I hardly recognized it as beef brisket: a pile of shredded meat soaked in vinegary sauce. If you dislike sloppy joe–style messy meats, then avoid the brisket and the menu item called "shredded," which is pulverized pork soaked in sauce. Both pack a lot of flavor, but don't expect naked brisket in the Texas tradition or pulled pork in the western Kentucky style.

For nonbarbecue pleasures in Monroe County, you can get a huge grilled hot dog at Collins Barbecue in Gamaliel. I ate mine dipped in their hot sauce and topped with crunchy vinegary slaw. And while in Tompkinsville, you really should stop by Dovie's Cafe and eat one of their famous breadcrumb-cut hamburgers fried in soybean oil, served on waxed paper. The thin burger patties float in the oil as they fry. They'll squeeze some of the grease out if you want, but no worries—there's plenty of flavor (and grease) left inside a *squozed* or *stomped* hamburger. And yes, you probably should try at least one barbecue egg, which comes—as David Arms jokes—from a barbecued chicken.

So here are a few of the places in Monroe County to get your shoulder fix. Eating in the restaurants and shacks can be fun, but if you are just passing through Monroe County, or if you live a far piece from it, I recommend getting a shoulder plate from at least three places and driving on down to the Old Mulkey Meeting House to have a sampler tasting at the picnic tables underneath the mature shade trees. And please note that the weekends are the best time to find these places open.

Just know that if you make a special trip to Monroe County or Cumberland County or Barren County to get barbecue, chances are you're going to be eating grilled meats. If you come with that expectation, you're less likely to be disappointed. I happen to love this barbecue style of grilling over hickory and sopping with vinegar sauce, as it takes me back to childhood. And when I've taken friends from out of state to eat at Smokey Pig in Bowling Green to get this style of barbecue, or taken them on road trips to Glasgow or Tompkinsville, they've always enjoyed it. It's good, and it's something particular to this small region.

Backyard BBQ

Randy Walden is the current owner of this barbecue establishment known as Paul and Nora's back in the early 1990s. That's when I'd travel down to Tompkinsville from my home county of Barren and sample the T-ville flavors. On one trip with my friend Marc Maggard, we walked into Paul and Nora's soon after they'd opened and I ordered a shoulder plate and asked the man to "dip the hell out of it."

He asked, "How hot you want it?"

"Hot as you can get it."

"I can get it pretty hot."

"Dip the hell out of it," I said, confident in my ability to take whatever heat he could dish out.

I don't know what kind of wicked magic that barbecue doctor did in Paul and Nora's kitchen that day, but that shoulder plate plumb near burned a hole in my head. Maggard and I took our Styrofoam plates of shoulder and beans and vinegar slaw down the road and popped them open at a quiet home construction site. It was summertime, and the sun beat down on us as we looked out over the cattle fields while biting into dip-drenched slices of pork shoulder. Sweat popped out on my forehead and my tongue went numb, and I kept eating the stuff after the endorphins kicked in. It's a good memory, and I'm amused now to think what a kick that barbecue man must have had while fixing our plates. I think his name was Rosie. I imagine him saying, *I'll show these boys a thing or two about hot.*

In late 2011 I returned. The dining area has expanded and been spruced up, but the recipes remain the same under Randy's ownership (he's the grandson of Paul and Nora). Shoulder remains the biggest seller, but they also grill pork chops, hamburgers, chicken breasts, tenderloin, half chickens, and hot dogs. Country-style ribs, thickly sauced shredded pork, and ham round out the menu. Side dishes are basic: two kinds of slaw, beans, tater salad, and fries. A BBQ egg—a boiled egg pickled in Monroe County vinegar dip sauce—costs 50¢.

Pit worker Jesse Bowman gave me a tour of the cooking area out to the side of the restaurant. Smoke filled the sky as they burned down slabs of hickory in a big stove. They cook on an open pit using burned-down hardwoods, mostly hickory. Chicken halves cook for three hours on a normal day, although they can "be done" in two and a half hours on a busy day. Shoulder slices can cook in ten to fifteen minutes on a hot grill on a busy night, but twenty to thirty minutes if not rushed. All the side dishes but the fries are homemade.

The hot-dipped shoulder plate—setting me back only $6.50—came with three slices of grilled shoulder swimming in spicy-oily vinegar sauce, yellow potato salad, baked beans, and two slices of white bread served in Styrofoam with a plastic fork. The BBQ egg was pickled, very salty, and tasted of the dip sauce. The dining room is very clean, with high-backed booths, wood paneling, and outdoorsy scenes of birds, deer, and hillsides. At the Saturday lunch hour most of the eaters were men—no surprise.

My companion Jeanie tried the shoulder and started coughing. "A little spicy," she said. "It's got a bite to it. Oh, my God—my nose is going to be running all day."

The dip sauce gives shoulder its distinctive flavor. Without it, shoulder is rather tame, in my opinion, as it doesn't soak up much smoke in that brief time of grilling. In short, I wouldn't eat much shoulder without getting it heavily dipped. The potato salad was a good creamy one, with pimentos, green pepper, onion, and a slight sweetness. The beans were not doctored up very much—just regular beans not too far removed from the can.

They also grill pork tenderloins and then finish them in the oven. The half-inch-thick sliced tenderloin was tender and had more smoke flavor than the shoulder. Jeanie, who cooks her own pork tenderloins at home, said about the tenderloin with the mild vinegar sauce, "That rocks." Jeanie grew up eating long-smoked pulled pork in the Hopkinsville area. I respect her tastes. And I agree—even though the tenderloin was a little dry, as lean grilled pork tends to be, I really enjoyed it when dipped in that tasty mild sauce.

As far as grilled shoulder goes, this stuff is about as good as you're going to get. The sweet tea—with free refills—is incredibly sweet for my palate, but Jeanie said it was "just right."

When pulling away from Backyard, which is located on the eastern outskirts of Tompkinsville, I noted the cemetery across the road. And Jeanie said, "If you have a heart attack after eating your barbecue, they know where to put you." Thanks, Jeanie. Thanks for reminding me of the hazards of my hobby.

Open: Thursday–Saturday, 10:00 a.m.–8:00 p.m.; Sunday, 10:00 a.m.–7:00 p.m. (or until sold out)

2768 Edmonton Road; 270-407-5435

R & S Bar-B-Q

This little barbecue joint is one of my favorites, in part because I visited this location when I was just a boy, and later in high school, and more recently as a still-growing (in the belly) man. It's located down in the valley from the old Monroe County high school. A house trailer stands across the road next to a pile of tires. When I ate there in high school, it was just a small cinderblock shack, and the dining area was full of smoke from the indoor pit behind the ordering counter. Back then, smoke leaked out into the rest of the shack and out the door when you entered. But that building burned in 2001, and they rebuilt a slightly larger structure in the same location. Now, a layer of smoke doesn't hover in the dining room. There's a mixture of old tables of different colors—yellow, orange, blue—and the walls are painted yellow with tributes to African Americana on the walls, including a photo of Barack Obama. A television played *Dr. Phil.*

The folks who run R & S have inherited a long family tradition of barbecue. Ms. Anita Hamilton owns the place now—one of the only female-owned and female-operated barbecue places I've visited. She reminded me that the place was called Tooley's back in the 1960s and '70s. It was handed down to Alex Tooley in 1971. He ran it until the mid-1980s. Anita bought the place in 1990 and has been there since. I reminded her that when I visited back in the old days, smoke rolled out into the dining room.

"You couldn't see," she said. After the 2001 burn, they took care of the smoke problem—effectively eliminating some of the old-school shack atmosphere but making dining in much more pleasant.

I asked Anita if she and Norman Hamilton over at Hamilton's Bar-B-Q in Burkesville were kin, and she said they were first cousins. Anita's friendliness is disarming, and she's beautiful, with striking freckles on her face and a penchant for dressy fashion. I've never seen a better-dressed pit master in all my barbecue adventures.

Out back, stacks of hickory provide the fuel for this great barbecue. You can see the wood being burned in a big steel drum. Then coals are taken from the drum and shoveled under the rack inside the building that holds the meat. The hickory wood comes out of Livingston, Tennessee.

When I'm in T-ville, I'm all about the shoulder, but for the purposes of research I also tried ribs and chopped pork with a sweetish tangy sauce already on the meat—a bit too sweet and saucy for my liking. The big spare ribs, though, were real good, imbued with a lusty smokiness from cooking over hickory coals and distinctive tanginess from Anita's vinegar dip. Anita said if you want spareribs, you have to get there early. The potato salad had sweet pickles in it. The green beans were nicely seasoned and long cooked until soft in the way I've eaten them at many rural Kentucky mothers' tables. The macaroni salad was pretty good, with a distinct flavor of onions. The slices of pork shoulder were smoked to a pretty crispy brown, tender, and peppery. Because of the considerable smoky flavor, I was surprised to learn that a piece of shoulder cooks in about forty-five minutes—the benefit of thin slicing and having so much surface area to soak up the smoke. So, for the price of $5.75, I got three slices of shoulder, two sides, and two pieces of white bread—the value of eating in a town lacking a highly accelerated economy. (There are lots of forestry industries in Monroe County, hence the availability of the hickory. A Kingsford charcoal plant is located several miles east of Tompkinsville.)

Anita told me a fascinating story about the origins of Monroe County barbecue sauce. One of her ancestors passed through a slave camp in Cave

City, Kentucky, and someone at the camp gave him the sauce recipe. The folks at this particular camp came from North Carolina. Now, barbecue in Monroe and a few surrounding counties looks a whole lot like eastern North Carolina barbecue, saucewise—a blend of vinegar, lard, butter, salt, cayenne and black pepper.

I asked Anita what sets the different barbecue places apart, since they're all getting shoulder from the same place and cooking it in a similar manner using similar sauce.

"Personality," she said. "Customers are always laughing and talking with us. I love people. We want you to feel at home." Anita and her daughter Samantha sure deliver on sweet hospitality, real good ribs and shoulder, and fine homemade sides.

Open: summer hours: Tuesday–Saturday, 10:30 a.m.–7:00 p.m.; winter hours: Tuesday–Saturday, 10:30 a.m.–5:30 p.m.

217 South Jackson Street; 270-487-1008

Red Barn Bar-B-Q

A full-service large restaurant, Red Barn is located south of Tompkinsville, tucked back behind Save-a-Lot grocery. Floors are black and white tile. Big windows look out onto woods, and the dining room is open and lit by fluorescents. The menu includes a shoulder plate for $6, chicken halves or breasts, tenderloin, pork chops, country-style and baby back ribs, hot dogs and hamburgers, and an extensive side-dish selection.

The three-quarter-inch-thick grilled tenderloin was one of the best meats I ate in all of Tompkinsville, reminding me of western Kentucky–style pork, with good smokiness and tenderness. The salty grilled cabbage was delicious and was a perfect complement to the pork. My friend Jeanie and I both raved about this flavor combo. The tenderloin bark was truly magnificent. I wanted to order a whole plate of tenderloin bark. The green beans were strangely vinegary, but I liked them. (Marketta Dubree, who runs the front, is originally from Cumberland County, and she told me the green beans are from her grandmother's recipe.) The half chicken was very tender and goodly smoked with some crispy skin on the outside.

Marketta's husband, Gary, mans the pits. He cooks whole tenderloins two to four hours and then slices them to order. He burns down hickory slabs

221

in a barrel outside and brings them in to shovel underneath the pits. When he begins grilling in the morning, he cooks shoulder first when the grill is hottest. When the shoulder is done and the fire has died down some, he does pork chops and hamburgers. Gary hickory smokes the ribs and applies sauce while they cook to keep them moist. Pit temps range from 350° to 500°—real hot compared to western Kentucky slow-cooking methods.

Red Barn originally opened in Columbia, but after a fire on December 14, 2008, destroyed Adair County's only Monroe County–style barbecue place, the Dubrees came back home. Now, some of their old customers from Columbia drive all the way down, one hour to the south, for a meal. The Dubrees got them hooked on Monroe County style. They've been serving barbecue for ten years and have been at the Tompkinsville location since May 2009.

Marketta said she and Gary will probably be in the barbecue business until "we have to come in with canes and walkers." As Jeanie talked Marketta into standing for a photo with Gary, Jeanie said, "Y'all act like you like each other," and Marketta said, "We've stuck it out for twenty-six years and we work together, so either we really love each other or we're two of the most stubborn people that's ever been born."

If you want your barbecue hot, ask Gary to skim it off the top, where the pepper floats. And do try that smoked cabbage with the pork loin—a dreamy combination.

Open: Thursday–Saturday, 10:00 a.m.–8:00 p.m.
313 South Main Street; 270-487-9000

Frances' Bar-B-Que

Probably the restaurant with the most name recognition in Monroe County, Frances' has been serving up thin-sliced pork shoulder with a distinctive dip since 1977, when Frances Arms built her restaurant after leasing another barbecue place down the road for eleven years and developing a loyal following. The original Frances' was in Hestand, several miles south of Tompkinsville on the road to Moss, Tennessee. I used to stop there on my way to visit Reuben Schwartz, the Amish eyeman (iridologist) and herb seller located in Vernon, a bucolic community in a remote valley of the Cumberland River. Reuben would gaze into my iris with his magnifying glass and suggest vinegar baths and herbs to cleanse my liver, boost prostate health, and so on. I'd get Reuben's prescription for optimum health and then drive up to Frances' and load my colon with grilled pork shoulder and fries. I could always do Reuben's prescribed colon cleanse later.

The original place burned down on Good Friday 2009, much to the disappointment of loyal patrons near and far (someone placed a bouquet of flowers at the burn site), but reopened nearer to town a year later. I tried the new location in fall 2011, along with my photojournalist sidekick Jeanie Adams-Smith.

Owner David Arms, a jovial storyteller, gave us a tour of the pit area. He was grilling slices of picnic ham over charcoal for a couple's fiftieth wedding anniversary party down in Tennessee. "We do a lot of wedding rehearsals, family reunions, and at Christmas and all that, and here's why. You get forty pieces for $40. I don't know if you're a Bible-reading man or not, but it does say in the Bible 'Feed the hungry.' Now I got that covered. *There are a few more things that I might need to work on, but feeding the hungry I have covered*," David said. He delivered the line so smoothly I expected he'd used it before. Like I say, a born storyteller spinning tales in an endearing south-central Kentucky twang.

David turned the pieces of ham as he talked. "You can get more sauce taste and charcoal flavor by dipping and flipping," he said. He goes through sixty to eighty twenty-pound bags of Nature Glo Old Hickory Charcoal Briquettes each week. "Me and my mother and wife have cooked over 1 million pounds of sliced shoulder," he said. He started working the grill at age eleven. "We broke every child labor law there was."

We ordered a mix plate (your choice of three meats) with beef brisket, sliced shoulder, and chicken (dipped hot) with hash brown casserole and mac and cheese. We also tried the dry-rubbed smoked chicken. The brisket is cooked on a gas-charcoal rotisserie smoker. Frances' is the only place in Monroe County serving brisket. The mix plate came with two pieces of sauced shoulder, a chicken leg and thigh, and a heavily sauced and shredded brisket. The chicken was sweet and peppery, and the thinly sliced shoulder with tangy sauce was very tender. The standouts were the sliced shoulder—the top-selling item at Frances'—and the tender, salty smoked chicken. The hash brown casserole was rich, cheesy and moist, with buttery cracker pieces (like Ritz crackers) mixed in.

Frances,' like other Monroe County joints, gets its shoulder from Ross and Ross meat processors in Tompkinsville, who get their pork from Indiana Kitchen pork supply headquartered in Delphi, Indiana. Shoulder accounts for 60 percent of Frances' sales.

David left the pit area and sat with us awhile to spin a history of Monroe County barbecue. Here are some highlights.

"Before it got so fancy like my grill is back there, people would take bedsprings and build a wooden fire on it and burn the paint off and sterilize it, and they'd cook on those bedsprings."

"Everybody claims to have the first vinegar-based recipe. All I know is my daddy pretty much trumped 'em. He said a 110-year-old black man give him his recipe and he's dead now, prove him different. That's what he always claimed."

David started making the sauce in 1982–83. He tweaked the sauce using weights and timers to make it consistent throughout ongoing batches. "I ain't talking bad about nobody's food," he said, "but a lot of your chain restaurants have proven bad food will sell as long as it tastes the same at ever one of 'em across the United States. So if you got good food and get a repeat on it, people will continue to come."

About his methods of barbecuing, David said, "The process we use, you really have to stay on top of the game. It's labor intense. You can't shortcut nothing or you'll be throwing meat away." It takes him thirty to forty-five minutes to grill eighty to ninety slices of shoulder. "My philosophy is that you dip and flip. You get tired of that, you flip then dip," David snickered.

David brought me a BBQ egg out and said, "I invented that." The boiled egg had soaked in vinegar dip until well pickled. "I tell everybody you know how you get a barbecued egg, right? Barbecued chicken." David said it started out as a joke. His friend owned a package store, and David noticed the guy had an ever-disappearing jar of pickled eggs on the counter. David saw potential profit there. He joked with his mother that he was going to sell enough barbecue-sauce pickled eggs to send his son to college. He said he's sold three dozen per week for twenty-something years, so the egg business "pretty much has" paid the college bill. I did the math, and David's not pulling my leg. According to my calculations, three dozen barbecue eggs yields about $15/week profit. After twenty years, that's over $15,000 profit. Pretty good for something as humble as a pickled egg from a barbecued chicken.

David greeted people in the restaurant. "How you doing, hon?" "Have you been waited on?" Watching David's easy way of talking with his customers, I understood why, in addition to the good food, people returned to Frances' time and again.

I asked David how long he intended to stay in the barbecue business, and he delivered an answer in his trademark wisecracker style: "I don't know. Until my crooked uncle straightens up?"

Open: Thursday–Sunday, 10:30 a.m.–8:00 p.m.
418 East Fourth Street; 270-487-8550

Gamaliel

Collins Barbecue

In arQtectural terms, this barbecue establishment most definitely qualifies as a shack. You walk in and order at a small counter, and the smoke from the open pit behind the counter fills your nostrils and sometimes singes your eyeballs. The only seating is an outdoor picnic table. Out back, Wormie burns down hickory slabs in a barrel and brings shovelfuls of hickory coals into the shack and shovels them underneath the meats. He flips pieces of sliced pork shoulder and sops them with vinegar pepper dip in the Monroe County style. Flips and dips, flips and dips.

At Collins Barbecue, named after the original owners, the sliced shoulder is the thing to get. If you like it hot, Wormie will satisfy, skimming the dip right off the top where the spices gather, and as your taste buds take in that smoke-licked shoulder and fat-infused vinegar dip, your sinuses will open up. If you like it real hot, ask for "suicide"; moderately hot, "dipped"; just a little hot, "sprinkled." Wormie also grills big hot dogs (which he'll also dip), chicken, and big spareribs. The ribs I tried on a late Saturday afternoon had been held above water (steamed) in an oven. Wormie served them with his vinegar dip ladled on. They were tasty, but the pork shoulder with Wormie's hot dip is what I'll order time and time again.

Wormie served me some pickled bologna from a big jar. He pickles it in vinegar, hot sauce, and jalapeños. "I do it just for me," he said. "Guess what? I get tired of barbecue."

Wormie grilled shoulder, while my friend Jeanie Adams-Smith documented this slice of life with her great eye and high-powered digital camera. The exhaust fan hummed loudly. The hickory coals browning the pork smelled real good.

I said, "You think this smoke's gonna get ya finally with all the cooking and smoking?"

Wormie said, "Probably does," but admitted that it probably didn't matter, what with the three packs of cigarettes he helps a friend smoke each day.

He likes cooking the pieces of shoulder about thirty minutes. "The longer you cook 'em the better off you are," he said.

You might be squirmy eating barbecue cooked by a guy named Wormie, and I wouldn't blame you, but you can't fault him for a name that was thrust upon him. I asked the man how he wanted to be named in my book, and he said, "Wormie because nobody won't know me if you don't." He told me how to spell the name. I said, "It's kinda like Madonna. Everybody knows who she is, but nobody knows her by Ciccone or whatever."

When I asked how he got his nickname, Wormie said, "Well, you do not really want to know," but then immediately launched into his story. I should mention that in local dialect "wormy" means scrawny. And now, for your reading pleasure—transcribed as authentically as possible from a digital voice recording—a story from one of my favorite characters in the barbecue world.

Seriously. I'll tell you how it was. I worked as a butcher. I *cut* for all these barbecues. Okay? And uh, this woman, elderly lady—we'd deliver to older folks who didn't have no car and what have ye, and run charge accounts and what have ye, so uh, she come by and she'd ordered a sack of potatoes, and she wanted some seeds and stuff, you know, which we done that, you know—we's just a little ole small store, you know—anyway, she ordered her groceries. Told us what she wanted and everythang, well, I goes out and I get my little buggy and I go pick everythang up she's supposed to get—she'd just stopped down there at the feed store and asked me to pick up fertilize and all this stuff that we don't carry, you know, so that's what I done. And when I got over there, them potatoes that she'd ordered had not got delivered to the store yet. Okay? But I had some other people need some stuff, so I went over there and picked it up. And I made me a little circle, you know, and took all these old ladies and gentlemen and whatever their stuff. I left hers for last. I went to unloading everything, got it all done. I left her ticket for her. I even put her milk and stuff in the refrigerator for her, her eggs and all that. I mean I'm a nice man. She said, "Will you put that lightbulb in for me?" Well, I done that. You know? And before I could get back to the store, which wudn't three minutes, she called down there and said, "*You tell that little wormy son of a bitch get my damn taters over here!*" Of course God and everybody was in there and they heard it! That's how I got my name. It stuck with me!

I looked at my boss and I said, "I'm going to tell you *one* thing: my *daddy* always told me if anybody ever called me a son of a bitch and I didn't whoop 'em, he's gonna *stomp my ass!*" 'Scuse my language. I told him, "I'm going back and I'm going to tell that little lady a piece of my mind."

He said, "She's traded with us for about forty years. If you go over there you're fired."

I said, "Well, I just quit."

He said, "Wormie . . ." And they started calling me Wormie! I've carried that name for a good twenty years or longer. I worked for that man for twenty-two and a half years.

And that's the story Wormie told me of his naming.

As Jeanie and I took our leave after an hour of good-time chatting, Wormie handed me my sacks of spareribs and sliced shoulder to go and shouted, "Thankee! Have a goodun! Come back! Give me a call now! If you get ready to come and you want a big order or anything like that, call and say, 'Worm Dawg, I'm on my way.'"

Open: Wednesday–Sunday, 9:00 a.m.–"until we run out"
531 East Main Street; 270-457-2828

Southern Lakes Region

Burkesville

Capps BBQ

The small town of Burkesville, seat of Cumberland County, lies on the highway to Dale Hollow Lake. The curvy drive on the John Muir Highway down to Dale Hollow is beautiful: cattle and hay rolls in the fields, good stands of hardwoods, rustic barns with quilt patterns painted on them, and modest-sized country homes. The Kingsford charcoal plant near Summer Shade and a few lumber companies testify to the importance of trees in this area. I'll bet that many locals don't know why this is called the John Muir Highway. Well, the little bearded tree hugger walked from Indiana to Florida in 1867 and passed through this part of Kentucky. Muir describes his adventures in journals published posthumously in 1916 as *A Thousand-Mile Walk to the Gulf,* a classic of southern nature writing.

Outside Summer Shade—one of the nicest town names I've ever encountered—I drove past a home with plastic deer in the front yard. Christmas wreaths and red bows decorated these deer, very sissy. Just east of Summer Shade, I passed one of many signs erected by Evangelist Dewey Cooper. This one read: WARNING: JESUS IS COMING—ARE YOU READY? Such signs appear regularly along roadsides in this region, very much a part of my cultural upbringing. Southeast of Summer Shade, the land changes dramatically and starts to look more like eastern Kentucky. Many homes are heated with wood, smoke rising from the chimneys. Roads twist and snake through the substantial hills, and the old crumbling barns remind you of a time when tobacco crops paid the mortgages in this small-scale farming region.

At one point, Dale Hollow reservoir held the world-record smallmouth bass. I've passed through Burkesville several times en route to Dale Hollow, but until December 2011 had never laid eyes on Capps BBQ because it lies on the north side of town. Look for a small cement-block building painted red with one picnic table outside. Inside, another small table sits near the ordering counter. This place is mainly takeout.

On the cold day I visited, Mr. Willard Capps, a gray-bearded man wearing woodsy camouflage coveralls, was grilling pork chops in a covered garage area offside the shack. Smoke rose from an old steel cooking box with a heavy hinged lid on it. He's been selling meat in Burkesville for thirteen years, with shoulder being his biggest seller.

I'd just butchered two hogs earlier that week, so Willard and I talked hogs for a while. He said that back in the day, his daddy didn't want to kill a hog until it weighed about 600 pounds. Our biggest hog, named Red Bud, weighed 444 pounds at slaughter time. Willard said that if you want to cure hog meat, you need some age and fat on it. "A little 225-pound hog ain't big enough for me to do what I want to do with it." He went on, "People used to didn't waste nothing about a hog. I remember my mama made that souse meat? Ever part was just about used."

Willard cooks with Kingsford charcoal and said he can't tell the difference between it and fresh wood coals. But he admitted that he could taste gas when people grilled over it. He basted the pork chops with sauce as they sizzled.

Willard said he started barbecuing on the riverbank, ever since he was big enough to get out to fish and hunt. "I barbecued about everything they is to be barbecued. Even tried frog legs one time. They didn't turn out too good."

"What's the strangest thing you ever grilled?"

"Probably groundhog."

"I've done that," I said. "Mine didn't turn out too well."

"It's too lean. Rabbit's too lean, too."

"I bet if you wrapped bacon around there it might work."

"That'd probably turn out alright."

Willard said he'd sold grilled bologna awhile, but that the profit margin was much higher from selling a shoulder sandwich.

"You ever try any rainbow trout on a grill?" he asked.

"Yeah," I said. "White River in Arkansas. Cooked them right up at the campsite."

"They're good. Flake right off the bone."

The menu is simple: shoulder, pork chops, shredded pork, chicken, hot dogs, hamburgers, and the standard sides: slaw, baked beans, and potato salad. The thin-sliced shoulder and pork chops were good. Willard's dip sauce made with colored vinegar was sweeter than some I've tried.

Open: Wednesday–Friday, 10:00 a.m.–7:00 p.m. (a bit longer in summer)

920 North Main Street; 270-864-9429

Hamilton's Bar-B-Q

Located in a cinderblock building with vinyl-siding facade, not far off the town square in a residential neighborhood, Hamilton's is the real deal. Smoke blows from a big steel exhaust chimney jutting from the side of the building. A screened porch with tables for semi-outdoor dining runs along the front. From inside the porch, you can see a sign that says "Alpine Motel" on top of a nearby hill. "Alpine" might be a bit of exaggeration, as Burkesville is hardly mountain country, but the town does have the flavor of an eastern Kentucky town, tucked as it is within the foothills of the Appalachians known as the Cumberland Plateau. Just a little bit east of Burkesville, heading toward Albany on Highway 90, the hills grow longer and steeper, and before long you get to Harper Mountain, one of the westernmost mountains in this lake region of south-central Kentucky. Keep heading east and the mountains start popping up all over the place and get taller and taller.

Inside, the menu mounted high on the wall lists sandwiches and plates. Choices are, simply, meats cooked on the open pit you can view from the ordering counter. Seeing the long, rectangular iron grates elevated to belly level and enclosed by concrete blocks and bricks, with a bed of coals underneath and slices of shoulder, half chickens, and a whole pork tenderloin browned from the smoke got my stomach juices rumbling. In addition to these meats, they sell pork chops, shredded pork, hot dogs, and ribs. No side dishes are listed on the menu, but I spied the words "apple pie." And sure enough, right there on the counter lay homemade fried apple pies wrapped up in plastic foil, just begging me to take a couple home.

Not seeing any sides on the menu, I chose a shoulder sandwich. Elisa, traveling with me on this day, said, "Let's try the tenderloin. I'm curious," and I agreed, even though I was suspicious about tenderloin because it's a very lean meat and dries out easily. I watched a big bearded man wearing jean shorts and a reversed ball cap slice thick pieces off the whole tenderloin. He said, "You want 'em dipped?" and I replied, "Dip 'em good."

This man, who, I later learned, is Norman Hamilton, went about his work with a sense of cheerfulness. He served up our sandwiches at the counter and said, "Anything else?" and Elisa asked for a plastic bottle of cold sweetened tea from the cooler behind the counter just because his cheerfulness made her want to spend more money.

We took the sandwiches outside and sat at a plastic table on the porch. A long counter runs along the front of the porch, and you can sit there and look out upon the Cumberland County Maintenance Garage. I unwrapped the aluminum foil to reveal the beautiful shoulder sandwich, two slices of browned and still-moist shoulder nestled between two slices of white bread. Some beads of amber grease clung to the foil. The shoulder pieces, thicker than the norm, were hot off the hickory pits. You could really taste the smoked meat, as it wasn't overwhelmed by a sauce.

Elisa popped the top of a Styrofoam takeout box, and inside the pork tenderloin sandwich looked much the same, except the tenderloin was two pieces of lean pork sliced one-inch thick with a slim band of tasty browned fat on the edges, drizzled with a tangy vinegar-based sauce. I took a piece of tenderloin and bit into it, and my bias against that lean cut of meat was shot all to hell. It was juicy, tender, laced with moderate smoke, and bursting with flavor from the seasonings and dip sauce.

As we pondered the popularity of tenderloin on menus in this region, Elisa posited that tenderloin, like chicken, might be favored by women who want a leaner cut of meat. We'd been told recently by Gerald Judd at Mama Lou's in Uno that a lot of women don't like barbecue, and that was why he served breast of chicken.

As we finished our sandwiches, a man eating inside when we arrived came out onto the porch and said, "Good food here, isn't it?" I agreed, remarking it was my first time. He said, "If you get a plate, you better take part of it home with ye. They give you three big pieces of shoulder or tenderloin and big sides. It's as good as there is around." The sides, I learned, are beans, slaw, and potato salad.

The dining area of the restaurant exudes the aura of a barbecue shack. In the men's restroom, the floors are uneven, and vinyl contact paper looking like wood is pasted to the floor. The sitting area is furnished with old vinyl booths and plastic tables with folding chairs; the floors are concrete, and the walls are painted cinderblocks and paneling. Big fans cool the room. On the walls hang pictures of the Tuskegee Institute National Historic Site and Rev. Martin Luther King Jr.

Customers kept filing in through the front door, ordering food, and then moving to the dining room to eat it. Norman talked with me between filling orders. Norman and his wife, Pat, have been in the same location since 1979, when they bought the building. They opened the restaurant part-time for a while (Norman had a full-time job at a factory in Glasgow), but then had to close for six years after Pat was burned in a fire. People still called them at home asking when they would open again. Norman decided to retire from the factory at age fifty and do barbecue full-time. He credits Pat for making things work. "It's been a business when she started running it," he said. "When I was running it I played a lot of softball. I opened whenever I got ready to barbecue, because I had a job, and mostly then it was on Saturdays and Sundays. And people started out, 'Well, he's got good barbecue but he's never open.'" Pat brought steadiness to the business. Now they are open consistently three days a week.

Norman suggested he might be ready to retire from barbecue before long, and he looked over to his granddaughter Logan and said, "She could take this business to the next level." I saw a little embarrassed smile cross the fifteen-year-old's face. More people walked in and ordered their Saturday night dinners. I thanked Norman, and he invited us to come back again with a big smile and a handshake.

Watching Norman turning pieces of shoulder and saucing meats, smelling the rich odor of browning shoulder and the sizzle of fat on coals, and seeing those half chickens and whole pork tenderloin laid out on the grates—I couldn't help myself and ordered a half chicken and one of those fried pies to go. Norman filled my order and rang me up and thanked us again. I dug into the barbecued chicken outside, sitting on the bedrails of the Ford Ranger. The chicken was good, tasting of smoke and dip sauce, nothing more. It had cooked longer than I like, but that's the nature of chicken and ribs. If you get them at the perfect time, then you are in for a divine experience. If they sit a while, well, you'll get meat that's drier than it should be. I did like the chicken, though. But my favorite was the pork tenderloin (to my surprise) and the shoulder.

If Logan doesn't take up the barbecue heritage from her grandparents I sure hope somebody does. The Hamiltons cook low and slow, the meats are excellent, and the place pleases my penchant for homey shack atmosphere. The steady stream of customers confirmed the talk I'd heard about how good it was, but I didn't really need more proof than my taste buds, which said, "More please!" We drove away and cracked open that apple pie—we were not far down the road before we wished we'd purchased two of them.

I returned to Hamilton's in December 2011 to try that tasty tenderloin again, along with two more homemade pies, and I spoke with Pat awhile. She sliced the tenderloin right off the pit, so the meat retained the juiciness. One of Pat's customer's—a big guy wearing a Hamilton's BBQ cap and chewing on a toothpick, his little daughter at his side—testified, "Ain't much no better than what you're gonna eat right here. I cook myself and I'ma tell you somethin'. It's in ye sauce, and it ain't get much better than what's right here."

The man, Henry Pruitt, said he'd eaten all of the barbecue in the area—and that everybody used the same meat, but Norman's sauce was just superior to all others. "It's in the sauce. You can take two beautiful women and put 'em side by side—what makes that woman, though?"

"It's subjective," I said.

"It's the attitude! It's how she presents herself. One is going to be better than the other because of her attitude. Am I right or wrong? It's the same thing about this right here. Put two good cooks on that grill right there, one of them's going to be better than the other because of the sauce."

I asked what Norman did differently with his sauce.

Henry said, "I don't know, brother. I wish I did. I can drank the sauce. It's in the sauce."

Open: Their sign says, "Usually open at 9:00 a.m. Thursday, Friday, Saturday"

211 Hill Street; 270-864-9446

Hot Rod B.B.Q.

South of Burkesville, on the main road to Tennessee, this joint adds deep-fried side dishes, a spicy slaw, and a super-hot ghost chili sauce (upon special request) to the typical grilled meats found in this part of the world. I tried the pulled pork, sliced pork shoulder, and half chicken. I can't recommend the pulled pork, because it's the same pre-sauced stuff that most barbecue places in this region sell, often called "shredded" on menus. I wasn't too fond of the chicken, either, as I found it overcooked (the bone pulled right out from the meat, as if stewed) and too saucy. If you like chicken falling-apart tender with sauce on it, however, you'll probably like the chicken here. It's tasty—just not my preferred style.

On the upside, the shoulder sandwich at Hot Rod is a great food deal: $3 got me three slices of shoulder, dipped hot upon request, with white bread. The aroma of the dip—the way it flared my nostrils with a distinctive vine-gary tang—reminded me of eating hot chicken wings. I also like the Hot Rod slaw, a mayo slaw with barbecue baste (dip) mixed in.

Deep-fried offerings are strangely absent at barbecue joints in south-central Kentucky. Baked beans, slaw, and potato salad are expected, but it's rare to find fried items such as corn nuggets, buffalo chips, onion petals, mac and cheese wedges (fried macaroni and cheese!), and fried pickles. Hot Rod has them. Even though I'm not usually wowed by food-service frozen things, it's hard not to like buffalo chips—waffle fries dusted with "buffalo" spices.

I appreciate how the young folks who opened this place in April 2011 are doing something a little different from other barbecue places in the region. The dining room is spanking-new clean and decorated in an automotive mo-tif. NASCAR played on the television. Aluminum diamond plate—the shin-ing metal often seen on truck toolboxes, bed liners, bumpers, and trim—runs along the bottom of the cement-block walls, which are painted brick red above.

Chad Pruitt and his older brother Jimmy, owners, and Todd Cash, head cook, are the men behind the Hot Rod. They burn down hickory wood and shovel coals under the meats through a trap door from the outside, so they don't ever have to bring ash into the kitchen. Todd was a fry cook before he and Chad decided to open the restaurant, and he brought his frying savvy with him to the new venture. When I expressed my preference for unsauced pulled pork, Chad said when they first opened they weren't saucing the pork, but locals wanted it sauced, so they changed to suit the local tastes. Todd admitted that he too prefers pulled pork sans sauce, but "We couldn't give it away without the sauce on it."

This is interesting—yet another connection between these south-central Kentucky counties and Appalachia, where they also want their pork heavily sauced. (You can get the pork pulled from Boston butts without sauce upon request.)

I asked, "How are the fried pickles going over?"

Chad said, "The more people try the fried pickles down here, the more who loves 'em. But it's hard to get 'em to eat it. That's what we're trying to do—something a little different than everybody down here. Just got to give it time."

I should mention that Hot Rod recycles cans. In the wasteful Styrofoam-filled world of barbecue takeout, that's a pleasant surprise.

After closing down for a winter holiday, Hot Rod opened in spring 2012 for their second season. On the phone they said they'd made improvements since I visited during their early weeks of operation. I'm glad they've survived a year in these tough economic times, and I look forward to trying them again.

Open: Thursday, 11:00 a.m.–6:00 p.m.; Friday–Saturday, 11:00 a.m.–8:00 p.m.; Sunday, 11:00 a.m.–6:00 p.m. (closes sometimes during winter—call ahead)

3830 Celina Road; 270-433-9696

Columbia

Brad Simmons, headman of Lucky Dog BBQ catering based in Danville and organizer of the first-ever Kentucky State BBQ Festival in fall 2011, told me that he was living in a "barbecue wasteland" in central-east Kentucky. I know what he means. If you draw a line straight down the map from LaGrange (northeast of Louisville near the Ohio River) to Burkesville (down next to Tennessee on the Cumberland River), you've pretty much marked the line between Barbecue Dreamland and Barbecue Wasteland. Just look how thick the first part of this book is, with barbecue places galore in the western part of the state, but tapering off—with pockets of barbecue riches, like around Louisville—the farther east you venture. Consider the Green River Lake area. Joe Barbee's Breast and Butts Que in Columbia is currently the only game in the region, and Joe's good barbecue is available only on the first and third weekends of each month from March to December. No wonder people in Columbia drive all the way down to Tompkinsville to eat at Red Barn for their open-pit grilled meats. Monroe County has five barbecue joints. Cumberland County to the east has four. Clinton County to the east has zero. Russell County to the north of Clinton: zero. Adair County bordering Russell County to the west: one. And here it is, the current sole offering of barbecue around Green River Lake.

Breast and Butts Que

Joe Barbee used to cook on the Kansas City Barbecue Society competition circuit, until his then girlfriend twisted his arm to get off the road and open his own barbecue place. "She hated KCBS. Hated the people, didn't like anything about it." So he quit the circuit and opened his own place on April 1, 2005. That date was prophetic, as Joe was *fooled* by this woman—she wiped out his bank account. Joe had to borrow money to pay his suppliers. Joe says he moped around a couple of weeks, but then his daughter Susan Barbee-Harvey said, "Look, if this place means that much to you, I'll help you out some, but I can only do it a couple of weekends a month."

"She's the reason we're all here," Joe said, giving Susan a sideways hug.

Breast and Butts (B & B) is a family operation that focuses on quality. "We prep the meats just like at a contest," Joe said. "We wash everything. We use our own rubs. We let the meat sit a while before putting it on the cooker. We use an Ole Hickory cooker. It's the most dependable. The cookers are a lot smarter than the people running them," he noted, talking about the barbecue competition circuit, where a bunch of inebriated guys are apt to open the cooker doors far too often to peek at the meat, letting heat out and screwing up the process. "Just let it alone," Joe said.

I ate a sampler platter that came with one slice of dry-rubbed boneless shoulder, a few bones of baby back ribs, a chicken breast/wing, pulled pork from Boston butt, one of Ol Joe's Ky. wings (a smoked ham shank), potato salad, baked beans, and slaw. I also tucked away a good portion of a huge "loaded BBQ potato." All meats were tender and flavorful, with the ham shank ranking highest on my flavor/tenderness scale. Joe's take on sliced shoulder, using a dry rub instead of vinegar baste, sets him apart from the Monroe County style to the south (I liked it, but prefer the grilled vinegar-dipped shoulder of Monroe County to Joe's shoulder pieces, which cook, like everything else, on the gas-fired rotisserie). The beans are excellent. Because of the lack of deep smoking that I prefer, this is barbecue that benefits from the addition of sauces. Two of them were available at the table: Ol Joe's Original (a sweet and tangy tomato-based sauce with pepper kick) and Ol Joe's Mustard Barbecue sauce (like the original, with added mustard seed). Joe's distinguished cowboy visage—blue jean shirt, full-brimmed hat, and a wizened face with full mustache that puts me in mind of the actor Sam Elliott—graces the bottles. I imagine Joe as a ladies' man—a tall drink of Kentucky water.

When I entered B & B on a Friday afternoon around 3:00, a group of middle-aged men talked and laughed at a nearby table. As I worked on that sampler platter and big potato, several other folks came in to dine, including a woman from Michigan who teaches at the local Lindsey Wilson College. She likes B & B so much that she was loading up with it to take back to her family in the North for the holidays.

The atmosphere is welcoming: a big open dining room with long folding tables decorated in plastic tablecloths (a Christmas candy-cane design in December), metal folding chairs, tiled floor, and, best of all, walls decorated with over one hundred framed black-and-white photos of local history—some of it Joe Barbee's family history. For example, there's a weathered advertisement for the Columbia & Campbellsville Stage Line, J. B. Barbee, proprietor. There's memorabilia, such as aprons from Joe's five years on the

Kansas City Barbecue Society contest circuit. He competed at the prestigious Jack Daniels Invitational in 2004 and 2005. And then there's plenty of funny stuff to catch the eye, like the mounted rabbit with deer antlers (a jackalope?) and a sketch of Abe Lincoln and Jeff Davis standing side by side and encircled by the words "Kentucky boys with attitudes." I spent thirty minutes looking around Joe's restaurant and still didn't see everything. It's like a local history museum.

Joe's an entrepreneur with the gift of liquid speech. He walked me around the restaurant, telling stories about people in the old black-and-white photos. "This man here's from Adair County," Joe said, pointing to a photo. "He won the national fiddle contest."

Joe's history in barbecue goes back to his youth. "I was raised on Tennessee-line barbecue." In the late 1950s and early '60s, Joe went down to Dale Hollow reservoir for fishing and houseboating and got his first taste of grilled sliced pork shoulder. "Mercy. I'd never eaten steak that was that good. Then when I got married and had kids, I'd get up on Sunday morning and drive to Pea Ridge and buy Ruth Willis's barbecue and bring it back and have it in the oven for Sunday lunch when we got out of church. I raised my kids on it."

Years later, in the 1990s, Joe spent time in New Orleans learning how to fry turkeys. (He fried ninety-three of them for Thanksgiving 2011.) In 1999, he went to the Kentucky Bourbon Festival in Bardstown and met Bear Woods of Backwoods Barbecue and tried the Kansas City style. Joe loved it. He asked Bear to teach him how to do it. Joe spent the next several years on the circuit, learning the trade while cooking with the J-Mack team from far western Kentucky. "I learned enough to be dangerous."

By the way, the stuffed potato with pulled pork on top was fabulous. When I go back to Breast and Butts, I'll get that potato, an order of Ol Joe's Ky. wings (the smoked ham shanks), and the great baked beans and vinegar slaw.

Open: Seasonally, March–December, every first and third weekend on Friday and Saturday, 10:00 a.m.–8:00 p.m. (open for forty days per year—get it while you can!)

824 Campbellsville Road; 270-384-2360

Russell Springs

FishTales

In June 2012, Susan Mirkhan, owner of J. J. McBrewster's in Lexington, opened FishTales at Wolf Creek Marina, right on the placid waters of Lake Cumberland. Despite the fishy name, this lakeside restaurant will also feature smoked meats. It's one of the last places you can get barbecue as you head east in southern Kentucky toward the Cumberland Gap.

Dine with a view of the big lake. Kentucky is beautiful from the Mississippi River to Appalachia, and Lake Cumberland, even though an impoundment, is a lovely jewel among the diamonds.

Open: Tuesday–Saturday, 11:00 a.m.–10:00 p.m.; Sunday, 11:00 a.m.–3:00 p.m.

782 Island Ramp Road; 270-866-3437

Breast and Butts Que's World-Champion Ribs

Joe Barbee's got some well-earned opinions about rib smoking, because in 2005 he won first place in ribs at the Jack Daniel's World Championship Invitational Barbecue down in Lynchburg, Tennessee. (Joe was competing on the J-Mack Cookers team, based in Bardwell, Kentucky.) When Joe offered to tell me how to cook ribs, and I gladly agreed to listen, he rolled out a tale that included hints, tips, and some strong opinions. I'll try organizing his spiel into an easy-to-follow form.

1. Don't use baby backs! Use a St. Louis–style rib, because it's from an older, larger hog and has more fat content with better marbling and flavor. Besides, baby back ribs are strangely curved and have sharp bones that poke through the foil when you wrap them after smoking.

2. Pull the membrane from the underside of the rib. (I find that sliding a butter knife under the membrane in the middle and lifting up allows me to insert a finger underneath to hold the ribs down. I then work the membrane loose and pull up and off.)

3. Shake a dry rub generously and evenly on both sides of the ribs. Joe recommends his own brand, Ol Joe's Barbecue Rib Rub, available

---

online at www.jpsaucehouse.com. Joe's rub ingredients include salt, sugar, paprika, spices, dehydrated garlic, and black pepper.

4. Let the rubbed ribs rest at least 2 hours or overnight in the refrigerator.

5. Bring ribs to room temperature, or at least to 50°F. Start your smoker and get the fire up to 250°.

6. Place ribs on the smoker bone side down and cook at 250° for 4½ to 5 hours. When the barometric pressure is low, the ribs will cook quicker. Cool, eh?

7. Joe says the next step is very important. In his words: "*Leave it the hell alone.*" Don't be opening the lid to check them every 30 minutes. "The smokers are smarter than we are." Joe says you want that constant pressure caused by a steady temperature in a closed area.

8. Pull the rack of ribs up after 4½ hours. If it breaks apart, then it's done.

9. Brush the rack lightly with your favorite rib sauce. Would you believe that Ol Joe recommends his own sauce? You can buy a bottle at Breast and Butts Que in Columbia.

10. Wrap tightly in aluminum foil and put into an insulating plastic or Styrofoam "cooler" (not cooled in this case) to keep the ribs warm. Let them steam and tenderize in the foil for at least 1 hour; 2 is better.

11. Cultivate the Buddhist mind, which means try to quench your desire to tear into those ribs before they are finished doing what needs to be done. "It takes discipline to do this, to wait that long," Joe says.

12. Take ribs from cooler. Unwrap foil. Get your fingers sticky. Eat up.

Derby Region

Leitchfield

Big Kahuna Bar-B-Q ("Ride the Sweet and Spicy Wave")

The barbecue safarian could easily pass up Big Kahuna, and that would be a shame because the Big Kahuna special—a half-pound of thinly sliced smoked beef from a "special" cut of steer layered up on a garlic-spread hoagie roll and topped with a sweet and spicy sauce with strong hints of molasses—stands as one of the tastiest and oddballish creations I've seen at a Kentucky barbecue restaurant. Owner Frank Hewes, with roots in Los Angeles and Texas, brings beef into pork country and gives it a far west of West Coast flavor with his rubs and sauces, including a sweet Hawaiian sauce made with passion fruits like coconut, mango, and pineapple.

Frank's place is tucked back in the corner of the small Southgate strip mall, and his smoker is out back, which makes it easy to overlook. Originally serving out of a portable trailer dressed up like a log cabin and parked at McCubbin's Furniture, Frank—after three years in this location—was forced to find a permanent spot. The health department, enforcing the old law, said a portable business could not remain in the same location for over fourteen days, and he couldn't return for at least thirty days. So Frank needed three locations to set up, and he didn't want his customers to have to chase him around town. Frank asked, "Can I be permanent?" and the health department said yes, but you have to put your trailer up on a pedestal and hook up to a sewer and add two public restrooms. But there was no sewer on the bypass, and they wouldn't allow him to have a septic tank. Frank recounted, "My options were to go belly up or look for a new place. And this is my passion. So we found this place and I did all the remodeling myself."

With a career in construction under Frank's midlife belt, he and his wife, Sheral, retired to Kentucky because they wanted to live on a lake. After touring several states they chose Rough River Lake north of Leitchfield. But Frank's longtime passion is barbecue, so his retirement morphed into this new vocation. His construction skills served him well as he remodeled the interior of his restaurant with high-backed wood booths and wooden tables in a big open dining room. In the background a sound system played Skid Row, the Proclaimers, the White Stripes, and kindred music at a pleasant volume. I complimented Frank on the ambience of his restaurant, and he said, "I wanted you to come in and feel like you were at home." All the walls are wood paneling and photos of Hawaii landscapes—like tall waterfalls and sea foam smashing into coastal boulders—hang in each booth. Frank said these photos were taken in June 2010 on their twenty-fifth wedding anniversary trip. Pointing to the largest photo near the front door, he said, "That's the beach where we renewed our wedding vows." That sweet story isn't the only indication Frank is a romantic: he and Sheral opened Big Kahuna on Valentine's Day, 2007.

In addition to the Big Kahuna special, I ordered a pulled-pork sandwich and a "pig wing"—a shank end of ham with four to six ounces of meat smoked deeply. The pork sandwich was a real filler-upper—hickory-smoked kalua-style pork pulled from Boston butts piled high on a large braided bun and served with sauce on the side. The pork was moist and juicy, nicely salted, with a moderate smokiness. I liked the deep brown sweet sauce with notes of onion and black pepper, and the hot sauce was remarkable—of medium thickness with sour notes and something that reminded me of Italian dressing. Frank said later (when I fished for sauce secrets) that there wasn't any Italian dressing in his sauce.

The Big Kahuna special—that thinly sliced smoked-beef sandwich—is Frank's signature item and not to be missed, but what I really loved (in addition to the Big Kahuna beef) was the humorously named pig wing. That ham shank soaked up loads of smoke, and the meat was sweet and tender as can be—bursting with flavor—and went wonderfully with Frank's fruity Hawaiian sauce. I could eat three pig wings with a couple of sides (like fried onion rings) and be real happy. If you request it, any of the sandwiches can be served on the hoagie roll and toasted and brushed with the garlic spread in the style of the Big Kahuna sandwich.

Other menu items are brisket, pulled chicken, and ribs—all smoked by Frank on a big iron smoker housed out back in the original traveling log cabin. The St. Louis–style ribs are available on Fridays and Saturdays. On a later trip to Big Kahuna, I got a full rack of these ribs and took them home. Elisa and I dug into them and found them deeply smoked and tender, with a nice crispiness to the bark. We loved the ribs with Frank's sweet Hawaiian sauce.

Side dishes include tangy baked beans, mac and cheese, mayonnaise slaw, and a spicy award-winning chili. And if you're feeling a bit freaky, you can request some of Frank's super-hot sauce, made from a mixture of ghost chilies and habaneros, or try his cheesesteak sandwich, a twist on the Philadelphia original that uses slices from his special beef and sautéed onions and jalapeños instead of the standard bell peppers. I daresay this is probably one of the only cheesesteaks you'll find on a menu in middle Kentucky. As for the super-hot sauce, it's plenty hot, but Frank has tamed it down to less than half the potency of his initial concoction, which was putting blisters on people's lips. He was afraid he was going to have to require people to sign a waiver to avoid litigation.

Frank learned culinary skills from his mother, who made her son cook with her when he got into trouble instead of grounding him. "So she taught me how to cook, and there were times when I'd get in trouble a little bit on purpose, just so I'd have to cook." He prepared food for big family functions for years before getting into barbecue full-time.

I asked how the people of Grayson County had taken to his regionally unique style of barbecue. Frank said, "We've lived here now for eight years, and I couldn't find a beef barbecue. Everything was pork. My roots are from Texas and California, and beef is the way you do barbecue out there. Here in Grayson County they didn't accept the beef, so I was giving free samples of my beef away. And then people were going, 'Oh my God, this is amazing.' So now my Big Kahuna sandwich is my #1 seller."

Frank's incredibly knowledgeable about barbecue. He's eaten it all over the country, and he's had to change all his recipes from the West Coast—where he cooked with oak because they couldn't get hickory—to adapt to the smoke flavor imbued by the local Kentucky hickory, which, thank the Lord, is abundant. "I had to change my recipe for everything," he said, "because oak is so overpowering. The hickory is more mellow and gentle. I had to reinvent my rubs and sauces when I came here to Kentucky."

I sure enjoyed speaking with Frank, who seems to be as laid back as his logo: a pig on a surfboard wearing flowery board shorts and flashing the "hang loose" symbol with his human thumbs and pinkies—about the most anthropomorphized pig I've ever seen. When I explained my project, Frank said, "Well, I'm from California—I don't do Kentucky barbecue," and I said that was alright, he'd passed the test with his carefully tended smoky meats and creative twists on beef barbecue.

I know Californians get a bad rap for all kinds of reasons, and I've heard jokes about California sliding off into the Pacific. Well, central Kentucky is lucky to have this West Coaster choose us over other states with lakes. A belated welcome, Frank. You've given me a reason to reroute my travels when heading toward Louisville and parts north.

Open: Monday–Saturday, 11:00 a.m.–9:00 p.m.
338 South Main Street; 270-287-7649

Clarkson

Smokin' Rednecks Bar B Que

Open since August 2011, owner Gary Preston, wife Glenna, and "the Redneck Team" bring atypical barbecue offerings and dinnertime karaoke to small town Clarkson, conveniently located near the Wendell H. Ford Western Kentucky Parkway southwest of Elizabethtown. I asked Jason Clemmons, the restaurant manager, what he recommended, and without batting an eye he said, "The pulled-pork pizza."

I asked, "Are you serious?"

Jason took me over to another table to show me a family dining on the pizza. They offered me a slice. It was good—a thin pizza with pork on it. A man at the table said, "The pulled ham is good, too." Jason then launched into a description of the pulled-ham sandwich with "homemade horsey sauce." "We smoke the precooked ham for eighteen hours," Jason says, "and pull it apart just like pork butt. It comes with melted cheddar or a slice of pepper jack cheese on it."

I said, "I'm not sure I need any cheese on my barbecue."

Jason asked the guy at the table, "Is the horsey sauce and the ham good?"

The man garbled something through a full, chewing mouth.

"His new favorite sandwich, he said," Jason translated.

The pulled-pork pizza and pulled-pork sandwich are the biggest sellers.

Meats at Smokin' Rednecks cook on an Ole Hickory gas unit. I tried a bit of several meats. The thin-sliced rubbery brisket and mushy pulled pork lacked the smoky flavor I desire, and the smoked ham was very salty. The standouts, though—worth driving for—were the Jason's pride sandwich and the spareribs. The sandwich was a huge, smoked, Italian-spiced sausage ground with meat from rib trimmings (the tips), served on a foot-long toasted bun with grilled onions and green peppers, slathered in barbecue sauce. Not traditional barbecue, but entirely filling and flavorful.

"We trim our own ribs," Gary said. "We can buy spareribs cheaper than we can buy St. Louis cut." Gary's ribs come dry or wet. Everything is homemade. "It's not real barbecue if you don't do it in house."

They're preparing to put in a full buffet with meatloaf, fried chicken, and the like. Ribs won't be on the buffet because they're so expensive. Pork is at an all-time high, Gary said, because China just bought 89 percent of the U.S. pork market. "Pork is a traded commodity. You have to shop around if you want to be successful. I want fresh. You got to give the customer the best product you can give them. If you don't have consistency in a restaurant, it will kill you."

At 5:00 on a Saturday, a family ate underneath a Louisville Cardinal on one side of the restaurant; across the room, another family ate underneath a Kentucky Wildcat. The place gradually filled with customers over the next hour, and the calm that I had entered gave way to laughter as tables filled and people prepared for karaoke at 7:00. A middle-aged gent named Mike at the next booth, who looked like he'd leapt right out of a Lucky Charms cereal box, said he'd driven down from Big Clifty, as he often does, to sing Elvis's "Hound Dog."

Gary is a good marketer, and he sells sauces under the Smokin' Rednecks brand: Sissy sauce (mild), Almost a Man sauce (medium), and You the Man sauce (hot). The sauces are thicker tomato-based sauces containing Worcestershire sauce, garlic and onion powders, corn syrup, and vinegar. The hottest, my favorite, contains a 52 percent blend of hot peppers. I'm fond of sauces heavy on vinegar and pepper, and this one satisfied. They even do a Redneck Wing Challenge with a Superman sauce (containing pepper extract) that requires the signing of a waiver to eat. You have one hour to eat eight chicken wings drenched in this devilish sauce. Winners get them free; losers pay $12. The next morning, everyone's a loser.

"You can bring a grown man to his knees with that," Gary said. "Remember: whatever goes in must come out. The only thing I suggest is to eat a big bowl of ice cream, so the next day you can say, 'Come on, ice cream!'" Only five people had completed the wing challenge when I visited in November 2011.

Gary recently returned to Kentucky, where he has family roots, from Florida. Gary's an unforgettable character—a big guy with a food-loving belly and long ponytail who juggles several business ventures at a time. His line of Redneck sauces are in high demand—when I visited they were sixteen thousand cases behind in orders—and in Leitchfield he has a thousand-seat music theater in the works, and he's recently talked with the *Deadliest Catch* folks at the Discovery Channel about doing a show out of Dutch Harbor, Alaska. The Alaskans will teach Gary about crabbing, and Gary will teach them about redneck barbecuing.

Gary's a hoot to talk to—a gregarious fellow with a flair for fun food and an atmosphere with a sense of humor. And Jason Clemmons, Gary's right hand at Rednecks, is a devoted salesman who believes in their products. These fellows understand hospitality. And although I've had better pulled pork and brisket elsewhere, I've rarely encountered such creative barbecue concoctions at Kentucky restaurants.

I highly recommend that big homemade sausage, Jason's pride—especially if you're fond of meat in tubular form—and also the smoked rib tips and ribs, which are dusted with a distinctive dry rub (which Gary sells) and glazed with sauce. You won't find rib tips at many places in the Bluegrass, or barbecue pizza either. Wash it all down with seriously sweet tea.

Open: Tuesday–Friday, 11:00 a.m.–8:00 p.m.; Saturday, 10 a.m.–"until the last person is out the door"

117 West Short Street; 270-242-3692

Louisville

I was a bit suspicious about Loo-a-vul as a barbecue town—after all, it's almost in the North—but Louisville has impressed me with its variety and quality, and in a few cases rocked my well-traveled barbecue world.

Louisville's a melting pot of U.S. regional barbecue styles. Ole Hickory Pit serves up pork and mutton cooked on masonry pits in the traditional western Kentucky style (the owners have Paducah roots). Texican's in Crestwood, inspired by the owners' time in Texas, brings awesome brisket and hot links to pork country. Frankfort Avenue Beer Depot serves up a wet brisket they dub "Louisville style." Rite Way fixes a slaw-on-top pork sandwich, and Scotty's Ribs and More serves juicy dry-rubbed ribs, both sandwich and ribs reminiscent of west Tennessee barbecue. Smoketown USA wowed me with their Flintstone beef ribs, the only beef ribs I encountered when tripping all over the Commonwealth. And the young culinary-school talents who own Hammerheads are taking Kentucky barbecue to a strange and wonderful place, smoking up scrumptious lamb ribs, Peking duck, and pork bellies.

Louisville, our largest city, stands as the only urban space in Kentucky. Lexington, with a population of around three hundred thousand (less than half of Louisville's), is more suburban, a sprawling university town. Louisville feels like a real city, with distinctive neighborhoods and a multicultural populace. I expect Louisville's rich barbecue offerings have something to do with the geographical diversity of its residents, while Lexington, home to transplants from Appalachia—a region lacking a strong barbecue tradition—has fewer barbecue offerings. Three of my favorite Lexington barbecue restaurants, after all, are owned by people with western Kentucky roots.

Welcome to Kentucky's funky-fun city for a pan-regional barbecue tour.

Rite Way Bar-B-Cue

I pulled the Ford Ranger up to the curb at Rite Way at dusk, and the neon sign hanging above the front window of this old two-story house in a West End neighborhood beckoned me inside. But before I could walk up the crumbling concrete steps to open the glass door, Terry, wife of owner and pit master Wesley Johnson, opened the door and welcomed me.

Open since 1942, Rite Way is a place to visit for funk, nostalgia, and neighborhood vibe. They still have the original phone number and an old rotary phone used for many years. A Xeroxed photo of President Obama and family decorates the back of the antique cash register on the counter. Old poster menus still hang on the wall, with only the prices painted over and changed throughout the years. The defunct deli cooler made me wonder if it ever held cold cuts and cheeses, or maybe raw meats for sale. A table near the door was covered in dozens of funeral programs, most with photos on the front.

"That's our death table," Terry said. "That's our customers who have passed." I thought it was really sweet, albeit a bit unsettling. Most folks don't want to be fronted with the specter of death before digging in to a pork sandwich, spareribs, or a chili-drenched Coney dog—Rite Way's best-selling items. And that's pretty much the whole menu.

Wesley's grandfather David started Rite Way during World War II. He had only a sixth-grade education and couldn't get financing, but he made it happen. When David died in 1982, Wesley's dad took over. Wesley's run the place since 2007, and he's worked there since he was a child, never had another job. He's now in his forties. Three generations of Johnsons have lived upstairs. Wesley still cooks on the original pit from 1942, using mixed hardwoods like hickory, oak, and maple. He also makes the slaws and sauces. Wesley tends the pits in back and makes sandwiches, while Terry takes care of the front. They run the whole show.

The pork sandwich was served with a dip sauce drizzled on it, so that the juices soaked down through the bun. The addition of slaw on top made this one messy sandwich, best eaten with a fork if you're wary of wet fingers. Boston butts are smoked using real wood and then brought inside and sliced on a deli slicer. Butts that have cooked longer will shred on the slicer. The meat on my sandwich had cooked for a shorter time—chewy slices instead of velvety shreds. The ribs were coated in the same thin vinegary sauce and served on a foil-lined plate. Hotheads can drizzle the bloodred table sauce on their barbecue, but go sparingly, as this stuff is potent enough to overwhelm the meats—a serious peppery hellbroth.

"I guess Wesley will take it with him when he dies," Terry said about the sauce. "Nobody knows the recipe. I don't even go around when he makes it." In the hot and humid summer months, customers who eat the hot sauced sandwiches sit in Rite Way with wet rags on top of their heads.

While Terry talked and I ate, a couple came in, and Terry introduced me. The giant of a man, six foot three, named Big Eddie Bowe, has known Wesley since childhood. I learned that he often eats Coney dogs dotted with hot sauce and that many customers come in for the same item regularly prepared in the same way by Wesley. "Wesley know how to dot it," Big Eddie said. "I don't spread it. There's some guys come in here and get a pork sandwich and the meat is just flaming red. That's some dangerous stuff right there."

Rite Way does mostly a takeout business and specializes in serving food into the late night, way past when most barbecue places close. Some customers recall a time when Wesley's grandfather and dad stayed open until 4:00 a.m., and men who'd been drinking would come in to "kill their stuff." The kids and grandkids of these patriarchs remember the wet brown bags filled with juicy barbecue they brought home.

"What keeps me coming down is the customers," Terry said. "They're remarkable. They can't get any kind of barbecue like they get here, and they keep coming. We have a lot of customers been coming for a long time, and now their grandkids are coming and their kids are coming."

When I left with a full belly and my mind swimming with Terry's stories of local lore and family history, the green-and-red lettered Rite Way Bar-B-Cue sign was glowing brighter than ever against the dark November night.

Open: Monday, 12:00 p.m.–8:00 p.m.; Tuesday, 12:00 p.m.–9:00 p.m.; Wednesday–Thursday, 12:00 p.m.–10:00 p.m.; Friday–Saturday, 12:00 p.m.–12:00 a.m. (sometimes closes from 3:00–5:00 in the afternoon if business is slow)

1548 West Catherine Street; 502-584-9385

Jimbo's Bar-B-Que ("The Sauce Is on the Side 'Cuz There's Nothing to Hide")

When living in southern Indiana for a year, I often observed the hillbilly flavor of the area, including the local dialects. Driving the country roads around Stinesville, I got lost and stopped to ask a yokel—ratty jeans, sleeveless T-shirt, work boots, crew cut—for directions. As I pulled away, I asked, "What's a Hoosier, anyway?" and he said, "That's me!"

My father, Ken Berry, said, "A Hoosier is a Kentuckian who learned how to cross the river." Maybe Dad was onto something, because Jeffrey Graf of Indiana University Libraries, researching the history of the word *Hoosier,* notes that it "was a term of contempt and opprobrium common in the upland South and used to denote a rustic, a bumpkin, a countryman, a roughneck, a hick or an awkward, uncouth or unskilled fellow. Although the word's derogatory meaning has faded, it can still be heard in its original sense, albeit less frequently than its cousins 'Cracker' and 'Redneck.'"

I bring this up because Jimbo's Bar-B-Que is a rare case of barbecue moving into Kentucky from Indiana. Maybe it's not too strange, though, as the original Jimbo's was in Corydon, Indiana, not too far west of Louisville across the Ohio River and at about the same longitude. This second (and now only) Jimbo's is located in southwest Louisville, right across from Iroquois Park, one of the largest public spaces in the city, and four miles south of Churchill Downs. Owners Nikki and Bob Barringer, Louisville natives, came to the business in 2004 after Bob's father, Bob Sr., bought out the original Jimbo over in Corydon. They bought a bar and transformed it into the current family-friendly restaurant.

Since its inception, Jimbo's has done open-pit barbecue, but in 2012 the Barringers bought an Ole Hickory cooker and are making the transformation. The barbecue I ate in May 2012 came from the open pit.

I sat out on a deck under blue skies during the lunch hour at one of several picnic tables shaded by Blue Moon Brewing Company umbrellas. Nikki said they sometimes have live bluegrass music on the weekends on the patio. I joked about them serving beer at a family barbecue place, and Nikki said, "This is a very Catholic community. It's a family-type atmosphere, but you can get a beer if you want."

My lunch began with a basket of beautiful fried green tomatoes—seven slices of tomatoes bought from local Amish folks, dipped in seasoned batter, and goldenly fried, served with a tangy blend of ranch dressing and hot sauce. They are served seasonally. I thought, *I regret that I have but one stomach to give to my country,* because these tomatoes were the first food other than coffee to touch my lips that day, and it was going to be a full day of eating, and I just wanted to finish that wonderful basket. Willpower won out in the end.

Tracy Barringer, Bob's sister, came out to check on me. She said when she was growing up in Louisville's southwestern Pleasure Ridge Park area, fried green tomatoes, fried zucchini, and fried squash were their Saturday night snack.

My belly juices awakened by the green maters, I was now ready to tackle Jimbo's sampler: two baby back ribs, two spareribs, two chicken wings, and pulled beef, chicken, and pork sliders. I also had to try the bar-b-que wrap and potato salad. The wrap is a flour tortilla, grilled and stuffed with pork, beef, or chicken (I chose beef), baked beans, slaw, dill pickles, onions, and barbecue sauce. The brown grill marks on the white tortilla make for a nice presentation and pleasant crispness. The wrap packs a lot of flavor in a convenient takeaway form. The overall effect was great. Some of the beef flavor came through, but merged with primary flavors of beans and slaw. The wrap comes with one side item. It's a good bet if you aren't hankering for pure barbecue but want a filling twist on barbecue to go.

The sampler, served in a foil-lined plastic basket, was enough food for two, especially if combined with the fried green tomatoes. The pork reminds me of Whitt's, the Nashville-based franchise—flaky, salty, and not extremely smoky. All the sandwich meats—beef, pork, and chicken—were on the dry, flaky side. Sandwiches are served with dill pickles and raw onion rings. When I tried the sandwiches with Jimbo's peppery, tangy, semi-thick tomato sauce, pickles, and onions, I found them good—which means that, for my tastes, the flaky meats aren't the star of this platter.

That award goes to the smoky, tender, dry-rubbed baby backs, the best thing on the plate. They were cooked just right, with a mahogany bark and the flavor of a peppery dry rub.

So upon returning to Jimbo's, I'd get a basket of fried green tomatoes during the growing season and a four-rib baby back rib dinner with the creamy red-skinned potato salad (more sour than sweet from the dill pickles and mustard) and the homemade banana pudding (which is actually offered as a side!). Runner-up is the pork sandwich.

Considering the name, you might expect to walk into Jimbo's and find a hillbilly fellow in overalls, but as Nikki pointed out, Jimbo's is an all-girl operation, "three in the front and three in the back." I got to meet the whole crew. They tolerated me while I snapped photos, intrigued as I was by an all-female crew, a rarity in barbecue—so often the passion of obsessed men.

Thanks for the hospitality and good food, ladies.

Open: Tuesday–Thursday, 11:00 a.m.–8:00 p.m.; Friday–Saturday, 11:00 a.m.–9:00 p.m.; Sunday, 12:00 p.m.–7:00 p.m.

801 West Kenwood Drive; 502-375-1888

Shack in the Back BBQ

My buddy Dixon and I were traveling south from Hoosierland on I-65 and feeling a hunger, and Dixon said, "I'd like to stop and get somethin' to eat when we get to barbecue country." Dixon's a Mississippi Delta boy who has lived in his home state for over four decades—never lived anywhere else—but had visited me in Kaintuck two years earlier and knew we had some fine barbecue.

The previous day I was giving blood in a Red Cross mobile unit on Indiana University's campus, and the woman checking my blood pressure told me it was high. "Well," I said, "I'm writing this book on Kentucky barbecue, see . . ." and she said, "I'm from Louisville." I asked her about Louisville barbecue, and she said I had to go to Shack in the Back in Fairdale, south of the big city. Ma'am, if you read this someday, my sincere thanks for the recommendation.

We pulled into the gravel parking lot behind the restaurant before dusk on a Saturday night and had a hard time finding a free spot among the swarm of vehicles. The Mike Willet band blasted an eclectic mix of tunes ("Day-O [The Banana Boat Song]," "Wasting Away in Margaritaville," "She Thinks My Tractor's Sexy") to diners eating outside under a covered patio. A smoking smokestack crowned by a steel cap in a birdhouse design with pig shapes cut from it rose from the pit area in the back of the restaurant. A copper-colored flying-pig weathervane rose from the roof. The driveway was lined with iron poles painted in racing flames with a sign hanging from a cable between posts that said, "Caution: hot BBQ." The property was full of fun touches like that.

Inside you'll find a small dining room and a log cabin decor, with photos of horses, black-and-white photos of old-fashioned scenes, pig decor (little ceramic pigs), and old Coca-Cola serving plates and cast-iron cookware on the walls. The logs look real because they are; Shack in the Back is housed in a restored log home from 1896.

My hopes heightened by the woodpile of hickory and fruit woods behind the restaurant, I walked to the counter and ordered up two meals for Dixon and me to share: a Shack sampler of ribs, smoked sausage, two small sandwiches (we chose chopped pork and chopped brisket), and a quarter-rack rib plate. Two sides came with each plate. We chose Nanny's potato salad, smoked baked beans, Wild Willie's coleslaw, and burgoo. We left the air-conditioned interior to go sit at a table on the patio. I love eating outside whenever the mosquitoes aren't biting too badly and it's warm enough. The music was loud, so if you prefer a quieter meal on a music night you might want to eat inside.

Our eyes nearly popped out when the food came. The sampler plate is a load of good eating. We halved the sandwiches and homemade smoked andouille sausage, popped the plastic tops off the side dishes, and started tucking it away.

The pulled-pork and chopped-brisket sandwiches were served on small soft rolls. Both were good, with subtle smoke flavor and tender, moist meat. I learned after talking with the pitmen later that evening that they smoke briskets twenty-two hours, so when I return I'll get the sliced brisket for the full smoky flavor of it. For my tastes, I found that the pork sandwich benefited from a drizzle of the "tangy" sauce.

As for sides, Dixon loved the slaw, a mayonnaise dressing mixed with fresh-sliced cabbage and carrots. I can see why they'd be proud of the slaw, as it would be easy for them to pop open a gallon of pre-made slaw and plop it onto plates, and this slaw, like the potato salad, was made at the restaurant. The pleasant crunch of the slaw and fresh taste made for a nice palate cleanser between bites of barbecue, but I let Dixon have most of it as I prefer vinegar slaws. The potato salad was a good creamy one with a taste of mustard. Our favorite sides were the smoked beans and burgoo. This particular burgoo was more like a stew; they didn't grind it into slurry as seems to be the fashion in Owensboro. Dixon hadn't had burgoo before—it's not common outside of western Kentucky, and the closest comparable taste I've found is the Brunswick stew of Georgia—and he liked it a lot.

We both had eyes for ribs, so we saved them for last—sort of worked up our appetites tasting through the other offerings, including the wonderful andouille sausage, which we both loved, as it was both spicy and smoky. We also tried the smoked chicken wings and—I'm serious—what's called a smoked "turkey rib"—a special cut of white-meat turkey that includes the scapula bone and the attached muscles. The chicken wings are slightly sweet with a pretty amber color, nice and crispy. I hardly ever get wings at a barbecue place, but these were great, tasting of honey and spice and smoke. Dixon said, "That's definitely what I want out of a wing." The turkey rib was also smoky and spicy, but without the sweetness of the chicken wings. Dixon loved the turkey rib, said it was his favorite thing on the plate. I also loved the full-on flavor. I'll get the turkey rib appetizer, which comes with five "ribs" and north Alabama–style white sauce, next time around.

And then the baby back ribs. We were already getting full when we started on them, but they were mighty fine still, with a tasty dry rub and sweetness from, we think, honey. The ribs were superbly tender and still had some pull on the bone. Dixon said, "If you like sweet ribs, these are great." That's true, but I have to qualify that, because these ribs weren't covered with barbecue sauce like so many midwestern ribs. You sauce your own at Shack in the Back, and they are tasty enough with smoke and rub that you don't need much sauce. I gnawed every last morsel of meat from the bones, even though my personal tastes lean toward more spice, salt, and smoke. But if you want good, tender, sweet ribs not coated in barbecue sauce, then you will probably eat these right up. They were pink in the middle from the smoke but still firm. As Dixon said, "You can't ask for any more than that."

Barbara and Mike Sivells, owners of Shack in the Back, have roots in Niagara Falls (Barbara's home city) and Hoptown (that's Hopkinsville). Barbara has lived down here for over twenty years. Hopkinsville is vinegar sauce country, and Barbara's personal tastes, fashioned by her childhood in Niagara Falls, where people drizzle vinegar on fried fish and eat vinegar and salt chips, lean toward the tangy as well. But Barbara said the folks in Louisville didn't take to their original vinegar sauces, so they've shifted to a tomato base and sweetened them up. When they opened in September 2006, the Sivellses started with open pits, but now they have a wood-fired rotisserie cooker that they load with meats for the slow and low smoking with hickory, apple, and cherry woods. They still cook the wood down to coals and shovel them underneath the meat—the old-timey style of barbecuing still common in western Kentucky. It's a pleasure to see such care taken just south of the big city.

The pitmen were lounging by the smokers this late Saturday night, and they showed us around before we hit the interstate south. These fellows were real ambassadors, lauding the freshness of the ingredients they use and telling me how many people have visited from all over the southern states, including Texas, and "bragged about" how good the food was at Shack in the Back. I enjoyed their enthusiasm because it was well earned. These hospitable folks

---

Shack in the Back BBQ's Sweet Sop

Barbara Sivells said of this recipe, "We mainly use it to toss our chicken wings in after they come off of the pit. We also glaze our bologna and baby back ribs with it before we serve them. My husband, Mike, thinks the sop is great on everything. That's why he named it *sop*. . . . He says, 'It's so good that you'll sop it all up with your bun!'"

5 pounds dark brown sugar
1 lemon, juiced
6 ounces honey
¼ gallon cider vinegar
2 tablespoons black pepper
2 tablespoons onion powder
2 tablespoons garlic powder
¾ tablespoon cayenne pepper
½ tablespoon habanero pepper sauce
½ tablespoon crushed red pepper
2 tablespoons Spanish paprika

Mix vinegar, honey, and lemon juice in pan over medium heat. Whisk in all spices thoroughly. Heat mixture until it comes to a boil. Add brown sugar, stirring constantly until completely dissolved.

---

made Kentucky proud on this night, and Dixon said as much. We both left with stuffed bellies, and as we drove down the road Dixon said, in his slow drawl, "Man, I'm feeling the pure barbecue bliss right now." I agreed that it was one of my best barbecue meals ever.

Open: Tuesday–Thursday, 11:00 a.m.–8:00 p.m.; Friday–Saturday, 11:00 a.m.–9:00 p.m.

406 Mt. Holly Road, Fairdale (Take exit 125 off I-65 and head west on Gene Snyder Expressway for two exits to New Cut Road. Exit and take a left. Shack in the Back is a short drive down the road on the right. Be careful when using a GPS to find this place, because mine led me astray.); 502-363-3227

www.shackinthebackbbq.com

Doc Crow's Southern Smokehouse and Raw Bar ("The Freshest Flavors of the American South")

Upscale barbecue in a downtown location, Doc Crow's is the swankiest restaurant featuring smoked meats I've visited, which says more about the high dive factor potential of barbecue than about Doc Crow's. I've eaten at fancier restaurants—just not ones specializing in barbecue.

The prices are surprisingly reasonable, though, considering the prime Main Street real estate and the money the owners sunk into remodeling this historic building that once housed whiskey barrels. In May 2012, a pulled-pork sandwich—a pile of smoked pork, tobacco onions, slaw, and pickles on a quality buttered and toasted bun—with house-made chips cost $7. Substitute fries or a side (like the superb mac and cheese cooked in béchamel sauce and nicely browned after baking, or fresh green beans cooked al dente with pieces of stewed tomatoes, diced onion, and house-made bacon) for $2 more. A half rack of dry-rubbed baby back ribs with Texas toast cost $12. These babies, served naked, reminded me of ribs I ate when judging a Memphis Barbecue Network rib contest (meaning, they were competition-quality ribs, hard to achieve in a restaurant). The tender brisket, eight ounces of thick-sliced beef cut from the whole smoked brisket, not just the flat, served on Texas toast and topped with rings of fresh onions, a few slices of pickle, and a complementary tomato-based sauce, cost $8. *Man v. Food* devotees might go for "the Bubba": a half-pound steak burger topped with pulled pork, beef brisket, fried green tomato, onion rings, a fried egg, slaw, and barbecue sauce. For the vegetarian in your group, there's a smoked portobello and fried green tomato sandwich, "topped with slaw on a toasted brioche bun," for $7.

The concept is pan-southern, so in addition to smoky meats they serve seafood po'boys, fried catfish, shrimp and grits, seafood gumbo, and desserts like bread pudding in bourbon sauce. A raw bar stands just inside the entrance, and oysters of the day are listed on a chalkboard. When I visited, three varieties of Virginia oysters were on ice. Behind the bar, the taps feature blue-collar beer like Pabst Blue Ribbon and boutique brews like Bluegrass Brewing Company's Bourbon Barrel Stout. A top-shelf bourbon selection includes such seldom-seen treats as Pappy Van Winkle's Family Reserve 23 Year Old Bourbon.

Oh, Kentucky. You've given the world some gustatory delights.

Doc Crow's is a huge place, running the length of a whole city block, and various sections of the restaurant have a distinctive feel. The front part, looking out onto Main Street, is casual, with wooden booths and tables and old brick walls painted white. The high ceilings remind you that this old building once held aging bourbon barrels (it was a bonding warehouse for bourbon whiskey). The midsection is an open-kitchen concept, exciting and busy as chefs plate food and servers deliver it. Beyond it, a section with six cushioned booths, stained wood, a black color motif (booths and wall panels), and subdued lighting (small lamps on the booths) seems designed for intimacy. In the back, two large rooms with floor-to-ceiling windows provide ample space for big parties or family dining. Beautiful wood floors add to the classy, comfortable ambiance. It's worth noting that the acoustics of this old bonding warehouse—the high ceilings and brick and woodwork—amplify sound. The restaurant was probably at 10 percent capacity when I visited during a midweek lunch hour, and I noted the way people's voices echoed in the front dining section. If desiring a quieter dinner on a busy night, you might prefer one of the six booths near the back.

Open since February 9, 2011, Doc Crow's is the brain child of wine expert Brett Davis, MS (master sommelier) and his colleagues in fine dining— Culinary Institute of America graduate Michael Ton (a French-trained chef) and Steven Ton, brother-owners of Basa, a modern Vietnamese cuisine restaurant on Frankfort Avenue in Louisville. Steven is one of the "godfathers of the craft cocktail in this region," according to Brett, a native of Knoxville,

Tennessee. How many chances do you have to eat barbecue at a restaurant developed by a Vietnamese chef with French culinary chops, a cocktail wizard, and a wine guru?

I asked Brett why experts in fine dining would open a restaurant specializing in pan-southern cuisine. He said, "When we open restaurants, we go into the location and figure out what they want to be. So we walked into this location and this is the historic whiskey row. You may have noticed we have a wall of 150 whiskeys. So we started with whiskey. What's the natural food for that? Well, barbecue. You got to have barbecue with that. But we didn't just want to be a barbecue joint. We all lived throughout the South, so we decided to do a southern concept. I lived in New Orleans and Savannah awhile, and Michael talked about doing more seafood. So we said, 'Okay, let's do a coastal southern concept,' so it's land *and* sea here. You have the barbecue, and we sell more raw oysters than any restaurant in the region. So we're not just a barbecue joint."

Meats are cooked on a Southern Pride unit at a "medium to medium-minus" level of smokiness "on purpose," Brett said, "because we like tasting the meat." The sandwiches and ribs were served on metal trays on top of brown butcher paper—an attractive and sensible way to eat barbecue, as the butcher paper absorbs dripping fats and sauces.

I told Brett I loved the mac and cheese—was pleased to get a side dish that tasted fresh and creative—and he said, "We use a béchamel sauce. There's a little French influence to that. We don't have a lot of secrets here. We don't think there are a lot of secrets to barbecue."

Right? Quality meats cooked with wood smoke at low heats (except for chicken) until appropriately tender. Not much of a secret to that.

Get the picture? Tender, moderately smoked meats and quality sides developed by classically trained chefs, merged with a top-shelf whiskey selection in a classy atmosphere in downtown Derby City, along with fresh oysters flown in regularly.

Got a sweet tooth? The Wilber's sundae splices together pig, cow, and corn (whiskey): "Brown butter praline ice cream with Bourbon caramel ribbon atop cinnamon pork rinds sprinkled with candied bacon topped with a Bourbon cherry." They use Comfy Cow ice cream, a Louisville shop that handcrafts ice cream, using the finest ingredients, in four-gallon batches.

Open: Monday–Thursday, 11:00 a.m.–10:00 p.m.; Friday, 11:00 a.m.–11:00 p.m.; Saturday, 5:00 p.m.–11:00 p.m.
127 West Main Street; 502-587-1626

Doc Crow's Southern Smokehouse and Raw Bar's Mac and Cheese

1 pound elbow macaroni cooked al dente
4 ounces Gruyère cheese
4 ounces Vermont cheddar cheese
½ cup of béchamel sauce (recipe follows)
Freshly ground black pepper to taste
Salt to taste

BÉCHAMEL SAUCE
5 tablespoons butter
4 tablespoons all-purpose flour
4 cups milk
2 teaspoons salt
½ teaspoon freshly grated nutmeg
2 fresh cloves

In a medium saucepan, heat the butter over medium-low heat until melted. Add the flour and stir until smooth. Over medium heat, cook until the mixture turns a light, golden, sandy color, about 6 to 7 minutes.

Meanwhile, heat the milk and cloves in a separate pan until the liquid is just about to boil. Add the hot milk to the butter mixture 1 cup at a time, whisking continuously until very smooth. Bring to a boil. Cook 15 minutes, stirring constantly, then remove from heat. Season with salt and nutmeg.

Gradually fold in half of the cheeses until a silky smooth consistency has developed. Mix in the elbow macaroni, spread mixture evenly into casserole dish, and top with the remaining cheese.

Preheat the oven to 475° and bake for 7 minutes or until a golden crust is formed.

Hammerheads

This neighborhood bar specializes in creative smoked meats like lamb ribs, duck tacos, and PBLTs (pork belly, lettuce, and tomato sandwiches). I've raved about the place to my foodie friends. Owned by two young chefs who met in culinary school—Oldham County native Adam Burress and Chase Mucerino from Dickson, Tennessee—Hammerheads takes barbecue to exciting new (or maybe old, as in Old World) places. After all, I expect to find duck on menus in France but not in a basement pub in an industrial section of Louisville.

Before opening Hammerheads, Chase and Adam worked at several restaurants around Louisville, honing their culinary skills. Adam was a *sous-chef* at Ceviche, an upscale Latin restaurant, for five years, and during that time he asked his food rep friend to supply him with off-the-beaten-path ingredients to play around with. "We had three *sous-chefs*," Adam said. "My job was just to play with shit and come up with specials. He sent me lamb ribs one time, and I'd never heard of lamb baby backs. I did 'em, loved 'em, and I was like, 'When I open a restaurant, I don't care what it is, I'm having 'em.'"

When I arrived at opening time, 5:00 p.m., the place was already busy with workers bustling about preparing for the Wednesday evening crowd. I took a barstool at a counter by the entrance, fronting big windows that look out on the small houses across the street and the sidewalk picnic tables. By 6:45 the hostess had to tell people that no tables were available. They've been open only since December 2010, and already they're serving 150–200 people in a four- to five-hour dinner shift.

Meats smoke on cylindrical steel tank units off to the side of the pub, perfuming the neighborhood with smoke from chunks of hickory and cherry wood burned in the fireboxes outside the main cooking chamber. When trees are cut at a local park, the workers bring loads of wood to Hammerheads. The double-barreled smoker, sitting on a portable trailer, came from outside Panama City, Florida. This particular smoker works on a "reverse flow" design, where the firebox and smokestack are on the same side of the unit, creating a convection effect in which the smoke has to pass over the meats twice before exiting the smokestack. This results in some super-smoky meats.

And what fabulous meats they are. They smoke whole briskets after cutting off the tail ends (which they grind into hamburgers). Hungry for a burger? They grind all meats in house and offer elk, venison, lamb, chorizo, and Angus burgers. They try to get meats from local sources when possible. Signature dishes include tacos with soft-shell crab, duck, beef, or pork. I loved the deeply smoked duck. The BBQ lamb ribs were served, like everything else, on an attractive wooden board and garnished with spring greens and a brown herb-infused sauce—the Hammerhead version of a barbecue sauce that's closer to a Daviess County mutton dip than to a Kansas City sauce—but really, this sauce is in a class of its own, hard to compare to conventional flavors. The pink lamb ribs were beautifully smoked and tender. If you're not afraid of fat and love the flavor of lamb, get them. Likewise, the decadent PBLT sandwich, along with a big basket of French fries cooked in duck fat, made a perfect meal. The PBLT was four thick strips of pork belly—sliced much thicker than typical bacon—with a deep smoke ring, served on Texas toast with lettuce, a slice of tomato, and sun-dried tomato aioli. The duck-fat fries

Hammerheads' Smoked Duck Tacos

Adam Burress and Chase Mucerino said they were glad to contribute recipes for this book. Well, they did, but it's clear these guys are chefs and not cookbook writers. I imagine much of their cooking relies on intuition. I've actually padded the "recipe" they sent me, adding smoking temperature, for instance. In short, this isn't much of a recipe. You have to experiment with spice proportions on the wet rub, for example, and figure out how to make the aioli. But I'm including it here for the adventuresome cook and to give a recipe snapshot of Hammerheads' freaky take on barbecue.

1 whole white Peking duck
Wet rub: sweet chili sauce, garlic powder, onion powder, curry powder, adobo
Corn tortillas and garnishes

Mix together wet rub and slather on the duck. Smoke indirectly with cherry wood at 220°F for 4 to 6 hours, then cover with foil and roast for about 3 to 4 hours. Pull the duck and serve on grilled corn tortillas with pico de gallo, cilantro, and jalapeño-lime aioli.

were rich and perfectly crisp. Oh, I began my meal with a scrumptious pretzel croissant dipped in homemade beer cheese made with Founders Double Trouble ale. The croissants are made by Klaus Riedelsheimer at his cottage industry, the Pretzel Baker, just up the street from Hammerheads. If you want, they'll serve your PBLT on one of Klaus's pretzel buns.

What else? They have crab cakes and smoked catfish, chicken and waffles, shrimp and grits, baby back ribs, panko-breaded deep-fried mac and cheese balls with Hollandaise sauce, a smoked cheddar grit cake, smoked mac and cheese, jalapeño-apple slaw, French fries tossed in truffle oil, and bacon brownies. Beer drinkers can cleanse the palate with several draught options, like St. Bernardus Tripel, Founders Double Trouble IPA, or Mahr's Ungespundet lager.

As I worked my way through these delights, the setting sun filtered through the windows and lit upon the cheerful yellow-painted walls, and middle-aged folks sipped beer from tulip glasses along the long bar. A little while later, at 7:00, people clad in shorts and sandals stood behind these folks, talking and laughing but unable to sit because the place was packed.

This place is just awesome. Local touches fill the restaurant. For instance, the draught beer taps are ten individual funky pieces crafted at a local art glass studio. The food is gourmet but the atmosphere is laid back and quirky, fun and convivial. Get there early if you want a table. Look for the hammerhead shark mounted above the entrance.

Open: Monday–Saturday, 5:00 p.m.–late
921 Swan Street; 502-365-1112

Smoketown USA

One of the funkiest barbecue restaurants you'll find anywhere, Smoketown USA caters to lovers of deliciously smoked meats and to vegetarians, and the building that's home to this artful establishment is a big brick structure built in 1862 that's been, over the years, a grocery, a seed and feed store, and a blacksmith shop. Now it's a barbecue destination and rotating yard sale, as Eric and Lynn Gould, owners, decorate the walls and ceilings with "an ever-changing array" of funky junk. The tall interior walls are old brick with various colors of paint that's been applied over the past 150 years—which Eric discovered after scraping the walls with a shovel and decided to put polyurethane over it to keep the weathered look. Your eyes can hardly take in all the artwork, much of it abstract, and pottery and mobiles hanging from the ceiling. The restaurant's located in urban Louisville, not far from downtown in the historic Germantown/Smoketown community.

Eric and Lynn bought the building in 2002 and then spent several years rehabilitating it. "The floor was like a total roller coaster," Eric said. "We had to put new beams underneath. New heating, air, plumbing, electric, everything." They opened for business in May 2007.

"Everything here is for sale," Eric said. "If you like the table, chairs, salt, pepper, art. Everything turns. It just flows."

I said, "So you are the owner, right?"

"I'm the owner and my wife owns me."

Eric cooks out back on a big iron unit using the indirect heat of mixed hardwoods. Meats are seasoned with salt, pepper, and garlic and browned for one and a half hours before steaming in the smoker for four more hours. "So simple," Eric said, "but simple is good. They put so much schlep on things sometimes, they're losing money and they're losing style. Because sometimes you just need to get the basics of what meat is."

I had to try the appropriately named Flintstones, *huge* beef ribs that made my jaw drop twice—first when I saw the price ($23) and second when the server, Crystal, carried them to the table and set them in front of me. Then I understood the price tag: these ribs could feed two to three people, as four bones came with the order, each wrapped with a healthy mass of meat. I wonder how much each rib weighs. I'm thinking about a half pound. The Flintstones rank highly in my "memorable meals" list, as I've just not eaten anything like them anywhere else. While traveling in Texas I've eaten beef ribs, but none of them were as huge and meaty as these at Smoketown. Oh, my, and talk about tender. The fat and flesh melt in your mouth. Get ready for sticky fingers from the sweet glaze.

The beef ribs were served with two sides and my choice of sweet or jalapeño cornbread. The mac and cheese competes with the best I've eaten, full of garlic and black pepper and a two-cheese sauce, and the savory soul greens are mixed greens (mustard, turnip, collard) cooked in a veggie base with marinated tomatoes, black-eyed peas, jalapeño, and Tabasco. The menu advertises that "most of our sides are vegetarian friendly, seasoned with spices and roasted vegetable base." Their cornbreads incorporate half cake and half corn-meal, so it's like a little dessert. The jalapeño bite with the sweetness was distinctive and really good. "It's silly to get rid of 10 percent of America," Eric said. "Think about it: at almost every business, you got a vegetarian in there."

Eric David Gould is a funny guy—a Jewish fellow with Chicago Polish ancestry (his grandfather, he said, worked for Capone), wearing a black apron over farmer's overalls and a baseball cap on his head. Philosophically chatty, Eric mills about talking with customers when not taking orders or tending the smoker.

In a word, Eric knows food and has an eye out for his clientele, with the vegetarian sides and the portobello mushroom sandwich, my first time seeing one of these at a barbecue place. Eric can serve tofu "burgers" if he wants and I'll still respect his craft, because those Flintstones made a true believer out of me. I wonder what the pork ribs, pulled pork, and brisket are like. Guess I'll just have to return to find out! But I'd probably just dive into the Flintstones again, as I'm not in Louisville often and those beef ribs were truly extraordinary, competing with Knockum Hill's huge pork chop and Hammerheads' smoked lamb ribs and duck tacos to claim the title "Most Innovative Barbecue in the Bluegrass."

Open: Tuesday–Thursday, 11:00 a.m.–9:00 p.m.; Friday–Saturday, 11:00 a.m.–10:00 p.m.

1153 Logan Street; 502-409-9180

www.smoketownusa.com

Frankfort Avenue Beer Depot & Smokehouse ("Louisville Style BBQ")

This bright-red pub with two huge barrel smokers out front was jamming during a Saturday lunch hour. I got a kick out of the sports bar atmosphere. Aquariums are mounted near the ceiling, and ductwork is exposed. Out back on a patio sit picnic tables near a wacky play area called Beerhalla, cluttered with cornhole boards, putt-putt golf, and ping pong tables. Inside at the bar, men watched football on big televisions. I noted kids, women, and a young couple eating at tables farther back from the bar.

It's a watering hole, so there are plenty of domestics and imports to choose from, along with a full bar. I was surprised to see Falls City beer on

Smoketown USA's Multipurpose Dry Rub (a.k.a. 3-2-1 Mix)

Eric David Gould says that his barbecue methods are simple and good. I agree. Eric kindly shared the dry rub mixture he sprinkles on all of his meats before smoking and steaming them at temperatures between 275 and 325°F. I've mixed dry rubs at home that contain ten or more ingredients. Eric's contains only three. The heavy proportion of garlic makes this rub unique—one of the secrets, I think, of those fabulous Flintstone beef ribs at Smoketown USA.

While many dry rubs make a good tenderizer for through-the-night marinating, this one, Eric says, should be applied close to the time of smoking.

3 cups granulated garlic (or garlic powder)
2 cups ground black pepper
1 cup fine salt

Mix ingredients together. Sprinkle on beef, pork, and chicken right before smoking.

Smoketown USA's Mac and Cheese

This delicious version of an old favorite is courtesy of Eric David and Lynn Gould.

1 pound macaroni, cooked and drained
1 cup canned cheddar cheese sauce
⅓ brick Velveeta
1 cup whole milk
⅓ stick butter
3-2-1 mix (see the Smoketown's Multipurpose Dry Rub above)

Cook macaroni a little on the firm side and rinse with cold water after cooking. Put macaroni in a 13 x 9–inch pan that has been sprayed with cooking spray.

Mix all ingredients except macaroni in a glass measuring bowl. Heat in microwave for three or four minutes. Stir and continue to heat and stir until well blended. Pour over cooked macaroni. Bake in a preheated 325° oven for 20–30 minutes (check on it at 20 minutes).

tap, thinking that this cheap lager had gone the way of the dinosaurs, but discovered that the old Louisville brewery is back in business with a new vision after being watered down by corporate brewers over the past decades. The new taste—an American pale ale this time around—returns to the old vision of Ben Schrader, who founded the brewery in 1905 to create competition for a local monopoly on beer production. Check out the fascinating story at the Falls City website (fallscitybeer.com). It's only proper that an established Louisville sports bar would serve the local brew. It's a good cheap brew to go with your barbecue.

All meats are hickory smoked at 350° for six to eight hours on the big barrel units. They do pork pulled from Boston butts, chickens, baby back ribs, and a "Lou-a-vul beef brisket" (meaning it's wet, sauced before serving). They also offer smoked burgers and brats, and sometimes they smoke salmon, making the place a hot spot during Lent. (Louisville's a big Catholic area, like Owensboro and northern Kentucky, setting it apart from the Protestant wilds of the rest of the state.) They've a range of caloric appetizers (fried cheese balls with horseradish sour cream, saucy wings, battered and deep-fried green beans, battered and deep-fried sliced onions), chili with their own smoked meats, ham-rich bean soup, and sides such as broccoli and cheese, mac and cheese, and green beans. The brisket slow-roasts in a pan, and the dry-rubbed ribs are wet mopped with a dip of cider vinegar, Worcestershire sauce, and their dry rub during the first four hours of cooking. Most sides are homemade. The bean soup, served with cornbread, was voted "best in Louisville" in a *Courier-Journal* readers' poll; the soup includes a whole smoked spiral ham that's cooked down slowly all day with the beans.

My cousin Jason and I ordered sandwiches and sides. The brisket sandwich was a mound of meat heaped up three to four inches between a buttery browned bun. The pre-saucing gives it the appearance of a handsome sloppy joe. By itself the meat has the texture of roast beef, with some good bark on it. I liked it, but it is more roast beefy than briskety. The potato salad was magnificent, red-skinned potatoes mixed with creamy mustard-mayo sauce and chunks of celery. I also loved the salty green beans with a spicy pepper kick, cooked down with bacon and pulled pork, so tasty I drank the bean juice. You have to love salt to appreciate these beans. I think they might also have some barbecue sauce in them. The pulled pork was also heaped on a good bun, tender and moist with a moderate smoke flavor, served without sauce. Because the pork needed salt, I added some mild table sauce, a complexly flavored concoction with an onion crunch, sweet fruity notes, and chili pepper. Sandwiches are served with pickles. The barbecue wasn't the best I've ever had, but the sandwiches were hefty in the hand and very good, and the sides were excellent. I think if they reduced the cooking temperatures and smoked the butts longer, the meats would be juicer and smokier and make this one of my favorite places in Kentucky.

And by the way, the women who took care of us were as sweet as southern tea. Thank you, ladies.

Open: Monday–Wednesday, 11:00 a.m.–10:00 p.m.; Thursday–Saturday, 11:00 a.m.–11:00 p.m.; Sunday, 12:00 p.m.–10:00 p.m. (kitchen hours—bar hours are longer)

3204 Frankfort Avenue; 502-895-3223

Ole Hickory Pit

Multiple stacks and humongous wheels of hardwood fill up the yard space behind Ole Hickory Pit. This isn't what I expected from a suburban barbecue joint. I thought wood would be hard to come by in the city. Kenny Ramage, proprietor, uses big firebrick pits in the style found in Paducah and other western Kentucky barbecue towns. The brick holds the heat better, according to Kenny, and makes it easier to hold a constant temperature. Of course, the purveyors of modern barbecue might argue that a gas-electric oven holds a constant temperature as well. True. But you won't get that magical quality of fat dripping down on ash and then radiating back up into the meat unless you cook over wood.

In the back of Ole Hickory I met Richard, who has tended the pits for twenty years. His shift starts at 5:30 a.m. He slow-smokes Boston butts and beef briskets for fifteen hours and mutton leg quarters for eight hours, using hickory, oak, and ash. Richard has smoked so long that he goes by "feel," not a temperature gauge. I asked Richard how long he planned to keep tending the pits, and he joked, "I'd like to quit right now!" before adding, "But this place is family owned and they're good people, and that means a lot."

The most popular items at Ole Hickory Pit are the hand-pulled chicken and pork. Kenny and his son Tyler are barbecue purists, meaning that they don't add a bunch of seasonings to the meat. Time, heat, and smoke are their major ingredients. They smoke, as Tyler says, with "any wood that bears a nut," despite the hickory in their title. They used to smoke with 100 percent hickory, but it's getting harder to find. Sometimes they have to get hickory shipped in from Tennessee. Tyler says that any nut-bearing tree will yield a similar flavor to hickory, so now they mix woods.

Their quarter and half chickens, which cook four to six hours on the pit, as well as their pork ribs, come right off the pit with no seasonings added. The flavor of smoke, skin, and meat of the chickens is magnificent. To the chopped pork, pulled chicken, turkey, and mutton they add a very light vinegar-based sauce to prevent dryness, but it doesn't affect the natural flavor much at all. You can get any of the meats on toast, hoecakes, or bun. The pork and mutton sandwiches at Ole Hickory are good, and the chicken off the pit is real good. The pork sandwich came with a healthy portion of pork with some bark mixed in on a lightly toasted bun. I prefer more smoke, so on my next visit I'll request more bark. The pork has a good vinegar tang from the sauce that's already mixed into the meat. I was surprised to find mutton on a menu in Louisville, and the mutton sandwich satisfied me with its distinctive gamy flavor. The mutton was sauced, and the flavor soaked into the bun. In short, if you like mutton, you'll be happy to find it here in Louisville. If you haven't tried mutton, that special meat of far-western Kentucky, then you should. Put "Try mutton" on your bucket list.

Homemade side items include barbecue and white beans, slaw made fresh every day, potato salad, mac and cheese, fried apples, and green beans. I also sampled an oddity called "fried corn on the cob" for the first time in my life. It's a simple concept, really. Take an ear of corn and throw it into a deep fryer. It was hot and tasty with butter on the outside. I laughed about it. I mean, who ever thought of deep-frying corn!

The hospitality at Ole Hickory is superb, in part because Kenny and Tyler are such amiable folks. I really loved the family atmosphere. Tyler, the oldest of three sons in the Ramage family, told me the story of their barbecue history. On the wall behind the counter hangs a photo of Kenny Ramage with his father in front of their original barbecue place in Paducah in 1941, when a barbecue sandwich cost 30¢. Tyler's grandfather, a brick layer, built the pits at Kountry Kastle and Starnes in Paducah, the ones at Ole Hickory, and others in western Kentucky, and he worked at Kountry Kastle in the 1940s–60s. Kenny said his father was the one who started the barbecue on toast tradition of the McCracken County area, and also the split hot dog with chili on a toasted bun. Kenny's sister, Faye, owns O'Tyme Hickory Pit in Paducah.

When I asked Kenny what differentiates Louisville barbecue from western Kentucky barbecue, he said he didn't know how other people in Louisville cooked, but "if you don't see a hundred ricks of wood behind the building then you know there's something wrong. I mean, you can have a rick of wood on your place and fool anybody, but if you are actually cooking with 100 percent wood then you got to have a lot of it, right?"

I recommend getting the meats off the pit—which I prefer wherever it's an option—because the meat will be less adulterated by pre-saucing. Tyler said they used to do "off the pit" for each order, but their business is too booming now to do custom-chopped sandwiches for each order. He said they often serve 400–450 barbecue plates per day. Ask, though, and you may be treated to some off-the-pit action. The best way to guarantee meat off the pit is to go for a quarter or half chicken.

Open: Monday–Thursday, 10:00 a.m.–8:00 p.m.; Friday–Saturday, 10:00 a.m.–9:00 p.m.

6106 Shepherdsville Road; 502-968-0585

The Smokehouse BBQ

I stumbled upon this newish barbecue place south of Louisville in the Fern Creek area on the road to Bardstown, and I'm glad I did. Located in a converted Pizza Hut, the restaurant has a bar and televisions playing sports in all four corners. I ate a pork sandwich with homemade seasoned chips. The pork was served without sauce on a cornmeal-dusted bun. Four table sauces are labeled house, hot, spicy, and habanero. This is a family-style place with enough offerings to satisfy various tastes: salads topped with smoked chicken, smoked turkey, or grilled salmon; a turkey melt; a grilled burger; a walleye sandwich (an unusual find for central and western Kentucky, but popular in the northern parts of the state). Barbecue, however, forms the core of the menu, with loin back and spareribs, smoked chicken, and beef brisket. A combo meal comes with a quarter slab of ribs and another meat plus two sides. Meats are cooked out back on a Southern Pride unit.

The sandwich was a heap of pork, unsauced, on a good bun, lightly toasted on the inside, served on an oval plate alongside a pile of salty homemade seasoned chips. I also tried a loin back rib, juicy and smoky. When I return, I'll get a half-slab rib plate with fried potatoes and onions and rich collard greens seasoned with jowl bacon and bacon bits. Or maybe I'll get the brisket, very tender and sliced about half an inch thick, nice and fatty with a good bark on it, served with a horseradish sauce I found unnecessary and overwhelming. The ribs don't really need a sauce, but I did like the habanero sauce with the loin rib. Of all the sauces, I liked the spicy one with hints of molasses the best.

While eating I talked with a fellow who said he'd been back four times for ribs since first trying them just weeks before. The restaurant was pretty busy for 2:00 on a Saturday afternoon. I noted how customers talked between tables and booths—a pleasant community atmosphere. I walked over to a table to check out what a young couple was eating and got to see an "onion straw loaf" appetizer, a whole platter heaped with lightly breaded onions fried until crispy, served with petal sauce. Four people could sensibly share it. I also saw the peppered fried potatoes, and they too were loaded up on the plate. The Smokehouse is a place to fill up on good food for reasonable prices; big portions are their style.

When I visited in November 2011, Deb Hunter, who runs the place along with her husband, David, said they'd been in business for one year. She reported that the place is packed on Friday and Saturday nights. While I talked with Deb, two middle-aged women were paying and one said, "I'm so glad this place came here. Don't go nowhere."

"We're not planning on it," Deb answered.

David smokes ribs for six and a half hours, briskets for fifteen and a half hours, and butts for fourteen hours. He wraps the meats in foil, so they're not getting smoke all the time. He uses hickory but has also tried apple and cherry woods.

David used to run a barbecue place in Bedford, Kentucky, in Trimble County, where he cooked on kettle-type cookers, but he said the labor was

The Smokehouse BBQ's Collard Greens

Thanks to Deb and David Hunter for this simple but delicious recipe.

½ bushel collard greens, washed and cut into 1-inch strips
2 large onions, diced
1 large piece smoked jowl bacon, cut into large chunks
3 cups precooked bacon pieces
1 gallon water
3 tablespoons canola oil

In a stockpot, heat oil. Sauté jowl, onion, and bacon pieces until the onions are translucent. Add water and greens. Cover and cook until stems are soft. Salt and pepper to taste.

The Smokehouse BBQ's Habanero Sauce

Deb and David Hunter's hottest sauce balances tanginess with sweetness and finishes with a medium burn.

13 habanero peppers, washed and cut
2 cups onions, diced
⅛ cup canola oil
56 ounces ketchup
5 cups water
1 cup apple cider vinegar
⅛ cup lemon juice
⅛ cup chopped garlic in water
½ cup red wine vinegar
1 cup molasses
½ cup honey
1 cup Worcestershire sauce
½ pound dark brown sugar
Splash of ground cayenne pepper

Heat canola oil and sauté onion and habanero until onions are translucent. Add all remaining ingredients and simmer on low heat 30 minutes. Remove from heat and puree in blender.

too intensive—having to babysit briskets for fifteen hours and batches of burgoo for thirty hours. "You can't stop stirring on low heat," he said. "You stop stirring and it all burns."

Homemade sides, big portions, a family business, and very good smoked meats—there's a lot to like here.

Open: Tuesday–Thursday, 11:00 a.m.–9:00 p.m.; Friday–Saturday, 11:00 a.m.–10:00 p.m.; Sunday, 11:00 a.m.–8:00 p.m.

5414 Bardstown Road; 502-239-4422

Bootleg Bar-B-Q

A big billboard let me know I was close to Bootleg Bar-B-Q. You might miss it otherwise, as the joint stands about one hundred yards off the highway. I pulled into the gravel parking lot around 1:00 on one of the hottest days in Kentucky history. Actual temperatures soared to the high 90s, and the heat index was close to 120. My twenty-year-old Ford Ranger had no air-conditioning, so I was sweating plenty as this potentially air-conditioned oasis beckoned me from Bardstown Road (U.S. 31-E).

In business since 1991, Bootleg is a squatty shack of weathered barn wood and plywood, with a piece of pig art perched on top of the roof—the outline of a pig shaped from pink-painted steel with wings made from two yard rakes and welded together with pieces of farm machinery. Picnic tables sit under a covered outdoor eating area. The gravel parking lot was colored by catering vans with kitschy logos painted on the sides. Flames ran along the bottoms and back doors of one van, and happy cartoon pigs appeared to be looking out the windows. Another featured a cartoon bandit in overalls lifting a happy-looking pig in a red wheelbarrow. The biggest van—a blocky behemoth painted Plochman's mustard yellow—loomed over the smaller cars and trucks of customers.

Inside, I stood back from the ordering counter and pondered the extensive wall menu. A few rustic tables and chairs lined the windows offside the ordering counter—an intimate and homey place to eat. Nothing fancy, in a good way. Only three other customers were in the place when I arrived, but when I left an hour later, several more people were eating in the air-conditioned dining room—an impressive showing at 2:00 on a sweltering Monday afternoon.

Bootleg offers baby back ribs and spareribs, brisket (but they were out of beef), mutton (but they were out of mutton because their supplier raised prices). They have specials every day of the week. I ordered the Monday special: red beans and rice with a double-smoked sausage, a load of food for $4. I also got a quarter chicken dinner and "pulled pork" in a to-go container, because I was visiting friends in northern Illinois that evening and wanted to treat them to some Kentucky barbecue.

In a move that probably baffled everyone else in the air-conditioned shack, I took my tray of food outside to eat at the picnic tables in the sweltering heat. I like speaking into a digital voice recorder when taking barbecue notes, and if I'm solo I feel weird sitting around other people in a restaurant and talking to myself. People look at me strangely. I chose privacy over comfort in this case. Needless to say, nobody else was foolish enough to sit outside in the oppressive heat.

I started with the red beans and rice. The woman had lined a paper plate with a bed of rice and topped it with a "Creole" sauce that tasted to me much like marinara, topped with red beans and a roughly chopped kielbasa-like sausage, served with a bland white roll. The pieces of sausage were good, and as a cheap fill-up, this was a worthy dish. The shredded pork, unfortunately, came heavily sauced. The meat was tender and moist but not very smoky. It's the kind of shredded pork I expect from industrial food services like Aramark. Sure enough, for the past several falls, at the beginning of the new semester at Western Kentucky University, I've co-hosted an event called Barbecue with the Professors to welcome new students, and Aramark caters the event. The mediocre stuff that Aramark calls "barbecue" is shredded pork heavily coated in a thick sweet sauce—what I call "Yankee barbecue." I lived near Chicago a while, and that heavily sauced meat seems to be the ideal up there, whereas in western Kentucky the focus is on smoky meats, not the sauce. Bootleg's shredded pork reminded me of Yankee barbecue, which shouldn't surprise me, considering Louisville's geography just south of the Ohio River.

With the quarter chicken dinner, you choose a wing-breast or thigh-leg portion. White meat costs extra. You also choose two sides. I had potatoes two ways. The "down home tater salad" was cold and creamy, with mayonnaise, flecks of pepper, and dill pickle. I preferred the "twice baked potato casserole," whipped potatoes with cheese and chives. The chicken was pretty good, a breast and wing with a dry rub and a slight smoky flavor. The two plastic containers of sauce that came with the chicken dinner were dark brown in color, thick, sweet, tangy, and peppery. Because the chicken doesn't have much smoke flavor, a little sauce pepped it up a bit.

After lunch, a nice fellow named Paul Blandford—the day-shift manager who has worked for Bootleg for eight years, since he was age fifteen—showed me their propane-heated rotisserie cookers. Chicken wings with a sweet glaze and half chickens browned on the rotisserie. Baby back ribs cook for four hours at 250°, and spareribs cook for seven hours. I tried two spareribs and liked them very much—thought they were the best thing I'd eaten at Bootleg. They were tender, juicy, and delicious, with a dry rub and sprinkling of sugar on the outside, served with a sweet and tangy sauce with a hint of Worcestershire. I sucked the bones clean.

Paul said they use real potatoes for their mashed potatoes and gravy, and they serve a "cactus salad," spicy vinegar slaw. They also serve burgoo, that distinctive Kentucky stew, and try to keep it on hand all the time, but don't sell much of it. I was surprised to see both burgoo and mutton on the menu, and Paul admitted that they don't sell much of either.

When talking about the advantages of propane, Paul said, "It's a lot easier to maintain a temperature, plus you can cook overnight—you ain't got to sit here and stoke a fire or something." I think of Mr. Quarles at Mr. BBQ in Grand Rivers, who shovels hickory coals underneath whole pork shoulders for twenty-four hours. What a difference in labor costs, and what a difference in flavor. But apparently people don't much seem to mind that Bootleg cooks with gas and sauces their meats heavily, as business is good. Paul said they do as much business in catering as in the restaurants, and that their big catering customers include Jim Beam and Heaven Hill, both bourbon distillers; Zappos, a shoe outlet down the road; and weddings, graduation parties, and drug reps.

My final recommendation: Bootleg Bar-B-Q is worth a visit. After my disappointment with the heavily sauced shredded pork, I saw a sign above the ordering counter that says you can get meat without sauce if you ask for it. So, I'd be happy returning to Bootleg and getting some of those tender dry-rubbed ribs, and also trying their mashed potatoes and gravy and "spicy-hot cactus salad." The red beans and rice are worthwhile, too. The chicken wings with sweet glaze also looked good. They also offer desserts, including fruit cobblers, bread pudding, and MoonPies. Next time I'll sit inside the small dining area and enjoy the cool conditioned air.

Open: Monday–Thursday, 11:00 a.m.–8:00 p.m.; Friday–Saturday, 11:00 a.m.–9:00 p.m.; Sunday, 11:00 a.m.–8:00 p.m.

9704 Bardstown Road; 502-239-2722

Mark's Feed Store ("Friendly Folks Servin' Famous Food")

A Louisville success story since 1988, Mark's draws a crowd at its five area restaurants, each with a different look but serving the same food. You'll find the most interesting architecture at 1514 Bardstown Road—a remodeled old two-story brick building—and the coolest interior decor at the original Mark's in east Louisville, housed in a historic building that operated for over fifty years as Hancock's Feed Store.

I'd say the company motto, "Friendly Folks Servin' Famous Food," is fair on both points: the atmosphere is warm and hospitable, and Mark's ranks near the top of Kentucky's best-known barbecue brands. Moonlite would be first; Mark's is probably second.

I hadn't intended to review barbecue chains or franchises for this book, which is why you don't see Smokey Bones, Famous Dave's, or Whitt's. But Mark's Feed Store is such a well-patronized Louisville establishment that I decided to go there to see what the fuss was about. I chose the original location on Shelbyville Road because I'd eaten at the Mark's on Bardstown Road several years before.

I was pleasantly surprised to find that each Mark's location makes food fresh daily. Operations manager Mary Stebbins and Shelbyville Road manager Gary Dean gave me a thorough tour of the kitchen before the lunch rush, and I saw stacks of buttermilk pies made in house daily, and fresh-made baked beans and green beans (both enriched by chopped pork)—"We're not very vegetarian friendly," Mary said—and I saw a hot steam tray filled with burgoo (containing brisket, chicken, and pork), also made fresh daily. I met a kitchen worker named Fred, who's been with Mark's since they opened twenty-four years ago, back when they did open-pit barbecue. Mark's now uses Southern Pride rotisseries fed with locally sourced green hickory wood and cooks whole shoulders for their lightly smoked pulled pork. Shoulders cook for eleven to thirteen hours, briskets for nine to ten hours, chickens for three to three and a half hours. Mary said, "We're middle of the road when it comes to smoke flavor," because they are accommodating the tastes of a wide customer base, and frankly many people don't like intensely smoked meats.

The open pits caught fire back in the day before they switched to gas. Fred said, "It wasn't pretty." Fred's long staying power is proof that Mark's philosophy—"If you treat the employees well, they will treat the customers well"—works. Fred makes the buttermilk pies early each morning.

The decor is comfortable-nostalgic, with the original feed store cinderblock walls painted a pretty shade of red, and fifteen-to-twenty-feet-tall ceilings with exposed slats and rafters like an open barn. Ceiling fans keep the air moving. On the walls hang black-and-white historic scenes of men standing in front of old markets, agricultural landscapes, country roads, barns and windmills. Natural light comes in through the windows. The dining area is open and spacious—a family-friendly place with lots of booths and tables covered in blue and white checkered tablecloths. Country music played lightly in the background.

I ate through the "greatest hits" of Mark's menu and washed it all down with tall glasses of not-too-sweet iced tea (so good I drank a couple quarts of it). I started with the burgoo and a corn muffin. The thick burgoo, made from a roux, tastes much different than those found in Owensboro. It's good, a rich, gravy-like stew of corn, peas, beef, pork, and chunks of chicken. I ate baby back ribs glazed with sauce; honeywings (breaded fried chicken wings glazed with a honey sauce); half-inch-sliced beef brisket moderately smoked; mildly smoked moist pulled pork (normally served with a mustard-based sauce, unless you request it dry); onion straws; fried dill pickle chips; fried corn; potato salad; and blackened chicken pasta made with bowtie pasta and smoked, pulled, diced, and sautéed-blackened chicken, with shredded carrots, purple cabbage, and a creamy-Italian type dressing.

The potato salad, made fresh daily, is in high demand; the Shelbyville Road store sells about six hundred pounds of it on Easter and Christmas Eve. I surely see why. This potato salad wins top honors for Best Potato Salad in Kentucky according to my own personal taste preferences: boiled and cut red-skinned potatoes and hard-cooked eggs coated in a dressing of sour cream, with touches of celery seed and green onions (I'm guessing—they didn't give me the recipe). This is similar to how I make potato salad at home.

I'd totally return to Mark's and get the burgoo, beef brisket, chicken pasta salad, thin and crispy onion straws served with a dip of ranch dressing and hot sauce, the *divine* potato salad, the crispy fried pickle chips, fried corn, and crispy-crusted sweet buttermilk pie. I wouldn't get the pulled pork (not smoky enough for me) or ribs (too saucy and not smoky enough for my liking). If I could choose only one meat and two sides, I'd get brisket, potato salad, and chicken pasta salad. And if I had company, I'd share an order of onion straws or fried pickles, and most definitely get another slice of that buttermilk pie. They also do a buttermilk crunch, one of their most desired desserts, according to Mary, who described it as "the buttermilk pie served in a cold mug with ice cream, caramel, and nuts." She added that Mark's has free desserts on Monday nights.

Mark's impressed me with their from-scratch sides, comfortable neighborhood atmosphere, and friendly service. I now understand why they are so beloved in Louisville. While the meats lack the deeply smoked real barbecue flavor I prefer, I was nevertheless pleasantly surprised by the overall quality of the food.

Open: Monday–Thursday, 11:00 a.m.–10:00 p.m.; Friday–Saturday, 11:00 a.m.–11:00 p.m.; Sunday, 11:00 a.m.–10:00 p.m.

11422 Shelbyville Road; 502-244-0140

www.marksfeedstore.com

Bobby D's Grill and Barbecue

Located in east Louisville in a small strip mall, Bobby D's is owned and operated by easygoing local boy "Bobby D" Draughon, who greets customers with a hearty welcome when they walk into his restaurant. Keep your eyes open, because this commercial district prohibits advertising signs, and my GPS unit just got me in the ballpark of the restaurant.

The interior is pleasant, with ample seating, tile floors, big windows that let in sunlight, flat-screened televisions, and sports bar decor. Bobby D's was formerly Pit Stop Bar-B-Que, which has a history in Louisville going back to 1980. After several ownership changes, Bobby opened in the current location in June 2007, using Pit Stop's original barbecue menu and adding other items.

"We do all homemade sides," Bobby said. "Our green beans are cooked with our pork." It's a hands-on family business. Bobby's daughter Chelsie staffed the register, and Josh Fontaine, a friend of Bobby's son Robert, cooks and plates food.

I watched Bobby meander through the restaurant at the lunch hour to check on customers.

"You doing alright, buddy? Good."

"How we doing today? You doing alright? Can I get y'all anything?"

Born in California, Bobby has lived in Kentucky since age five. "I was a navy baby," he said. "I'm a Kentuckian now." Bobby drew me in with his languid speech—a blend of hillbilly and laid-back surfer dude. I expect he lets few things ruffle his feathers—although he admitted to getting upset if his barbecue isn't cooked just right. "I'm about the passion of it. I get upset when something cooks a little bit long, or if it's not perfect. You got to be hands on. You have to have a passion for what you do no matter what you do."

Bobby smokes meat on a Southern Pride gas unit using indirect heat and hickory wood. Boston butts cook for sixteen to twenty hours; naked brisket flats cook fourteen to sixteen hours. He smokes whole split chicken breasts and uses the white meat for pulled chicken (a favorite with women, he said). His extensive menu includes such nonbarbecue items as salmon burgers, fish, buffalo-style chicken salad, and a Philly cheese steak that's received compliments from natives of that city. Bobby said the extensive menu was necessary to do business in that area.

"We're real versa*tile*," he said. "We get a lot of groups in here. If one person doesn't like barbecue, it will deter a whole group. That's why I have the salmon burger and loaded potatoes. It's a fifty-count potato, real big. We put bacon, butter, sour cream in it, load it with meat, put cheese on top, and cover [it] in our barbecue sauce. It's to die for, man." Bobby said he's had guys from Texas come in and say, "I want some fat on that," talking about the brisket. "Not out here," Bobby said. "I smoke the flat of a brisket and shave it down pretty lean." Apparently, East Side Louisville folks are watching their waistlines, and Bobby's adjusted to suit local tastes.

I ate a "Pit Stop Combo" with shredded sauced pork (reminiscent of the style served in the southern counties of Barren and Monroe), chopped sauced brisket, sliced brisket, and meaty pork spareribs that had good texture and flavor. I also ate a loaded potato topped with chopped brisket—so big it took up the whole blue plastic plate it was served on (the blue plates were served on red cafeteria trays). Considering that the restaurant is decorated heavily in University of Kentucky and University of Louisville gear, these blue plates and red trays appeared to be a shout-out to Kentucky's biggest sports rivalry. The hot and mild sauces reminded me of thickened tomato soup with vinegar added—not my style, but lovers of mild tomato sauces might like it. Of the side dishes, I enjoyed the green beans and baked beans. The ridiculously huge potato loaded with big flavors was a meal in itself and a good food bargain. The shredded pork surprised me—I could still detect the smoke flavor through the sauce, even though the butts were cooked in a gas unit. The chipped brisket would make a good sandwich; it reminded me of the chopped mutton served at Owensboro restaurants—meat chopped or ground finely and mixed with sauce. It doesn't look pretty but is rich enough to taste through sandwich bread. The sliced brisket was tender and had a moderate smoke flavor. The best thing I tried was the super-meaty dry-rubbed pork spareribs tasting of thyme or some similar herb like oregano. For $10.50 (fall 2011 prices), you can get a rib dinner with two sides or a loaded potato. I'd go for the ribs with loaded potato and leave stuffed and happy. Ribs marinate in the dry rub for twenty-four hours before getting eight to nine hours on the smoker.

By the way, you can request meats without sauce, and when I called Bobby six months later, he said they're serving meats drier these days and customers are taking to it. Some older customers still want it heavily sauced, though. I'm guessing wet barbecue is old-school Louisville style, since I've eaten saucy meats at other established Louisville locations, like Hickory House, over the years. The new Bobby D's also serves different home-cooked lunch specials each week, like meatloaf, country-fried steak, boneless pork chops, and big burgers ("3/4 of a pound with everything in the garden on it").

At the end of my meal, Bobby invited me outside to see a fourteen-point buck his son Robert had killed that morning up in Henry County. The deer took up the whole bed of Robert's truck, and I thought how strange it looked in the parking lot of this strip mall. Bobby was obviously proud of his son. He stood in the parking lot and waved to me as I drove away, hospitable to the end.

Open: Monday–Friday, 11:00 a.m.–7:00 p.m.; Saturday, 11:00 a.m.–3:00 p.m.
13303 Magisterial Drive; 502-253-6740

Scotty's Ribs and More ("Home of BIG BUBBA's Bub-Ba-Que")

My most embarrassing moment on my barbecue safari occurred at Scotty's. But before I tell you about it, I just want to say: Scotty's serves great food prepared with care. I love the "where everybody knows your name" hospitality and Scotty's passion for the food he serves, from the breading on his fish to the rubs on his meats. Everything is freshly made and one of a kind.

Owner Roy "Scotty" Scott is a character, a youthful seventy-two years of age in 2012 and still stoking his custom smoker with split hickory and cherry, working the fryer in the kitchen, and plating food. He said, "You can't find people to work these days. There are some that are on drugs and all that crap," so along with steady employees Angel and Jim, Scotty serves customers as he's done since May 6, 1986.

I asked Scotty if he'd ever been written up in the big Louisville paper, the *Courier-Journal,* and without batting an eye he said, "For drunk driving and beating the hell out of a ninety-year-old lady." I might have been offended if everything else about Scotty's demeanor didn't seem so sweet. He calls his place "Redneck, Kentucky," and says he's chief of police and mayor. He sells T-shirts emblazoned with the Big Bubba Redneck Kentucky logo.

Scotty is picky. Regarding food quality, he said, "I try to get the best stuff on the market." People on restricted diets can eat his pork ribs because he trims so much fat from them before smoking and then grinds his own sausage with the trimmings to use in stromboli and on pizza. (Well, the restaurant name does specify "Ribs and *More*.") His fried chicken and fish have a "one-of-a-kind certificate of authenticity." The chicken wings marinate in "special stuff" and they test-fry them to see if they are up to par and then use the chicken/fish breading on them. They hand-cut fries daily. Huge hamburgers are smoked on the pit and are bigger than the bun. The hot or mild sauce is always served on the side.

I spoke with a man sitting at the bar, who praised Scotty's barbecue, fried chicken, and pizza. "Best chicken in Louisville. I sit here a half hour waiting for it, so that tells you what I think about it." This grand fellow, Ed

Norris, played football for the Colts "back in the day, a hundred years ago." He said when professional golfers come to town to play at the Valhalla Golf Club next door, they pack Scotty's place.

Scotty's has a full-service bar. Photos of Kentucky basketball players line the walls, along with a framed guitar autographed by Brad Paisley, the singer-songwriter. You can sit in booths, at tables, or on red stools at the bar, or at tables in a dining area separated from the bar. Angel, our server and enthusiastic promoter of all things Scotty, said, "You got to get Scotty to show you his pit. Once you see it, you'll be like [she laughs]—cause I was like, 'That's a—'"—here Angel broke off abruptly, then resumed, "and he said, 'Yeah,' because Scotty's friend was an engineer and he said that's how they should do a pit so that's how they did it."

Angel's story created a sense of mystery. She set me up for the pit viewing but refused to reveal the punch line, whatever it was that made her say, "You ain't going to believe it. It's the coolest thing." I remarked, "You're being rather secretive," and Angel said, "I don't want to spoil it; I just want you to look at it and see if you realize what it is." My mind may be a bit twisted, but I was expecting something a little ribald—a barbecue pit that *looked* like something else, because Angel had said, "Once you see it, you'll be like, ha ha!" What could be so outrageous about this mysterious pit that it conjured such joyful laughter from Angel?

The food came. The good pulled pork from Boston butts had nice bark and smoke, and this was a time when the pork actually was enhanced by a drizzling of sauce. The hot sauce was distinctive: sweet, tangy, and peppery with a creeping heat. The mild sauce was a thick tomato sauce, reminding me a bit of marinara with a vinegary tang. The smoked beans contained meat and a special sauce. The burger was awesome, like having a burger at home but even better because the meat soaks up so much smoke. The inside of the burger had a nice pink smoke ring. My cousin Jason Berry, who lives in Louisville and accompanied me on this initial Derby Region leg of my barbecue tour, said of the burger, "It's good as I've ever had." The fried corn was a half ear, blackened on the outside, sweet and smoky. I liked it a lot. The hand-cut fries and beer-battered onion rings were fresh and crispy. The meaty St. Louis–style ribs, which smoke for four hours over hickory and cherry wood, had great smokiness and dry-rubbed flavor.

After eating, I said to Scotty, "Your food shows some good love and care," and he replied, "You have to love what you're doing." He said the burger is ground fresh daily by a local butcher. Scotty gave me some history, including how his pit was designed by an engineer friend. He must heat it to 220° before it will draw, and once it's up to temperature the damper on the pit will open and close to maintain a steady 220°. Scotty took us out back to see the pit.

Remember, Angel had prepped me for this. So out back, Scotty showed us the unit. He said, "Now go around to the side of it and tell me what that is." I looked, I faltered.

Scotty said, "Well, what is it?"

I couldn't say. My mind was blank.

I finally said, "Well, my imagination is lacking a little bit here. It *kind* of looks like a scrotum and a penis."

At this, Jason, the quiet one, cackled. Scotty urged, "Look at the side of it. Look at the outlay of it. What is it? What is that made of!"

I said, "Aw, you mean the material?"

Scotty raised his voice and with a touch of exasperation said, "*What does it look like to you?*"

Finally, Jason broke his silence and saved me. "It's a dumpster," he said.

Scotty started laughing. And then I, the thickhead, said, "Oh, *I* see. I thought you were trying to make a joke. Oh, I see now." Well, shucks, a cigar is sometimes just a cigar.

And sometimes a smoking unit is just a dumpster. It's the craziest homemade barbecue apparatus I've seen out of the 160 barbecue places I've visited in Kentucky. Scotty has used it for twenty-six years. The shed that encloses it is brand new, because the old shed recently caught fire. Scotty had the lid of the dumpster up and took a sample of meat out for a customer. "I got to running my mouth and forgot about it," Scotty said, "and fire jumped up and *boom!* Flames shooting out everywhere!" Fortunately, the flame didn't spread to the bar area.

I walked away and said, "Well, I just can't believe it—a dumpster smoking machine."

As Jason and I drove away from Scotty's, Jason looked over at me and said, "A scrotum and a penis!" and we laughed until tears came to our eyes.

Open: Monday, 4:00 a.m.–10:00 p.m.; Tuesday–Wednesday, 10:30 a.m.–10:00 p.m.; Thursday–Saturday, 10:30 a.m.–11:00 p.m.

14049 Shelbyville Road (about one mile east of I-265, in Shelby Station Center, a strip mall with a highly visible Papa John's Pizza); 502-244-6868

Pewee Valley

Jucy's "Hickory Smoked Texas Style" Smokehouse

When you walk into Jucy's and order at the counter, you can view a whole beef brisket on a wooden cutting board through the counter glass and watch an employee chop or slice it to order, and also see the side dishes, like fried potatoes and onions, mac and cheese, and green beans. The potatoes and onions are pretty unusual for a barbecue restaurant. They boil new potatoes and chop them up with skin on and fry them on a grill with onions and spices. The saucy pintos cooked with ham hocks are also delicious and something you won't find often at Kentucky barbecue places. The top-quality Angus brisket cooks sixteen hours in a modern steel rotisserie unit using hickory wood for smoke, and they rub it with spices before smoking. They also do pork spareribs smoked for seven hours, pulled pork from Boston butts smoked sixteen hours, pulled chicken, smoked turkey breast, smoked pork tenderloin, and honey-glazed hams. Their pit is going twenty-four hours a day, six days a week.

Open since 1996, Jucy's is a full-service restaurant with intentionally rustic decor: Texas longhorns are mounted above the menu, and the walls are covered with vintage signs, deer antlers, an armadillo, horseshoes, a mounted bass, the ass of a deer, old photos of airplanes, license plates from Texas and Kentucky, and a painted concrete floor. Barn wood covers the interior and exterior of the building, and several racks of wood are stacked in front of a chain-link fence that keeps patrons out of the pit area. It's a comfortable place.

The sliced brisket sandwich was a generous helping of meat on a regular hamburger bun. The meat had a decent smoke ring, and the smoke flavor lingers in the back of the throat. The table sauce is different than what I'm used to, sort of like A-1 steak sauce. The brisket was good, with a nice blend of meat, fat, and bark mixed on the sandwich. If I were on the road and hungry, I'd be mighty happy to come into Jucy's and get the brisket sandwich. The brisket was firmer than some I've tried, for example, the brisket at Coldwater Two in Murray, Kentucky, so I'm guessing that Jucy's doesn't wrap the brisket in foil to break down muscle tissue. Not wrapping can be a good thing, because steamed brisket can turn into the texture and flavor of roast beef, but the tenderness in naked briskets is more difficult to achieve. I also like the appearance of a naked brisket better, because the dry rub remains gorgeously blackened on the outside. The pork spareribs had some pull to them—a little dry and chewy—with a good smokiness.

Tommy Hiltzman owns Jucy's, which he named after "slow, juicy barbecue." Tommy comes from east Texas and values homemade food (indeed, he starts with dried pintos for his "country beans") and high-quality meat. Jucy's is just across the highway from the train tracks. Look for the red metal roof and ricks of seasoned wood.

Open: Monday–Saturday, 11:00 a.m.–9:00 p.m.
7626 LaGrange Road, Pewee Valley; 502-241-5829

Crestwood

Texican's BBQ Pitt ("No Place Smokes Like Ours")

The mom-and-pop owners of Texican's, Dustin and Shirley Curtis, specialize in barbecue and homemade sides. I love this place—*one of the best barbecue restaurants in Kentucky*. I ate a three-meat and two-side combo with pulled pork, beef brisket, and cherry-smoked ribs, with cinnamon apples and home-fried potatoes. I also tried a chicken quarter, smoked sausage, and mac and cheese. I loved everything except the mildly flavored (but still homemade) mac and cheese. What can I say? I like big flavors.

Texican's has a quaint atmosphere: an old Cape Cod–style house with nice hardwood floors and windows looking out onto the highway and the railroad tracks. Because this place was built as a house and not a restaurant, seating is scattered throughout wherever they could comfortably fit tables. You place your order at the counter in the front room. I said how much I liked the atmosphere, and Shirley said, "Hard to believe we've already fed over a hundred people today." She said they get a lot of business from the schools and the Ford plant.

Team Curtis opened their current homey restaurant in May 2008 after five years cooking at festivals and serving from a small booth in Crestwood. Shirley was born and raised in that small town, and Dustin is from Anderson County. "I drug her to Sherman, Texas, for about nine years," Dustin said, "and I spent about seven of that trying to figure out how to do barbecue."

The cherry-smoked ribs had a rich smoke flavor and crispy-peppery exterior, and the meat pulled from the bone nicely. Dustin experimented with hickory for a while but said the flavor was overwhelming, so he tried cherry and found it smooth and sweet, so he stuck with it for the ribs. Local tree cutters keep him stocked in cherry wood. The tender, barky pulled pork had intense hickory smoke flavor, as did the brisket, which was well seasoned in a way that brought out the flavor of the juicy meat. Chicken quarters are rubbed with special spices and cooked over charcoal. They have won "best chicken" awards at local cook-offs; the trophies decorate a shelf in the front room. The chicken was tender and juicy with a great seasoned flavor. The cinnamon apples reminded me of Grandma's. I loved the skillet potatoes with toasty onions. Oh, and the smoked sausage took me back to my travels in Texas. This is one of the only places in Kentucky selling smoked sausages. All the meats were perfectly tender and deeply smoked on a heavy-duty steel custom unit outside. I recommend everything I've described, but my favorites of the meal were the brisket, pulled pork, spicy Louisiana-style hot link smoked two to three hours (Dustin said he fell in love with hot links in Texas), the red potatoes with crispy onions, and the fried apples. After I feasted, Dustin invited me outside to see the smoker. He feeds the fireboxes on the end of a long double-barreled tank unit with split quarters of hardwood, mostly hickory, and when he opened the lid on one side and I saw those deeply barked meats, my heart swelled—love at first sight, and that was *after* I'd eaten. Those butts and briskets were beautiful. You can see me fishing around for words to describe just how wonderful this barbecue was, but you just need to try it. Really. This is pure barbecue—meats served without sauce; meats so tender and delicious that sauce is nearly an outrage. If you must, they have a good, thick, deep-brown sauce with molasses notes. Dustin said it was the kind of sauce he grew up on in Anderson County. I said, "The good news is that your meats don't require sauce."

"That's my goal," he said.

I was fortunate on this day to be joined by Dominik Fuhrmann, a photojournalist for Fox 41 news out of Louisville. Dominik's wife, Heather, a Mississippi lady, had been my student at Ole Miss back in the 1990s. So after not seeing Heather for a decade, I met her in Louisville and was privileged to spend the day with her husband as he took video and helped me interview barbecue people.

Outside by the smoker, Dominik set up his camera and asked Dustin questions. Dustin said shagbark hickory was his preferred species, but he was making do with a load of pignut hickory, which can leave a bitter aftertaste.

Dominik asked, "What does it take to make good barbecue? What are the key ingredients?"

Dustin answered, "A lot of patience, a lot of love, and good wood. And seasonings to bring the flavor of that wood out. We do it low and slow and smoke all our meats for twenty-something hours."

And that, my friends, pretty much sums up this wonderful barbecue place.

Open: Monday–Friday, 11:00 a.m.–8:00 p.m.; Saturday, 11:00 a.m.–3:00 p.m.

6608 West Highway 146; 502-241-9227

www.texicansbbqpitt.com

La Grange

Big R's and Shannon's BBQ

In 2009 I ate at Big R's on Main Street in La Grange. Well doggone it, Big R (Randy Winstead) is doing more fishing these days while his daughter Shannon Pottie runs the show. She's done moved the restaurant a few blocks southwest, and I haven't been able to revisit. But Shannon says the food is the same, although they've added some new items like barbecue spaghetti and brisket pizza. Big R's opened in 2005, and Shannon became a partner in 2006, after a fifteen-year career in orthodontics. So here's my semi-outdated response to dining at Big R's on Main, with the address to the new place listed at the end.

A couple of blocks off the quaint downtown square of La Grange, right by the train tracks, stands a historic two-story home I never would have taken for a barbecue restaurant, if not for the sign out front. I was a little skeptical as I approached this well-kept house, as—well, I have to admit that I have a little shack fetish, some of the best barbecue I've ever eaten having come from rustic roadside shacks with no frills, just a limited menu and really good smoked meats. As for atmosphere, Big R's is about as far away from "shacky" as you can get. There's no huge disheveled woodpile out back, no rusted-out husks of cars lying nearby, no grease-smudged windows and plastic picnic tables. Big R's is quaint, semi-upscale, the kind of place you'd take a first date if you wanted to woo her with a barbecue dinner. Forgive me for saying it, but it's the kind of place a lot of women I know would like. I'd take my mama there.

My cousin Jason Berry and I sat at a cafe table underneath a big umbrella outside the entryway to the house.

I joked, "Who'd ever think we'd have European sidewalk dining in Kaintuck? Well, the town is called *Le Grange*," I said in my best Pepé Le Pew voice, pinching up the nose to sound stereotypically Frenchified, but it came out sort of faux-Cajun, like "Le Grawwwwnjuh."

Jason, a man of few words, said, "Yea-uh."

Randy Winstead, "Big R," studied the history of barbecue for a while before opening his restaurant. He began on small smokers, using one he built in his garage with a welder, and not long after he got his smoker done, his team, Big R's Blazing Butts, placed in the top ten in all meat categories in a Kansas City Barbecue–sanctioned contest. This gave him confidence to keep cooking. He sold barbecue on street corners off his smoker for charity events, and then his hobby turned into a business. Their current building is their third; the original location seated 20 people; the second place seated 40 people; now they can seat 102 people. They don't advertise, so word of mouth is bringing an increasing number of patrons to dine on Big R's meats and homemade sides.

Randy has worked on the railroads as a career, but when he retires fishing and barbecue will remain his hobbies. He said of his barbecue passion, "If you don't get excited every time you open that smoker lid out there, you probably ought to find something else to do. You just gotta have the love for it. Every time I open the door on that smoker I get excited to see what it looks like and how it comes out."

Big R's serves seriously good food. I asked them to make up a sampler platter, so we got to try several meats and sides. Randy mixes up different dry rubs for pork, ribs, chicken, and brisket, and they have one sauce. He smokes big briskets (ten to thirteen pounds) and ten-pound Boston butts at 225° for twelve hours, using a mixture of hickory and cherry woods. He pulls the membrane off the back of the ribs and rubs them and smokes them at 230° for three and a half hours. They also smoke a sausage link made upriver in Cincinnati, and Randy said it's catching on. The half rack of baby back ribs had a good smoky flavor and appropriate tug to the tender meat, and the medium-sweet tomato sauce on the outside was caramelized like beautiful candy. Jason and I were real happy with the ribs. The good baked beans included a portion of smoked pork. *The baked potato salad is ridiculously marvelous.* Loaded with much of the stuff you'd get on a stuffed baked potato, like bacon, sour cream, and chives, it could be a meal in itself if you had a whopping bowl of it. The sweet potato casserole is also mighty nice. The coleslaw was fresh but didn't have much vinegar in it, and I prefer a vinegar slaw. The pulled chicken was a chopped chicken breast with very little smoke flavor, not my style. The chopped brisket with a rich, dark tomato sauce on top was pretty good. The pulled-pork sandwich was a whopping heap of lightly smoked tender meat with some bark mixed in, topped with a tomato-based barbecue sauce and served on a regular hamburger bun. The sandwich was good. I just like more smoke, and on chopped pork I prefer a vinegar sauce. This sauce, like most in the Derby and northern Kentucky region, leans on the tomato too heavily for my personal preference.

In short, if you want a place with a relaxed atmosphere and sweet family-run hospitality and some great side dishes, like that potato salad that I find myself dreaming about sometimes and the flavorful sweet potato casserole, combined with a real good rack of baby back ribs, then you should give Big R's a try. Randy's middle daughter is a pastry chef who makes different cakes.

Note to the thirsty traveler: this barbecue place sells a variety of domestic beers, wines, and fruity coolers.

As noted at the beginning, Big R's has recently transformed to Big R's and Shannon's BBQ. The new hours and location are listed here.

Open: Tuesday–Thursday, 11:00 a.m.–8:00 p.m.; Friday–Saturday, 11:00 a.m.–9:00 p.m.

213 South First Street; 502-222-0058
www.bigrsbarbecue.com

Shelbyville

Ken-Tex Bar-B-Q

Open for twenty-five years, with three different owners (the original owners were Texans), Ken-Tex slices meat to order on a cutting board. They use a gas-wood custom-made hybrid rotisserie cooker, using only hickory. A substantial amount of wood is stacked out back. The brisket smokes at a very low 175° eight to ten hours. The pork loin smokes six to seven hours. They also serve meaty pork spareribs by weight, so you can try just one rib if you want. (Mike Mills, barbecue legend and owner of 17th Street Bar and Grill in southern Illinois, says: "Life is too short for a half rack." True, but when on barbecue safari, sometimes the belly can't hold even a half rack.) On Fridays they serve salmon. Pork butts smoke for thirteen to fourteen hours. You can get brisket and pork chopped or sliced. They make their own rubs, sauces, mayo slaw (the local preference), pinto beans, potato salad, and a popular item called "longhorn stew," sort of like a burgoo with all of their meats and some vegetables in it. The hot sauce tasted of chili powder and packed nice heat. The real good brisket was super smoky and peppery, mighty similar to the fine briskets I've sampled in Texas.

Personal choice: if you get the brisket at Ken-Tex, just get the meat only. The sandwich was served on a monotonous white bun, nothing special, which detracts from the wonderfulness of the meat. I'd leave off that tasty but strong sauce, too, as it overwhelms the meat. The meat is good enough to stand on its own, so I'd just get a pound of that fine brisket and some complementary sides. The single pork sparerib I tried had a real good smokiness and a rich exterior flavor, but was overcooked and chewy. I watched the young Mr. O'Brien slice the rib off on the cutting board, and the whitened bones were exposed at one end where the meat had drawn up—a sign of cooking at too high a temperature. The rib was good—fine on flavor, but not as tender as it could be. Of course, I tried only one. The sliced pork—a pork loin sliced thinly—was a little dry, but what can you expect from such a lean piece of pork? I personally don't know why anyone would mess with smoking a pork loin, anyway, unless you want a very mild-flavored nonfatty barbecue. The loin was pretty good. This is for the type of folks who don't like heavy smoke and like to add flavor with sauces.

Ken-Tex is a smallish restaurant. It used to be even smaller. They've moved up from barstools to a family eating area. Plain wood paneling decorates the exterior and interior of the building. I like the atmosphere—not too fancy, with the simple aura of a barbecue shack. But it's still a sit-down restaurant. Conveniently located off I-64, it's a good stop for hungry souls traveling between Louisville and Lexington.

Open: Monday–Thursday, 11:00 a.m.–8:00 p.m.; Friday–Saturday, 11:00 a.m.–9:00 p.m.; Sunday, 11:00 a.m.–8:00 p.m.

1163 Mount Eden Road; 502-633-2463

Northern Kentucky River Region

There's not much barbecue in northern Kentucky other than chains like Smokey Bones and Famous Dave's. I ate at four barbecue places in this region, and only one made the cut, Tina's in Carrollton. Two places didn't make my highly subjective good list because they serve a heavily sauced sloppy joe–style pork sandwich. The other place that didn't pass muster served way-saucy ribs that tasted old, along with beans and potato salad right out of food-service jugs. Now, if I had world enough and time, I'd return to these places and sample other things on the menu. It's highly possible they have good ribs or chicken, for instance. If I'd known at the time of visiting that mom-and-pop barbecue of any kind is such a rare find in the upper counties of the Commonwealth, I'd have stuck around longer and worked harder to find something good. On the other hand, why should one have to work so hard to find good barbecue? It's all over Louisville and in the central and western parts of the state, and Lexington is now home to several good barbecue restaurants.

Tina Stephenson recently closed her restaurant's doors after nearly twenty years, but she's still catering. Her home catering business is located just four miles from Kentucky Speedway in Sparta. She said to call ahead if you want some barbecue.

As homage to Tina, the smart-talking pit boss of the Northlands (of Kentucky), I include this original review from summer 2009.

Carrollton

Tina's Bar B-Q

I nearly screwed up majorly when, after a full day of barbecue touring I pulled into Tina's parking lot, looked at the nondescript metal building next door to a fitness center and hair salon, didn't see a woodpile, didn't smell any smoke, and almost drove on down the road. Oh, but that would have been a mistake, especially since Tina's offers about the only nonfranchised barbecue you can find in this part of the world, and Tina knows how to make meats tender and flavorful, period.

I specifically asked for bark, so my real good pulled-pork sandwich had a lot of tasty outer meat between two garlic-buttered and grilled pieces of Texas toast. The mustard slaw on the side had cabbage and pickle in it, and the first bite reminded me of good sauerkraut. I wouldn't want it on my sandwich, though. The sauces include an extra-hot that's very vinegary with a lot of pepper in it, just the way I like it. (Tina said the man who makes the hot vinegar sauce is from Glasgow, and that when that sauce was gone, maybe it's gone for good. Glasgow is my hometown. No wonder my taste buds were so fond of the vinegar-pepper sauce). The mild sauce is tomato based. The baby back ribs had a good smokiness and a tasty dry rub added to the flavor. The spicy, smoky brisket was sliced paper thin like roast beef (much different than the thicker sliced brisket I've eaten in Texas). Tina prefers her brisket moderately cooked. I asked her what is the advantage of preparing brisket this way (thin sliced, less time on the smoker) compared to the long-smoked and thick-sliced way, and Tina said simply, "I like it better this way, so that's the way I cook it." Her substantial sandwich list includes a smoked turkey Reuben and "Beef-N-Swiss" served with "horsey mayo." Sound familiar? When I tasted the thinly sliced brisket, this menu item made sense, since the meat could be easily layered on a sandwich like those available at the franchise roast beef places. But Tina's gives you beef that actually looks, tastes, and smells like beef. What a concept!

After eating I went up to speak with Tina at the counter. She was busy serving people and getting things ready for the dinner crowd, but she answered my questions while bustling around. When I praised the tenderness and barkiness of the pork, she said, "You requested bark? They don't know what that is here," and I said, "Well, I told them to give me the blackened meat on the edges," and she busted out laughing.

I asked, "Where did you get your barbecue ways? How did you learn your trade?" and Tina described her learning methods: "Stick it in there and see what comes out."

Tina, who comes from a family of butchers and meat smokers, has been barbecuing for sixteen years. She operates a Southern Pride rotisserie cooker, using hickory and red oak. She smokes butts for eighteen hours, and the briskets average about eight hours. She uses dry rub on the ribs, and the butts go on the smoker without any seasonings. When she first started, she rolled the butts in a dry rub and the folks up there in northern Kentucky (Tina debated with me about the geography, saying she lives in "central" Kentucky and that "northern" doesn't start until you reach the Boone County line) said it was too spicy, so she cut back, and cut back, and finally just put them on without seasonings and never got any more complaints from the locals.

Tina has a sassy wit and ready laugh. Her fluorescent green menu shouts in bold letters at the top: "We do not have burgers or French fries." Describing her meats on the menu, she notes that the smoked turkey is "shaved," the beef brisket is "shaved and spicy," and the pulled pork—and this really makes me chuckle—is "pork pulled apart." I'm guessing this description is for the folks stopping in off Interstate 71 who just might not be familiar with barbecue lingo.

ADDENDUM: As noted above, Tina still does barbecue catering. If you want to try some smoked meats from northern Kentucky (sorry, Tina, but I'm calling the geographical boundaries here), give Tina a call for a catering job.

Tina Stephenson: 859-567-5887

Bluegrass Region

Frankfort

The finale of my statewide barbecue tour took place in the state capital, capping my journeys with a touch of symbolism. The big cemetery in Frankfort—the one with great views of the capitol building and the Kentucky River—holds at least some of the relocated bones of Daniel Boone, along with an impressive monument. Boone explored unfamiliar territories. I've explored new barbecue territories. The connections are stunning! Where's my long rifle?

Staxx ("Our Food Really Staxx Up")

I'm glad the lawmakers in Frankfort finally have a local place to eat barbecue, the food of the people.

When I met Frankfort dweller Charlie Winter at Staxx on May 24, 2012, the restaurant had just celebrated a one-year anniversary. A family affair, Staxx is owned and managed by Dan Liebman, designed by his girlfriend, Susan (she's responsible for the interior decor and exterior landscaping), and supported in the kitchen by Dan's son Joe. (Another son, Ben, just finished his first year of college at Western Kentucky University.) Soul and blues tunes played in the background, jiving with the Stax Records motif that colors the restaurant. (Stax Records originally recorded blues, soul, and gospel artists in Memphis.) Photos of old Frankfort hang on the walls, along with Stax record posters and maps from Dan's late father's map collection.

Born and raised in Frankfort, Dan worked in equine journalism for years before making the shift to the restaurant business. Dan recognized that Frankfort "desperately needed barbecue again." Dan and Charlie talked about the old days of Frankfort barbecue, when they visited the Pink Pig and Capitol Bar-B-Que. When younger, Dan would help Newton Vance stoke the barbecue pits at Capitol, burning the wood down and shoveling the coals underneath the meats in the west Kentucky style. At Staxx, they use a Southern Pride unit to cook the meats, stoking it with split hickory supplied by a local woodworker.

Charlie and I sampled around the menu, and, having similar tastes for smoky barbecue, here's what we liked most.

The smoked andouille from Savoie's Sausage in Opelousas, Louisiana, had a great bite and crispy skin. "I'm totally all over that sausage," I said to Charlie.

The crispy and peppery smoked chicken wings, rubbed with plenty of brown sugar to make a beautiful caramelization, also packed bold flavors. The smoked turkey was excellent, tender and surprisingly zesty. As I've said throughout this book, I like big flavors. At Staxx, the big flavors are found in the sausage, wings, smoked turkey, and red-skinned potato salad. I also liked the St. Louis–cut ribs served with blackberry sauce. Seriously, a thin sauce tasting of blackberries with some sweetening, like a blackberry dip. I hadn't eaten barbecue condiments this weird since trying Bad Bob's raspberry-infused sauce with ribs in Murray at the beginning of my barbecue odyssey three years before—my travels bookended by ribs served with fruity sauces.

Daniel Boone, pioneer of the territories. Wes Berry, pioneer of Kentucky's smoky meats. If I could only have such a regal monument when I die, without the battling over bones.

Staxx offers several barbecue sauces, in addition to the singular blackberry dip. The extra-hot sauce reminds me of a Hickman County vinegar-cayenne sauce, just a little bit thicker. Joe said regulars often mix sauces, blending the "Spicy" sauce with the "Carolina Twang." Dan said Kentucky's current governor, Steve Beshear, is partly responsible for the vinegar sauce at Staxx. Governor Beshear is from Hopkins County. They like their vinegar sauces over there.

The jalapeño corn muffin, made with cornmeal from Weisenberger Mill in Midway, Kentucky, was also mighty fine. I ate that muffin along with the tender spareribs dipped in blackberry sauce, then sat back, contemplated the world, and called it good.

For dessert, I sampled two "jar desserts" made in small mason jars by a local woman: a "chocolate crunch" and a "strawberry cheesecake"—fun, cakey, creamy treats. Although I'm a lover of cheesecake, I liked the chocolate crunch the most. You can reuse the jars later for home canning.

Thank goodness that the Cradle of (Official) Power in the Common-

Charlie's Bourbon Chipotle Barbecue Sauce

My fellow barbecue lover Charlie Winter joined me on a trip to some Bluegrass barbecue joints and helped me celebrate the finale of my barbecue tripping at Staxx in Frankfort. Charlie has been seeking out the best in Kentucky barbecue for longer than I have and mastering the smoky arts at his home in Frankfort. He's generously shared his recipe for a barbecue sauce with a healthy dose of bourbon, Kentucky's native spirit.

Charlie writes: "Not only do I like my smoked meat with a bourbon chipotle barbecue sauce, I smoke all my meat in my homebuilt bourbon barrel smoker. I have spent many years creating barbecue sauces, but I think this one is smoky, savory, sweet, and spicy with an added kick."

1 cup Heinz ketchup
¼ cup white vinegar
¼ cup water
¼ cup molasses
3 tablespoons honey
1 tablespoon chipotle ground pepper
1 tablespoon freshly ground black pepper
¼ cup Kentucky bourbon

Combine vinegar, water, and ketchup in a nonaluminum saucepan over medium-high heat. Use a whisk to blend until smooth, then add all remaining ingredients. Once the mixture comes to a boil, reduce the heat and let simmer uncovered for 30–45 minutes, stirring occasionally. If you like your sauce with more heat, add more chipotle pepper to taste.

wealth once again has a place to get some good barbecue. I've often thought that barbecue can bring people together. Witness the multicultural Barbecue on the River festival in Paducah. At barbecue places, you can see people in office dress eating next to construction workers. It's time for the Donkeys and Elephants to get down to Staxx, share sauces across the tables, and get some good things done.

Open: Monday–Thursday, 11:00 a.m.–8:00 p.m.; Friday–Saturday, 11:00 a.m.–9:00 p.m.; Sunday, 11:00 a.m.–8:00 p.m.

11 Carson Place; 502-352-2515

Lawrenceburg

Tony's Bar-B-Que Barn

One Sunday while on the road, I stopped at this nicely kept full-scale restaurant, mighty hungry, and sat with a crowd of people who, I'm guessing, were having their post-church lunch. It was cold in the barn on this hot August noon. The interior decor is a lot of wood. It's a tall-ceilinged barn with rafters that run the length of the restaurant, with red-and-white checkered window treatments and livestock motifs on the walls.

I ordered a combination platter with pulled pork and dry St. Louis–style spareribs. I got two ribs, nicely tender, highly seasoned, salty, with crispiness on the outside from the pepper and salt. I liked the external crispiness, which set these ribs apart from many I've eaten. The pulled pork is long strips of pork shoulder with a mild flavor, tender, not sauced. There was some bark in it, but the smoke flavor was mild. The ribs are the way to go for flavor. The sauces, hot and mild, are semi-thick, sweet, and tangy. The sauce complemented the pork well, but the ribs didn't need any sauce—they were good on their own. The wide-cut green beans were good, as were the fried okra and vinegar slaw. I also liked the sugary stewed tomatoes and the cornbread salad, two things I'd never seen at a barbecue restaurant in Kentucky. Two pieces of cornbread came with my meal, and I also tried the burgoo, made with meat, potatoes, tomatoes, and carrots, which cooks down about twelve hours.

After eating I spoke with Tony Howard, originally from Owensboro (hence the burgoo on the menu). Tony's been in business at this location since 2003. Much of Tony's family is from Whitesville, just east of Owensboro, which he described as "a Catholic community that barbecues *all* the time." I asked Tony how his methods differ from those back home, and he said, "We serve pulled pork and pulled chicken. We don't have sliced or chopped meat, and we don't serve mutton, which I grew up on. This area doesn't like the taste of mutton."

He serves the chicken in sauce. Whole shoulders are dry rubbed and smoked fourteen hours with hickory at 225° on a gas-wood unit. The ribs are hickory smoked to 170–175° in an outdoor smoker to tenderize them and then cooled and held in the refrigerated walk-in until someone orders them. Then—and this is where that interesting crispy texture comes from—they are heated on the steak grill. Tony's son figured out this method to avoid holding ribs in a steamer and accordingly losing some of the fat and flavor. Heating per order like this takes about fifteen to twenty minutes, which isn't the most efficient method of serving ribs, but I liked the result. The ribs are rubbed with seasonings before they go on the smoker and again on the grill during the reheating. Some au jus is added for moisture. Several "real picky rib connoisseurs," regular customers, like the ribs real well, so "we're stuck with it," Tony said, meaning this method of rib prep.

We started talking woods, and Tony said he liked a combination of hickory and sassafras, but the folks in the Bluegrass Region think sassafras is too strong, so he uses only hickory. I said I liked sassafras, and he said, "That's why you like Old Hickory barbecue in Owensboro—they cook with hickory and sassafras. Western Kentucky people wouldn't say sassafras is too strong."

Tony also does the barbecue for the "Beast Feast" at the local Sand Spring Baptist Church. People bring him elk, deer, pheasant, wild turkey, and so on, and he smokes all the game at 225°.

I said business looked to be good, and Tony said, "We're doing alright. We're not getting filthy rich, but we're halfway there—we're getting filthy."

Open: Monday–Saturday, 11:00 a.m.–9:00 p.m.; Sunday, 11:30 a.m.–3:00 p.m.

1435 North 127 Bypass; 502-859-3030

Tony's Bar-B-Que Barn's Cornbread Salad

Trinca Barnett, a native of Anderson County, started working at the Bar-B-Que Barn in 1996, when she developed this recipe. I asked what inspired her, and Trinca said it's something she "threw together to make something tasty with leftover cornbread."

12 pieces leftover cornbread or hoecakes
½ cup green onion
1 whole red tomato, chopped
1½ cups shredded cheddar cheese
2 cups mayonnaise

Simply, you just mix it all together. When Trinca told me her ingredients over the phone, she just assumed I knew how to make cornbread. She's right. I like to add chopped jalapeños to my batter.

Dressed-Up Cornbread Salad

For those splurging times, I've played with Trinca's recipe (see above) and substituted 1 cup sour cream for 1 cup of the mayonnaise and added ranch dressing spices (1 tablespoon parsley plus 1 teaspoon each of garlic powder, onion powder, onion flakes, dill weed, salt, and black pepper) to the mayo and sour cream to make the dressing. I've also added 2 cups cooked black-eyed peas or pinto beans, sliced black olives to taste, cooked corn cut from the cob, crumbled cooked bacon (at least a 12-ounce package—the more the better!), chopped green peppers, additional chopped tomatoes, additional cheeses (like pepper jack), and—this is nice if you like heat and vinegar—some sliced pickled jalapeños.

Layering the ingredients in a large glass bowl makes for a pretty dish. First crumble ½ of the cornbread on the bottom, then layer the other ingredients, topping with 1 cup of dressing. Repeat this layering one more time, with the dressing on top, followed by a scattering of chopped green onions. The flavors marry after a couple of hours in the refrigerator.

Harrodsburg

Dunn's BBQ and Catering

The sign into Harrodsburg says "1774," honoring this town's long history—at least long for the USA. Considering they've had so long to get their act together, it's even sadder that Harrodsburg hasn't developed much of a barbecue tradition over the years. Dunn's is the only game in town.

A family business since 1981, Dunn's started simply enough, with two couples pooling money to buy $400 worth of building materials to make a collapsible concession stand to take on the road to sell barbecue at festivals and such. Since 1991 they've had a regular catering and walk-in business in a modest block building—what used to be an old country store—across the road from warehouses of the Heritage Tobacco Group.

Inside, there are a few tables for dining in, attractive old wood floors, and wall posters announcing Dunn's victories at the Fort Harrod Beef Festival: first-place professional steak in 2007, third-place burger, first-place brisket. A Bible near the ordering counter was open to Psalm 68–69, right next to another sacred text—the Kentucky Wildcats 2011–12 basketball schedule.

Sid Dunn, the young fellow running the place when I entered at opening time, was busy filling a catering order (80 percent of their business comes from catering), but he had time to make us a couple of pork sandwiches and a platter of brisket. Sid had recently returned from a missionary trip to post-earthquake Haiti. He's the nephew of the original owners. They've cooked for William Shatner, Al Green, Smokey Robinson, and the Four Tops. Photos of these celebrities hang on the wall.

"I'm doing Rand Paul next week," Sid said.

Sharon Dunn, one of the original owners and an elementary school teacher, came in after a while. I asked Sharon about the lack of barbecue places in the Bluegrass Region, and she said she didn't really know why, but acknowledged the slim pickings. "Just seems like people aren't much interested in it." Her brother Herbert, a minister, loved barbecue and was the real driving force behind the Dunn family's business. Their original goal was to sell enough barbecue at events to help finance trips to NAACP meetings. Then they sold meats at Pioneer Days and the Mercer County Fair, and the business just grew over the years. Back in the old days, Sharon sold barbecue out of a duplex, living in one side and serving barbecue out of the other side. That was before they moved into the current location.

The shredded pork from Boston butts cooked ten hours was heavily sauced meat on a hamburger bun. My traveling companion, Charlie Winter, called it "crock-pot pork" and said he'd eaten roadside sandwiches in Mississippi that tasted similarly. The brisket, which smoked at 200° for twelve hours on a Southern Pride cooker, was sliced thinly and served with a sweet brown sauce. It was good, like smoky roast beef. Charlie and I liked the brisket best. Sid uses cherry and apple wood mostly. They also had grilled chicken, ribs, and fried fish on the lunch menu.

"Brisket is just now catching on here," Sharon said. They've had it on the menu the past four years. "Now that's one of the main things they order," she said. We talked about how food shows on television are spreading regional specialties like brisket around the country.

Dunn's style of sauced pork isn't my favorite, but the brisket was tasty, and they are about the only thing going—excluding caterers—in the central Kentucky region that includes the counties of Jessamine, Mercer, Washington, Marion, Casey, Lincoln, and Boyle. I appreciate their staying power in a tough business.

Open: Monday–Thursday, 11:00 a.m.–2:00 p.m.; Friday, 11:00 a.m.–8:00 p.m. (Friday is their big day—Sid said their hours were sometimes longer. Call ahead.)

726 Cane Run; 859-734-3675

Danville

The Kentucky State BBQ Festival

Barbecue. Beer. Bourbon. Such is the stuff that the Kentucky State BBQ Festival is made of. Get there on the second weekend in September to fill your belly with smoky meats prepared by national experts, representing various barbecue styles, and to sample Kentucky Proud products from the Bluegrass region and beyond.

I ventured to Danville's Constitution Square in 2012 to interview the pit masters and sample all the tasty delights I could cram into my gullet in a day. The whole historic square swarmed with people lined up to sample meaty offerings from such barbecue celebrities as Moe Cason of the Ponderosa BBQ team from Des Moines, Iowa; Melissa Cookston of Yazoo Delta Q from Nesbit, Mississippi; Shelly Hunt of Desperados Barbecue from Angola, New York; Carey Bringle of the Peg Leg Porkers BBQ team from West Tennessee; and Craig Kimmel of Firehouse BBQ from DeLand, Florida. Additionally, festival organizers Brad and Cindy Simmons served up tasty treats like smoked beef ribs from Lucky Dog BBQ in Danville (luckydogbbq.com). You want to try the only beef ribs served in Kentucky outside of Smoketown USA in Louisville? Then get to the Kentucky BBQ Festival in September and visit Lucky Dog BBQ, a catering service that serves some of the best pork and beef in the Bluegrass.

This festival rocks for a few reasons. One, at many so-called barbecue festivals, the only people who eat the meats of the masters are certified judges. Not so at this big block party. Oh, no. Here, if you are willing to wait in long lines, you can smack your lips on some of the best Q in the country, prepared by folks featured on such television programs as *BBQ Pitmasters.*

But it's not all about barbecue. I wandered Constitution Square and sampled Kentucky Ale brewed by Alltech, a brewing and distilling company in Lexington; ate beer cheese; chatted with Kentucky Fried Chicken spokesperson Colonel Bob Thompson, looking dapper in his white suit; sampled excellent charcuterie from Marksbury Farm Market, a small-scale butcher and abattoir in Lancaster, Kentucky; took home a bourbon barrel stave from the Kentucky Bourbon Trail, sponsored by the Kentucky Distillers Association; interviewed eccentric Hoosier Tom Fischer, headman at bourbonblog.com ("the enthusiast's resource for all things spirited"). And I tasted—get this—weird and wonderful *pulled-pork cupcakes* from the Twisted Sifter, a cake shop in Danville.

Not decadent enough? Then indulge in a cigar dipped in bourbon from the Kentucky Gentlemen Cigar Company (kentuckygentlemencigars.com), a tobacconist based in Lawrenceburg. Who says you need to go to Mexico to buy good cigars imported from Cuba? We got the tobacco, climate, and bourbon to make a distinctive product right here in the Bluegrass.

The Kentucky State BBQ Festival raises money for the regional United Way. In 2012, their Friday night Bourbon Barrel Art Project auction (barrels sponsored by local businesses and art patrons and painted by local artists) earned $16,000 for the charity. I enjoyed the auction immensely, watching folks get into bidding wars for barrels and sampling delicacies prepared by the pit masters. My favorite find was the "Firecrackers" prepared by Craig Kimmel—jalapeño peppers stuffed with cheese, wrapped in bacon, smoked, and topped with a sweet-savory barbecue rub and sauce. Can I get a hallelujah?

Quality vendors of special regional products and excellent barbecue define the Kentucky State BBQ Festival. The 2012 festival, in its second year, attracted a very impressive forty thousand people. I asked Lucky Dog BBQ master and festival chair Brad Simmons to encapsulate the festival in a few words, and he said, "People who come to a barbecue festival are ready to eat the food, and if you're going to put all that time and passion into the barbecue, why would you *not* want to share that with the people? That's the whole concept of the festival!"

Amen, my barbecue brother. That should be the slogan of barbecue festivals far and wide.

Georgetown

Fat Boys BBQ

You've got to look real hard to find good barbecue east of Interstate 65, the north to south artery splitting Kentucky roughly in half, but the long drives to find smoked meats do offer scenic rewards, like when traveling Highway 460 between Frankfort and Georgetown, and the road winds through lush green fields bordered by old stone fences. And yes, pretty horses are a common sight in this country.

Fat Boys is located north of Georgetown, "out in the country," to use the language of my upbringing, even though the rustic log building from the 1800s isn't too far north of Georgetown's thriving downtown. The exterior looks something like a homegrown Cracker Barrel, with rocking chairs and a wagon wheel and a wooden Indian on the porch. The interior has weathered wood floors, wooden paneling, and rustic decor like iron skillets and old Coca-Cola advertisements hanging from the walls. Customers eat at long folding tables with metal chairs.

Fat Boys does custom catering; they'll smoke up a whole pork shoulder, beef brisket, city ham, whole turkey, whole chicken, country ham, bologna—seems that if it walks or flies, they'll smoke it.

I arrived pretty late on a Saturday morning and ordered a sampler platter for brunch. I got three baby back ribs, brisket, and pulled pork with two sides and a roll. The only sauce on the table was Texas Pete, the hot pepper sauce made in North Carolina. The cowboy beans were small pintos with meat cooked in with them. The server brought Sweet Baby Ray's sauce to the table, an affront to well-smoked meat, in my opinion. The pork was heavily sauced, not the style I like. It was juicy and tender, of stringy texture, with a very mild smoke flavor. If I had it to do over, I'd ask if I could get the meat unsauced. The good brisket had some nice bark on it and a hint of smoke; it reminded me of crock-pot roast beef, real juicy and fall-apart tender, but wasn't as smoky as I like. The pork ribs had a nice smoky pinkness and good flavor from the dry rub. The ribs were real good.

Brothers Frank and Johnny West, the smoking team at Fat Boys, cook on a long cylindrical iron tank unit with a side firebox. Originally from Magoffin County in the Appalachian Mountains, they learned how to smoke meats from a Texan and have been honing their skills since 2000. They live right over the hill from the restaurant. Using local hickory, they smoke butts and briskets for eighteen to twenty hours and ribs for nine hours. They make their own dry rub for the ribs and butts. The butts smoke for two to three hours and then get double wrapped in foil for the rest of the cooking.

When I said to Johnny, "I noticed that y'all pull your brisket," he replied, "It ain't pulled, it just falls apart."

Speaking with me out by the smoking unit, Frank asked, "You ever tried smoked bologna?" and I said no, but mentioned that when in far-western Kentucky the previous weekend I'd noted some places smoking bologna and hypothesized that this liberality of meats is a distinctive characteristic of Kentucky barbecue. Being a border state, we're a hodgepodge of barbecue styles.

Frank agreed. "If it can be smoked, we smoke it. We smoked goat last week."

One of their favorites is smoked-bologna salad—a blend of four-hour-smoked bologna, mayo, and pickles. Because they also serve breakfast, they have people who request pulled-pork omelets and smoked-bologna omelets. "If I got it, I'll fix it," Frank said.

Their most popular items are pulled pork and ribs, but brisket is increasing in popularity. When I visited Fat Boys in July 2009, they'd been open at that location for only five months, even though they'd done catering and competitions before going whole hog into the restaurant business. When they started, they sold only one brisket per day, but because of word of mouth and customer loyalty, the demand for brisket had increased eightfold in that five-month period. They were selling thirty pounds of pulled pork daily.

I asked how long they intended to stay in the barbecue business, and Frank said, "Hopefully until I die. You gotta love it, because it's too much work. It's constant, all day long—there's always something to do, somebody always hollering, 'We're out of this or out of that.' And it's usually 110° in here."

In summary, Fat Boys gets my applause for family atmosphere, cool location, congenial hospitality, and real good pork ribs. The cowboy beans were rich, simmered in their own broth, with some kind of meat—appeared to be sausage—cooked in. The fried okra was great. The cornbread, a big round piece, was good. You might like the brisket and pulled pork—I mean, the meats smoke for a heck of a long time—but maybe some of the intense smoke flavor I like dissipates through the wrapping in foil, what some people call the "Texas crutch." Everything was tender and tasty, though. It's a full-service restaurant, serving steaks and catfish and other dishes. But since we're talking barbecue, I'd stick with the baby back ribs and brisket.

Open: Monday–Sunday, 7:00 a.m.–8:00 p.m.; Friday–Saturday, 7:00 a.m.–10:00 p.m.

2176 Cincinnati Road; 502-867-1031

Lexington

Billy's Bar-B-Q

In business since 1978, Billy's has earned a reputation for being one of the best places to eat barbecue east of Interstate 65. Part of that success should be credited to the western Kentucky roots of the originators, Billy Parham and

Bob Stubblefield, who learned their trade from friends in Murray, Mayfield, Paducah, and Owensboro—four of the best per capita barbecue towns in the state. Billy's is a full-service restaurant with a laid-back, fun atmosphere. My cousin Jason and I walked into the air-conditioned comfort of Billy's for lunch on a hot summer day. The lighting was nicely dimmed, and strings of small, clear bulbs, like holiday lighting, crisscrossed the ceiling and paneling along the booths. Many posters decorate the walls from musicians who have played in Lexington. A boar's head is mounted on the wall (and also serves as Billy's mascot, featured on the menu and on the sign outside).

We took a booth, and before you know it I was sipping a draft Kentucky Bourbon Barrel ale from a tulip glass—kind of frou-frou for a barbecue place, but I liked it. A sweet server took our order and the food came promptly. Billy's menu is extensive. You can fill up on all kinds of goodies not usually found in barbecue shacks—"appeteasers" like spicy beer cheese, deep-fried pickle chips, catfish strips, or a cup of burgoo—but you better save room for Billy's smoked meats and side dishes.

We split a pork plate—a whopping bunch of pulled and chopped pork, probably three-quarters of a pound of it, and also a jumbo mutton sandwich, with meat heaped on a big sesame seed bun with dill pickles and red onions (I removed these before eating). The pulled pork had a lot of bark and smoke flavor. It was a little dry and chewy, but the flavor was good. The hot sauce was a thin and vinegary pepper sauce that worked nicely with the pulled pork. I was happy and surprised to find mutton in Lexington. I prefer mutton naked off the pit, but for sauced and sandwiched mutton this was good. It was chopped less finely than at Moonlite Bar-B-Q Inn in Owensboro, a place famous for mutton, and I prefer Billy's coarser chop. The "ho-made" onion rings using fresh onion slices (they cut the onions there) were fabulous—crunchy and lightly breaded. We both loved the garlicky, buttery cheese grits that came heaped up in a bowl. The cornbread was really sweet. They smoke baked beans for three hours. They grind cabbage for the slaw. They cook and mash potatoes for the potato salad. In short, we were both impressed with the homemade quality of Billy's food. I saw servers carrying platters of heaping plates and bowls, so it seems to be Billy's custom to give plenty of food for the money.

After eating, I went back to talk with the young men doing the smoking. They gave me the rundown. Whole shoulders and beef briskets smoke for twelve hours in a gas-wood hybrid cooker using local hickory wood for smoke. The gas heats the unit up to cooking temperature, and then they throw on the wood, and the gas kicks on when the wood burns low to maintain a constant temperature. They slather pork fat on the wood, letting it soak in overnight, so when burning it they approximate the drip flavor you'd get from shoveling coals underneath the meat in the old-fashioned way—a clever way to add flavor to meats cooked in a gas-fired oven. The meaty slabs of St. Louis–style ribs, smoked three to four hours, had a beautiful rosewood color from the dry rub and smoke, and the flavor right off the pit was wonderful. They hold the ribs in a walk-in cooler and reheat them in a steam tray on their stovetop. I can't say how good the ribs are after being held a while, but if you get them fresh off the pit, oh, have mercy. The chopped brisket was good—smoky and tender.

When driving away, Jason said you could go back to Billy's and make a great meal of dry-rubbed ribs, cheese grits, and onion rings. Agree. I'd also like to try the deep-fried pickle chips with horseradish sauce and mustard-style potato salad.

Open: Monday–Saturday, 11:00 a.m.–10:00 p.m.; Sunday, 11:30 a.m.–9:00 p.m.

101 Cochran Road; 859-269-9593

www.billysbarbq.com

Ky. Butt Rubb'in BBQ ("Ain't No Fancy Gas Smoker Here!!")

Don't let the strip-mall surroundings deter you; I had a good time and a great meal at this barbecue-and-more restaurant. I lucked into Butt Rubb on a Saturday afternoon when the University of Kentucky Wildcats were playing the University of Tennessee and got to observe customers, employees, and co-owner Leigh Pence (a Fayette County native) watching the game—that crazy Wildcat fervor rampant all over the state, but of course especially strong in Lexington, home of the Big Blue. I used to hear Ole Miss fans call UK the "Big Poo." They're just jealous.

I sat at a high-top table near the bar for a good view of the television and spoke with New Jersey native James Myers, a University of Kentucky student and part-time barkeep, who talked me into a sampler platter with burnt ends (not always available but, lucky for me, were on this day) and potato salad. I chose the three-meater and rounded out the platter with smoked sausage, four bones of St. Louis–cut spareribs, and onion rings cut and breaded in house. I also sampled the beef brisket and pulled pork—they do call themselves Butt Rubb, after all. Garlicky Texas toast rounded out the meal.

Ky. Butt Rubb'in BBQ has been open since June 23, 2009. I asked Leigh what they do best, and she said, "My husband does all this marvelous food. This is all he's ever done since he was fifteen, was cook. It's all good. Everything smokes sixteen to eighteen hours. All hickory all day."

Leigh told the pure-dee truth. The onion rings were crispy and melted in my mouth like cotton candy. The red-skinned potato salad had flecks of celery seed, boiled egg, and a creamy dressing that was not sweet, thank goodness, and was one of the best I've ever had (thank you, James from Jersey, for steering me toward it!). The ribs were nicely charred on the topside but tender throughout, reminding me of the famous Rendezvous ribs in Memphis. Ribs smoke for six hours, and before serving Greg Pence, Leigh's husband, "flashes them on the grill to caramelize the sauce a little bit." The sliced smoked sausage, which comes fresh from Troyer Foods in Goshen, Indiana, tasted like a Polish or English breakfast sausage. The cubed burnt ends from beef brisket flats burst with salt and smoke, very tender and delicious, and I loved them with the Texas toast. This might be the *only* place in Kentucky serving burnt ends. I hadn't eaten them since I visited Kansas City years ago and was glad to try them again. They *were* very salty—so if you are averse to salt, keep this in mind. Finally, the rich, tender, smoky chopped pork reminded me of some of the best in western Kentucky. Table sauces are sweet and thick. The "Hot Like You" sauce has a good peppery kick. They also have "pig wings" on the menu—one of a few places in the Commonwealth smoking these, and also one of the only places outside the Hopkinsville-Owensboro corridor serving burgoo. I also tried the white sauce, which tasted much like the concoction made famous by Big Bob Gibson's in north Alabama.

A lovely young woman taking a break at the bar, Abby Davis from Frankfort, overheard me exclaiming about the basket of fried dill pickle spears she was snacking on, and she shared one with me. I dipped that crispy pickle into the mayonnaise-based white sauce and felt my heart flutter slightly. Abby, one of a few young people working that day, said, "I keep things exciting here. I give good advice on what to get."

Butt Rubb, like Sarah's Corner Cafe across town, shows their enthusiasm for University of Kentucky athletics. On the wall by the front door hangs a framed autograph of Joe B. Hall, coach of the 1978 NCAA basketball championship team, who thanks Butt Rubb for the "great dinner," and posters of UK men's basketball and football teams plaster the wall by the bar. A playing card of Jay Shidler, "the Blond Bomber" from that 1978 team, is displayed in a frame, next to his words: "I've always loved good 'butt,' & you can't beat this 'butt' rubb'n BBQ." An illuminated sign in the back dining room features a pig massaging another's pig's hams, next to the caption: "After the Wildcats Kick Butt noth'in Beats a Butt Rubb'in."

I asked Greg, a Boonesborough native, how he came up with the name. He said, "Well, we use Boston butts and I put a rub on it. It started out as a joke and stuck."

Greg smokes with hickory wood on big custom barrel smokers out back, and when I asked what kind of species of hickory he used, Greg schooled me in woods, revealing just how much he'd experimented over the years. "I can't pronounce it," he laughed. "There's only like sixteen [species]!" He mostly uses shagbark hickory, but sometimes will smoke with the diamond-patterned mockernut hickory, which is "okay," according to Greg. He doesn't like pig nut hickory, calling it "pretty bland, a white wood that doesn't put out the right kind of smoke." Someone brought Greg a load of red hickory. "The taste was good, but everything in there looked like you'd been smoking with cherry. Everything was just *red*. I didn't want to use that anymore."

In the summertime, business is so good that Greg fires up all three of his big smokers. "It gets nuts as soon as school is out. In four months we'll be balls to the walls."

By the way, #2-ranked Kentucky pulled it out in the end, beating Tennessee 65–62, to the great relief of a crowd gathered around the bar. The Wildcats went on to win the NCAA championship in 2012. Looks like a good time for a Butt Rubb'in.

Open: Tuesday–Friday, 11:00 a.m.–8:00 p.m.; Saturday, 12:00 p.m.–8:00 p.m.
450 Southland Drive; 859-277-0099

J. J. McBrewster's

Business has been cooking at this Lexington eatery since Guy Fieri brought his big personality and posse of cameras into the kitchen of this barbecue restaurant whose owners have western Kentucky roots, the *only* place in Kentucky I've found that serves—get this—*goat!* (Call me envious of a guy who gets paid to go eating around the country and you wouldn't be lying.) Guy marked this territory with a signed poster and a spray-painted stamp on the wall of his sunglassed visage and trademark spiked hair beside the words "Guy ate here," along with his signature. No, I'm not jealous. Really.

Located in a strip mall next door to Domino's pizza and a Chinese restaurant, J. J.'s offers barbecue classics with a suburban twist. For example, barbecued meats are served on ciabatta buns with a side of chips or an apple, or you can get a panini. The pig bark panini is pulled pork, bacon, and provolone served on a ciabatta loaf. The nicely named goatini is BBQ goat and provolone on ciabatta. They also offer several "stuffed spuds" (the phat spud is a potato with pulled pork or chicken and baked beans, topped with cheese), salads, and soups.

But barbecue still makes most of the menu, and I, along with buddy Mark "Action" Jackson (a Memphis native who teaches at Transylvania University in downtown Lexington), tried a range of it: pulled pork, goat, mutton, and brisket. We also tried the creamy slaw, potato salad, "maple glazed baked beans," green beans, and mac and cheese. Four table sauces allow for sampling. The cutely named melon sauce (which doesn't have melon in it) ranks highly on my list of clever barbecue sauce creations. You can watch owner Susan Mirkhan make it on the YouTube clip of Fieri's *Diners, Drive-Ins and Dives* broadcast.

Of the meats, Mark and I praised the thick-sliced brisket the most, finding it tender and flavorful throughout. They smoke the whole brisket, which means extra-juicy, delicious fattiness for flavor and moisture, on an Ole Hickory cooker using hickory wood for about twenty hours, as they do with all the meats except chicken and salmon. The brisket soaked up enough smoke to satisfy me, and the seasonings seeped deep into the meat. Moreover, since this is the only place I've found in the Commonwealth serving barbecued goat, I suggest you try it, but know that this goat was chewy and stringy, as was the mutton—especially the external barky pieces. Both were slightly sweet and well seasoned, but I think these meats could benefit from regular basting with a dip. Both meats were improved by drizzling on some of the Daviess County dip, a thin Worcestershire-based tangy sauce. The pulled pork was tender and had a good fluffy texture, but it lacked the deep smokiness I prefer. This is often my response to pork cooked on gas-wood hybrid cookers. Mark agreed. We both thought the western sauce—a tangy, sweet, peppery, orange-colored sauce reminding me of the mild sauce at Knoth's Bar-B-Que over by Lake Barkley—added necessary flavor to the mildly smoked pork. Of the sides we tried, I liked the baked beans seasoned with onions, sugar, and spices the best. The potato salad was sweet, "almost a fruity sweet," in Mark's words. I didn't try a dessert but was tempted by such homemade sweeties as banana pudding, pig picking pie (peanut butter pie and chocolate fudge), and cobblers (blackberry, peach, or pecan).

J. J.'s has a welcoming family atmosphere. Friendly employees greet you when you walk in the door, and the open dining room is clean and bright, with walls painted UK blue, mustard yellow, and rusty red. Windows let in natural light. Floors are carpeted. Mellow music plays throughout the dining room—at least until the University of Kentucky basketball game begins, as it did during our meal. A plaque on the wall from the Lexington Humane Society thanks J. J. McBrewster's for their donations. The Mirkhans are dog lovers who named the restaurant after their rescued bulldog. She calls him Mac. The sandwiches at J. J.'s are named after him.

Susan, who grew up in Eddyville, came over to speak with us after we finished our meal. We bragged on western Kentucky barbecue awhile. Susan said the sweet peppery sauce had been made in her family for at least eighty-two years. The recipe was found in her great-great grandmother's Bible. Susan compared it to honey mustard, and then told me a funny story about the sauce. Her uncle, Harold Crady, was a successful insurance man who cooked barbecue on the river in Eddyville on Saturday nights. "It was a passion for him; it wasn't something he could make any money doing." Uncle Harold would cook on the riverbank with Mr. Knoth.

The plot thickens. "So Mr. Knoth stole the recipe?" I asked.

"Harold gave it to him. Everybody knows the sauce as Knoth's, but ironically enough it goes back a lot further than that. What's funny is that years later my dad married into the Knoth family. Hugh [Knoth] made his sauce with white vinegar, and my uncle made his with apple cider vinegar. There's a very big argument about which sauce is better. You can't even tell the difference, but anyway . . .

"Western Kentucky deserves a lot of recognition for barbecue. When I was growing up, you didn't eat burgers. You didn't eat turkey. When you had an affair, you ate barbecue: pork shoulders and mutton. It didn't matter if it was Christmas or a family reunion in July—you ate barbecue. So I would go to my Knoth's side of the family, and they'd be like, 'You didn't go over there and eat any of that Crady's barbecue, did you?' And then I'd go over to Crady's house, and they'd go, 'You been over at Knoth's eating that barbecue?' It was never a Hatfield and McCoy kind of thing, but I got to live it because I was going to both households.

"My family has always hand-pulled barbecue. We hand-pull all of our meats. One of the most popular things is to take your shoulder or butt and throw it in a big commercial blender and let it tear it apart, and then you go through it and pick out the gristle and things. But we hand-pull ours. During a slow period we smoke over a ton of pork a week."

Susan keeps goat on the menu because it was featured on *Triple D,* but she said, "It's extremely expensive and difficult to get. We don't make one dime on it." She's been getting goats from local farmers, and the supply has been strained. There just aren't enough goat farmers around. But Susan is committed to supporting local farmers. A Kentucky Proud banner—an icon stamped on Kentucky-made products—hangs on the wall near Guy Fieri's photograph. Susan gets produce from local sources whenever she can.

Talking about the dearth of barbecue in the Bluegrass Region and eastern Kentucky, Susan said she'd met many expatriates from western Kentucky who've been "longing for" the barbecue of home. "When I'd been open like six months, a guy said, 'I feel like I've gone home and had my dinner.' That's a nice compliment."

Susan has put a lot of heart and family history into her barbecue restaurant—from sauces to soup recipes, and through donations to the Humane Society and by supporting local farmers. It's a clean family place with something on the menu for everyone.

Open: Monday–Saturday, 11:00 a.m.–9:00 p.m.
3101 Clays Mill Road, Suite 301; 859-224-0040
www.jjmcbrewsters.com

Mary Lou's BBQ

Entrepreneur and barbecue man John Dance opened this new place in April 2012, and I haven't had the chance to eat there. John used to own Good Ol' Days BBQ Farm in Versailles. John's got some strange ideas about smoking woods—at least strange in Kentucky. He told me, "I like to smoke with blackjack oak when I can get a load from north Florida. Texas and Oklahoma also have this species, also known as turkey oak." The menu at Mary Lou's says they do "Texas Style BBQ" and smoke with hickory. The stripped-down menu includes pulled pork, brisket, pork ribs, and—something out of left field—pineapple blue cheese coleslaw.

John named the place after his childhood and current sweetheart. He said, "Mary Lou and me have been together since seventh grade. I told her I was finally serious and named my place after her. When a southern boy names his barbecue after his lady, you know it's serious."

I've read positive reader reviews of this new barbecue place, with one native Texan praising the beef brisket, andouille sausage, and smoky beans.

Open: Monday–Saturday, 11:00 a.m.–8:00 p.m.
226 Walton Avenue; 859-252–4227 (4BBQ)
MaryLousBBQ.com

Neal's Smoke Box

I've been surprised over the years to find good barbecue at service stations. When I lived in Oxford, Mississippi, awhile, the best ribs in town came from a place called B's, housed in a Shell station south of the town square. To get some of the best barbecue in western Kentucky, you'll have to walk through the doors of Heaton's Citgo station in Princeton. And you'll find some of the best stuff in the Bluegrass Region inside a Shell station, formerly a Chevron, in southeast Lexington, close to I-75.

I started with a brisket sandwich—three slices of well-smoked peppery beef coated with a heavy sauce that reminded me of KC Masterpiece. The pulled pork was tender and also saucy. The brisket was extremely peppery and salty, reminiscent of beef jerky, but unlike jerky it was very tender. Both sandwiches came on untoasted industrial hamburger buns.

In brief, Neal's Smoke Box knows how to smoke a brisket, but I'd just get the meat without bun or sauce, both of which detracted from the good flavor of the meat. That's not always the case, of course. Sometimes these elements—meat, bread, sauce—work together, like the magnificent hoggy sandwich at Mr. BBQ in Grand Rivers, which comes on a good hoagie bun brushed with garlic butter, toasted, with a thin peppery sauce on the side. So run into the Smoke Box, get a big plate of brisket, ask them to leave off the sauce (if they will), and also try the meaty spareribs that Neal smokes on the huge steel unit outside the store, and get some of Kelly's homemade side items like the green beans and sweet potatoes. That's a good meal.

Neal's Smoke Box has one of the most engaging origin stories I've heard. When I stopped by during summer 2009, they'd been in the Chevron station for only three months, but they'd already been selling barbecue at the Lexington Farmers Market for seven years. The owners, Kelly and Neal Harris, started the business to raise money to build the Ruby E. Bailey Family Service Center in Lexington, whose mission is to help families and children in need, including literacy learning, after-school tutoring, and feeding programs. Their goal is to "help break the cycle of government dependency," said Kelly.

Neal does the smoking, and Kelly makes the green beans and macaroni. "Mommy's the mac queen," Kelly said. She said her greens and sweet potatoes come from five generations of cooking know-how, passed down daughter to daughter from the family's origins in Meridian, Mississippi.

You can top off your meal with one of Kelly's homemade cinnamon rolls. Oh, yes.

UPDATE: Neal's Smoke Box closed in late 2012, but you can eat the same barbecue, homemade sides, and desserts at the Harrises' Wagon Bones Grill.

Wagon Bones Grill

In 2011 the Harrises of Neal's Smoke Box opened a new place, Wagon Bones Grill, which serves pulled pork, sliced brisket, ribs, chicken, grilled corn, mac and cheese, and more. It's located downtown near restaurants such as Nick Ryan's Saloon and Stella's Kentucky Deli. I stopped by on a Saturday morning at 11:00, one hour before official opening time, and the smoker outside was cold and nobody was inside. It was winter, though, after one of the only snowstorms of the season.

Sharon Thompson, food writer for the *Lexington Herald-Leader* for over thirty years, interviewed Kelly Harris when Wagon Bones Grill opened and did a short write-up on her "Flavors of Kentucky" food blog. Describing their barbecue, Kelly said, "We smoke our meats for hours and use a Memphis-style with the Western Kentucky spin dry rub to form a savory crust. Then pull them by hand for the ideal mix of crusty, smoky tender and juicy meat from the inside out. Then we finish them with one of our homemade sauces: a tangy, semi-sweet barbecue sauce or our Western Kentucky dip sauce to complement the spicy rub and smoky meat."

Business is so good, Kelly said when I called in May 2012 to request a recipe (she politely declined to share), that they plan to open another restaurant in Midway.

Open: Tuesday–Saturday, 11:00 a.m.–8:00 p.m.

591 West Short Street; 859-523-2400

Red State Barbecue

Scott Ahlschwede, DVM, an equine veterinarian who owns this quaint restaurant north of Lexington, chose the name after watching the elections one year and noticing that all the states listed as red on the electoral map were good barbecue destinations. Lefties, no worries. Barbecue transcends political divisions.

The interior offered a toasty welcome from the winter cold. A blue and white UK Wildcat lamp hangs above the thick-slab wooden bar top. The menu is scribbled on a big chalkboard behind the bar. A stuffed wildcat mounted on a piece of driftwood stands on a mantel, next to a wall of fame: signatures and testimonies from famous visitors, including six foot eight Kenny "Sky" Walker and seven foot one Sam Bowie, who kindly marked the top of his head on the wall so we lesser mortals can see just how shrimpy we are by comparison. How do I know the heights of these former UK basketball players? Google, perhaps? Unnecessary, for both men listed their vertical blessedness as a part of their signatures. I've been thinking about a personal stamp for my own barbecue fame—maybe cholesterol levels or blood pressure readings?

I approached the bar and struck up a talk with Jennifer Wiglesworth, an artist who manages Red State to support her art habit. She said some customers asked if they were communist because of the name. That had crossed my mind also, but I expected George Bush red instead of Fidel Castro red. Turns out the place is neither—at least not belligerently. If the owner has a political agenda, he hides it well. He's from Texas, but his place pays homage to Kentucky's favorite basketball team all over the walls of the place.

Open since November 5, 2010, Red State has already established a good following. Jennifer said, "Our lunch business is fabulous. Today they were lined out the door for an hour straight." That's about all the advertisement you need. In addition to the regular menu meats, which I discuss below, they also do weekend specials like whole smoked prime ribs, whole smoked turkeys, smoked salmon with a honey barbecue glaze, and smoked meatloaf. All meats smoke on a Fast Eddy's by Cookshack rotisserie pellet cooker.

My old friend Chip Barton, from my hometown of Glasgow, blew in from the cold, and we ordered a couple of "two-meat" plates—one with ribs and pulled pork, the other with brisket and pulled chicken. Our sides were potato salad, beans, mac and cheese, and corn pudding. I loved the thick-sliced brisket with ample fat left on it, and also the spareribs seasoned with thyme, oregano, and other spices. The mac and cheese was great—very cheesy macaroni shells from a roux base, extremely caloric and satisfying. The corn pudding was also rich. The baked beans—long-cooked pintos with chili pepper—were good. The potato salad was nothing special. The pulled pork was flaky with a moderate smoke flavor, and the pulled chicken—well, hell, I just don't understand why people order this stuff. Why did I order it? One can always hope . . .

So, my perfect meal at Red State: a two-meat plate with brisket and ribs, mac and cheese or corn pudding and baked beans (which provide a good flavor contrast to the rich and cheesy macaroni and pudding dishes). Oh, the sauces aren't necessary for the delicious brisket and ribs, but of the three table sauces—Memphis sweet, Texas spicy, and Carolina mustard—I found the Memphis sauce the most complex and fresh-made tasting.

The temperature was 23°F when Chip and I said good-bye and went our separate ways down the highway, my belly full and my spirit lifted by the renewal of old friendship and the making of new ones. Thanks, Jennifer, for making us feel at home.

Open: Monday–Thursday, 11:00 a.m.–8:00 p.m.; Friday–Saturday, 11:00 a.m.–9:00 p.m.; Sunday, 11:00 a.m.–8:00 p.m.

4020 Georgetown Road; 859-233-7898

www.redstatebbq.com

Sarah's Corner Cafe BBQ

A short drive east of Lexington on Highway 60, Sarah's smokes up some of the best barbecue in the state and serves it up in a homey country-store atmosphere. LD and Ralph Egbert, realtors, opened Sarah's on May 29, 2009, naming it after their beloved dog Sarah Jane, whom they met in 2003 at an animal shelter. Photos of Sarah grace the menus. In one, Sarah's looking humiliated in a University of Kentucky–colored dog sweater. LD and Ralph are huge Wildcat fans, having moved to Lexington from western Kentucky to be closer to the sports action. They show their fandom with their Blue Wall, a corner of the restaurant painted Wildcat blue with photos of UK legends hanging on the walls. They even put Rick Pitino up there, forgiving him for his perfidy. I guess winning five of six SEC tournaments and an NCAA national championship earns a lot of forgiveness.

Out by the highway for advertising, a big tank unit smoker with a firebox on the side for indirect cooking was parked. The meats they smoke up on there are oh-so-good. Charlie Winter and I shared a "Sarah's sampler" with three meats and three sides. Charlie said (and I agree) that the very meaty baby back ribs were some of the best he's had in a while (and Charlie is a barbecue freak like me). They were moist and smoky, as good as I've ever had at a restaurant. Charlie called them "outstanding" and said his father-in-law would call all the meats "larrupin'."

"What?"

"Larrupin'."

"What are you saying, Charlie?"

"Good. Larrupin'."

Charlie's father-in-law is from Scottsville, near my old stomping grounds, and I'd never heard of this word. He'd sprung a new one on the English professor. According to the Urban Dictionary, *laruppin'* describes "food so tasty it makes your tongue slap your brains out."

Charlie said, "I could eat my weight in those ribs."

The thick-sliced beef brisket was real good, and the pulled pork was smoky and tender. I liked the peppery bark on the pork and the distinctive smoke flavor. I told LD that the barbecue sauce reminded me of Knoth's sauce over in the Land between the Lakes, and she just smiled. The greens were rich and full flavored, like Grandma's, with a lot of pot likker, and the hash brown casserole was cheesy. Pones of cornbread rounded out the meal.

Sometimes LD and Ralph go wild and smoke pineapple and shrimp and Italian sausages. The day I visited she'd just made a homemade potpie using beef brisket.

"What do you do with smoked pineapple?" I asked.

"Eat it!"

Well.

LD and Ralph have roots in Princeton (in the heart of western Kentucky barbecue country) but lived in Paducah for eight years before moving to Lexington in 1985. Ralph used to manage Old Town Tavern, and LD worked for Starnes BBQ in Paducah. Her father used to run Knoth's.

Ooooooooooh. No wonder LD smiled when I said their sauce reminded me of Knoth's.

I asked LD about the east-west barbecue divide in the state, and she said, "I just don't think people have the time and patience. You got to watch that smoker. You can't just put the meat in there and cook it. It takes eight to ten hours to cook those Boston butts. You just can't rush it."

Can we infer by LD's hunch that western Kentucky people move at a slower pace—got more time for setting around watching meat cook slowly—than the people around Lexington?

The country-store atmosphere at Sarah's makes for fun dining in. I liked looking at the photos of dogs and cats on the walls. The Egberts actively support the Lexington Humane Society. Their personal story on the menu says, "Our pets (all thru Humane Societies) have given us great joy."

A sign above the door leading to the restroom states boldly, "This ain't *Wendy's*—You'll eat it any way we fix it." Gladly. These folks know good food.

Get to Sarah's Corner Cafe. It's larrupin' good!

Open: Monday–Friday, 8:00 a.m.–6:00 p.m.; Saturday, 8:00 a.m.– 4:00 p.m.

4300 Winchester Road; 859-309-1220

Sarah's Corner Cafe BBQ's Smoked Shrimp with Pineapple and Vidalia Onions

3 pounds shrimp, peeled or unpeeled (both ways work well)
10 medium-sized Vidalia onions, quartered
6–7 pounds pineapple chucks, with juice
Spicy dry rub (with cayenne, black pepper, paprika, etc.) to suit
    your taste

Spray large foil pan with cooking spray. Add onions and dry rub to pan and place on smoker at 250°F for 1 hour. Add pineapple and shrimp, shaking on additional dry-rub spices. Smoke for about 20 minutes or until shrimp is pink. Serve with barbecue sauce.

Sarah's Corner Cafe BBQ's Zagnut Ice Cream

1 cup sugar
3 cups heavy cream
1½ cups half and half
1 tablespoon vanilla
6 Zagnut candy bars, crushed

Mix everything together and put into an ice-cream maker. Turn freezer until the cream hardens, usually 20–30 minutes in my Cuisinart ice-cream maker.

Richmond

BC's Backwoods BBQ

Brandon Rousey opened BC's in May 2012 after running another barbecue place for four years. Meats like beef brisket, ribs, and sausage smoke on a custom offset pit. Brandon also does whole-hog catering. I haven't had the chance to try his barbecue, but I'm including BC's here to let you know it exists, and because I expect that a man cooking whole hog knows what he's doing.

Open: Monday–Saturday, 11:00 a.m.–9:00 p.m.

1900 Berea Road (From I-75 take exit 83 toward the Bluegrass Army Depot for three and a half miles. Turn right onto U.S. Highway 25 South for one and a half miles. BC's Backwoods BBQ is on the left in the Bluegrass BP.); 859-575-4023

Gridiron BarBQ

Husband-wife team Jamal and Jillian Davis opened this football-themed restaurant in fall 2010. From Orlando, Florida, Jamal came to Colonel Country on a football scholarship and met Jillian, a Hart County native attending Eastern Kentucky University on a basketball scholarship (she's the first woman from Hart County to get a Division I basketball scholarship). Now they have two children and have established a home in Richmond. Jamal says he gets barbecue advice from his uncle DC Charles in Valdosta, Georgia.

Gridiron is one of those barbecue places I recently discovered and don't have time to visit before submitting this book to the publisher. I regret that, especially since there's so little barbecue in eastern Kentucky. Menu items include pulled pork, beef brisket, pulled chicken, spareribs, barbecue sides, and various pies. Jamal uses homemade rubs and cooks meats in a Southern Pride unit fired with gas and hickory. Pork and brisket are the most requested meats. Butts smoke from twelve to fourteen hours; briskets for fourteen hours. Jamal doesn't wrap the meats because he doesn't like how it makes them seem "like they were baked in the oven."

Richmond folks like their meats heavily sauced. Jamal said, "They love to sauce it to death." If so inclined, you can ask for sauce on the side. Jamal will be glad to oblige. That's how he likes to eat his own barbecue, after all.

By the way, they named their potato salad—Jamal's grandmother's recipe—after a regular customer who loves the stuff. Jamal explained, "I told her if she comes in here one more time this week, then I'm naming the potato salad after her." She came in not just once but three more times. Now you can get "Kelli Jo's touchdown" potato salad.

Open: Tuesday–Saturday, 11:00 a.m.–8:30 p.m.
711 Big Hill Avenue; 859-624-5002
www.gridironbarbq.com

Appalachian Region

I stopped at the fire department in Winchester, Kentucky, east of Lexington in Clark County, to get recommendations for barbecue places in the area. A fireman, whose name I never got, talked to me awhile about barbecue in the mountains. This fellow, originally from Morehead in Rowan County, said mountain people were smoking whole hogs regularly and having big parties where they smoke lots of meats. He has a custom cooker he built himself—a "redneck rig" he called it—assembled from various found items, including a food warmer from a restaurant, and it has lots of racks in it for laying meat, and there's a hook in it for hanging a side of hog. He said grocery stores in the area, like the Kroger in Morehead, sell out of brisket because it's in such high demand from locals. In short, he said there's plenty of meat smoking happening in the mountains—just not at established restaurants.

I had to beat the bushes a bit to come up with the small list that follows. I've not read any authoritative study that explains why barbecue is deeply entrenched in western Kentucky but hard to find (I'm talking places selling it to the public) in the eastern part of the state. I've known for a long time that self-sufficient mountain dwellers kept and killed hogs. Linda Garland Page and Eliot Wigginton's *The Foxfire Book of Appalachian Cookery* lists all kinds of recipes for pig parts, things like head cheese and scrapple, and how to cook the "rooter" (snout), chitlins (intestines), brain, and other "nasty bits" (shout-out to Anthony Bourdain), but there's very little mention of barbecue. "Back-bones and Ribs" can be "stewed like chicken parts or barbecued or canned."

Well, there's one mention of barbecue. There's even a recipe for barbecue sauce in the cookbook with more vinegar than ketchup, which looks good to me. But the one "barbecue" recipe in the book calls for pouring barbecue sauce over chicken, covering it in foil, and baking it until tender. I know people in the upper Midwest whose idea of barbecue is very similar to that— baked or crock-potted meat.

In another book, *Appalachian Home Cooking: History, Culture, and Recipes,* Mark F. Sohn, a professor at Pikeville College, gives a recipe for "Country-Style Barbecued Ribs." Most of the recipe is a tomato-based barbecue sauce that's poured over the ribs before they are tenderized in a "slow cooker" for five to nine hours. I'll bet they're tasty, but I just can't call meat that doesn't touch smoke "barbecue."

My hunch is that resourceful mountain people needed to preserve their hogs for longtime consumption, not just blow it all on one decadent barbecue, while wealthy landowners in the flatter lands of western Kentucky could afford to kill a whole hog and have it barbecued for a picnic. Or maybe the Catholics, who have been cooking up sheep and hogs at Fancy Farm for 130 years and took root in the western parts of the state, have something to do with it. I'm going to keep looking for answers.

Morehead

Pop's Southern Style Barbecue

Adam Ferguson, the young owner/operator of Pop's, named it after his "grandfather-in-law" (his wife's grandfather). A Floridian by rearing, Adam moved to Kentucky "to get away from the hustle and bustle" of Orlando. His father was from eastern Kentucky, and when Adam visited when he was younger he really liked it. "My wife and I just wanted a change," he said, "so we told my parents we were moving to Kentucky. They got excited and they moved too. I miss the water back home, but I don't miss Florida."

He smokes butts for sixteen to eighteen hours on a homemade cooker made from an 850-gallon propane tank—the kind my grandparents used out in the country to heat their home. Pops—"I've known him since I was probably five years old," Adam said—made the smoker for him as a birthday present. "He had no idea I'd open a restaurant with it. I thought Pop's was catchier than Adam, so we named it Pop's. He's always been real nice to me. He taught me quite a bit about barbecue."

The meats at Pop's come with some natural juices, but there's a truly hot (and one mild) table sauce available. The meats are so good they don't need sauce, though. "I wrap my shoulders after they are about halfway done to keep them from drying out," Adam said. "Some barbecue guys are totally anti-wrap. I use blended hickory and white oak. I tell the guys who cut my wood to only cut dead standing. There's not quite enough hickory around here to supply 100 percent hickory, plus I've always used a lot of oak—especially down in Florida there's not a whole lot of hickory. We actually use orange wood down there too—it gives real good flavor."

"What do you think white oak gives the meat?"

"I think it's mellower than hickory. I prefer that to the real strong flavor. Your hardcore barbecue people probably like it stronger toward the smoky side. I shoot for the middle of the road and try to please everybody."

Pop's is Adam's first food-service adventure, and he says the business is doing real good. In addition to barbecue, they sell a lot of catfish. He also does pork loin, brisket, and baby back ribs. He smokes the whole brisket and slices it to order. He also sells a lot of thin-sliced smoked turkey breast. On Saturday nights they do "wood-fired prime rib." "We cut our own steaks. We do sirloin, New York strips, and rib eye."

Adam ran a produce department for a Super Target before coming to Kentucky. He noticed the lack of barbecue in the Morehead area, and one morning on the way to church they passed a building. Adam told his wife, "That would be a good place for a barbecue restaurant." The following week they drove by and there was a sign out front: "For sale or lease." So they started up the business. Pop's is truly a family affair. Adam's mom, Lori, was running the hostess station/cash register and checking on customers while I plowed through a load of diligently prepared food.

Adam brings his Florida ways to Appalachia in the form of seafood. "We do jumbo tiger shrimp and scallops. Every once in a while I get lobster. I've gotten two-and-a-half-pound Dungeness crabs in. I just try to fill what's missing in the area."

I sampled baby back ribs, smoked pork, sliced beef brisket, a fried catfish fillet, and thin-sliced smoked turkey breast, plus baked beans, slaw, and fried pickled jalapeño pepper slices (hand-breaded at Pop's) with ranch dressing for dipping. I topped the meal with a ridiculously rich and wonderful Amish fried pie—homemade chocolate pudding stuffed into a pastry shell, fried until crispy and served with two scoops of vanilla ice cream, whipping cream, and chocolate drizzled on top. The dessert alone is worth driving a good piece for. I'm not even a big sweeties guy, but I ate every bit of this pie, and that was on top of the full barbecue plate. Of the rest, the brisket was my favorite—nicely browned and barky on the outside, tender throughout, with an intense flavor from sixteen hours of smoking—and the lightly breaded fried catfish melted in my mouth. The smoked pork was tasty but wet and mushy from the wrapping in foil. The fluffy moistness of the pork would be a great addition to hoecakes. I prefer my pork pulled in larger pieces, but this was still really good, reminding me of Mississippi-style barbecue. It went well

Pop's Southern Style Barbecue's Cheese Potatoes

Adam Ferguson writes, "This dish travels well on a folded beach towel. Wrap with a second towel for long road trips. Stays hot and ready to serve for over an hour. Your family and friends will be looking for you and your old Dutch oven for parties to come."

#12 size cast-iron Dutch oven
10 pounds russet potatoes, sliced ¼ inch thick
2 ounces bacon grease
1 bulb garlic, chopped
1 pound butter
2½ pounds Velveeta cheese, cubed
1½ ounces salt
1 ounce black pepper

Preheat oven to 375°F. Heat Dutch oven on stovetop and add bacon grease. Add potatoes and garlic to hot grease. Cook until browned and fragrant. Add butter and salt to the Dutch oven. Turn potatoes gently until coated with butter. Put Dutch oven in an oven and bake for 1 hour with lid on. Add Velveeta pepper and fold potatoes without mashing them. Cook for an additional 10 minutes.

with the buttered Texas toast. I also enjoyed the tender and smoky baby back ribs. All the meats had a distinct smoke flavor except for the turkey, which was rather mild. The baked beans were creamy with pork mixed in and the slaw tasted crispy and fresh. Everything was of top quality. The meats didn't need sauce, but there is a hot barbecue sauce with a true kick at the table.

Adam uses 100 percent wood. I asked, "What temperatures do you cook at?"

"I usually sear it—hit it about 350—and once it sounds like you're frying bacon, I put the damper on and pull it back down and let it finish off at 250."

In addition to barbecue, Pop's delivers burgers made from "Kentucky-raised certified Black Angus" ground in house. They have a crazy food challenge—a five-pound hamburger.

Adam is really hands-on with his cooking. The brisket I liked so much was the first he'd cooked on a new smoker, and he wasn't entirely happy with it. "Next time I'll nail it," he said, saying the brisket was "a touch dryer than I wanted it to be." I agreed with his assessment, but the brisket was still nearly perfect.

Pop's is located near the intersection of Highway 60 and 801 (the road to Cave Run Lake). It's worth the hour-plus drive from Lexington. Get the brisket and ribs, and *do* save room for the fried pies made by some local Amish folks. I loved the chocolate version—just absolutely, ridiculously good.

Open: Tuesday–Thursday, 10:30 a.m.–8:30 p.m.; Friday–Saturday, 10:30 a.m.–9:30 p.m.; Sunday, 12:00 p.m.–8:00 p.m.

110 Kentucky Avenue, State Road 801; 606-784-6378

East Point

Pit Stop BBQ

The billboard reads "C. M. Clark's Pit Stop BBQ." The C stands for Christian, appropriately named because his parents are missionaries who came to the mountains to do good works, including starting a nondenominational church in the tiny community of Warbranch in Leslie County. Christian followed them to the mountains. He's originally from a small town in New York State but has lived all over. Perhaps that accounts for Christian's off-center approach to barbecue and decor. He competes with Big Bubba Buck's in Munfordville for my Funkiest Shack award. The best part of the funk is the sky-blue school bus outside the shack that Christian has decked out in tables for fair-weather dining. A sign on the bus window says, "Eat in." Stumps of wood form the base of tables, and Christmas lights dangle from the bus windows. The bus, like the shack, sits in the shadow of a tree-covered mountain.

Inside the shack, which Christian built from the ground up, hang more Christmas lights, including the red chili pepper lights illuminating the ordering counter. An octagonal sign on the wall says, "Stop and pray." Pit Stop is a barbecue place in progress. Christian is building on a dining room and taking woodworking classes in Paintsville to learn to make solid walnut tables, and he's acquired booths from a Mexican restaurant in Ohio that he'll eventually install. His "wallpaper" is rusted metal roofing screwed horizontally to the walls of the dining room. Recycled materials are all over the place. He laid the pretty wood floors himself with lumber from a sawmill down the road. "I'm working with a small budget," he said. "If I can build it myself, I will."

He started in April 2009 with a basic smoker and worked some festivals, saved his pennies, and has been gradually building his business into a fun family eatery. He will eventually have karaoke on weekends. He said summer is hopping, with people stopping by for grilled corn and cold ice cream.

Mr. Clark, who earned a restaurant management degree at the age of twenty-five, specializes in chopped lean meats—pork, chicken, brisket, and turkey—and surprising side dishes like smoked sliced red potatoes and garlic/sesame roasted carrots (sort of hoity-toity for a barbecue joint, especially a rural one). He also smokes spareribs. The meats come sans sauce, and each has been seasoned by a different rub. Four sauces are available at a help-yourself counter. A "Sammich" gets you meat on Texas toast or a bun. The "Trinity" sandwich comes with three different meats. I really liked the cider vinegar bite of the potato salad and loved the candied crust of the spareribs hot off the big barrel smoker outside. The ribs were very tender with *big* flavor from the dry rub and smoke.

"I want to bring something here that isn't here," Christian said. "I want kids and family to come. I want high school kids to come for karaoke competitions on weekends. I sponsor CADA—Citizens against Drug Addiction—locally and in Floyd County, and I want them and other groups to have their meetings here."

Christian appears to have the servant's heart of his parents. I wish him years of success in bringing his special brand of family-friendly funk to Appalachia.

Open: Tuesday–Saturday, 11:00 a.m.–5:30 p.m.
24 Little Paint Creek; 606-889-6462

Prestonsburg

Pig in a Poke BBQ

If you're driving to far-eastern Kentucky from Lexington on the Mountain Parkway, fill up your gas tank. It's a lonely road with few exits and plenty of curves. When I made the trip, those old mountains—home to some of the earth's most species-rich forests—snuggled the road, dusted with snow. As I crossed into Magoffin County, the inclines rose up higher and steeper. I entered Prestonsburg at the lunch hour on a Friday and passed businesses on the main strip through town: a pawn shop, Family Dollar, Ace Hardware, Cash Express, Kentucky Mountain Bride, School of Hair Design, KFC, Taco Bell, Wendy's, Hardee's, Dairy Queen, McDonald's, Arby's. Is it any wonder that family-owned restaurants stand out like oases in the fast-food monocultures of small-town America? Thank goodness for barbecue places, which more often than not are still mom and pop.

Such is the case with Pig in a Poke, owned and operated by Brian and Tammy Cramer since 2007. I must admit that my expectations for this restaurant weren't high after reading negative Google reviews—most complaining of poor service and about drunken patrons at the bar. I'd imagined a real dank dive-bar atmosphere. I was pleasantly surprised when I entered Pig in a Poke to discover a dining room with quality booths and tables, well-kept wood floors, a pleasant mauve and white paint scheme, and a cool spiral staircase leading upstairs from the downstairs dining area. The dining area upstairs—which does have a full bar with beers on tap—was built with even more gorgeous wood. Shades of brown create a relaxing, classy feel, from the dark brown slats of the cathedral ceiling to the wooden tabletops and bar seating. Nice chandeliers hang from the ceilings, and several flat-screened televisions provide many good viewpoints to watch UK games. There's even a second-floor balcony in the Deep South style for outdoor sitting. Imbibers can get a Kentucky Bourbon Barrel ale on tap and relax in one of the lounging chairs and gaze across the road at the Archer Clinic of the Highlands Health System. If you eat too much barbecue and get abdominal cramps, care is available a hopskip away.

During the lunch hour, the clientele appeared to be primarily well-dressed businesswomen. It seems to me that if you want family dining, eat downstairs; if you want a lively bar atmosphere, go upstairs. And if you're opposed to a rowdy bar atmosphere, then go at lunch. People were on good behavior.

I sat at the bar upstairs and spoke with Mr. Cramer, who was eating a lunch of pig nachos topped with buffalo-sauced chicken breast meat hand pulled after four hours of smoking. I told him I'd heard that eastern Kentuckians like their sauce with a little barbecue in it. He said 99 percent of his customers wanted their meats sauced, "the more the merrier," but you could get the meats "dry," without sauce, upon request. The honey sauce is the one that gets applied to most meats before serving.

I was glad to be the 1 percent in this case.

"When I started here," Brian said, "I wanted to put a shoulder out there—I wanted to pull it off the shoulder and serve it to you plain and let you put sauce on it, but that just went south right away. People were like, 'Man, I want the sauce on it.'" And so the heavily sauced barbecue culture was established.

The "Little of Everything" came with baby back ribs, pulled pork, pulled chicken, pulled brisket, sides of loaded potato salad and slaw, and a nice square of sweet cakey cornbread. The food was good, with my favorites being the well-seasoned brisket and the excellent loaded potato salad made with leftover baking potatoes and other rich stuff. A variety of Cattleman brand sauces in squirt bottles are available, along with one sweetened spicy vinegar sauce that's passed around upon request. The pork (a shoulder-butt combo) and briskets smoke twelve hours on an Ole Hickory cooker using hickory wood. The meats go on naked, mostly, with only a salt and pepper rub applied to the brisket. "People tell me I'm losing money because of the bone," Brian said. "But anything cooked with the bone in it, it's gotta be good." Amen to that.

The tasty chopped brisket was my favorite meat—very tender with some good fat mixed in with the lean—and I sure relished that loaded potato salad. I could make a whole meal off a pile of the potato salad, the brisket, and the sweet baked beans (a blend of pinto, northern, kidney, and regular baked beans). They also serve big baked sweet potatoes. "Some of them look like footballs," Brian said. The sweet cakey cornbread was nearly like a dessert. Brian said the mountain folks had to come around to it—they were used to dried cornpones—but now people ate whole baskets of it. "I kinda think it's messing up my dessert sales," Brian said, laughing. Half-pound hand-patted burgers, sixteen-ounce charbroiled rib-eye steaks, fried pollock and chips, brats, grilled portabellas, and more round out the menu. Brian wanted to appeal also to the "mother-in-laws who don't like barbecue."

In his former job, Brian traveled all over Kentucky building traffic intersections and maintaining freeway lighting. "I was able to frequent quite a few barbecue restaurants and see how other people were doing it, which was really kind of beneficial." His stops included Smokey Pig in Bowling Green, where Brian lived for a year (eating high on the hog but staying low on the chain at Motel 8 near I-65). On weekends he returned home and sold barbecue out of the end unit of a motel. He rented the room, which had a three-bowl sink and other stuff to satisfy health code requirements, and cooked on Brinkman smokers. He said when people were lined out the door he knew he was on to something. "By 1:00 I'd be sold out," he said. "I called it 'Pig in a Poke' because a poke's a bag and you could only get it to go."

Eventually he bought the big building of his current location (it was an apartment complex with four units) and remodeled the heck out of it. There's a really cool elevator, like a dumbwaiter, that transports food from the kitchen to the upstairs bar area.

"How'd you become interested in barbecue in the first place?"

"I love to smoke," Brian said. "I love to smell it. I love to sit and drink a beer and just stare at it."

About using a gas-wood hybrid cooker, Brian said, "It isn't real in the sense that it's not smokers that you have to stand and tend to all day and all night, but in this business, as much as we sell, it's hard to mass-produce without something like an Ole Hickory pit or Southern Pride. I feel pork should taste like hickory, so we load it down with wood all the time to keep that smoke going. The Ole Hickory pit has been kind of a godsend because it's a lot easier. But if you don't see a stack of wood out back, then you really aren't smoking. You gotta have wood."

Brian summed up his philosophy: "The beauty of barbecue is that everybody does do things their own different way. Barbecue is a way of life. You don't buy it in a bag. We're constantly cooking here."

ADDENDUM: In 2011, Brian opened a second location down the road in Pikeville, serving the same fine food.

Open: Tuesday–Saturday, 11:00 a.m.–8:00 p.m.
341 University Drive; 606-889-9119

"Wrap it up, son!
The sun's almost up."

I'm nearly out of gas. The Ford Ranger died, and I've eaten at nearly every barbecue place in the state. I gained twenty-five pounds and lost twenty of them. I've talked with some wonderful people, soiled several shirts with dripping grease and sauces, improved my photography skills, and cultivated some strong opinions about what makes excellent barbecue.

It's common in books such as this to ponder the future of the subject at hand. Here's a stab at it.

In "A History of Barbecue in the Mid-South Region," a chapter of Veteto and Maclin's *The Slaw and the Slow Cooked,* barbecue historian Robert F. Moss traces the development of barbecue traditions in the middle South, paying special attention to Arkansas and Memphis. He writes, "The region's barbecue is best looked at not just as something to eat but as a social institution. It has long had a remarkable power to bring people together from diverse walks of life, helping them to celebrate important events, debate contentious issues, and have a good time." Reading this, I think of Kentucky's long-standing barbecue festivals and summer church picnics, key events in the cultural life of many western Kentucky communities, including the huge Fancy Farm picnic in Graves County that kicks off the political election season. I've watched young people helping the well-seasoned pit tenders at these events, promising that the traditions will carry on.

While I expect the festivals will keep going strong, using the same cooking traditions they've used for years—especially at the International Bar-B-Q

Festival in Owensboro, where the (mostly) church teams still cook mutton on open pits and stir huge cauldrons of burgoo—I can't say what mom-and-pop barbecue shacks, joints, and restaurants will look like in fifty years. Some of my favorite barbecue in the state is prepared by men in their seventies. What happens when the venerable old-school barbecue masters like Red Grogan, Cy Quarles, and Oscar Hill finally hang up their hickory-coal shovels?

I expect barbecue to remain an important part of Kentucky cultural life—the festivals and picnics—and also to evolve as a food culture. While there might be a decline in traditional western Kentucky style as the old pit masters retire, a move away from the masonry pits toward less labor-intensive methods, I don't think cooking with wood is going to disappear. First, you have several younger pit masters keeping the masonry pit coals alive, people like Ricky Prince in Bardwell, Ray Leigh in Future City, and Eric Binson in Benton. Moreover, plenty of barbecue folks are cooking with big tank units or homemade steel pits fired by huge piles and stacks of wood, still abundant in Kentucky, fortunately for us: men like Marc Hatcher at Pit Stop BBQ south of Murray, Dave Webb of Dave's Sticky Pig in Madisonville, and Dustin Curtis at Texican's BBQ Pitt in Crestwood. I expect the convenience of the manufactured cookers—the popular Ole Hickory and Southern Pride brands, for example—will draw more people into the barbecue business, as less humanpower and wood are needed to cook meats on these units—and because of this there might be some watering down of barbecue, a move toward less smoky meats. But maybe we've seen this trend already, based on the spread of barbecue chains like Famous Dave's and the success of Louisville's Mark's Feed Store, which offers good-quality food across the board but measures only mild to medium on the smoky scale. And most barbecue fiends I know love the smoke. That's what makes it *barbecue* instead of "oven baked."

I've also noted the increasing popularity of beef brisket and expect this trend to continue, and I hope along with it the importation of other delights associated with Texas, like smoky sausages. Furthermore, considering the wild success of Hammerheads in Louisville—open for less than two years but packing the house nightly—I predict we'll see the spread of "new" (as in new to most Kentuckians) barbecue styles—more smoked lamb ribs, pork bellies, and duck. And I've a hunch that Alton Brown, Bobby Flay, Guy Fieri, and other national food personalities are playing a considerable role in shifting the barbecue styles of this still-rural state, as the Internet and television bring faraway foodie expertise and international flavors into our homes. Take, for example, Hot Rod B.B.Q. in Cumberland County, Kentucky (home to 6,850 people, according to 2010 census numbers—95.4 percent "white," 2.6 percent "black," 0.1 percent "American Indian"). I'm pretty sure they didn't create their super-hot barbecue sauce made with ghost chilies out of thin air. Maybe one of the owners traveled to India, where the so-called ghost chili thrives. But I'm guessing the doctor of this sauce got the idea from popular media like *Man v. Food.*

Finally, as Kentucky—an overwhelmingly Caucasian state—becomes home to more and more immigrants from Mexico, Burma, Bosnia, and south Florida, I expect (and hope) to see *barbacoa* and other "new" styles adding to and transforming the Commonwealth's established and proud traditions. I just love barbecued beef tongue, garnished with cilantro and lime, on top of corn tortillas. Yes, please. I'll have some of that.

Wes's Great Kentucky Barbecue Feast

Favorite Dishes from My Travels

B ritish celebrity chef Marco Pierre White toured the United Kingdom several years ago searching for special foods. His discoveries, televised as *Marco's Great British Feast,* culminated in a huge meal featuring the best of British cuisine. In this spirit, I offer you Wes's Great Kentucky Barbecue Feast—a collection of my favorite smoked meats, sides, and desserts from my tour of the Commonwealth.

Meats

Beef Ribs

Smoketown USA, Louisville

Brisket

Hickory Heaven Bar-B-Q, Marion
Mama Lou's Bar-B-Que and Gifts, Uno
Old Hickory Bar-B-Q, Owensboro
Texican's BBQ Pitt, Crestwood

Chicken (halves or quarters)

Ole Hickory Pit, Louisville
Split Tree Barbecue, Alvaton

Chipped Mutton

Thomason's Barbecue, Henderson

Chipped Pork

Peak Bros. Bar-B-Que, Waverly

Duck, Lamb, and Pork Belly

Hammerheads, Louisville

Monroe County–Style Sliced Shoulder

Backyard BBQ, Tompkinsville
Collins Barbecue, Gamaliel
Frances' Bar-B-Que, Tompkinsville
R & S Bar-B-Q, Tompkinsville
Smokey Pig Bar-B-Q, Bowling Green
South Fork Grill, Glasgow

Mutton

Bar B Que Shack, Hopkinsville
J & B Barbecue, Henderson
Old Hickory Bar-B-Q, Owensboro

Pork Ribs

Dave's Sticky Pig, Madisonville
Ky. Butt Rubb'in BBQ, Lexington
Larry, Darrell & Darrell, Mayfield
Old Hickory Bar-B-Q, Owensboro
Sarah's Corner Cafe BBQ, Lexington
Scotty's Ribs and More, Louisville
Southern Reds Bar-B-Que, Pilot Oak

Pork Shoulder / Boston Butt / Chops

Carr's Barn, Mayfield (pulled pork from whole shoulder)

Harned's Drive In, Paducah (pork on toast)
Knockum Hill Bar-B-Q, Herndon (the big loin chop)
Leigh's Bar-B-Q, Future City (pulled pork from whole shoulder)
Mr. BBQ & More, Grand Rivers (pulled pork from whole shoulder /
    hoggy sandwich)
Pit Stop BBQ, Murray (pulled pork from Boston butt)
Prince Pit BBQ, Bardwell (pulled pork from Boston butt)
Red Grogan's Bar-B-Q, Clinton (pulled pork from whole shoulder)
Woodshed Pit BBQ, Hopkinsville (pulled pork from whole shoulder)

Pork Tenderloin

Hamilton's Bar-B-Q, Burkesville
Red Barn Bar-B-Q, Tompkinsville

Sausages / Hot Links

Shack in the Back BBQ, Louisville
Staxx, Frankfort
Texican's BBQ Pitt, Crestwood

Shaved Beef

Big Kahuna Bar-B-Q, Leitchfield

Side Dishes

Barbecue Potato

Hardware Cafe, Cunningham

Baked Beans

Dave's Sticky Pig, Madisonville
KP's Smokehouse, Central City
Thomason's Barbecue, Henderson

Burgoo

Bar B Que Shack, Hopkinsville
Old Hickory Bar-B-Q, Owensboro

Cheese Grits

Billy's Bar-B-Q, Lexington

Cornbread

Mama Lou's Bar-B-Que and Gifts, Uno

Corn Pudding

Red State Barbecue, Lexington

Fried Okra

Mr. BBQ & More, Grand Rivers

Fried Onion Rings

Billy's Bar-B-Q, Lexington
Ky. Butt Rubb'in BBQ, Lexington

Green Beans

Doc Crow's Southern Smokehouse and Raw Bar, Louisville
Mama Lou's Bar-B-Que and Gifts, Uno

Grilled Cabbage

Red Barn Bar-B-Q, Tompkinsville

Hash Brown Casserole

Backwoods Bar-B-Que, Paducah
Frances' Bar-B-Que, Tompkinsville

Mac and Cheese

Doc Crow's Southern Smokehouse and Raw Bar, Louisville
Smoketown USA, Louisville

Mixed Greens

Smoketown USA, Louisville

Potato Salad

Big R's and Shannon's BBQ, La Grange
Brothers Barbecue, Murray
Frankfort Avenue Beer Depot & Smokehouse, Louisville
Ky. Butt Rubb'in BBQ, Lexington
Mark's Feed Store, Louisville
Ole South Barbecue, Owensboro
Pig in a Poke BBQ, Prestonsburg

Skillet Potatoes and Onions

Mama Lou's Bar-B-Que and Gifts, Uno
Texican's BBQ Pitt, Crestwood

Slaw

Bar B Que Shack, Hopkinsville
Dave's Sticky Pig, Madisonville

Desserts

Banana Pudding

Dave's Sticky Pig, Madisonville
Old Hickory Bar-B-Q, Owensboro

Buttermilk Pie

Mark's Feed Store, Louisville

Fried Amish Pie

Pop's Southern Style Barbecue, Morehead

Homemade Ice Creams!

Ruby Faye's Bar-B-Que, Clinton
Sarah's Corner Cafe BBQ, Lexington

Old-Fashioned Fried Pies

Hamilton's Bar-B-Q, Burkesville

Acknowledgments

I'm grateful to my parents, Ken and Linda Berry, for abundant care, affection, and freedom to explore the woods, streams, cattle pastures, moss-filled ponds, and tobacco barns of cave country during my long, wonderful childhood. Dad, I've learned much from you, including patience, humility, and the pleasures of heavy outdoor labor—all those days hauling in wood and harvesting tobacco. Mom, I admire your grace, humor, devotion to family, and culinary know-how. I trace my love of food back to your kitchen—the wonderful mixture of good country cooking blended with surprises like pan-seared chicken topped with steamed broccoli, crabmeat, and béarnaise sauce.

I'm also proud of my grandparents Willis Reid and Gladys, the hub of the big Berry family, and have fond memories of salty-nutty country ham, biscuits with rich gravy, and black-skillet potatoes—of hulling beans and shucking corn in the shade of the sugar maple with Pa Pa, while the pressure cooker rattled in the hot kitchen—and days and nights fishing and frogging in the spring-fed pond and trout-stocked Peter Creek that bordered the land. The Berry family killed hogs in the fall, and Pa Pa fed me cracklins from the black iron kettle, the beginnings of my porcine proclivities.

This project was supported with a Junior Faculty Research Grant from Western Kentucky University. Special thanks to the committee who awarded the grant back in 2008; to Karen Schneider, chair of WKU's English department, for getting my last-minute grant application pushed through while I was away teaching in China; to Tomitha Blair, who processed multiple travel forms; and to the benefactors of WKU who make such grants possible.

(Dear Karen and Kevin—wishing you many peaceful hikes in your Colorado retirement.)

Hugs to Dale Rigby and John V. Glass III (and the entire Glass clan) for putting me up when I needed a place to stay; to Jason Berry for hospitality during my many trips to Louisville; and to Mark Jackson for the Lexington home away from home.

Gratitude to the traveling partners mentioned within these pages, others not mentioned, and some gone from my life, but not forgotten.

Jeanie Adams-Smith journeyed with me to Monroe County, took another journalistic trip to Hopkinsville and Grand Rivers, and provided awesome images for this book. I'm grateful for your friendship, generosity, and photographic magic. Also, thanks for loaning me Abby's future camera!

Joe Michael Moore of Barren County—I can't thank you enough for donating your hog expertise and many hours of hard labor while teaching us how to transform our two living hogs into four huge country hams, loin chops, sausage, ribs, Boston butts, and bacon. I know pigs so much better, inside and out, now. We're grateful for your kindness and gentle touch. You're an excellent teacher, and your country sausage really is the best I've ever eaten.

A big hickory-smoked chicken, double dipped, to Shane Wood for writing a story about this book for WKU's *College Heights Herald;* to photojournalist Dominik Furhmann for following me around Louisville with audio and camera equipment and putting together a well-edited barbecue piece that aired on WDRB Fox 41 in Louisville during Thanksgiving week 2011; to Bruce Bjorkman, host of *Cooking Outdoors with Mr. BBQ,* out of Portland, Oregon, for having me on his show; to Jimmy Lowe for the story in the *Glasgow Daily Times;* and to Gaye Bencini for the lunchtime conversation and resulting story in the *Hickman County Times.*

A kettle of burgoo to southern food aficionado John T. Edge for recommending the University Press of Kentucky and for inviting me to jawbone about barbecue at the Southern Foodways Symposium in fall 2012.

Appreciations to Ashley Runyon and the whole team at the University Press of Kentucky for seeing this book through and dealing with my need for extended deadlines so I could squeeze in *just a few more* barbecue places.

Acknowledgments

Thank goodness for copyeditor Robin DuBlanc, who combed through this manuscript packed with nonstandard English, multiple variations of the word *barbecue,* and potentially offensive wisecracking. She whipped it into shape while retaining the original spirit.

To the folks at Cricket Press in Lexington—thank you for the original cover art!

I've learned about food and travel writing from many experts in the field. A hearty Kentucky bourbon toast to Anthony Bourdain, John T. Edge, Peter Kaminsky, Jeffrey Steingarten, and Calvin Trillin for taking me on culinary cultural tours and making me want to ride shotgun. Special thanks to the barbecue writers and photographers whose books showed me the possibilities of such an undertaking: Vince Staten and Greg Johnson, Lolis Eric Elie and Frank Stewart, Mike Mills and Amy Mills Tunnicliffe, and John Shelton Reed and Dale Volberg Reed.

I received gracious, helpful manuscript guidance from Elizabeth S. D. Engelhardt, author of *Republic of Barbecue;* Maggie Green, author of *The Kentucky Fresh Cookbook;* and John Shelton Reed, coauthor of *Holy Smoke: The Big Book of North Carolina Barbecue.* Thank you, friends. The book is better because of your feedback.

The recipes contributed by barbecue people I met during my travels have enhanced this book. Thank you all for sharing your expertise and secrets.

Finally, to the many folks across the Commonwealth of Kentucky who generously shared stories, barbecue knowledge, and good food (somehow managing to continue working while I fumbled around learning to take decent photos)—my heartfelt admiration and gratitude. You are too many to mention individually, but the stories and photos inside this book are a tribute to your art.

Selected Bibliography

I've read a pile of books about barbecue, southern foodways, and meat in general. The following have been the most inspiring and influential. From some I've learned barbecue history, culture, and conflict; from others, how to write about food.

Adams, Carol J. *The Sexual Politics of Meat: A Feminist-Vegetarian Critical Theory.* New York: Continuum, 2000. Print.

Aidells, Bruce. *Bruce Aidells's Complete Book of Pork.* New York: HarperCollins, 2004. Print.

Bjorkman, Bruce. *The Great Barbecue Companion: Mops, Sops, Sauces, and Rubs.* Freedom, Calif.: Crossing, 1996. Print.

Bourdain, Anthony. *A Cook's Tour: Global Adventures in Extreme Cuisines.* New York: HarperCollins, 2001. Print.

————. *Kitchen Confidential: Adventures in the Culinary Underbelly.* New York: Ecco, 2000. Print.

Bourette, Susan. *Meat: A Love Story.* New York: Putnam, 2008. Print.

Davis, Ardie A., and Chef Paul Kirk. *American's Best BBQ: 100 Recipes from America's Best Smokehouses, Pits, Shacks, Rib Joints, Roadhouses, and Restaurants.* Kansas City: Andrews McMeel, 2009. Print.

Early, Jim. *The Best Tar Heel Barbecue: Manteo to Murphy.* Winston-Salem: Privately printed, 2002. Print.

Edge, John T. *Southern Belly: The Ultimate Food Lover's Companion to the South.* Chapel Hill: Algonquin, 2007. Print.

Elie, Lolis Eric, ed. *Corn Bread Nation 2: The United States of Barbecue.* Chapel Hill: U of North Carolina P, 2004. Print.

Elie, Lolis Eric, and Frank Stewart. *Smokestack Lightning: Adventures in the Heart of Barbecue Country.* New York: Farrar, Straus and Giroux, 1996. Print.

Engelhardt, Elizabeth S. D. *Republic of Barbecue: Stories beyond the Brisket.* Austin: U of Texas P, 2009. Print.

Fearnley-Whittingstall, Hugh. *The River Cottage Meat Book.* Berkeley: Ten Speed, 2007. Print.

Finley, John. *The Courier-Journal Kentucky Cookbook.* Louisville: Courier-Journal and Louisville Times, 1985. Print.

Graf, Jeffrey. "The Word *Hoosier.*" Indiana University. Web. Sept. 21, 2012.

Kaminsky, Peter. *Pig Perfect: Encounters with Remarkable Swine and Some of the Great Ways to Cook Them.* New York: Hyperion, 2005. Print.

"THE KENTUCKY BARBEQUE: Some of the Picturesque Phases of the Great Political Picnics; NOTED ONES OF OTHER DAYS; How Whole Animals Were Cooked and Vast Quantities of Burgoo Pre-pared and Eaten." *Louisville Courier-Journal* Nov. 7, 1897: n. pag. Web. Apr. 19, 2011.

Lee, Matt, and Ted Lee. *The Lee Bros. Southern Cookbook.* New York: Norton, 2006. Print.

Lilly, Chris. *Big Bob Gibson's BBQ Book: Recipes and Secrets from a Legendary Barbecue Joint.* New York: Clarkson Potter, 2009. Print.

Midkiff, Ken. *The Meat You Eat: How Corporate Farming Has Endangered America's Food Supply.* New York: St. Martins Griffin, 2004. Print.

Mills, Mike, and Amy Mills Tunnicliffe. *Peace, Love and Barbecue: Recipes, Secrets, Tall Tales, and Outright Lies from the Legends of Barbecue.* Emmaus, Pa.: Rodale, 2005. Print.

Moss, Robert F. *Barbecue: The History of an American Institution.* Tuscaloosa: U of Alabama P, 2010. Print.

Page, Linda Garland, and Eliot Wigginton, eds. *The Foxfire Book of Appalachian Cookery.* New York: Dutton, 1984. Print.

Pollan, Michael. *The Omnivore's Dilemma: A Natural History of Four Meals.* New York: Penguin, 2007. Print.

Reed, John Shelton, and Dale Volberg Reed. *Holy Smoke: The Big Book of North Carolina Barbecue.* Chapel Hill: U of North Carolina P, 2008. Print.

Sohn, Mark F. *Appalachian Home Cooking: History, Culture, and Recipes.* Lexington: UP of Kentucky, 2005. Print.

Staten, Vince. *Jack Daniel's Old Time Barbecue Cookbook.* Louisville: Sulgrave, 1991. Print.

Staten, Vince, and Greg Johnson. *Real Barbecue: The Classic Barbecue Guide.* Guilford, Conn.: Pequot, 2007. Print.

Steingarten, Jeffrey. *The Man Who Ate Everything: And Other Gastronomic Feats, Disputes, and Pleasurable Pursuits.* New York: Vintage, 1997. Print.

Stern, Jane, and Michael Stern. "Mutton, Honey." *Gourmet* Nov. 2006. Web. Sept. 21, 2012.

————. *Roadfood*. New York: Broadway, 2008. Print.

Trillin, Calvin. *The Tummy Trilogy*. New York: Noonday, 1994. Print.

Veteto, James R., and Edward M. Maclin, eds. *The Slaw and the Slow Cooked: Culture and Barbecue in the Mid-South*. Nashville: Vanderbilt UP, 2011. Print.

Warnes, Andrew. *Savage Barbecue: Race, Culture, and the Invention of America's First Food*. Athens: U of Georgia P, 2008. Print.

Index